Understanding Collapse

Understanding Collapse explores the collapse of ancient civilisations, such as the Roman Empire, the Maya, and Easter Island. In this lively survey, Guy D. Middleton critically examines our ideas about collapse – how we explain it and how we have constructed potentially misleading myths around collapses – showing how and why collapse of societies was a much more complex phenomenon than is often admitted. Rather than positing a single explanatory model of collapse – economic, social, or environmental – Middleton gives full consideration to the overlooked resilience in communities of ancient peoples and the choices that they made. He offers a fresh interpretation of collapse that will be accessible to both students and scholars.

- An engaging, introductory-level survey of collapse in the archaeology/history literature.
- Ideal for use in courses on the collapse of civilisations, sustainability, and climate change.
- Includes up-to-date case studies of famous and less well-known examples of collapses.
- Illustrated with twenty-four black and white illustrations, five line drawings, sixteen tables, and twenty-two maps.

Guy D. Middleton studied Ancient History and Archaeology at Newcastle University, where he won the Shipley Prize. For his Ph.D. at Durham University, he studied the collapse of Mycenaean states around 1200 BC. His works on collapse include: 'Nothing lasts forever: Environmental discourses on the collapse of past societies' (*Journal of Archaeological Research*, 2012) and *The Collapse of Palatial Society in Late Bronze Age Greece and the Postpalatial Period* (2010). He also has a B.A. in Humanities and English Language and an M.Ed. in Applied Linguistics and has worked extensively with international students. As well as teaching at universities in the United Kingdom, he has lived and worked in Greece, Korea, and taught for some years at the University of Tokyo, Japan. He is now a Visiting Fellow in the School of History, Classics, and Archaeology at Newcastle University.

Understanding Collapse

Ancient History and Modern Myths

GUY D. MIDDLETON
Newcastle University, UK

CAMBRIDGE
UNIVERSITY PRESS

University Printing House, Cambridge CB2 8BS, United Kingdom

One Liberty Plaza, 20th Floor, New York, NY 10006, USA

477 Williamstown Road, Port Melbourne, VIC 3207, Australia

4843/24, 2nd Floor, Ansari Road, Daryaganj, Delhi – 110002, India

79 Anson Road, #06-04/06, Singapore 079906

Cambridge University Press is part of the University of Cambridge.

It furthers the University's mission by disseminating knowledge in the pursuit of education, learning, and research at the highest international levels of excellence.

www.cambridge.org
Information on this title: www.cambridge.org/9781316606070
DOI: 10.1017/9781316584941

First published 2017

Printed in the United States of America by Sheridan Books, Inc.

A catalogue record for this publication is available from the British Library.

Library of Congress Cataloging-in-Publication Data
Names: Middleton, Guy D., author.
Title: Understanding collapse: ancient history and modern myths / Guy D. Middleton (Newcastle University, UK).
Description: New York, NY: Cambridge University Press, 2017. | Includes bibliographical references.
Identifiers: LCCN 2016023884 | ISBN 9781107151499 (hardback) | ISBN 9781316606070 (paperback)
Subjects: LCSH: Civilization, Ancient. | History, Ancient. | Social change – History – To 1500. | Complexity (Philosophy) – Social aspects – History – To 1500. | Resilience (Personality trait) – Social aspects – History – To 1500. | Human ecology – History – To 1500. | History – Errors, inventions, etc. | Social archaeology. | Environmental archaeology. | BISAC: SOCIAL SCIENCE / Archaeology.
Classification: LCC CB311.M43 2017 | DDC 930–dc23
LC record available at https://lccn.loc.gov/2016023884

ISBN 978-1-107-15149-9 Hardback
ISBN 978-1-316-60607-0 Paperback

To Yoshie and our baby Elise Saki, and to my parents Jennifer and Denis, and my family and friends

The great old days have gone, and all the grandeur of earth; there are not caesars now or kings or patrons such as once there used to be, amongst whom were performed most glorious deeds, who lived in lordliest renown. Gone now is all that host, the splendours have departed. Weaker men live and occupy the world, enjoy it, but with care. Fame is brought low, earthly nobility grows old, decays, as now throughout this world does every man.

The Seafarer. In R. Hamer.
A Choice of Anglo-Saxon Verse

The myth is of even more importance, historically, than the reality ...

Bertrand Russell.
History of Western Philosophy

Contents

Figures and Maps

Tables

Preface

This book developed naturally out of the years I have spent studying collapse. I first became interested in collapse on a tour of Greece with the British School of Archaeology in Athens in 1999; there I decided that, if I could, I would study Late Bronze Age (LBA) Greece and end of the Mycenaean palace period for a PhD. That study, done at Durham University, brought me to other collapses – I looked at the Hittites, an imperial state close in time to the LBA Greeks which collapsed at around the same time, as well as the Classic Maya, who, with their land of many interconnected states and kingdoms, seemed in some ways more comparable with the handful of Mycenaean states that existed in Greece. I looked at the collapse of the Western Roman Empire too, which seemed similar in kind to that of the Hittites both in the possible causes of collapse and its aftermath. And so I began to wonder about collapse in general, about the possibilities and problems of comparative studies of collapse, and to think of collapse as a problem area in its own right to be studied and investigated in archaeology and history generally.

But when I started studying collapse, I soon realised that there was no accessible general summary or introduction, as there are for, say, the archaeology of empires or ethnicity, gender or trade, or some other theme; yet there was a vast literature spread through numerous more or less separate fields of study, from environmental policy to geology, as well as the distinct subfields of archaeology, delineated by culture, period, region, or theme. The basic idea that there was no easy way in to such a tangled field stayed with me, and led me to this project by way of a paper written for the *Journal of Archaeological Research*, in which I (rather optimistically) sought to review recent work and ideas on collapse, and really learnt how much was going on. With this book, I hope to provide that introduction; an easy, hopefully interesting, up-to-date point of entry to the study of collapse. That said, the aim of the book is not to 'solve' once and for all the 'mysterious' collapses of past civilisations or introduce some new 'grand theory' – I, and many others, do not believe there to be one 'solution' that can usefully apply across the board – but rather to question the idea of collapse, and introduce the variety of ways in which such collapses have been seen and explained by scholars.

In the book, I focus on past collapses known from both archaeological and textual sources, and it should become clear that the sources available and the history of study of a given area both construct and influence our knowledge and views of any particular collapse. This is why I have opted for a case study approach rather than a thematic one. It has been said that there is a divide between archaeology and history; as Lester L. Grabbe has put it: 'textual scholars largely ignore archaeology, and archaeologists seem to believe a flat, uncritical reading of the text is fine', but this is an overstatement.[1] My tendency, bred by studying both ancient history and archaeology, is to think more inclusively, and though I will refer to both archaeology and archaeologists and history and historians, I regard them as overlapping fields, with people from both engaged in researching the past and constructing history and historical narratives, and therefore sometimes dealing with collapse.

Theories of history are important – they underpin our every thought, whether we know it or not. Collapse challenges our theories of history for it forces us to interpret evidence and shape narratives of cultures, polities, and sites on a variety of scales, temporal and geographical. Often collapse figures in grand historical narratives – the collapse of the Western Roman Empire, for example, ushering in a dark age out of which eventually developed the nations of modern Europe (to grossly oversimplify). In the late twentieth and early twenty-first century, a tendency has been to see collapse as an environmental issue, with collapse blamed on climate change or anthropogenic environmental damage ('ecocide'). A hundred years earlier it was often, though not exclusively, seen in terms of migration; theories thus change with the times. But as we shall see, collapse is rarely so easy to explain as these dominant theories would suggest.

PLAN OF THE BOOK AND JUSTIFICATIONS

The book follows a simple plan. The first chapter introduces collapse as a 'hot topic' in current affairs and as a constructed narrative that has a long history in our culture. The subsequent chapters each take an instance of collapse as their subject, running in roughly chronological order; we shall encounter the Egyptian Old Kingdom, the Akkadian Empire, the Harappans, Minoan Crete, Mycenaean Greece, the Hittite kingdom, the Western Roman Empire, Mesoamerica and Teotihuacan, the Classic Maya, the Andes, Angkor and the Khmer, and Rapa Nui (Easter Island) – introducing the context and presenting and evaluating a range of explanations (Figure 0.1).

The case study approach taken here needs some justification. Both Joseph Tainter and Jared Diamond adopted such an approach in their books on collapse, so the format is one favoured by authors writing about collapse.[2] However, Tainter's case studies were, for the most part, exceptionally short and lacked contextual detail, without which any discussion of collapse makes little sense except to specialists in that particular field. Plus, his longer case studies were written to validate his own grand theory of collapse, rather than as critiques of previous explanations. Diamond's case studies were also written with his own environmental slant in mind, rather than as objective enquiries. The case studies in this book offer contextualising detail – background on the history of the field and on the society being discussed, sometimes detail on how the field has developed, where I think relevant, as well as critically examining the proposed causes of collapse. I have tried to strike a balance in doing this, though some will undoubtedly think there to be too much or too little of one thing or another. Furthermore, I offer no grand theory – rather I am interested in what each collapse was or was not and how people have tried to explain what was happening. I hope that this approach will provide a good introduction to each collapse, and to general ideas about collapse, allowing the reader to judge the theories for themselves, rather than trying to persuade them of one particular view. The case

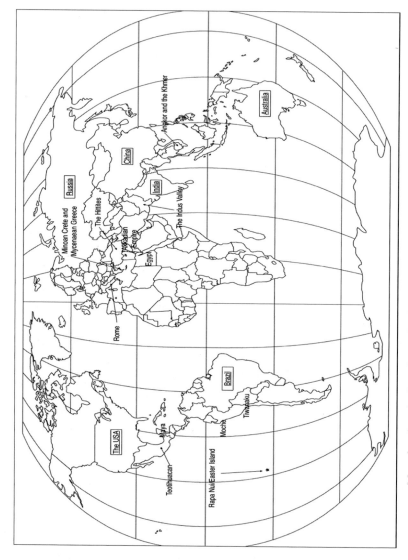

FIGURE 0.1. Map showing the locations of cultures discussed in the book.

study approach also means that readers are free either to read the book from beginning to end or just to dip in to read the parts that interest them or which they are studying.

Some justification for the choices of case studies may also be necessary. The examples have been chosen for their fame, interest, and variety, and for the work done on them, and for their 'archaeological' and, in some cases, primarily 'prehistoric' nature; others could have been used instead. Norman Davies, for example, in his *Vanished Kingdoms: The History of Half-Forgotten Europe,* deals with fifteen historical polities that have come and gone in Europe from the fourth century AD to the fall of the Soviet Union in 1991.[3] Undoubtedly, we could study at least some of these in the guise of collapse, examining the archaeological changes that political and social change drove. However, none of those primarily historical examples is examined here. There are also no examples from North America, even though the Ancient Puebloans (Anasazi, etc.), from the American southwest, and the Cahokians from the Mississippi Valley are fairly well known and discussed archaeological examples of collapse.[4] Collapses, state fragmentation, and dynastic change in China, Korea, and Japan – all of which, like ancient Egypt and Mesopotamia, experienced periods of unity and disunity, often referred to as 'intermediate' or 'warring states' periods – are also not discussed, and no examples have been drawn from the Indian subcontinent, with its many empires and states.

The examples chosen are therefore somewhat arbitrary, and so I make no claim to comprehensiveness – a work that was truly comprehensive would really be a study of global archaeology and the history of human societies from the dawn of human civilisation to the present. Even with more modest aims, and despite devoting a chapter to each case, it has still been necessary to be both brief and selective, though hopefully not too partisan. While collapse is defined in different ways by different authors, the examples I have chosen have all been labelled 'collapses' by scholars, though, as I try to show, there is variation in what happened and how their histories have been interpreted and explained. I hope to make it clear in this book that sweeping pronouncements that collapses can be explained by climate change[5] cannot be generally true, since collapse happened around the world at various times (that is, they do not all synchronise with climate 'events'), and clearly in some cases (take the collapse (or fall) of Carthage, for example, or the end of the Vandal kingdom in North Africa, or the destruction of the Aztec or Inka Empires) were simply caused by other people.

A word about style. In writing about these collapses, I have very deliberately tried to represent the voices and opinions of the scholars who have contributed to their study and to our understanding of what might have been happening. Collapse is a field that has its own cast of characters and it is helpful to know them. Some may find it heavy going, with a lot of names, facts (sometimes), and opinions, but I have attempted to weave together their different ideas into a coherent and, I hope, interesting narrative, with my own critique presented as well.

Finally, I hope the book will appeal to a wide audience – primarily as an introduction to 'collapsology' for students and for the interested reader, the first of its kind. I also hope that it will be read and be stimulating for experts in each field covered. No doubt the latter will find a lot to disagree with, but even this is a positive, since it can help push along collapse studies by forcing all of us to think more carefully about what we are investigating and how we explain it to others. It is difficult to find a format and style appropriate for such a wide intended audience, but again, I hope I have struck a reasonably acceptable balance that will please some, if not all.

Each collapse has its own story within its particular field of study, and books, chapters, and articles will continue to be written about each one, but I hope with this book at least to offer a way into this fascinating subject.

Acknowledgements

It is only possible to write a book of this kind, one that summarises and synthesises, argues, critiques, and interprets, because of the hard work and dedication of many other people – those who uncovered the evidence, translated the texts, and put forward their own ideas and theories; I gratefully acknowledge my debt to them and hope not to have misrepresented them here. Whilst I hope to have acknowledged the ideas of others in the usual ways, it is an inevitable outcome of research and reading done over years that ideas become mixed together and their origins become cloudy and obscure – more than once I have reread something I first looked at years ago and found that it expressed my own thoughts perfectly; I offer my apologies for any omissions.

I would like to offer specific thanks to several people and institutions. George Cowgill and Gary Feinman (and several anonymous reviewers) were encouraging and helpful as I wrote my review article on collapse for the *Journal of Archaeological Research*, the research for which informed this book. For reading specific chapters, spotting errors, and making helpful suggestions, I thank James Aimers, Trevor Bryce, George Cowgill, Oliver Dickinson, Jan Driessen, Arthur Joyce, J. M. Kenoyer, and Norman Yoffee. James Whiting read and gave feedback on an early draft and Richard Carter-White, a later draft. I owe special thanks to fellow collapsologist Arthur Demarest for his enthusiastic response to the book at the review stage and for his many pages of helpful and stimulating comments on the whole text (and for the many emails that followed) – especially for bringing me up-to-date on the Maya collapse.

I am also pleased to offer my thanks to Miroslav Barta, Richard Blanton, Jan Boersema, Sarah Clayton, Jonathan Conant, Robin Coningham, Norman Etherington, Ute Frank, Mark Gellner, Felix Hoflmayer, Rosita Holenbergh, Mark Hudson, Maria Iacovou, Gyles Iannone, Arthur A. Joyce, J. M. Kenoyer, Bernard Knapp, Stan Loten, Thalia Lysen, Margaret Maitland, Naoise Mac Sweeney, Joseph Maran, Simon Martin, Nadine Moeller, Tobias Muhlenbruch, Alistair Paterson, Benny Peiser, Cameron Petrie, Joshua Pollard, David Potter, Jane Rempel, Jerry Rutter, Jim Shaffer, Michael E. Smith, Keir Strickland, Lars Walloe, Harvey Weiss, Kate Welham Sue Wiles, and Ruth Young, who kindly sent me copies of their work, allowed me to include their illustrations, and/or pointed me in useful and interesting directions. Louisa Verwey at the Cory Library for Historical Research, Rhodes University, kindly located and sent me a very interesting and hard-to-get paper.

This book was begun in Tokyo, where I was a Project Associate Professor at Tokyo University between 2008 and 2015, and completed in Newcastle upon Tyne as a Visiting Fellow in the School of History, Classics, and Archaeology at Newcastle University. I would like to thank Jakob Wisse for kindly granting me this position at Newcastle.

At Cambridge University Press, I would like to thank Asya Graf for her enthusiasm for the project and for her cheerful help and support to the end. Thanks also go to Mary Catherine Bongiovi, who saw the book through to completion as well as to Kanimozhi Ramamurthy and the staff at Newgen for their careful work on the text. I also thank the anonymous readers at Cambridge for their comments on the draft; I hope to have improved the work in light of these.

On a personal note, this book would probably not have been completed without the moral support of James Whiting and Richard Carter-White. Thanks must go especially to Yoshie Nakata, who put up with me and collapse for years. Goblin Face and Miss Pemberton provided love and a (sometimes) welcome feline distraction as the book was completed.

1

Introducing Collapse

The fall, like the rise, of a civilization is a highly complex operation which can only be distorted and obscured by easy simplification.

Mortimer Wheeler[1]

CLIMATE APOCALYPSE IN THE NEWS

As I sat down to work this morning with Radio 4 on in the background, I was intrigued to hear the BBC's newsreader announcing that the riddle of the mysterious Classic Maya collapse had finally been solved.[2] I waited with baited breath to hear what the latest explanation would be, thinking it must be a slow news day for ancient history to have made it into the news mix. A moderate drought, she explained, was enough to cause the collapse of Maya civilisation around 1,100 years ago, which, she added, led to the Maya cities and pyramids being swallowed up by the rainforest. The announcer confided that, although solving the Maya collapse had long been a problem, archaeologists generally now preferred drought as the cause.

The whole report probably lasted no more than two or three minutes, an impressively short time in which to explain the fate of a long-lived and complex civilisation that had existed for hundreds of years, several times longer than modern nations like the United States or Australia. It was a problem that, as she rightly pointed out, had puzzled archaeologists and the curious for years. But I wondered what exactly I and other listeners were supposed to understand by 'collapse' and by 'Maya civilisation' – dramatic images of lost and abandoned cities reclaimed by nature were evoked, but would we all

be imagining the same thing? I was curious too about which archaeologists she was referring to, and who had decided that 'most' of
them preferred this conclusion. I briefly wondered whether I would
no longer be obliged to complete this book about collapse ...

So, I diligently looked up the original paper that the news report
was based on, just published in the journal *Science*.[3] The paper was
somewhat less definitive than the news report, but its argument was
still clear enough. I found that the authors, two oceanographers,
had studied the existing palaeoclimatic data, drawn from physical
samples taken from three locations in northern Yucatan, Mexico.
Like other researchers before them, they suggested that chemi-
cal analysis of cores taken from lake bottoms and from stalactites
('speleothems' – stalactites and stalagmites or cave calcites) indicated
periods of reduced rainfall in Late Classic Maya times (the eighth
and ninth centuries AD). This, they said, would have reduced the carrying capacity of the land, the amount of food that it could produce,
which would in turn have caused the population to fall catastrophically, triggering 'significant societal disruptions'.

Rather than a new solution, this sounded like a well-known story of
collapse due to some kind of environmental change with which human
society could not cope, the main difference being that the authors were
claiming that a more moderate reduction in rainfall could be blamed,
rather than the massive droughts suggested by others. If a modest
reduction in rainfall could have this effect, it suggested that the ecology
and hydrology of the Yucatan Peninsula, the home of (some of) the
Maya people, were particularly sensitive to change; a plausible hypothesis. But, given the long history of research on the problem of the Classic
Maya collapse, and the number of publications, scholarly and popular,
as well as television documentaries and even films on the subject, was
that it? Rainfall slightly reduced, Maya collapsed and disappeared?

I was still left wondering what the authors really thought the Maya
collapse was, and if this moderate reduction in rainfall could be
enough to explain it. The news story had suggested a point of collapse
around 1,100 years ago, *c.* AD 900, and the disappearance of the
Maya, whereas the authors of the paper actually noted, quite rightly,
that 'the disintegration of the Classic Maya Civilization was a complex process' taking two centuries. But their account still seemed very
much to imply some kind of terrible event that would have involved
a lot of death and unpleasantness. Did they imagine that many Maya

simply died at once, that it was ultimately a kind of Malthusian population collapse? And what were these 'societal disruptions'? Their statement that the collapse 'involved a catastrophic depopulation of the region' seemed clearly enough to indicate that it was an ecological collapse they were thinking of, of the kind biologists might identify in any species or ecosystem.

I was left with an image of an empty landscape, and a population wiped out by a terrible natural disaster, yet it is difficult to square this with the idea of a complex two-century process of change, which the authors had introduced. Two centuries is a long time, time enough for significant changes in ways of life and attitudes, in political geography, and in material culture to occur. Admittedly, it can be hard to conceptualise past periods of time; as George Orwell said 'when you look backward things that happened years apart are telescoped together'.[4] The stories implied some kind of 'back to square one' blow, from which the Maya, the few who survived, would have to start again amongst the ruins of their former glory. In this account, a fairly typical story of apocalyptic collapse involving a terrible disaster and death with a handful of survivors eking out a living in a post-apocalyptic age, the ancient Maya were helpless victims of circumstance.

The Maya are not the only ones to receive this treatment, although they are a perennial favourite – enigmatic, exotic, mysterious. In 2012, for example, *The Times of India* proclaimed that 'Climate killed Harappan civilization', a story also based on a research paper published in the *Proceedings of the National Academy of Sciences of the USA* (*PNAS*).[5] The paper argues that a reduction in monsoon rainfall affected the complex river flows of the Indus basin, with rivers getting smaller, becoming seasonal, or even drying up completely. The agricultural basis of the Harappan urban sites was undermined. Yet there was no sudden ending, no killing stroke executed by the climate; the authors state soberly that: 'since approximately 3,900 y ago, the total settled area and settlement sizes declined, many sites were abandoned, and a significant shift in site numbers and density towards the east is recorded'.

Another similar story, entitled 'Climate change: The great civilization destroyer' appeared in the *New Scientist* in 2012, this time about the Mycenaean Greeks of the Late Bronze Age, *c.* 1200 BC.[6] This article, again based on a research paper, wanted to add the Mycenaean collapse to the list of peoples, societies, and civilisations supposedly brought to an end by climate change.[7]

These stories, and others like them, seem to represent the public image of collapse in the early twenty-first century and the cutting edge of archaeological and historical research. They tie in with our concerns over current climate change, and also with the vivid images we have of drought and famine. What these stories remind me of, and presumably others, are the graphic images of the victims of the tragic droughts and famines in Ethiopia in the 1980s. These came to international attention through the harrowing television reports shown around the world, which many in developed countries, seeing such things for the first time, found so shocking. Those images, and more recent ones that still appear regularly on television, seemed to show people stricken and emaciated, in abject poverty, with no food, water, or hope, people for whom circumstances were intolerable and for whom normal functioning society had ceased, people who would, without international aid, die where they sat, starving and thirsty. Would the Classic Maya, Harappan, and Mycenaean collapses have looked like this?

STORIES AND COLLAPSE

Probably not. The problem with collapse in the news and in many popular articles is that the stories they tell are grossly oversimplified, offering a caricature of history, a mythic version of historical change for our sound bite society; they are infotainment at its best. As we have seen already, one issue is the way that scientific research is transformed into news. In the first place, certain kinds of scientific research are more likely to get published in high-profile journals, and thus to catch the attention of news services. Journals such as *Nature*, *Science* and *PNAS* choose to publish novel and especially interdisciplinary research, research that has definitive results and conclusions – hard science style. Thus stories about new climate change linked to the fate of ancient societies are much more likely to reach a wide audience than a more circumspect paper in an archaeological journal.

Then the headline language used to describe collapse in popular sources (in the press as well as in documentary films) frequently serves to obscure the complex historical processes that were at work, turning them into cataclysmic events, and presents the peoples, states, or societies (and peoples) in question as static two-dimensional entities that could be wiped out in a blip. Too often, such reports, and the science papers on which they are based, fail to really consider what they are saying. What do we mean by collapse and what do we mean when we talk about the Classic Maya, the Harappans, or the Mycenaean Greeks, their cultures, their societies, and their civilisations? If we frame the questions simplistically, we are likely to get simplistic and unsatisfactory answers.

Despite their lack of substance, these stories have a great and understandable appeal, and it is worth thinking about this a little. What such stories really represent is a kind of quest romance, a kind of story as ancient and appealing as the oldest stories we know, which historian Ronald Hutton explains is 'one of the most popular and effective modes of expression for historical or archaeological research'.[8] Researchers are heroes on a quest, who undergo a journey in which they apply their knowledge and skills, and eventually, and triumphantly, solve a seemingly insoluble historical conundrum.

Collapse stories appeal to our narrative desires in other ways too. They can be seen as both tragedy and parable. Tragedy originated as a specific kind of theatrical performance in ancient Greece, and tragic stories dealt with big and serious themes; plays were not simply 'art', but actively mirrored the politics and society of contemporary life and functioned 'as a powerful medium for the communication of ideas'.[9] They had a standardised plot in which the hero's journey is followed, his actions leading to a climax and then finally to a resolution, often the death of the hero.[10] Read 'ancient civilisation' for 'hero' and we have a story of rise, zenith, and fall – stories of collapse which are blamed on human degradation of the environment seem to fit this pattern.

In tragedy, the hero usually makes a mistake, which leads to his fate; sometimes these errors are brought about by outside factors, such as divine intervention, but at other times there is some fatal character flaw. So in collapse we can see external factors blamed or errors made by the society that collapsed. Just as in tragedy, where the *mechane* allowed gods to enter the stage through the air, revealing the act of violence that resolved the play, collapse is often 'explained' by *deus ex machina*.[11] Just as tragedy was a social art, witnessed and consumed by ancient audiences, our stories of collapse are spectacles, shared and consumed by modern audiences.

Aristotle thought tragedy served an emotional or psychological purpose. He suggested that 'through pity and fear' there would be catharsis, an emotional purging in the audience.[12] Nietzsche, thinking of tragedy, wrote of 'that lust which also involves the *joy of destruction*'.[13] Others have suggested that tragedy provokes *Schadenfreude*, that in fact audiences enjoy the horrors of tragedy and the sufferings of its fictional hero, a kind of enjoyment which, however morally questionable it may be, seems real and commonplace.[14] Does our witnessing of apocalyptic collapse, whether in print, on television, or on film, somehow fulfil us emotionally? Do we enjoy the spectacle and revel in stories of the destruction of others?

Perhaps. Nowadays this may be most evident in popular blockbuster films that project views of apocalyptic collapse with causes that reflect contemporary concerns. In recent decades, we have been treated to global disaster threatened by colliding comets in the 1998 film *Armageddon*, where disaster was narrowly averted through technology and guts, and also by the film *Deep Impact* where the ending was much more bleak, with millions perishing. In 2004 there was *The Day After Tomorrow*, a film which depicted a sudden climate change and the onset of a new ice age almost overnight. In 2009, *2012* focussed on global disasters such as earthquakes and tsunamis, which killed millions, caused by the heating of the Earth's core by solar flares – a select few humans were able to save themselves in a number of 'arks', built in secret in China. The 2011 film *Contagion*, in more of a documentary style, explored the effects of a global pandemic, which caused the breakdown of social order; the film reflected real contemporary fears about possible pandemics such as SARS and H1N1 flu.

Other myths of apocalyptic collapse too come to mind from our shared past culture. The flood myths shared by numerous cultures around the world are often taken to suggest that floods had a profound effect on people in the past, strong enough to warrant being passed down in stories, although floods, like other themes can have metaphorical rather than literal meanings.[15] The flood myth recounted in the Mesopotamian Epic of Gilgamesh, and later the Christian Bible, have even inspired people to search for a real catastrophic geological event that may underlie the story – some suggest the flooding of the Black Sea.[16]

Also from the Bible we have the story of Sodom and Gomorrah, recounted in Deuteronomy 29:23. The cities were destroyed by God in his anger at the wickedness and vice of their inhabitants. But other kinds of destruction were also foretold. In Isaiah 17:1–2, a prophecy of the destruction of Damascus is given, in which it is predicted that the city will become a heap of ruins. The destruction of the mercantile city of Tyre by Nebuchadnezzar was also graphically prophesied in Ezekiel, which describes the utter destruction of one state by another. Destruction is a consequence of wrongdoing – a precursor to our modern environmental stories of collapse.

The Atlantis myth is a story of catastrophic and apocalyptic collapse *par excellence*. It has been a part of Western culture since Plato composed it in the early fourth century BC; we know it from his *Critias* and *Timaeus*.[17] However, it is probably better known now than ever before; Alan Cameron notes it as the inspiration for over 20,000 books.[18] A Platonic myth rather than a Greek myth, invented by a man devoted to exploring order, a crafter of ideal societies, and political utopias, the story relates how Atlantis, a fictional ideal state located on an island in the Atlantic, fell from grace as its once blessed and virtuous people grew corrupted and greedy over time, eventually trying to enlarge their empire and conquer the world. For this hubris Zeus wanted to punish them, and the ancient Athenians, who in contrast to the Atlanteans were still virtuous, defeated them in war, freeing all the conquered and enslaved peoples, and averting the threat from the invaders. Afterwards, 'there were earthquakes and floods of extraordinary violence, and in a single dreadful day and night all your fighting men were swallowed up by the Earth, and the island of Atlantis was similarly swallowed up by the sea and vanished'.[19]

Interpretations of the Atlantis myth abound as people make the story conform to their desires, but it seems clear enough that Plato, in the fourth century BC, was teaching his fellow Athenians (and others) to be mindful of their ambition and their priorities.[20] They had been embroiled in the creation of an empire and had had a major conflict with Sparta, which led to defeat at the end of the fifth century BC. He perhaps wanted them to recall their ancestors in the earlier fifth century who had, somewhat against the odds, defeated the enormous might of the invading Persian king. Athens was the focus of the story; Atlantis represented an undesirable, avoidable fate. The

story elaborates the age old aphorism that pride comes before a fall –
much like the story of Croesus and the Delphic oracle.

Alan Cameron notes that 'it is only in modern times that people have taken the Atlantis story seriously; no-one did so in antiquity'.[21] Indeed, many have 'believed', including the British prime
minister and Homeric scholar William Gladstone, and have tried
to associate the Atlantis myth with 'real' history.[22] K. T. Frost in
1913 wrote that 'The search for Atlantis has given rise to so many
conflicting views (most of them palpably absurd) that few scholars are prepared to take it seriously', before offering his own view,
about which most modern scholars would express equal scepticism,
that the story represented Minoan and Mycenaean history.[23] Frost
noted that while 'it seems ... futile to seek for the geographical or
geological site of a huge island now submerged. On the other hand
a political and national disaster, a cataclysm in the usual instead
of in the literal sense of the word, can destroy an ancient civilisation as completely as any flood'.[24] But despite his comments others
have continued to look, and to make associations with the archaeological, geological, and historical evidence of the Late Bronze Age
Aegean, in particular the eruption of ancient Thera and its effects
on Minoan Crete.

An interesting example of an apocalyptic story from the pre-
Hollywood blockbuster days that ticks the same boxes, and shows
that our modern disaster discourse is no new thing, is the volcanic
disaster narrative.[25] This was a type of entertainment devised by pyro-
technical entrepreneurs, who produced 'volcano entertainments',
spectacles with painted backdrops and sound effects, which became
popular in the nineteenth century, but which originated in the eighteenth. They reflected increasing interest in geology and the natural
processes of the Earth combined with excitement over the excavation
of the buried city of Pompeii, which began in the 1740s.

In the 1880s, one such show, called *The Last Days of Pompeii*,
was toured by the Pain family, who were fireworks manufacturers
(Figure 1.1). It visited New York and London, among other places.
In its first performance at Manhattan Beach, Coney Island, the show
attracted more than a thousand spectators, with later shows attracting up to 10,000. In June 1889, the Pains put on a modified version of
the show, announced in the *New York Times* (9 June 1889):

FIGURE 1.1. Graham Charles. Fireworks at Manhattan Beach – 'The Last days of Pompeii'.
Source: *Harper's Weekly* 25 July 1885, 476. General Research Division, The New York Public Library, Astor, Lenox and Tilden Foundations.

Beginning next Saturday night, 'The Last Days of Pompeii' will be presented nightly by Mr Pain at Manhattan Beach. It is not to be a revival of the show which he gave under the same name in 1885, but a much more elaborate and magnificent affair. There will be 400 people on the stage, a ballet of 36 dancers trained by Batiste Cherotte, master at the Metropolitan Opera House, a male chorus from the same place, soldiers, acrobats, jugglers, tumblers, wire-walkers, and others to assist in making the picture of a fete day. The display is to culminate in the destruction of the city by the fires of Vesuvius.[26]

In addition to their romantic and tragic appeal, stories of collapse are ideal fodder for the creation of modern parables for our time – especially parables of human relationships with the natural environment. Examples of this are not hard to find, and they are frequently repeated in the literature, becoming factoids that purport to be straightforward historical facts. One noted environmental writer, Lester Brown, for example, in his book *World on the Edge: How to Prevent Environmental and Economic Collapse*, used as examples ancient Sumer and the Maya. The former collapsed because their successful irrigation systems eventually led to high salinity, resulting ultimately in food shortages and collapse. The latter chopped down too many trees, leading to soil erosion, and again, food shortages. Brown draws an explicit parallel between past and present: 'for us it is rising carbon dioxide concentrations in the atmosphere that are raising the global temperature, which could ultimately shrink grain harvests and bring down our global civilization'.[27] The lessons we are to learn from the past are clear.

None of this is to say that there is only one 'correct' version of collapse that exists to the exclusion of all others, nor that the academic archaeological version (not that there is 'one' single version) is the best – in doing history there are many stories and perspectives that can be usefully brought into play. But it is important that we recognise the constructed nature of our ideas about collapse. I think Stephanie Moser puts it best:

The notion that researchers are solely responsible for creating meaning about the past is a false assumption that diverts our attention from the fact that representations have their own unique conventions and ways of communicating. Thus knowledge is not simply created by researchers and then diffused into popular culture (i.e. a one-way process); it is also created by many other kinds of discourse which in themselves shape the ideas of researchers.[28]

Our thinking on collapse, and the stories we tell of it, popular and academic, are reflections of our own times and concerns. As we read back through accounts of collapse from different times, we can see this influence clearly.[29] But we must beware of over simplifying or skewing our accounts of past collapses just to turn them into lessons for modern society.

What I hope to have shown so far is that we often see collapse in very particular ways, which are structured by how we share knowledge – through stories or narratives. Collapse stories often bridge information and entertainment, fulfilling our needs on a variety of levels. Scientists are problem-solving heroes, societies are tragic characters, destined to fail, and collapse is a lesson to be learnt from. There is nothing inherently bad about this – it is human nature to make everything into a story. But if we really want to know about collapse, we have to begin by trying to see past the popular stories. A result of this, and one that many might find unsatisfying, is that we may end up without straight answers or simple plausible-sounding storylines; we might have to admit that sometimes (or a lot of the time) we do not know what happened or who or what was to blame for something that we think was going on.

WHAT IS COLLAPSE?

Before we get too far along, we should think about what collapse actually is and what kind of things can collapse. Assumptions about and lack of definitions of collapse are two of the problems in how it is represented. Very often, the implication is that collapse is some kind of apocalyptic event – everyone starves and the monuments of a civilisation decay and are lost only to be rediscovered much later on, posing a riddle to explorers and archaeologists. As Joseph Tainter suggests, many 'authors assume that we know what it means, without individual, cultural, or temporal variation'.[30] However, there is no guarantee that we are in fact all sharing the same idea of what collapse is.

Describing the Maya collapse, archaeologist Arthur Demarest takes the problem a step further, blaming controversies over interpretation not only on assumptions about what collapse is, but also on confusion over what is collapsing:

Recent discussions of the collapse of civilizations have demonstrated that terminological ambiguity creates much of the controversy regarding comparative issues, including differences in the interpretation of specific cultural historical episodes. The meanings of terms such as 'collapse' and 'decline' are far from obvious. Furthermore, ambiguity about what precisely is 'collapsing' (e.g. 'civilization,' 'state,' 'kingdoms,' 'tradition,' 'society') generates more disagreement than do problems of historical or archaeological interpretation.[31]

But there are definitions of collapse, and of what it might apply to, and I shall introduce and discuss some of those next.

Joseph Tainter's 1988 book *The Collapse of Complex Societies* is still probably the most referenced book on collapse; the author has written much about collapse, complexity, and sustainability. His definition of collapse goes like this:

Collapse ... is a *political* process. It may, and often does have consequences in such areas as economics, art, and literature, but it is fundamentally a matter of the socio-political sphere. *A society has collapsed when it displays a rapid, significant loss of an established level of sociopolitical complexity.* The term 'established level' is important. To qualify as an instance of collapse a society must have been at, or developing toward, a level of complexity for more than one or two generations. The demise of the Carolingian Empire, thus, is not a case of collapse – merely an unsuccessful attempt at empire building. The collapse … must be rapid – taking no more than a few decades – and must entail a substantial loss of sociopolitical structure. Losses that are less severe, or take longer to occur, are to be considered cases of weakness and decline.[32]

Tainter sees collapse very specifically as a political process connected to the degree of complexity of a society. Human societies become more complex as a response to the problems and opportunities that they face, and through collapse they become less complex.[33] Collapse then is a rapid process of simplification – where rapid means not instantaneous, but perhaps a few decades. Importantly, in Tainter's way of thinking, collapse itself is an adaptation not simply a failure.

What does this definition apply to? In his main examples, Tainter writes about the Western Roman Empire, the Classic Maya, and the Ancestral Puebloans of southwestern North America. These are three quite different entities, operating at different scales. The first was a large empire; the second a group of independent but competitive states of varying size making up what we could call a 'culture zone'; the third is a smaller single culture. So in Tainter's view, political collapse can happen to a range of 'things'. We might wonder, however, whether all of these are really comparable.

George Cowgill and Norman Yoffee discussed what collapse applies to in another key publication from 1988, *The Collapse of Ancient States and Civilizations*. They suggest that we should 'clearly differentiate between *state, society* and *civilization,* and use the last term in a specifically *cultural* sense'.[34] Collapse occurs within civilisations, which are the 'cultural tradition[s] in which the state is embedded,' consisting of 'literature, customs, languages'.[35] To some, this may seem like academic semantics, but it is important. Often we read or hear about the collapse of civilisations, but Roman, Maya, and Ancient Puebloan civilisations did not collapse at all – all three survive, transformed, to this day. It is specific political regimes that collapsed, social systems that changed, and religious and ideological systems that were transformed and/or rejected.

Take another example – Mesopotamian civilisation. Jane Rempel and Norman Yoffee asked the question, 'did Mesopotamian civilisation end?' They emphasised that while politically Mesopotamia contained many different states and empires over the years, which rose and fell, and eventually the whole region fell prey to even bigger empires passing through Persian and then Macedonian and Greek hands, 'Mesopotamian civilization did not undergo a similar collapse.'[36] That is not to say it did not change, it certainly did – it transformed over long years, but it did not collapse in the blink of an eye. The cuneiform writing tradition could be taken as an index of the presence of Mesopotamian civilisation and its disappearance as late as the third century AD could be said to mark the end of Mesopotamian civilisation.[37] But this single indicator is an arbitrary one – a civilisation is a set of features that transform at different rates (and with different implications for the people and societies in question).

There is no need to see such transformations as decline – the value of cultural items and practices such as writing changes, as do the ways people seek to construct their personal and cultural identities. Likewise with the end of the Western Roman Empire. Its political system collapsed in the fifth century AD, its territory fragmenting into multiple independent states, but Roman civilisation did not collapse. It had always been changing, and this did not end abruptly with the death of the last Western emperor; the Roman heritage remained alive, being reused, reinterpreted, and transformed by the people who inherited it – in the twenty-first century the Americans still place importance on the concept of liberty, and retain senators and a senate.

What about famous examples of collapse such as the Greenland Viking communities, or the lost city of Roanoake, or Rapa Nui? In the former case, we have two communities that were eventually abandoned – but these did not collapse in Tainter's sense, and the latest research suggests they were abandoned by their inhabitants in good order rather than that they fell into chaos and calamity with everyone starving to death or killing each other.[38] With Roanoake (the City of Raleigh, on Roanoke Island, Virgina), the English settlement founded in North America in 1587, we have an example of a mystery – another settlement abandoned – but again not a collapse in the view of many.[39] And what about Easter Island? Whether there was a collapse – a simplification of Rapa Nui society – at some point before Europeans arrived is controversial, as we shall see later on. In all these examples of supposed collapse, what probably happened is far less dramatic than the apocalyptic stories we are often presented with.

Many authors who write about collapse cite Tainter in their own lists of references, but not everyone strictly follows his definition of collapse. Jared Diamond, one of the most well-known popular writers on collapse, gave a definition in his 2005 book *Collapse* that is clearly drawn in part from his reading of Tainter and other thinkers on collapse, but it differs in key respects:

By collapse, I mean a drastic decrease in human population size and/or political/economic/social complexity, over a considerable area, for an extended time. The phenomenon of collapse is thus an extreme form of several milder types of decline, and it becomes arbitrary to decide how drastic the decline of a society must be before it qualifies to be labelled as a collapse.[40]

The first thing we should note is that, unlike Tainter, Diamond emphasises 'drastic' decreases in population over a wide area and long period of time. This reflects not only the common view of apocalyptic collapse, but also Diamond's background in ecology and biology, where collapse is something that happens to populations in ecosystems (think of the mysterious 'colony collapse disorder' that has affected bee populations in recent years). This focus on population and disaster also follows from Thomas Malthus' influential *An Essay on the Principle of Population*, published in 1798, in which populations grow until they are checked by some kind of catastrophe. The focus on population in Diamond's definition is almost the opposite of Tainter's view that collapse is primarily a political process.

It is easy to imagine that a demographic collapse would be a terrible thing – something that would by its very nature have to be brought on by plague epidemics or famines caused by extreme droughts or climate change or damage to a society's supporting environment, which reduced its carrying capacity. Such a disaster would surely have serious repercussions for any society – even possibly bringing about its demise (though clearly the medieval European states survived the massive disruption and population loss caused by the Black Death). Thus, Diamond envisions the Greenland Viking's collapse as:

sudden rather than gentle, like the sudden collapse of the Soviet Union [the Eastern settlement was] like an overcrowded lifeboat ... famine and disease would have caused a breakdown of respect for authority ... starving people would have poured into Gardar, and the outnumbered chiefs and church officials could no longer prevent them from slaughtering the last cattle and sheep ... I picture the scene as ... like that in my home city of Los Angeles in 1992, at the time of the so-called Rodney King riots ... thousands of outraged people from poor neighbourhoods ... spread out to loot businesses and rich neighbourhoods.[41]

A focus on demographics conjures up a stereotypical descent into a dark age largely devoid of people and of the kinds of activity that comprise civilised life. Whereas for Tainter a political collapse could have repercussions in other areas of life and society, including being a cause of depopulation, for Diamond it is primarily depopulation that is collapse.

We have looked at two quite different visions of collapse, both drawn from works attempting to give general explanations of why collapse happens – one taking an economic perspective, the other an environmental one. But what about archaeologists themselves, how do they see collapse? In an important book about collapse and regeneration, from 2006, entitled *After Collapse: The Regeneration of Complex Societies*, Glenn Schwartz explains:

In the archaeological literature, collapse usually entails some or all of the following: the fragmentation of states into smaller political entities; the partial abandonment or complete desertion of urban centers, along with the loss or depletion of their centralizing functions; the breakdown of regional economic systems; and the failure of civilizational ideologies.[42]

This broad description is different again. It does not necessarily describe the simplification of a given society, unless we see the fragmentation of empires or states as simplification, nor does it necessarily involve demographic collapse, although this can be indicated by the abandonment of sites (but this can also indicate the nucleation of population at a few sites or a shift in subsistence strategies). But rather than insisting on a single meaning, it gives us a number of descriptive features of collapse that we can tie to specific examples, and these reflect well how archaeologists apply the term 'collapse' in practice.

A more recent definition from their 2012 paper is given by archaeologist Karl Butzer and environmental historian Georgina Endfield, who suggest that:

Societal collapse represents transformation at a large social or spatial scale, with long-term impact on combinations of interdependent variables: (i) environmental change and resilience; (ii) demography or settlement; (iii) socioeconomic patterns; (iv) political or societal structures; and (v) ideology or cultural memory.[43]

Although there is some overlap with the previous definitions, this one is different again, since it defines collapse as large-scale transformation with a number of possible impacts on five interlinked areas. One problem with this definition is that there is no idea of the timescale of such transformation – are such transformations rapid? Does collapse as transformation have to be measured in a few years, in decades, or can it take place over centuries, in which case how does it differ from plain 'change'? Also, can we equate 'demography' with 'settlement' – that is, equate population with how populations are spread through the landscape?

Another problem (depending on your point of view) is that state formation or ideological changes, such as new systems or ideologies of power, may count, in this definition, as episodes of collapse. Was the pyramid age of Egypt an era of collapse because of its new centralisation and a new system of ruler-focused monumental propaganda? Can either the founding of the Roman Empire (from an oligarchical republican system), the Christianisation of Rome (or indeed Europe), or the extension of the franchise to women in the UK, as profound real and ideological changes, count as collapses?

Finally, let us include a definition from the sustainability literature, as given by Marianne Young and Rik Leemans:

Let us define *collapse* as any situation where the rate of change to a system:

- has negative effects on human welfare, which, in the short term, are socially intolerable;
- will result in a fundamental downsizing, a loss of coherence, and/or significant restructuring of the constellation of arrangements that characterise the system; and

- cannot be stopped or controlled via an incremental change in behavior, resource allocation, or institutional values.[44]

This definition is drawn from the results of a Dahlem workshop, published in 2007 as *Sustainability or Collapse? An Integrated History and Future of People on Earth*.[45] These authors, as with some of the others, do refer to timescales – since change is normal, collapse represents a change in its rate where certain effects are present, including simplification and 'socially intolerable' effects on human welfare. It is also seen as an unstoppable process – one that cascades from changed situation to changed situation, taking the unit considered further away from a particular first set of circumstances.

The definition is reminiscent of the idea of failed or failing states, an equally inexact concept popular since the 1990s, which is of clear concern to policy makers seeking to ensure that states become or remain sustainable and do not collapse. Of these, Cojanu and Popescu explain:

There is a growing recognition of the threat to international security posed by failed and fragile states, often marred by serious internal conflict that also has the potential of destabilizing neighbouring states and providing ungoverned territory that can provide safe haven for terrorists.

The inability of their governments to provide basic services is considered a significant contributory factor. Poorly performing developing countries are linked to humanitarian catastrophes; mass migration; environmental degradation; regional instability; energy insecurity; global pandemics; international crime; the proliferation of weapons of mass destruction, and, of course, transnational terrorism.[46]

Socially intolerable conditions can be quite a tricky concept to define. It may simply mean that living conditions become much worse – intolerably so, for a given period of time. They may, however, become tolerable as people's expectations and values change. For whom (and for how many) do conditions have to be intolerable? The slave miners in the Roman world, the child miners of nineteenth-century Britain, or other exploited or socially excluded groups surely lived in conditions that others might find intolerable … But these were normal features of 'successful' societies that were not collapsing. We might also, when we take society to refer to an identifiable social unit like an empire or state, think of circumstances that the system itself, rather than its people, is unable to bear.

Most reasonable people would expect there to be some leeway in language usage; after all, we usually adopt or create terminology to help us think about the thing we are trying to describe, and not as an end in itself, as Patrick L. Gardiner reminds us:

Generalizations about revolutions, class-struggles, civilizations, must *inevitably* be vague, open to a multitude of exceptions and saving clauses, because of the looseness of the terms they employ ... But this is not to criticize such generalizations provided that they are not expected to do more work than they are fitted for. The scientific model of precise correlation is misleading in any attempt to comprehend the role of these generalizations in history, where they function frequently as *guides to understanding*.[47]

Each definition of collapse brings with it different observations, ramifications, and repercussions. There is little of the apocalyptic to be seen, except perhaps in Diamond's and Young and Leemans' ideas, and the demographic definition is not one that archaeologists or historians usually use, except in specific cases such as collapse of native populations during instances of European colonialism. Much more frequently, collapse is used to mean the fairly rapid ending of states (including empires and much smaller entities), which itself can involve fragmentation into smaller units, simplification of political and social systems, change in urban settings, redistribution of population in the landscape, and changes in ideology made visible in architecture and the arts.

Many archaeologists agree that collapse often affected the elite members of societies most – or at least most visibly – and that those least affected (at least in some ways) would be the peasant farmers that made up the bulk of the population in pre-industrial societies. Thus collapse could be 'socially intolerable' to the elite but welcomed by 'middle classes' or others. But it is also true that collapse would have had effects that ran through a whole society to some extent. Fragmentation could bring instability and conflict, driving down agricultural production, trade, and exchange, all of which might affect the population levels, while the end of rulership, its specific ideology, and all that went with it would have had its own set of economic and social effects.

At any rate, whenever we think about collapse, it is a good idea to be critical – not for the sake of argument, but in order to grasp more fully what we (and others) actually mean and what we are really exploring.

WHAT COLLAPSED?

In Tainter's definition, collapse is something political that can happen to any established society – ones that are both more complex and less complex. But in practice, people apply collapse to many different kinds of 'units', and so I want to take a step back and consider the kind of units that collapse is said to happen to and to think about the implications of this. This is important because many authors take a comparative view of collapse, yet it is not always clear why some examples of collapse are thought to be comparable with others. To begin with, it may be helpful to consider the variety of entities that we encounter in the modern world, if only to remind us of some of the different categories involved.

Nowadays, we tend to think about the world as carved up into fixed territorial political units that we call countries, states, or nations, and which we often refer to generally as 'societies', owing to their nature as politically and socially defined in-groups in which people imagine a common identity. These may often be the biggest unit for which we have certain legally defined relationships and statuses, and a strong sense of identification. Some states, Switzerland, China, the United Kingdom, or Spain, for example, are multi-ethnic and multilingual, while in others, such as Korea or Japan, more stress has been placed, in recent times at least, on ethnic and cultural homogeneity.

Of course, there are also bigger entities like the European Union, in which many Europeans are voting citizens, but it is unclear whether this legal and political entity is also something with which many of its citizens strongly identify, in contrast with their other identities. There are other concepts that are made use of, such as 'westernness', 'Arabness', or 'Asianness', which are grounded in cultural or behavioural commonalities and sometimes in the idea of shared cultural heritages – sometimes equated with that loose idea of 'civilisations'. Much of Europe, and therefore the USA and other recent states, share an origin rooted partly in Roman and classical heritage. Some transnational identities and institutions are neither 'national' nor 'ethnic' and are based instead on religious or other affiliations – Catholicism is a prime example of an enduring non-ethnic group identity, Islam is another.

'Nation' can also refer to people who identify themselves as a unit, on the basis of some (possibly imagined) shared descent, ethnicity, or 'national' identity, for example. Nations may be non-sovereign groups, or groups with a degree of autonomy either within one or several sovereign states – the 30 million Kurds who live in Turkey, Iraq, Iran, and Syria, for example, or native American groups, are nations. Tribal or aboriginal groups elsewhere, within states, may also sometimes be considered as nations. In the past, as in the present, states and nations do not necessarily overlap territorially – empires and states may incorporate different peoples in different ways. In classical Greece, the helots of Sparta, Messenian Greek slaves owned by the state, were part of the state only to the extent that the state claimed ownership of them, keeping them subjugated for centuries. Despite this situation, a Messenian identity continued to exist and the Messenian state was reconstituted after the battle of Leuctra in 371 BC.[48]

WHAT ARE WE COMPARING IN PAST COLLAPSES?

A brief glance at some of the examples rostered in comparative approaches to collapse shows that many different kinds of units are often considered together (Table 1.1). We can see empires, such as the Akkadian and Roman; cases that may be empires or states, such as Han China, Tiwanaku, and Wari; states like Uruk and Old Kingdom Egypt, and Axum. We can also see what may be best described as 'culture zones', including the Classic Maya, Crete and Late Bronze Age Greece, and Mesopotamia, which were made up of numerous independent states and other possibly non-state communities, which nevertheless shared a degree of cultural and sometimes linguistic similarity (probably the Harappan/Indus Valley societies fall into this category too).

Other units are included too – societies that might not be considered 'state level', such as the Ancestral Puebloans and Rapa Nui (Easter Island), and communities that were part of larger cultural groups such as the Greenland Norse. The very prehistoric 'Natufians' were not a people – the name refers to a more sedentary culture that appeared among hunter-gatherer communities in the Near East.[49]

TABLE 1.1. *Objects of study in works on collapse*

Tainter (1988)	Ancestral Puebloan, Classic Maya, Roman Empire (plus many other shorter case studies)
Yoffee and Cowgill (1988)	Classic Maya, Han China, Mesopotamia, Mesoamerica, Roman Empire
Weiss and Bradley (2001)	Natufians; Uruk; Akkadian Empire, Old Kingdom Egypt, Harappa IIIB; EBA III Palestine, LBA Greece, Crete; Moche; Tiwanaku; Classic Maya; Ancestral Puebloan
Diamond (2005)	Ancestral Puebloan, Greenland Norse, Easter Island, Classic Maya
Schwartz and Nichols (2006)	Angkor, Classic Maya, LBA Greece, Old Kingdom Egypt, EBA Syria, Tiwanaku, Wari
Redman et al. (2007)	Old Kingdom Egypt, China, Mesopotamia, Harappa, Bal He Kuk, Classic Maya, Hohokam
Costanza et al. (2007) (In the same volume)	Classic Maya, Western Roman Empire, Northern Mesopotamia
Butzer and Endfield (2012) (and others)	Akkadian Empire, Axum, Cyprus, Greco-Roman Fayum, Iceland, Greenland Norse, Islamic Mesopotamia, Old/New Kingdom Egypt, Norse Greenland, Classic Maya,

Source: Tainter, J. A. (1988). *The Collapse of Complex Societies*. Cambridge: Cambridge University Press; Yoffee, N. and Cowgill, G. L. (eds.). (1988). *The Collapse of Ancient States and Civilizations*. Tucson: Arizona University Press; Weiss, H. and Bradley, R. S. (2001). 'What drives societal collapse?' *Science* 291: 609–610; Diamond, J. (2005). *Collapse: How Societies Choose to Fail or Succeed*. London: Penguin; Redman, C. L. et al. (2007). 'Group report: Millenial perspectives on the dynamic interaction of climate, people, and resources.' In Costanza, R., Graumlich, L. J., and Steffen, W. (eds.). *Sustainability or Collapse? An Integrated History and Future of People on Earth*. Cambridge: Dahlem University Press and Massachusetts Institute of Technology, pp. 115–148; Costanza, R., Graumlich, L. J., and Steffen, W. (eds.). (2007). *Sustainability or Collapse? An Integrated History and Future of People on Earth*. Cambridge: Dahlem University Press and Massachusetts Institute of Technology; Schwartz, G. M. and Nichols, J. J. (eds.). (2006). *After Collapse: The Regeneration of Complex Societies*. Tucson: University of Arizona Press; Butzer, K. W. and Endfield, G. H. (2012). 'Critical perspectives on historical collapse.' *Proceedings of the National Academy of Science* 109(10): 3628–3631 - see also other articles in *PNAS* 109(10)).

It seems clear from the list that these are not all identical types of unit, but they are each supposed to have experienced some kind of collapse – the Western Roman and Akkadian Empires ended; the Easter Islanders descended into famine, violence, and chaos, losing their high culture; the Maya abandoned their pyramids and cities; and the palaces of Late Bronze Age Greece and Crete were burned and deserted. But are they really comparable, as some claim? To me they often seem to be very different, and so grouping them together, and even assigning the same causes to their collapses, as some wish to do, seems problematic. Imperial collapse – the fragmentation of a single unit into multiple units, seems different from a sudden depopulation, or to collapses that are said to happen across entire culture zones, which involve widespread desertion. An empire is a clear political unit, but a culture zone is not, even if states or units with a culture zone sometimes build bigger states (or empires) within it, as happened among the Classic Maya, Mesopotamians, and perhaps others.

Taking a cue from Arthur Demarest, I think we can divide up the units into five kinds, in a fairly arbitrary and approximate scheme, which may nevertheless help us to see things in a clearer light, and perhaps to understand problems in previous approaches to collapse where many examples are seen as straightforwardly comparable – an approach which helps generate definitions of collapse that are then necessarily very broad, and not necessarily very satisfying (Table 1.2). Any comparative account should surely pay attention to the nature and comparability of the units under investigation.

1. Individual Communities

Individual communities might include examples such as medieval British villages, or the two small medieval Norse communities in Greenland, as well as 'mysterious' disappearing colonies like the English settlement of Roanoke in North Carolina.[50] The latter two were not really self-sufficient or sustainable 'societies' in themselves, rather they were precarious and vulnerable outposts of established societies, which shared in an on-going parent culture. It can be noted that the constant and normal ebb and flow of British villages did not bring about, and does not represent, any widespread 'British' collapse.

TABLE 1.2 *Five units implicated in collapse*

1. Individual communities
2. Political units – empires, states, dynasties, chiefdoms, etc.
3. Cultural units, civilisations, ideologies, lifestyles ('archaeological cultures'? – Natufian types?)
4. Systems, including 'world-systems'
5. Populations, peoples

2. Political Units

By political units, I generally mean the kind of units that Tainter calls societies. Collapse is frequently associated with empires in which a particular state or group come to dominate other people and groups over a wider area. Empires are not simply nations but are processes that stitched together peoples and places often by force, setting in train numerous changes at home and in their provinces – recall the Roman poet Horace's famous claim that 'captive Greece took her savage victor captive, and brought the arts to rustic Latium' (*Epistles* 2.1.156).

Non-imperial (or not clearly imperial) states or 'kingdoms' also collapse (although a state can be considered as made up from smaller units, and is thus 'imperial' in a sense). Teotihuacan would be an example of this, but so would the Late Bronze Age Greek states such as the Pylos polity. Greek palace states seem to have been built up from smaller units, pieced together presumably through diplomacy and violence – in which we might always find those people and groups resistant to state building groups. Some Classic Maya rulers too welded together bigger units from smaller independent ones, gaining influence over other centres and over wider areas. Even Egypt, often seen as a unified upper and lower state (pharaohs wore the double crown representing unity), could decompose into smaller constituent parts.

Another area that can cause confusion is the notion of dynasties. In the history of some areas, such as China, Egypt, and Mesopotamia, it is customary to speak of dynasties. A dynasty is commonly thought of as a ruling family, or house, but the term 'dynast' really just means a powerful person (think of 'dynamo'). Historically speaking, dynasty is also a term used where we should really think of distinct political entities that were independent, rivalrous, and that effectively created new states or empires in competition with others. China from the Bronze Age Shang to the early modern Qing was really many different entities in the same way that the Ur III dynasty of Mesopotamia was different from the Akkadian Empire. Progressivists might think of the later states as 'evolved' from, or more developed versions of, the former, and of course there are connections, often deliberately made, between the later and earlier states. Nevertheless, it may be more helpful to remember that they were in some senses different entities and not simply earlier and later iterations of the same thing.

The Shang, for example, were only one 'dynasty' of ancient China, and the term Shang also refers to bits of material culture (bronzes in particular), a cultural complex, and even a people, their phase usually divided into three and based at perhaps successive sites including Erlitou, Erligang, and with the better known Late Shang at Anyang.[51] They were not alone in the area we know now as China – there were other polities with their own dynasties. Much later, the Qing dynasty in China, who originated among the northern Jurchen people, took around a century to incorporate its eventual territory into a single state.[52] Between Shang and Qing, during the Qin dynasty/state (221–210 BC), there developed concepts of unity in China, including the idea of *Zhongguo*, the 'Central Kingdom', of *tianming*, 'mandate of heaven', and *tianxia*, 'all under heaven', which could be adopted as principles of interaction, as ideologies, by subsequent diverse actors and ethnic groups, and the idea of a common cultural core was codified, preserved, and studied in literature.[53] Such notions of unity developed in Egypt and Mesopotamia too, to varying degrees – though it was stronger in Egypt.

3. Cultural Units and Lifestyles

Here we have to be careful as we enter the realm of type three, for type three units are not really solid political structures at all, rather they constitute nebulous categories that employ materials or other cultural features as the parameters of a definable unit. So although people have talked (and some still do) about Maya or Mycenaean Empires, neither the Maya nor LBA Greeks formed a single political society; they were connected, yes, and shared elements of material culture that allow us to consider them, in archaeological terms, as 'a culture' (which in archaeology never necessarily indicates 'a people'). But their inhabitants may never have shared a common ethnic identity, even if they spoke the same language, and likely they considered their identity in more local terms (as did the citizens of classical Greek city-states – and those Greeks did also eventually share a notion of common ethnic identity). Like Mesopotamia or ancient China, independent cities grew up together, converging to some extent through a process of mutual development and contact known to archaeologists as 'peer polity interaction'.[54] Colin Renfrew explains that this:

... designates the full range of interchanges taking place (including imitation and emulation, competition, warfare, and the exchange of material goods and of information) between autonomous (i.e., self-governing and in that sense politically independent) socio-political units which are situated beside or close to each other within a single geographical region, or in some cases more widely.[55]

What about civilisations? It is also common enough to find references to Maya, Mycenaean, or Roman civilisations, and, like culture (or the culture of a particular people), for which it is sometimes a synonym, it can tend to imply a unity that, while real enough in some ways, can also distort our view of complex and diverse cultures. Although there may sometimes be a close fit between what we term a civilisation and a political unit – ancient Egypt, for example – this is not always the case. The many independent groups of Maya, spread across their landscape, shared sufficient aspects of culture, which we deem complex and sophisticated enough for us to see them as a 'civilisation' distinct from others. But cultures and civilisations in these terms seem to be difficult to consider as collapsible units in the same sense as a structured human society – though they are certainly prone to change and transformation and can be affected by the collapse of political units within them, which drive particular aspects of material culture (say literacy or monumental architecture, for example).

Here we should recall the difference between states, societies, and civilisations. It seems clear enough that collapse is something that can best fit political units, human social groups of whatever scale and complexity, but that culture and civilisation are different – they are certainly capable of transformation that may sometimes be connected to collapse (and to state formation and increasing or decreasing complexity).

I mention lifestyles, which may seem an odd term to find here, because one of the key ideas underlying most ideas about collapse is that life and/or society gets worse, and becomes difficult or intolerable. This idea of things getting worse is inextricably linked with ideas of decline, and wherever literary texts touch on this subject, we have to consider the possible gaps between rhetoric and reality – discourses of decline are often found alongside what others categorise as growth, improvement, and progress. Young and Leemans include this 'discomfort' in their definition of collapse, with its implication that a previous way of life cannot be maintained even if it were desired; and this is perhaps in the forefront of our popular images of collapse as a forced and probably difficult or unpleasant change.

One example of this idea might be the Ik people of northeast Uganda, discussed by Tainter as a case of collapse. He based his discussion on anthropologist Colin Turnbull's dramatic and (in)famous 1972 account *The Mountain People*.[56] Elements of the Ik's seemingly extremely selfish and individualistic lifestyle and behaviour, such as allowing immature or elderly relatives to starve to death, shocked Turnbull; these aspects were built upon and discussed by scholars and playwrights, and attracted the attention of the reading public around the world.[57] The Ik appeared almost to be an anti-society, and to represent what could happen when a people were driven to extremes in order to survive, something along the lines of the boys' descent into savagery in William Golding's *Lord of the Flies*.

It has seemed to many that the Ik represented a classic collapsed society, one with potential to represent the future of humanity. However, this 'apocalyptic' and 'post-apocalyptic' situation came about not because of natural environmental factors, despite the fact that the Ik were affected by a two-year drought at the time of Turnbull's visit, but because they had been barred from their traditional hunting grounds and forced to change their lifestyle, and this left them much more vulnerable to the effects of any drought. Much about Turnbull's presentation of the Ik has been criticised, but the image of a spiral into savagery remains a popular image of collapse – one that now tends to be associated with Easter Island, amongst other examples.[58] The Ik collapse – it seems to fit in with some of our definitions – was an unintended outcome of the changing laws of a modern nation.

4. Systems

Culture zones, as well as political, social, and economic ones, are really interconnected systems.[59] A system is a network of some kind, and for places that form part of a system their maintenance (in some form) may become dependent on the survival of the whole or part of that system or its functions. Historians and archaeologists sometimes refer to 'world-systems', because these systems can be regarded as 'worlds' in themselves.[60] As such, different cultures (or 'civilisations') can be regarded as parts of a system, as well as systems in their own right. The eastern Mediterranean at the end of the Late Bronze Age is an example of such a system, in which states from Greece to Egypt and beyond interacted with each other, with transfer of goods and materials as well as ideas and people.[61]

Systems can break down (i.e., stop functioning in the same way) in a number of ways and for many reasons, and this can affect the ability of other parts of the system to function or continue in the same form. We know this from our experience in the modern 'globalised' world. For example, if there is no longer a demand for goods from place B in place A, an economic specialism in place B may become redundant, damaging its order. If place B's ruler is dependent on a particular return from place A in order to maintain his position at home, such a change in place A may cause collapse in place B. Systems collapse is, to some extent, a useful way of thinking about collapse, however, it can be difficult to assess the levels of interdependency in world-systems. In the end, we must consider how any change in the system was responded to by a given part of it and whether and why collapse may have followed.

5. Populations

Finally, collapse is an idea that is often applied to populations and peoples, where it means a drastic and sudden reduction to very low levels, with consequent social and political effects. This usage is very familiar from ecology – well known now through collapsing honeybee populations in colony collapse disorder, as mentioned earlier, but also from the study of population – demography – and from common usage.[62] Recently, for example, Steven Gray in *Time* magazine explained that 'The news this week that Detroit's population plunged more than 25 per cent to just 714,000 in the last decade shouldn't be surprising. The city's collapse is as well-documented as it is astonishing – the population peaked at nearly 2 million in the 1950s, driven in part by a post–World War II auto industry boom now long gone.'[63] But clearly the population of Detroit has not simply disappeared or been wiped out in any apocalypse, rather people have moved in accordance with their ability to make a living and their perceptions of opportunity. Should we expect anything different from past populations?

Although some anthropologists and archaeologists do focus on population-based or palaeodemographic issues – as in a recent volume edited by Patrick Kirch and Jean-Louis Rallu entitled *The Growth and Collapse of Pacific Island Societies*, for example[64] – it can be very confusing when collapse is used generally with the implication that it is primarily a matter of a catastrophic decline in population, as it may be in ecology. Even though conquests and political collapses can result in reductions in overall population in the longer term, and in the redistribution of people in a landscape – away from former capitals or central places – as well as changes in the visibility of people due to changing material habits, these are often effects of collapse or go hand in hand with it as a process. It may look like people are disappearing – but people then, just as now, were mobile and responded to what was happening around them. Population number and distribution can change without being a collapse or causing one.

Colonisation, on the other hand, has very clearly led to episodes of demographic collapse and consequent social collapse. For example, with a population of over three million Taino in 1492 when Colombus arrived at Hispaniola (now Haiti and the Dominican Republic), the population of the island soon crashed to a tiny fraction of that number within a few decades – the indigenous cultures, political organisation, and language largely disappearing too.[65]

There are many features of collapse that can result in population redistribution and decline – warfare uses up people, can reduce the number of elite people (which would affect the make-up, the material culture, and functioning of society), spreads disease, and can make it impossible for life to carry on as normal, disrupting agriculture and trade. Defeats and failures in state organisations, or accidental disruptions, can also lead to failure to maintain established agricultural or other systems that contribute to the corporate system – both those that underpin an elite, or elite support of the system, or those that contribute to subsistence in general; without these, there can be famine or a failure of confidence in the status quo. Ideological change too can lead to people moving out from formerly important centres. Populations may, over time, spread out and shrink to fit the resources available, or respond in other ways, such as seeking to expand and commandeer resources elsewhere.

We sometimes have the situation where population collapse and other types of collapse can appear to be the same or be similar, and this can lead to further conflation of two distinct processes. Consider the contrast between the depopulation of Detroit, which we know to be due to economic changes, and the fourteenth-century Black Death in Europe, in which disease killed perhaps half the population of Europe. Both are visible demographic changes. But although to an archaeologist the evidence of abandonment, and limited use of sites, may look the same, the reasons for change in each case are very different. Population change can be both a cause and consequence of other forms of collapse and social change, but demographic collapse or decline, even if it happens suddenly, need not cause political or social collapse.

WHY DOES COLLAPSE HAPPEN?

There are, of course, a host of explanations that people have put forward to explain collapse, and these will be discussed in the context of the case studies throughout the book. But we can look broadly at some ideas before we start.

Tainter explains collapse by referring to an economic theory, that of declining marginal returns.[66] In this theory, when the quantity of a particular variable is increased, 'output' initially rises rapidly, but then slows and eventually may decrease.[67] He expresses this in four moves: (1) Human societies are problem-solving organisations, (2) socio-political systems require energy for their maintenance, (3) increased complexity carries with it increased cost per capita, and (4) investment in socio-political complexity as a problem-solving response often reaches a point of declining marginal returns.

In other words, societies can initially do well by becoming more complex; adapting to circumstances increases their complexity, which allows them to cope. But societies constantly face challenges, and so by constantly adapting and becoming more complex, they can eventually become over-complex, no longer delivering any benefit, at which point they collapse into more simple systems. What is interesting in this view is that collapse is itself an adaptation – the simpler societies that arise out of collapse are better adapted, and they may themselves start along the path of increasing complexity, suggesting a cyclical process of collapse and regeneration (on some level). However, this explanation still requires a cause – what problems was a given society facing that tipped it over into collapse?

Nowadays, many people associate past collapses with the environment. Indeed, the volume mentioned earlier, *Sustainability or Collapse? An Integrated History and Future of People on Earth,* based on the results of a Dahlem workshop that involved archaeologists, historians, and sustainability experts, focussed on climate change, environmental damage, and collapse, looking at what might have happened to past societies and the threats and dangers faced by contemporary societies.[68] These studies build on old ideas. Almost a century ago, in 1917, Ellsworth Huntington proposed that climate change had undermined the agricultural base of the Roman Empire.[69] Huntington, pioneering scientific methods still used today, used data based on tree ring records as proxies for climatic conditions and changes. More recently, in 2001, Harvey Weiss and Raymond Bradley published a famous and influential paper in the journal *Science*, where they argued that many ancient collapses were probably caused by climate change.[70] This view has recently been reasserted by Michael Marshall in his 2012 article in the *New Scientist*.[71] This environmental approach to collapse is common, indeed it seems dominant, and this is no surprise given our own contemporary environmental concerns.[72]

However, many, though not all, archaeologists remain sceptical about climate change explanations of collapse – certainly when they are applied as single cause theories.[73] This is not because archaeologists are ignorant of these theories (indeed, some have pioneered them), or because they have closed minds, or are unwilling to consider different kinds of evidence, but simply because they view collapse as a human story, one that is much more complex than the equation 'climate changes = societies collapse'. Climate change, when it happens (as with earthquakes), can also have very different effects in different, even proximate, locations.

Another problem often pointed out is that it can be very hard to tie down climate changes with any chronological precision, therefore it is difficult to associate them securely with political and societal changes. In this vein, there has been a tendency among supporters of climate change explanations to see correlation as causation – that is, when evidence indicating possible climate change seems to coincide with collapse, it is assumed to have been a causal factor in that collapse. Despite doubts about climate change-based explanations, no archaeologist would deny that agriculture-based societies – all pre-industrial societies – would have been vulnerable to bad years – too much or too little rain, excess cold and frost, and so on, that would potentially cause social disasters and destabilise societies. Even so, complex societies are often geared to offset such problems, for example, by relying on polyculture rather than monoculture, which would reduce the chance of total crop failure, by storing produce as an insurance, and by arranging for imports of food. Often, there is also ambiguity over whether climate changes were sudden shocks (i.e., events that happened at a point in time) or less dramatic shifts over time (the average for a period differs from earlier and later periods' averages) – the former would clearly be harder to cope with.

Readers of environmental histories, such as Clive Ponting's *A Green History of the World*, originally published in 1991, will be familiar with the notion that ancient societies cause their own collapse by destroying their own supporting environments, perhaps by deforestation or over-intensive farming, or a combination of 'eco-cidal' behaviour.[74] This has been a theme of Jared Diamond's work too, not only in *Collapse*, but also in his book *The Third Chimpanzee* (1992), and in a 1994 paper entitled 'Ecological collapse of past civilizations'.[75] He advanced the idea that 'self-destructive abuse of our environment, far from being a modern invention, has long been a prime mover of human history'.[76] Others, such as Sing Chew, have focussed on this, advancing the idea of cycles of societal development, environmental degradation, collapse, and environmental recovery.[77] This line of thinking is found in archaeology too – American archaeologist Charles Redman's book *Human Impact on Ancient Environments* discusses a range of examples of proposed ecocide, including the Puebloan culture and Rapa Nui.[78]

There is nothing new in such theories, whose modern origins date back to the work of George Perkins Marsh and his 1864 book *Man and Nature* – Marsh gave historical examples of land degradation and warned that humanity might reduce the Earth to the barrenness of the moon.[79] Later, in 1916, Vladimir Simkhovitch advanced the theory that Rome collapsed because of agricultural exhaustion; his argument owed its origins to quotes from Latin writers on agriculture and to recent developments in agricultural and soil science.[80] But although humans have always modified the natural environment, and the modern agricultural and industrial revolutions have done this on an increasingly large and harmful scale, coincident with massive and unprecedented population increase, it is certainly far from clear that many, or indeed any, of the ancient states that collapsed did so because they caused environmental damage that undermined their ability to exist. Even so, climate and ecocide arguments for the fall of the Roman Empire, and other collapses, can still be found embedded in modern research and historical narratives even a century and more after they were first proposed, with scholars in many fields seeking to build up scientific, especially palaeoclimatic, data.[81]

Although Diamond set out to write his *Collapse* book explicitly focussed on the environment and collapse, where historical examples would provide instructive parables, he had to concede that he knows of no 'case in which a society's collapse can be attributed solely to environmental damage', and even that 'it would be absurd to claim that environmental damage must be a major factor in all collapses ... It's obviously true that military or economic factors alone may suffice'.[82] For this reason, he provides a number of factors that could cause or contribute to collapse, three of which are environmental: (1) Environmental damage, (2) climate change, (3) societal responses to environmental problems; other factors are (4) changes with trade partners and (5) hostile neighbours. Even so, the tone of the book is clearly geared towards the notion that collapse is often caused by environmental damage. He claims, for example, that 'deforestation was a or *the* major factor' in the Rapa Nui, Ancestral Puebloan, Classic Maya, and the Greenland Norse collapses.[83] Overpopulation should also be added to Diamond's list of factors, since it plays a key role in many of his explanations.

With both Tainter's and Diamond's 'grand theories', a precipitating factor is still often necessary to set off the spiral of collapse – invasion, inflation, and loss of tax revenues sparked the demise of the Western Roman Empire, whose complexity finally stopped paying off. With the Classic Maya, Ancestral Puebloans, and the Greenland Vikings, climate change tipped these societies into collapse. In a Malthusian scenario, Diamond has the Rapa Nui, Ancestral Puebloans, and Classic Maya societies overpopulated, deforesting their environments and causing soil erosion, which undermined the subsistence basis of their societies – as population increased, the capacity of the land to support it decreased. This brought about violence, depopulation, and collapse. The final factor was the failure of rulers and elites to manage the situation – a warning to our modern powers that be.

Explanations of collapse that rely on overpopulation and the outstripping of resources are known as 'overshoot' models, and these have been critiqued by Tainter in his 2006 paper 'Archaeology of overshoot and collapse'.[84] He suggests that there 'does not presently appear to be a confirmed case of overshoot, resource degradation, and collapse brought about by overpopulation and/or mass consumption'. Overshoot models strongly reflect contemporary interests, and, as Tainter suggests, 'many of the most ardent proponents are outside of archaeology'. A recurring criticism in the environmental turn is the tendency to see populations as either unwitting victims of natural circumstances, such as climate change, or as ignorant and irresponsible ecocidal architects of their own doom.

The model of apocalyptic ecological collapse and historical change *a la* Diamond has been questioned by archaeologists and anthropologists in a 2010 book, *Questioning Collapse*, edited by Patricia McAnany and Norman Yoffee, and contributed to by other archaeologists, and at a Cambridge archaeological conference held in 2010.[85] Diamond himself reviewed *Questioning Collapse* in the journal *Nature* and was unsurprisingly critical of it – this led the editors and authors of the book to complain to *Nature* about the conflict of interest in asking him to review their book, which was composed as a direct response to his work (Figure 1.2).[86] Other researchers have also questioned the idea of climate and ecocidal collapse. W. H. Wills, Brandon Drake, and Wetherbee Dorshow recently published a paper in *PNAS* where they conclude that neither ecocidal practices, such as deforestation,

FIGURE 1.2. Jared Diamond vs *Questioning Collapse*.
Source: Cartoon by Jim Hunt.

nor climate change caused collapse and depopulation at Chaco
Canyon. They warn that it 'should not be used as a cautionary story
about socioeconomic failures in the modern world'.[87]

Often collapse is presented, especially in the popular media, as
having a single major cause – whether it be a natural disaster like
climate change, drought, or ecodical environmental damage; or a
human cause like corruption, invasion, or popular revolt; or economic factors. A fairly representative list of causes, referring specifically to the Classic Maya collapse, but relevant in considering many
other collapses, has been compiled by James Aimers (Table 1.3).

Despite a popular fixation on finding 'the cause', archaeologists tend not to think about collapse in such a cut and dried way.
In his recent book on Late Bronze Age collapse in the eastern
Mediterranean, Eric Cline has quite properly explained how uncertain things can be:

There is little doubt that the collapse of the Late Bronze Age civilizations
was complex in its origins. We do know that many possible variables may
have had a contributing role in the collapse, but we are not even certain
we know all of the variables and we undoubtedly do not know which ones

TABLE 1.3 *Proposed causes of the Classic Maya collapse*

Environmental	Socio-political
• Climate change/drought	• Change in trade routes
• Deforestation	• Competition from Central Mexico
• Disease/plague	• External explanations
• Earthquakes	• Intersite warfare
• Ground slope change	• Invasion with/without resettlement
• Hurricanes	• Peasant/class revolt
• Insect infestation/plant blight	• Political–ideological pathology/
• Overpopulation/subsistence stress	fatalism
• Soil erosion/loss of fertility/ change to untillable savannah	
• Volcanic activity	

Source: Page 333, Aimers, J. J. (2007). 'What Maya collapse? Terminal Classic variation in the Maya Lowlands.' *Journal of Archaeological Research* 15: 329–377.

were critical – or whether some were locally important but had little systemic effect ... There probably was not a single driving force or trigger, but rather a number of different stressors, each of which forced the people to react in different ways to accommodate the changing situation(s).[88]

For Cline, causation is complex – and, as he points out, we often do not know how to weigh up the factors involved or even that we are aware of all of them. His sentiments apply just as much to other instances of collapse. Arthur Demarest too notes that causation is layered – many factors at different levels may be involved.[89] There may be proximate causes as well as deeper structural issues. The structure, for example, ideology, of a society could determine the range of responses to a given proximate problem. In collapse, we are likely to be seeing multiple factors (rather than competing mutually exclusive explanations), proximate and structural, feeding back into each other and responses may have had unpredictable outcomes – the situations would have been dynamic.

Finally, we must not forget the role that chance plays in survival or collapse and the role of human actors in reacting and shaping events. Herbert Kaufman reminds us of these:

Chance obviously played a large part in the success or failure of states ... A combination of favorable circumstances could catapult one system to the summit and keep it there for a long time; a sudden misfortune might drag a system from its day in the sun after a short interval. That is not to say that the people in positions of responsibility in the overarching polities had *no* influence on their own fate; their actions could certainly exacerbate difficulties or take advantage of opportunities.[90]

While people will always be tempted to create a grand theory, or push a particular explanation of collapse, the truth will always be more complex – perhaps more complex than we can reconstruct.

SYSTEMS, CYCLES, AND RESILIENCE

Some of the recent work on collapse emphasise that there are normal cyclical patterns visible in history – and suggest that the rise and fall of organisations like states or empires, or their formation and collapse, are inevitable and repeating processes. The theory of cycling is not new, as we saw earlier in this chapter, and like many theories, they themselves 'cycle' in and out of fashion.

In collapse studies, cyclical-type theories can be found coming from historical theory, from archaeologists, and from ecology and biology. In what follows, a few of the major contributions will be discussed, beginning with archaeologist Joyce Marcus' dynamic model. After that, we will look at the approach of scholars who adopt a world-systems approach. Finally, we will examine an approach that has come to the fore recently for its application to sustainability studies – that of resilience theory.

The Dynamic Model

One model that emphasises the constancy of change in human communities is known as the dynamic model. This was originally developed by archaeologist Joyce Marcus to describe an apparently recurrent pattern identifiable in Maya states, how they grew, extended their power, and fragmented into smaller states – consolidation, extension, and dissolution.[91] When other archaeologists noted that the model seemed to fit their study areas too, she extended it to other Mesoamerican cultures and eventually to the Andes, Mesopotamia, Egypt, and the Aegean. In her view it seemed at least to fit with what happened to many ancient states, if not all.

Marcus noticed that Maya states seemed to be dynamic – over time, they appeared to follow a pattern of formation, expansion, and breakdown. Maya chiefs competed with their neighbours, and out of this competition larger states were formed. Major states based at Tikal and Calakmul appeared when they managed to dominate their neighbours militarily and diplomatically. In this way they expanded their influence territorially over already existing cities, and also new sites were developed. However, these bigger agglomerations did not last long before breaking up again into more or less independent smaller polities. Subsequently, some of these smaller polities, like Dos Pilas, also expanded in the same way. At their largest, states had a four-tier hierarchy of sites – the top three had administrative functions and hereditary lords, eventually all broke down to have only three tiers.

Marcus argues that this model captures the rise of states in the Early Classic period and the breakdown of some of Maya states in the Peten region in a period known as 'the hiatus' (AD 534–593). States that formed in the Late Classic – second generation states such as Dos Pilas – were often based in areas that had been provincial parts of earlier states. These states also collapsed between AD 800 and 1000 (the Terminal Classic), but other states were being formed at the same time in Belize and the Puuc region of Yucatan. Later still, Chichen Itza, and then Mayapan, formed states which also collapsed, leaving the Maya region divided into sixteen regions with a dispersed population.

One advantage of the dynamic model is that it presents periods of state formation and collapse as a normal process. And as Marcus points out, what is interesting is the variation in the duration of peaks and troughs, which we consider in hindsight to be normal. For example, she suggests that Mesoamerican field archaeologists consider the 200-year 'peaks' – periods where bigger unified states existed – to have been normal, whereas Mesopotamian epigraphers consider the long periods of disunity, where Mesopotamia was fragmented into numerous smaller polities, to have been normal, with unified states or empires unusual and short-lived.[92] Similarly in Egypt, China, or Japan, 'intermediate periods' or 'warring states' periods represent 'unusual' episodes of fragmentation in 'normally' unified states. In the Korean region, we can also find patterns of unity and fragmentation as kingdoms were forged and fragmented.[93]

Similar episodes of unity and fragmentation can also be found in the Roman Empire.[94] The so-called third-century crisis involved

persistent internal warfare and invasion from the Levant all along the
northern borders of the Roman Empire to the North Sea. Between
the murder of Alexander Severus in AD 235 and Diocletian coming
to power in AD 284 there was a period of chronic instability in which
armies repeatedly raised generals to the position of emperor. It also
saw the fragmentation of the Roman Empire into three independent
state structures. In addition to the 'official empire', Postumus, governor of Lower Germany, founded the Gallic Empire in the west, which
lasted from AD 260 to 273, incorporating Germany, Gaul, Spain, and
Britain. In the east, Odenathus and his widow Zenobia expanded
Palmyrene power, briefly forging an empire within the empire that
stretched from central Anatolia to Egypt.[95] The Roman Empire was
reunified by Aurelian but suffered periodic secessions and was officially divided by Diocletian; thereafter it fluctuated between unity
and disunity and fragmentation.

However, some point out that it is obvious that polities would rise
and fall and that many do not go through cycles – they collapse, and
that is the end of it. Furthermore, the 'cycle' does not repeat in many
cases, thus it is not really a cycle. Demarest observes that the Maya
collapse was not a cycle, it was 'a unidirectional series of steps of
fragmentation', so the model is wrong.[96] The Mycenaean collapses
also led to the end of states and these did not regenerate – the rise
of Greek polities much later on was a distinct step in itself and was
based on new principles – we can only view it as a cycle if we take a
very broad, and not very useful, perspective. The model also does not
explain why collapse happens.

Asabiya and Secular Cycles

A view of cycles of change was developed in the fourteenth century
by the Tunisian Arab historian Ibn Khaldun (AD 1332–1406), who
outlined his view of the rise and fall of states in his *Muqaddima*.[97]
His theories have inspired and been taken up and extended by modern scholars such as E. N. Anderson and Christopher Chase-Dunn,
and Peter Turchin, with reference to the rise and fall of empires and
states.[98]

Khaldun thought that the property of *asabiya*, a kind of feeling
of group solidarity, was behind the successful formation of states.

Over time, though, following the process of formation, *asabiya* would naturally reduce, leading to weakness, fragmentation, and the collapse of a dynasty. New groups with stronger *asabiya*, often nomads from the desert margins, would take over and form new ruling dynasties – effectively new states – and the cycle would repeat. The scenario reminds me of a story told by Herodotus, in which it could be said that *asabiya* was generated.[99] In the aftermath of the Assyrian Empire, from which numerous peoples had been trying to gain their independence, Herodotus describes the rise to power of Deioces the Mede. Deioces made himself indispensible amongst the Medes by gaining a reputation for dispensing strict and impartial justice, and increasing the number of people obliged to him. He then withdrew his services, causing lawlessness to return, but by 'popular demand' he was asked to return as king – and ruled justly for fifty-three years.

Anderson and Chase-Dunn note the repeated invasions and takeovers of China by nomadic outsiders 'in regular Ibn Khaldun cycles'.[100] They apply these cycles to a number of ancient and more recent examples, including the Soviet Union and even the USA, both of which they claim have gone through classic Ibn Khaldun cycles, though the USA clearly has not collapsed. Without the element of invasion from the outside, they instead posit some kind of 'internal renewal'. They also draw Khaldun into world-systems theory and offer a host of more immediate explanations for collapse, which draw on ecological literature giving an important role to climate change, deforestation, disease, as well as war and shifting trade connections.

Turchin, a population biologist, focuses on historical dynamics – in his term cliodynamics, the mathematical modelling of historical changes – and looks at *asabiya*, demographics, and the territorial expansion and contraction of empires, taking a cue from the work of Rein Taagepera, who attempted to quantify such factors in the 1970s.[101] A key to his work can be found in a quote from George Puttenham in 1589, which expresses the cycle:

peace makes plenty, plenty makes pride, pride breeds quarrel, and quarrel breed warre: Warre brings spoile, and spoile povertie, povertie patience and patience peace: So peace brings warre and warre brings peace.[102]

In a later book, Turchin and Sergey Nefedov begin their account by discussing Malthus and demographic cycles, and develop a cyclical model of historical change involving expansion, stagflation, crisis, and depression, which they applied to various ancient and more recent dynasties and states, including the Roman Republic, Plantagenets, Tudors and Stuarts, and the Capetians. They attempted to quantify historical data and argued that 'the general implications of our results ... are that some sort of general regularities of the historical process appear to exist'.[103] They mention both state collapse and demographic collapse, for example, they note that medieval France and western Europe:

was literally crammed with people. The 'ecosystem' ... was strained to breaking point and on the verge of collapse. The collapse experienced during the fourteenth century was the result of a typical concatenation of famine, pestilence, and war.[104]

Is it really surprising though that we find that human societies have gone through similar processes? We might ask why the process led to collapse in some cases but not in others. And should we really identify a collapse in fourteenth century Europe? It depends on what we mean by collapse. Despite demographic collapse in the fourteenth century, states essentially continued their development, and populations later became larger than they had been before.

It is possible that Turchin's roughly three-century cycle could be applied to ancient empires such as the Hittites, and possibly others, and could reveal factors worth investigating further in examples of collapse. But we should look at each instance of collapse rather than assume the model to be correct. And how roughly or precisely do we measure three centuries? The Hittite state lasted a little longer than four, as did the Roman Western Empire, so can these count? Change and vulnerability rather than stability and strength may have been the norm in most cases – where we do find a period of apparent stability over the long term, it may be due to chance, as Kaufman suggested.[105]

These 'cliodynamic' works tend to be quite removed from the archaeology and primary history of past societies, dealing in big patterns and systems, and the more abstract they become, the less convincing (or surprising) they appear when scrutinised. Although Turchin and Nefedov clearly allow that phases of the cycle blur into one another, have different scales, and also allow for the actions of individuals, how the many different kinds of unpredictable contingent 'causes' can be included in a single model is unclear. Nevertheless, the patterns they identify may be real enough, taken as approximations, if unsurprising. Systems history can sometimes be accused of simply telling well-known stories in the language of a particular theory.

In some cases, especially in 'big' history, the facts of 'what happened' are not established enough (or can be seen from multiple perspectives rather than a single narrative) to draw off a theory at a higher level convincingly. The conclusions of historical demographics, especially when using data derived from archaeology, are notoriously ambiguous (basically applying a preferred formula to habitation or funerary evidence). Quantifying 'history' to develop 'scientific' theories of history is something people have tried to do, but it rarely goes uncriticised and is often not convincing. Take *asabiya*, for example. As Tainter points out in one review, 'states … inculcate something like *asabiya* in their armed forces'.[106] Roman soldiers' 'love' of their standards is well known, so why should the Roman Empire have collapsed when *asabiya* was strong? *Asabiya* in nomadic (or peripheral) groups was often not enough for them to effect a takeover. *Asabiya*, or a notion of common cause, is an interesting way of understanding or expressing the shared belief in a system that people can have, but it will never be straightforwardly quantifiable.

Sustainability, Resilience, and Resilience Theory

The achievement of sustainability is a current target for many human societies on a number of scales.[107] Nations seeks to promote and achieve sustainability in agriculture and food supply, economic growth, and power generation, while also attempting to create sustainable communities for citizens to live in. Sustainability is not just an aim at the national level, but also at an international governmental level, and amongst private companies, and others. Sustainability is promoted as a social good by charities, in education, in research, and in the media. A sustainable society is by definition one that will not collapse but will carry on indefinitely, being able to adapt to change; and because of this, sustainability studies are directly connected with the idea of collapse. The whole backdrop of human history is now seen as a database for studying the sustainability of human communities.

In the debate about whether collapse is a useful concept for thinking about past societies and historical change, the concept of resilience has come to the fore. It is a key theme in McAnany and Yoffee's *Questioning Collapse*.[108] However, resilience can also be a confusing concept, for it too, like collapse, seems to be used in different ways. Technically, *resilience theory* is a metaphorical description intended to model changes in ecosystems as long-term adaptive cycles. It incorporates ideas of change that occur on multiple levels and at different scales, including sudden catastrophic change.

Resilience theory was developed by C. S. Holling in the 1970s; although it was initially applied to ecology, it has since been applied by social scientists, including archaeologists, to try and understand a range of systems including economics and human societies.[109] It is currently a favoured approach to sustainability studies. In resilience theory, resilience is defined as:

> the capacity of a system to absorb disturbance and re-organize while undergoing change so as to still retain essentially the same function, structure, identity, and feedbacks.[110]

We can imagine this applied to societies that can retain some essential 'essence' of themselves whilst absorbing shocks, with collapse representing an inability to do so without losing the 'essence', resulting in changes of structure and identity. Again, the implication seems to be that 'disturbance' might equal external shocks to the system, rather than internal change.

Some archaeologists also emphasise human resilience, but in a more general sense, and they position this as oppositional to the idea of collapse. It indeed sounds obvious enough that something which is resilient is sustainable, and therefore not prone to collapse. In the words of McAnany and Yoffee[111]: 'on close inspection of archaeological evidence, documentary records, or both, it becomes clear that human resilience is the rule rather than the exception.' In this sense they are suggesting that human populations rarely disappear.

However, resilience theory does not really mean that collapse or other kinds of change are unusual or uncommon, but rather it includes collapse as part of a normal cyclical pattern that may be identified in systems of various kinds in which constant changes may be taking place on different levels. Collapse can lead to innovation and change, as Brian Walker and Paul Salt explain:

'Creative destruction' is a term now used to describe the disturbances that periodically punctuate the adaptive cycle. It breaks down stability and predictability but releases resources for innovation and reorganisation.[112]

This is similar to historian Shmuel Eisenstadt's statement in his chapter of *The Collapse of Ancient States and Civilizations*:

the investigation of collapse in ancient states and civilizations really entails identifying the various kinds of social reorganization in these types of societies and so viewing collapse as part of the continuous process of boundary reconstruction'.[113]

Thinking about societies from the perspective of resilience theory means firstly acknowledging that human societies are really social-ecological systems. Any society relies on ecosystems (of which they are part) for its existence. This means local environments, but also perhaps those further afield, and effects between ecosystems and social systems, which feed back into each other in complex ways. We also have to consider that any particular 'society' that we identify is just one possible arrangement of people and the environment.

Applying Walker and Salt's definition of resilience to a human society, we can think of resilience as a kind of buffering capacity: the more resilient a society is, the better it can sustain 'disturbances' whilst remaining identifiably itself. This means it should be flexible enough to change and adapt without disintegrating or transforming beyond recognition. For example, Japan was affected by a massive earthquake in March 2011, followed by a tsunami which devastated the north east of Honshu. But Japanese society was able to absorb or buffer many effects of this disaster through its economic and organisational capacities. Although changes and adaptations followed these events, Japan has not collapsed or transformed into a new entity (we might consider changes to energy production as 'structural changes' though). Other societies affected by disasters may not be able to sustain them without serious transformation or collapse, which then becomes an adaptive trait.

To lose resilience, then, is to become prone to collapse – Charles Redman, an archaeologist with a long interest in human–environment relations, notes:

the long-term history of human-environment interactions contained in the archaeological record reveals that many human responses and strategies, although apparently beneficial in increasing production in the short term (even over a few generations), nonetheless led to a serious erosion of resilience in the long term, resulting in the collapse of both environmental and social systems.[114]

Redman explains that in resilience theory change is episodic, rather than either continuous and gradual or chaotic, which is reminiscent of geological catastrophism. There are forces of stability which promote continued productivity and forms of capital and social memory, as well as destabilising forces which create flexibility, diversity, and opportunity. In combination, these may sometimes appear to create an equilibrium. Taking a fixed approach to maintaining 'constant yields' without attention to context leads to the loss of resilience – in other words, changing circumstances may render a once well-adapted system maladaptive – suddenly unable to function. From a sustainability point of view, being able to adapt is the key – not just maintaining the status quo.

The adaptive cycle is represented by resilience theorists as passing through four phases, usually represented 'scientifically' as a figure eight, beginning with exploitation (r), in which an area is colonised (a biological/ecological theme). This is followed by the conservation phase (K), in which energy and material continues to be accumulated and stored. In the omega phase (Ω), there is increased population and environmental degradation, which is followed in the alpha (α) phase by reorganisation. Collapse may be a feature of the omega or alpha phases, depending on how one interprets the figure.

McAnany and Yoffee's perspective on resilience becomes more clear when we read that:

Resilience means that some kinds of change, especially political change, can be quick and episodic, whereas other kinds of change, for example changes in kinship structures and belief systems, can be slower moving. Both kinds and different paces of change can coexist.[115]

In other words, it is again the definition or parameters of collapse that are in question, and as we have seen, collapse is sometimes defined as a political process, sometimes as a demographic one. The distinction made between such phenomena as kinship structures and belief systems and political change is a relevant one though, and it recalls a distinction made by anthropologists between 'great' and 'little' traditions. Great traditions are those that have been associated with 'civilisation', elites, and urbanism, whereas little traditions are regarded as more basic and fundamental ways of life in more rural subsistence settings. It is, as we have seen, principally the loss of things associated with great traditions, which we, in hindsight, often see as the 'essences' of a society, that often defines collapse – continuity may well be observed in 'little' traditions in many cases.

There seems sometimes to be a confusion when thinking of resilience and resilience theory. Collapse is a normal stage in the resilience theory model of a cycle of change, yet at the same time the property of resilience itself is a measure of resistance to collapse. Cultures can be resilient in the sense that they retain a recognisable form, but sometimes cultural or social change is an adaptive collapse to a different system, but with a resilient population, who may develop a very different culture.

Another problem in the way resilience theory is applied to archaeology is that it tends to retain and emphasise a biological or ecological focus – that is, it focuses on the human-environment system without paying too much attention to the complexities of social systems themselves or how these are represented by their material culture. This means that resilience theory tends only to be deployed in terms of subsistence strategies and patterns – population and human-environment relations in particular. Explanations of collapse tend to be based on imbalances or disturbances that come up in, and between, these systems, where short-term productive gains are usually said to create overpopulation. In that situation, any disturbance, such as a climate event, causes the collapse – a shock that the system cannot absorb without profound change.

In these explanations there is an aspect of internal and external causation: a social and developmental trajectory based on successful adaptation, but that renders a society unsustainable in the long run because of increased vulnerability to shock, usually an external event. These shocks do not need to be external events, nor, strictly speaking, does the narrative need to be based only on subsistence elements of the society. Social relationships and identifications are also defining elements in societies, and the breaking of these, for whatever reason, can also create collapse as a result.

There are two helpful aspects of the resilience theory model, though. The first is that it incorporates a reorganisation phase in the alpha stage of the cycle following collapse. For although it is common enough to see a post-collapse phase as some kind of dark age, this term often obscures what is actually going on at the time. Collapse itself can even be seen as a necessary reorganisation, an adaptation in itself.

Resilience theory seems reminiscent of catastrophism in that there is unpredictable episodic disruption to systems. Indeed, it could be argued that resilience theory simply offers a new way of talking about the same themes that have already been addressed in collapse studies. Collapse in the model of resilience theory still requires some kind of external disturbances, and it is argument about causation that collapse studies have tended to revolve around. So in the end, resilience theory may not offer anything very new in terms of explaining how collapse comes about.

AFTER COLLAPSE

In a 1999 work, Tainter discussed post-collapse societies.[116] It might be generally thought that 'dark ages' should follow collapse, but Tainter cautioned that, like the term collapse, it 'is ambiguous and should be used with care'; he associates it with the 'declines in literacy, writing, and communication that often result from collapse'.[117] But to archaeologists, 'dark ages' are also periods which we know less about because there are fewer remains (as well as texts) for us to see – but neither of these mean that there were no people, or that nothing was going on. The term 'archaeological invisibility' is useful here. Rulers and elites are usually more visible (materially speaking) than the majority of the population, so periods after collapse can seem darker as elite culture disappears. Tainter makes the important observation that collapse is something that often affects social elites and ruling classes more than other sectors of society – 'dark ages, for most people, were only slightly less luminous than preceding periods'. Archaeologist Colin Renfrew agrees that as well as a loss of central administration and a loss of social and political complexity, collapse has often involved the 'disappearance of an elite'.[118] This is something that many archaeologists agree on.

People who study collapse are not, therefore, interested only in endings. Schwartz and Nichols' edited volume *After Collapse: The Regeneration of Complex Societies* (2006), deals with both collapse and also its aftermath.[119] This focus derives not only from a dissatisfaction with the idea that collapse is just an ending, simply a prelude to dark ages, but also from the comments made by Shmuel Eisenstadt, quoted earlier, about collapse being a process of reorganisation.

Endings, he argued, were also occasions of restructuring, and of new beginnings; in every collapse, there is also continuity and innovation. Implicit in this view is that collapse is rarely the apocalyptic catastrophe it is often presented as; there are still people and social memories and bonds, these people remember the past and recreate or discard elements of it as it suits them in their negotiation of new and meaningful identities and relationships. And collapse is often followed by the continuation of complex society on a different scale, or of the eventual regeneration of complex or large scale societies.

One of the most useful general concepts to come out of the book, which deals with several specific examples, is an idea developed by Bennet Bronson, writing about collapse and regeneration in Southeast and East Asia.[120] He discussed how complex societies regenerate according to three patterns. First, there are two forms of 'false regeneration'. The first is when a new complex society arises in the same area as an earlier one, but there is no historical link between them. The second is when the centres of a regional society appear to collapse and new ones arise within a given area, but this 'intrinsically evanescent' system itself is stable or constant. Then there is 'stimulus regeneration'. In this case, the development of a complex society is based on people's ideas about the past – ideas which may not necessarily be accurate. For example, it may be remembered through folk memories or known (say, through impressive physical remains) that a more complex society once inhabited an area, which stimulates later rulers to try and develop a new one. The final type is 'template regeneration', in which there are sufficient memories, writings, and so on to make it possible to regenerate a complex state on the model of an earlier one. Bronson suggests that the best example of this is the repeated collapse and recreation of Chinese imperial dynasties – essentially different but very similar empires; 'the key was widespread literacy and the existence of accessible historical records that

provided a sufficiently detailed blueprint for the pre-existing system
to be more or less fully reconstructed'.[121]

WHY IS COLLAPSE IMPORTANT?

Many archaeologists actually shy away from collapse, partly because
it can attract a 'lunatic fringe' and can distract us from the serious
business of learning about or presenting the past. Many are dis-
satisfied with the popular versions of collapse but are rarely called
upon to give their own verdicts, at least outside of scholarly publications, conferences, and workshops. Most archaeologists' stories of
collapse would fit far less well into the modes of narrative described
at the beginning of this chapter. Nevertheless, history and archaeology are riddled with things we call (for better or worse) collapse,
with beginnings and endings, with transformations, and with continuities and discontinuities; for me, these cusps have always held
a particular fascination. What is it that makes period x period x,
and not period y? How and why did we get from one to the other?
To what extent do these periods exist only in our minds? These are
important, even key, questions for those who study the past.

Collapse, despite its mixed academic reputation, is one of the
challenging and exciting areas of archaeology, one that brings up
a host of other questions that require attention – including the
questions of what exactly it was that was collapsing and exactly how
collapse proceeded – what variables were present, how they might
have interacted, what forms it took, and why. A recent project to try
to determine 'archaeology's most important scientific challenges'
recognised the importance of collapse studies; the group came up
with a category of 'resilience, persistence, transformation, and collapse', and in it they set the question: 'can we characterize social
collapse or decline in a way that is applicable across cultures, and
are there any warning signals that collapse or severe decline is
near?'[122]

Another reason that collapse is important relates to the use of collapse as a parable or example to be learned from. Since it is a given
that people will seek to use historical examples to make cases about
the present and future, one way or another, and even that policy may
be based, to some extent, on historical examples, we should expect

that the history is as accurate as it can be. The descriptions we saw Lester Brown give in his book are the same as those presented in the European Commission's *Water for Life* initiative booklet, published in 2003.[123] That document, aimed directly at affecting our contemporary behaviour, reported how Sumerian civilisation was 'undermined' by food scarcity while 'overfarming, deforestation with soil erosion and loss of productivity' led to 'the complete demise of ... [Maya] society by AD 900'. These views of Sumerian and Maya collapse can indeed be found in some archaeological and historical writing, but these narratives can in particular be traced back to popular environmental histories of the 1990s and beyond.[124] They have become fossilised into 'new' books (and other media representations) by authors who are largely unaware of the breadth of archaeological research and views. For readers not up-to-date with the archaeology, their content might be taken as an accurate representation of current ideas.

As we look more closely at how collapse is conceived and explained, it becomes apparent that the reality of many popular collapse narratives can be less than satisfying. The Ethiopian famines with their devastating effects on human life and society were not simply natural disasters, not simply caused by a reduction in rain or environmental mismanagement that meant the population could no longer be supported. As Alex de Waal has stated, 'the repeated famines that have struck Ethiopia, and in particular the great famine of 1983–5 were in large part created by government policies', and this was during a period of some thirty years of civil war and political instability.[125] If we accept that the Maya simply died and their civilisation ended because of an environmental change, or we label them as ecocidal 'failures', we do a disservice to the people who lived at the time and after, and to their modern Maya descendants who still live, in their millions, in Mesoamerica to this day, and we also leave much of the stories of collapse and transformation untold.

FINAL THOUGHTS AND MOVING ON

This long first chapter has covered a lot of ground. So far, we have explored a little of how collapse is often presented to us via the news, and how such narratives of collapse tie in with the kind of stories we are used to and like to hear, whether they be in the realms of infotainment, spectacle, or tragedy. We have also explored some of the different ways that scholars define collapse and the things they apply the term to, taking a look at some broad explanatory, descriptive, and theoretical models of collapse. We have already encountered the idea that collapse is a complex phenomenon, as Mortimer Wheeler observed decades ago in his discussion of the Harappan civilisation, and as Eric Cline recently stated of collapse in the eastern Mediterranean in the Late Bronze Age.

As with other books and publications on collapse, we will examine a range of examples – fifteen to be precise – some well known, others less so. I hope to put in context what was collapsing, and examine the ways in which scholars have characterised what was happening and how they have sought to explain each collapse. I try also to refer to what happened next – the aftermath of collapse. Although no grand theory of collapse is presented, I take a critical perspective of ideas in each case, and, throughout each chapter, I hope to give the reader an idea of who is saying what and why – giving voice to those researchers who work on and think about collapse and transformation. Even though it is rarely, if ever, possible to be precise or succinct about a collapse, which some might find dissatisfying, I hope readers will, by the end of the book, feel better equipped to make up their own minds about collapse.

2

Egypt: The Old Kingdom Falls

> In Egypt ... the first Dark Age began around 2200 BC, when at the end of
> Dynasty VI Egypt, until then a very stable society, with seeming suddenness
> fell into anarchy ...
>
> Barbara Bell[1]

THE OLD KINGDOM

Egypt in the late third millennium BC is fairly well known to us through
both written sources and archaeology (Figure 2.1). These give us a window onto the personalities and events of the Old Kingdom period –
something we do not have for all our examples of collapse. The Old
Kingdom ran from around 2686 to 2181 or 2160 BC, depending on
whether the Seventh and Eighth Dynasties are included in the Old
Kingdom or in the First Intermediate Period (FIP), but all dates must
be thought of as approximate, since different scholars follow slightly
different schemes (Table 2.1).[2] Rather than dates, which can be confusing, Egyptologists tend to refer to dynasties, and it was dynasties three
to six that made up the Old Kingdom; but as mentioned, some scholars
include dynasties seven and eight as well. The Old Kingdom was the age
of Egyptian unification, centralisation, and strong rule, and, famously,
of pyramid building – it is sometimes termed the age of pyramids.

At the end of this period, around the beginning of the twenty-
second century BC, shortly after the reign of Pepy II (c. 2278–2184
BC; the end of the Sixth Dynasty), the Old Kingdom, in which all
of Egypt had been governed as a unified and centralised state,
collapsed. The centuries after this have often been portrayed as a

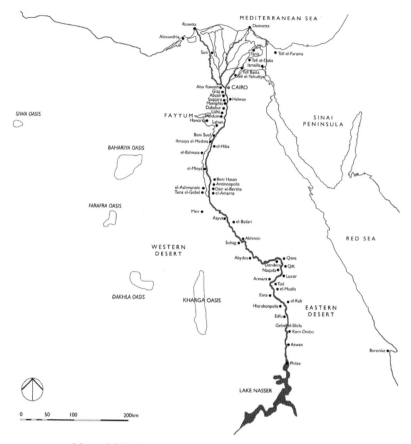

FIGURE 2.1. Map of Old Kingdom Egypt.
Source: From Ikram, S. (2014). 'Pharaonic history'. In Renfrew, C. and
Bahn, P. (eds.). *Cambridge World Prehistory. Volume I.* Cambridge: Cambridge
University Press, 280 (Map 1.17.1).

terrible dark age of chaos, political and social disorder, civil war, and
famine; it has even been thought that people turned to cannibalism
in their distress. Eventually though, order was restored and Egypt was
again unified, around 2055 BC, under the pharaohs of the Eleventh
Dynasty, who had originally ruled only Thebes; Mentuhotep II is
widely regarded as the first Middle Kingdom pharaoh.

In this chapter, we are concerned with the period between the
Old and Middle Kingdoms, the period which is known as the FIP.
We shall examine some of the textual and archaeological evidence
for this period and see how these have been interpreted by modern

TABLE 2.1 *Outline of Egyptian chronology*

Period	Dynasties	Approximate dates
Old Kingdom	Third–Eighth	2686–2160 BC
First Intermediate period	Ninth–Eleventh	2160–2055 BC
Middle Kingdom	Eleventh–Fourteenth	2055–1650 BC
Second Intermediate period	Fifteenth–Seventeenth	1650–1550 BC
New Kingdom	Eighteenth–Twentieth	1550–1069 BC
Third Intermediate period	Twenty-first—Twenty-fifth	1069–664 BC
Late period	Twenty-sixth	664–332 BC
Persian Egypt	Twenty-seventh = First Persian period [+ Twenty-eighth–Thirtieth] then Second Persian period	525–404 BC, 343–332 BC
Hellenistic Egypt	Ptolemaic kings	332–30 BC
Roman Egypt	Roman emperors	30 BC–AD 395

Source: Shaw, I. (ed.). (2000). *The Oxford History of Ancient Egypt*. Oxford: Oxford University Press.

scholars. What events could have caused the collapse of the apparently strong and flourishing Old Kingdom, and what were the dark ages of the FIP really like? But before we get on to that, let us look a little at Egyptian treatment of the dead, since this is one of the identifiable changes between the Old Kingdom and the FIP.

PYRAMIDS AND THE DEAD

The best known feature of ancient Egyptian culture, besides mummies, must be pyramids – especially the great pyramids of Giza. These three monuments were built by Fourth Dynasty pharaohs (2613–2494 BC) – the Great Pyramid built by Khufu attracts the most attention; it is a tremendous megalomaniacal monument to a ruler's power and status. As Toby Wilkinson points out, it was built with more than two million blocks of stone, which weighed more than a ton each, and it was the tallest building in the world until the Eiffel Tower was constructed in 1889.[3]

The great pyramids did not spring into existence from nothing; the pyramid form was developed over time over time. Khufu's father, Sneferu, constructed three pyramids.[4] His first was a step pyramid, built to surpass an earlier step pyramid built by Netjerikhet. But he

was not satisfied with this and some years later began work on a true
pyramid at Dahshur. Unfortunately, this monument started to sub-
side while it was still being built – cracks and fissures opened up in
the structure, and although the architects modified the plan and
the pyramid was completed, it was unfit for any purpose; it is now
known as the Bent Pyramid because of its skewed appearance. Finally
Sneferu constructed, successfully, the Red Pyramid.

Khufu's son Khafra also built at Giza – a smaller but more elevated pyramid that looked bigger than his father's.[5] His successor,
Menkaure, built the third great pyramid at Giza, which was much
smaller than the earlier two, but his successor Shepseskaf ended this
funerary tradition, building a mastaba tomb (the Mastaba el-Faroun
or Pharaoh's Bench) in the shape of a rectangular sarcophagus at
Saqqara, where the Third Dynasty pharaohs had been buried.[6] Fifth
and Sixth Dynasty kings found other ways to express their power and
position in Egyptian society.

It was not only royalty that constructed tombs. As the Old Kingdom
proceeded, members of Egypt's elite and the administrative class also
invested in increasingly elaborate tombs with features that were once
reserved for royalty alone. They also increasingly stressed their own
honours, roles, and achievements at the expense of kow-towing to
the pharaoh. There was something of a levelling taking place in the
material and ideological cultures, as represented by the funerary
evidence. As John Baines and Peter Lacovara point out, 'during the
decentralized intermediate periods, the difference in scale between
the tombs of king, elite and others diminished ...'.[7] We shall come
back to this theme later in the chapter.

Later pharaohs chose to build mastabas or smaller pyramids at
Saqqara – Pepy II, the last significant Sixth Dynasty pharaoh, had his
pyramid there, of which little now remains – but the 'Pyramid Age' of
the Fourth Dynasty ended with Menkaure, long before the FIP. From
the FIP, however, the practice of pyramid building ceased for two
centuries, marking a significant break in tradition.[8]

THE FIP IDENTIFIED

Both textual and archaeological sources mark out the existence of the FIP.[9] Turning to the texts, we can see that a break

in their history was recognised by Egyptians in later times. The Turin Canon, which contains a list of pharaohs reckoned by the Nineteenth Dynasty (around a thousand years later), gives a total after the Eighth Dynasty; this indicates that they considered there to be a break in the line of rulers after that. Another list, of Seti I, at Abydos, mentions no pharaohs between the end of the Eighth Dynasty and the Eleventh Dynasty, the beginning of the Middle Kingdom under Mentuhotep II. This is why there are two ways of reckoning the beginning of the FIP. Ancient Egyptians clearly believed that there had been breaks of some kind in their past, periods when the line of rulers had been broken. As we shall see, because of the nature of the written records that survive from this period, the FIP has often been characterised as a time of great scarcity and a dark age for Egypt.[10]

In the archaeological record, there are also signs of a break. Stephan Seidlmayer writes of the 'profound changes in the archaeological record, which were rooted in the Sixth Dynasty, and which reached their climax in the earlier half of the First Intermediate Period'.[11] At Memphis, the Old Kingdom capital, pharaohs and high officials had traditionally constructed mortuary complexes (at Saqqara), but this practice stopped after Pepy II. There was an increase in the number of burials, with more commoner burials and tombs of the provincial elite, both of which also became larger and better equipped with grave goods and decoration. Seidlmayer also notes 'fundamental changes in material culture' – there were changes in arts and crafts; pottery styles also changed, with an increased localism becoming apparent, with different styles becoming popular in Upper and Lower Egypt.[12]

IPUWER, ANKHTIFI, AND THE EGYPTIAN DARK AGE

So what was the FIP like? Barbara Bell suggested that it was a true 'dark age', an age of drought, famine, and collapse, coming to this conclusion from her analysis of textual evidence, contemporary tomb biographies, and literary works from later on in the Middle Kingdom.[13] One of the key pieces of evidence in the construction of the FIP as a dark age is the *Dialogue of Ipuwer and the Lord of All*.[14] In this text, a sage called Ipuwer is addressing a king. The dialogue is too long to quote in full, but the message of chaos and disorder can be gleaned from some representative lines:

The door keepers say 'let us go and plunder' ... The washerman refuses to carry his load ... A man regards his son as his enemy ... wrongdoing is everywhere ... The Nile overflows, yet none plough for it. Everyone says 'we do not know what will happen throughout the land.' ... Poor men have become owners of weath ... Hearts are violent, pestilence is throughout the land, blood is everywhere, death is not lacking ... Noblemen are in distress, while the poor man is full of joy. Every town says: 'let us suppress the power-ful among us.' ... The children of princes are dashed against walls ... Poor men come and go in the great mansions ... The king has been deposed by the rabble ... the land has been deprived of the kingship by a few lawless men ...[15]

The lament relates such details as the loss of royal power and tradi-tional governance, the loss in status of nobles and the rise in status of the lowborn, agricultural problems, an increase in lawlessness, more gangs and robbery, and foreign invasion and despair. It suggests that Egypt really was going through terrible times.

To understand the text better and grasp its significance, we need to consider the Egyptian worldview. The Egyptians had a concept called *ma'at*, which we can think of roughly as 'the way things should be'. Ipuwer describes how things were no longer the way they should have been in Egypt, how the world has literally been turned upside down, with traditional roles, attitudes, and circumstances reversed: for Ipuwer and the king, nothing was how it should have been or as it was before.

Biographies inscribed on tombs are another key source in the characterisation of the FIP as a time of drought, famine, and col-lapse. Toby Wilkinson quotes two, which seem to back up this pic-ture.[16] In one, a man called Merer explained: 'I buried the dead and fed the living wherever I went in this famine that happened'; another man, Iti, fed his hometown of Imitru 'in the painful years' and 'gave Upper Egyptian barley to Iuny and Hefat ... after feeding Imitru'. We get an image of dead bodies, hunger, and shortages of food – dire situations in which only a few men could organise relief and continue practices such as the proper disposal of the dead.

Perhaps the best-known biography is that of Ankhtifi, who was a powerful nomarch, or regional governor, during the FIP (Figure 2.2).

FIGURE 2.2. Ankhtifi of Moalla.
Courtesy of Getty Images.

Ankhtifi's tomb records the great deeds he accomplished during his
life – or those he claimed to have performed:

I fed/kept alive Hefat, Hormer, and (?) ... at a time when the sky was (in)
clouds/storm and the land was in the wind (and when everyone was dying)
of hunger on this sandbank of Apophis.

All of Upper Egypt was dying of hunger, to such a degree that everyone
had come to eating his children, but I managed that no one died of hunger
in this nome. I made a loan of grain to Upper Egypt ... I kept alive the house
of Elephantine during these years, after the towns of Hefat and Hormer had
been satisfied ... The entire country had become like a starved (?) grasshop-
per, with people going to the north and to the south (in search of grain),
but I never permitted it to happen that anyone had to embark from this to
another nome ...[17]

According to Ankhtifi, things were so bad in some places that people were forced to engage in cannibalism. Again, like *Ipuwer*, the text may refer to deteriorated environmental conditions, this time possibly encroaching sand dunes – 'the sandbank of Apophis'. But in Ankhtifi's nome no one starved, no one had to travel to find sustenance, and he could even spare grain to send it to other places. Ankhtifi, and others like him, had stepped into a power vacuum and were doing the job of the pharaoh.

What was the cause of Egypt's dire situation? Bell read the texts to refer in parts to natural disaster – to drought in particular, and to invading sand dunes: 'the desert is throughout the land' – and she argued that a low Nile was the cause of turmoil. She argues that Egypt experienced two severe droughts and famines, the first around 2180–2130 BC and the second again around 2000–1990 BC – 'the First Dark Age in Egypt, bracketed by two particularly troubled and dark intervals, each associated with a severe drought' followed by 'a period of strong government, cultural advancement, and general prosperity'.[18]

INTERPRETING THE TEXTS

The *Dialogue of Ipuwer* and the biographies seem to give a clear picture of Egypt in the throes of chaos. But how far should we trust this picture?

Scholars disagree about whether Ipuwer was a real historical figure; Egyptologist Fekri Hassan thinks that he was.[19] Hassan has argued that Ipuwer was probably a real man who was perhaps around twenty years of age at the end of the reign of Pepy II. He would thus have seen at first hand the collapse of central rule in Egypt and was able to record it for posterity. Like Bell, Hassan argues that the terrible collapse of the Old Kingdom was caused by a lower Nile around 2250–2050 BC.

But many other scholars regard the *Dialogue* as a much later composition, from the Middle Kingdom, when *ma'at*, right order, had been restored – the historical setting is a device and the poem 'is not historical'.[20] Its purpose was not to record historical events, but to contrast the desirable order of the present, when a strong pharaoh ruled a unified Egypt, with the apparent disorder of the past. The Ipuwer text, rather than being an eyewitness account of a disaster, draws on themes of order and disorder to promote a particular ideological view of the world – it laments disorder and provides a reminder to the pharaoh of how things should be; indeed, Ipuwer has been called by Alan Gardiner a 'die hard aristocrat' for his world view.[21]

Given that the text seems to be a much later composition and is clearly not at all neutral in its representation of the world, we should not put much trust in it as a historical record of the FIP. With its image of a world turned upside down, we can expect the *Dialogue* to stress things that were the reverse of the proper order – a lack of strong central rule, foreign invasions, the poor becoming rich, no one knowing one's place. For this reason we might suspect that lines like 'the desert is throughout the land' are also devices to stress the (undesirable) disorder and unusual circumstances of the past with the (normal and desirable) right order of the present, rather than being straightforward historical facts. The text actually tells us that 'the Nile overflows, yet none plough for it', which, if we were to accept as accurate, suggests not that a low Nile or desertification is the problem, but that the political or social situation is preventing people from carrying on a normal life of farming in the wake of the annual flood. The Ipuwer text really just lauds one political and social order over another.

Ankhtifi's biography, and the others we saw, are different. These are contemporary biographical texts of real people who were powerful in their own regions. But even these cannot be taken straightforwardly at face value. During the very real decentralisation that characterised the FIP, this class of biographies really took off, with local and regional leaders aping the pharaonic practice of recording their great deeds – and again, recording them in the sense of *ma'at* or what should be. While Ankhtifi and the others do certainly mention food shortages, they also stress their ability to cope with them and to maintain order in their own region, which is compared with hunger and disorder elsewhere. These local leaders wanted it known that they were successful managers who could, like the pharaoh in other times, feed their own people and even bail out other communities. These motifs are typical of this genre of text. They also tell us that, whatever the state of Nile was, food was certainly available during the FIP – there had to have been food if Ankhtifi was able to feed his armies and other regions!

It is also clear in the texts that life did not end in FIP Egypt. Regardless of whether or not there were droughts and food shortages, it is clear that for life to go on, and for local rulers to continue to rule, there cannot simply have been an apocalyptic collapse – drought or no drought. The population also did not disappear or die en masse – the collapse was one of central rule and a unified state based on the rule of a pharaoh.

Despite the different ways in which the key textual evidence can be, and has been, interpreted, Bell's influential picture of a massive drought and social dislocation is still widely repeated. Brian Fagan, in his popular book about climate change and past civilisations, describes how 'ancient Egyptian farmers abandoned their fields en masse in a frenzied search for food when droughts strangled the Nile flood in 2100 BC' – a view derived from Bell's account.[22] Much the same views are also repeated in William Burroughs' *Climate Change in Prehistory*.[23]

Given our own contemporary concern with the environment, the end of the Old Kingdom seems like a clear salutary case of a state collapse driven by climate change. But the stories of Ipuwer and Ankhtifi do not simply describe natural disasters and social chaos – a stereotypical dark age; they are open to very different interpretations that demonstrate the FIP was a thriving and vibrant period.

Contemporary biographical texts like those of Ankhtifi do focus on disaster, but it is there as a foil: 'tales of crisis served to legitimize the power of local rulers'.[24] The disasters were overcome by the ability and actions of local rulers. These rulers had arrogated power to themselves in lieu of strong central rule and justified it by making claims about their role and the efficacy of their rule – just as pharaohs constructed and justified their own positions and ideology by making claims of their own on public monuments.

SCIENTIFIC EVIDENCE

However, before looking again at the FIP, there is some scientific evidence that suggests a climate change event did happen, and that there were associated droughts in late third millennium BC Egypt. Michael Krom and colleagues studied sediment fluctuations in the Nile Delta over the past 7,000 years and concluded that a very dry spell did coincide with the end of the Old Kingdom.[25] Another more recent study by Christopher Bernhardt and colleagues was of the pollen record of the *Cyperacea* in the Burullus Lagoon in the Nile Delta.[26] They argued that this pollen was a marker of the Nile's flow and that a decrease in *Cyperacea* pollen indicated a decreased flow. They concluded that the Delta area suffered from several drought events.

However, although some Egyptologists agree that there were severe droughts at the end of the Old Kingdom and in the FIP, others are not so certain. Stephan Seidlmayer has suggested that 'independent evidence confirming climatic change during the First Intermediate Period is lacking' and reports evidence from Elephantine of increased Nile flow through the period.[27] Marc Van De Mieroop believes that our contemporary focus on climate change has influenced our views on the end of the Old Kingdom and the FIP; he remarks that 'the case for climate change is unproven'.[28] Karl Butzer is equivocal – 'it is possible but unproven that Nile failures may have helped trigger collapse of the old kingdom'.[29] Nadine Moeller has also expressed doubts, though she suggests that the positive evidence for a climate event is increasing.[30] More research will undoubtedly bring us closer to the truth of the matter.

But even if we accept that there was climate change and the Nile flow was reduced, did this cause the collapse of the Old Kingdom? Seidlmayer, an expert on the FIP, thinks not. He sees the evidence as indicating a drying tendency during the Old Kingdom, with increased aridification and lower Nile levels. But he also points out that the increasingly dry climate and lowering Nile in earlier times 'showed no signs of affecting the development of pharaonic civilization' and so wonders why any climate change would have caused the end of the Old Kingdom and brought about the FIP.[31] The collapse of the Old Kingdom is reckoned to have come about in 2184 BC or shortly thereafter, and the FIP lasted until 2055 BC; the scientific evidence for drying dates from 2250 to 2050 BC. There is a seventy-year lag (at least) before the end of the Old Kingdom, which is hard to explain if the drought was so devastating. We might also have to imagine Mentuhotep II successfully reunifying Egypt during a more arid phase, which would mean that an arid phase presented no obstacle to rebuilding the state. Accurate dating remains a problem in understanding the relationship between climate and historical trends and events.

ROOM AT THE TOP

Although the jury is still out on the matter of climate change and
its potential effects, there are other factors to consider, which relate
more to economic and social dynamics. One potential factor in the
collapse is rooted in the history of the Sixth Dynasty and concerns
legitimacy and the passing on of power.

The Fifth Dynasty pharaoh, Unas, died without an heir and was
succeeded by a commoner called Teti (the first Sixth Dynasty pharaoh), who married Unas' daughter.[32] In order to cement his authority, it was necessary for Teti to reward his supporters and curry favour
with members of the elite. This favour can be seen in the funerary
record at Saqqara, where richly decorated elite tombs crowd around
Teti's pyramid, showing off the high status accorded to his followers.
But it seems likely that Teti was assassinated in a palace plot – a mysterious king Userkara seems to have ruled for a short while until Teti's
son took power as Pepy I.[33] Userkara may have been related to Unas
as part of the extended royal family.

Pepy I also faced the threat of assassination in a plot involving
one of the royal wives. The biography of one of his courtiers, Weni,
who had risen from commoner to palace administrator, tells us that
he uncovered a conspiracy hatched in Pepy's harem. As Wilkinson
explains, the harem could be a focus of intrigue against the ruler.[34]
Weni was amply rewarded for his conduct.[35] He was made 'sole companion' of the pharaoh, and was later appointed governor of Upper
Egypt – a first for a commoner. On his death, he was allowed a stone
sarcophagus, which was usually a royal prerogative. Infighting and
intrigue in the royal family could cause instability at the heart of the
Egyptian state – it could also drive change in the way the state operated at the highest levels, in the ways pharaohs delegated authority,
and in material culture.

A SLIPPERY SLOPE? – THE RISE OF THE LITTLE PHARAOHS

Some scholars, like Wilkinson, argue that the ruling elite actually
contributed to the collapse of central authority by making changes to
the way the Egyptian state was run; the pharaohs sowed the seeds of
their own demise.

Old Kingdom Egypt was a highly centralised state based in the capital of Memphis, where the pharaoh, the high elite, and the apparatus of government were located.[36] Provinces were governed from the centre, but during the Fifth Dynasty (2494–2345 BC) rulers started appointing individual nomarchs, provincial governors who would actually reside in their nomes. We can see this change from a shift in burial patterns of governors from around Memphis to the nomes themselves – a shift which also brought markers of high culture more into the provinces. This move started a decentralisation of power and created new hereditary local elites away from Memphis.

Now these local elites, rather than just the Memphite government, could access and redistribute the produce of Egypt, and the nomarchs could act with a fair degree of local autonomy. With the powers they acquired, the nomarchs became, in effect, local pharaoahs – their powers over their, albeit much smaller, regions were the same in some ways as those the pharaoh had exercised over Egypt as a whole. Wilkinson writes that some began to call themselves 'great overlord'.[37] By the end of the Sixth Dynasty, after the long reign of Pepy II, the transition from centralised power to regionalised power was complete, and this provided the fracture lines along which the centralised state, now no longer really necessary for the running of things, would break down.

There is no need to see this localised system as less effective than a centralised one, nor to see it as 'un-Egyptian' or somehow not fitting into the scheme of Egyptian history. Local governors may well have been able to provide a more effective response to bad years and low Niles, or to any climate changes that took place, by being able to manage agricultural production and redistribution more closely, which is what the FIP biographies suggest.

Local economies became richer and more complex with these centres in place, and this may have shifted the balance of Egyptian society, creating a new point at which it could fracture into more local units. In fact, far from being unproductive, the end of the Old Kingdom and the FIP enjoyed a spread of wealth into the provinces – Egypt became more urbanised, with local populations becoming more apparent due to increased burial in local cemeteries. As Seidlmayer emphasises: 'rather than being an outright collapse of Egyptian society and culture as a whole, the First Intermediate

Period was characterized by an important, though temporary, shift in its centres of activity and dynamism'.[38]

A THRIVING CULTURE

In any case, regardless of whether or not there were low Niles or a drier period, life in Egypt did not grind to a halt at all with the end of the Old Kingdom, and FIP Egypt may not have been such a dark age as the texts of Ankhtifi or Ipuwer suggest at first glance. Seidlmayer provides a much more positive reading of the period: 'far from being a period of cultural decline, these turbulent years witnessed an upsurge of outstanding creativity'.[39]

He suggests that when focussing on the contemporary rather than later Middle Kingdom texts, it is 'difficult to subscribe to the traditional negative view of the period'. The Middle Kingdom texts about the FIP are 'pessimistic', they serve to justify royal rule and the social order after the period of disunity. Although certainly pessimistic, if we read Ipuwer positively, rather than simply as a disaster narrative, we actually have a picture of a lively period of social change and mobility. To think this social flux was a bad thing is to fall under the spell of the *Dialogue*'s composer and his 'aristocratic' view of what was right.

From an archaeological viewpoint, it has long been noted that there is a visible increase in commoner burials during the FIP; non-elite burials also changed in nature. Tombs became both larger in size and contained a greater number and variety of grave goods, for example, beads and amulets, alabaster headrests, and the greatest number of mirrors. As Ellen Morris states: 'non-elite interments exhibited more trappings of wealth in the First Intermediate Period than did or would their counterparts at any time when the state was strong'.[40] Many of the grave goods were items from everyday life, which surely suggests, as Seidlmayer points out, relatively favourable economic conditions.[41] Far from a terrible dark age, we might think that in the FIP commoners were doing just fine.

Not only were there bigger and better equipped graves, non-elite burials in the FIP contained elements that formerly only elite burials displayed, notes Morris.[42] Amulets with symbols referring to concepts of eternity and regeneration become common, as do religious texts, now found on non-elite coffins and on grave stelae.[43] This matches the comments in Ipuwer that the poor have become wealthy, but it contradicts the idea of a straightforwardly 'bad' dark age. In a more positive spin, the period has been noted as one of increased 'democratisation', at least in the sphere of religion.

THE REGENERATION OF THE STATE

The Old Kingdom lasted some eight centuries, a remarkable length of time for a state to endure. The two-century long FIP ended with the reunification of Egypt by Mentuhotep II, of the Eleventh Dynasty. The rulers of this dynasty had started out as kings of Thebes, and they were in competition with the Ninth and Tenth Dynasty rulers at Herakleopolis, but Mentuhotep managed, at last, to conquer Middle and Lower Egypt and create a new unified Egyptian state.

Like the Old Kingdom pharaohs, Mentuhotep, in an effort to create a new ideological scheme after the fractured FIP, had himself represented by statues in temples around Egypt, where he could be seen and worshipped. He was depicted, Ellen Morris describes, as being beloved by the gods, 'holding their hands, suckling from their breasts, and receiving from them caresses and gifts of eternal life', and he was also portrayed as a victorious ruler 'smiting' his enemies – a traditional pose for pharaohs.[44] In addition, he associated himself with the creator god Min by adopting the same pose, with right hand raised, left hand masturbating; Mentuhotep was the creator of a new Egypt.

But the new pharaohs, although they could mimic rulers from the Old Kingdom, whose monuments surrounded them, also modified their image to suit the new times. In this, they took a lead from the local rulers that had governed the fragmented Egypt of the FIP, rulers like Ankhtifi. They presented themselves as shepherds who took care of their people; statues with furrowed brows show the burden of responsible rule, and some even show pharaohs with overlarge ears – ears with which they could hear the prayers and concerns of their people.

These moves were calculated to appeal to a changed society. For although Mentuhotep was able to unify Egypt militarily, '99 percent or so of the people who had not and would not become part of the ruler's inner circle could simply have refused to participate in the state system'.[45] To this end, the privileges won by local elites and non-elite people in the FIP were not removed, and the trends, such as increased access to tombs and religion that had been set in motion, continued throughout the Middle Kingdom. The textual and archaeological record witnesses the emergence of a 'middle class'. A military victory was not enough; in order to set up a new stable kingdom, the pharaoh had to gain the consent of the wider elite and of the population at large. The Middle Kingdom was not simply the Old Kingdom mark two, it was a new and different state – because of the FIP.

FINAL THOUGHTS

The Old Kingdom came to an end probably because of the shifting locus of power in the state from the top to the regions, and the changes this brought about might have been exacerbated by increasingly arid conditions and a lower Nile. Local governors may have been better placed to rule their regions and to cope with such changes more effectively than central government, but power in any case had been devolving to them from the Fifth Dynasty onward. The collapse of the Old Kingdom was a political one – Egyptian civilisation did not disappear. Furthermore, the FIP was no terrible dark age, even if there were famines. What the contemporary and later sources tell us is that there was great social and economic mobility during the FIP; the poor and servile classes no longer simply accepted their lot. To some, the changes were horrifying, but we can imagine it being quite the opposite for others.

The long period of the FIP, during which a fragmented Egypt, with its smaller scale societies, continued to function, was eventually brought to an end by force. But even so, many of the social trends set in motion during the end of the Old Kingdom, which flourished during the FIP, continued into the Middle Kingdom.

THE SECOND AND THIRD INTERMEDIATE PERIODS

While Egypt was again reunified after the FIP, the Middle Kingdom too came to an end in what is known as the Second Intermediate period (SIP), which lasted approximately from 1700/1650 to 1550 BC, taking in the Thirteenth to Seventeenth Dynasties.[46] Once again Egypt fragmented into smaller units. The pharaonic government moved from Memphis in the north to Thebes to the south, while control over Nubia was lost. Northern Egypt was ruled by minor kings until a group known as the Hyksos took over northern Egypt, setting up a capital at Avaris, in the Nile delta. A description of this was recorded by Josephus, based on earlier sources: 'By main force they easily seized it without striking a blow; and having overpowered the rulers of the land, they then burned our cities ruthlessly, razed to the ground the temples of the gods ... Finally they appointed as king one of their number whose name was Salitis. He had his seat at Memphis, levying tribute from Upper and Lower Egypt, and always leaving garrisons behind in the most advantageous positions'.[47]

The Hyksos remain a somewhat mysterious people, but, based on the hieroglyphic renderings of their names, they were probably from nearby Syro-Palestine. Although often seen as militaristic invaders, the Hyksos dynasty may have originated from among the Asiatic migrant community; the archaeology of Avaris in the SIP suggests the development over time of a hybrid culture with both Egyptian and Asiatic features. Hyksos kings generally tried to present themselves as Egyptian rulers. Eventually Egypt was reunited by a strong military ruler Ahmose (Kamose), and Avaris was sacked and destroyed.

The Third Intermediate period (TIP) was again a time of fragmentation, this time lasting much longer, from *c.* 1069 BC to 715 BC. However, many local leaders seem to have been related and perhaps to have co-operated with each other rather than being in constant conflict – Marc Van De Mieroop suggests that 'it was not a period of chaos'.[48] These 'collapses' took place because of human factors and particular historical events; this should make us think twice before laying the blame for the FIP primarily on environmental rather than human socio-political factors.

3

Akkad: The End of the World's First Empire

Its canalboat towpaths grew nothing but tall grass, its wagon roads grew nothing but the wailing plant... No one walks among the wild goats and darting snakes of the mountain, its steppe where grew the succulent plants grew nothing but the reed of tears ... Akkad is destroyed!

The Curse of Akkad[1]

THE AKKADIAN EMPIRE

While we tend to view Egyptian history as periods of unity punctuated by fragmented intermediate periods, in Mesopotamia, disunity, or local independence, to put a different stress on it, was the norm, and the region, often a patchwork of autonomous states, was only occasionally unified in what we call empires. The first of these was the Akkadian Empire (Figure 3.1). This empire was welded together by Sargon of Akkad, who conquered the states of southern Mesopotamia around 2300 BC, but it collapsed after only about a century, around 2200 BC (Table 3.1). Even so, a precedent for empire-building had been set, and this would influence the course of Mesopotamian history for centuries to come.

The accounts of Sargon's origins in the sources tell different stories about him – as Aage Westenholz points out, this 'probably means that nobody really knew' the truth.[2] Some suggest that he was a nomad chief, others that he was a commoner, a cup-bearer in the palace of king Ur-Zababa of Kish. He may have usurped the throne in a palace coup – we do not know, but however he became king, he moved his base from the city of Kish to Akkad, a new capital he built for himself further north, possibly where Baghdad is now.[3] Sargon campaigned

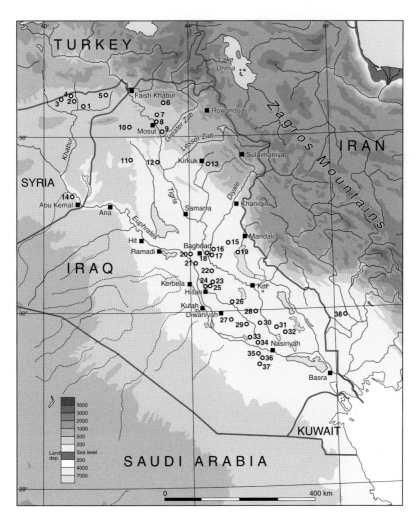

1. Tell Brak
2. Chagar Bazar
3. Tell Halaf
4. Tell Mozan
5. Tell Leilan
6. Bavian
7. Khorsabad
8. Nineveh
9. Nimrud
10. Tell al Rimah
11. Hatra
12. Assur
13. Nuzi

14. Mari
15. Tell Asmar
16. Khafaje
17. Ischali
18. Ctesiphon
19. Tell Agrab
20. Dur-Kurigalzu
21. Sippar
22. 'Uqair
23. Jemdet Nasr
24. Babylon
25. Kish
26. Nippur

27. Isin
28. Adab
29. Shuruppak
30. Umma
31. Girsu
32. Lagash
33. Uruk
34. Larsa
35. Al 'Ubaid
36. Ur
37. Eridu
38. Susa

FIGURE 3.1. Map of the Akkadian Empire and Mesopotamia.
Source: From Oates, J. (2014). 'Mesopotamia: The historical periods.' In Renfrew, C. and Bahn, P. (eds.). *Cambridge World Prehistory. Volume III.* Cambridge: Cambridge University Press, 1499 (Map 3.8.1).

TABLE 3.1   *The Akkadian and Ur III dynasties*

The Akkadian dynasty	Approximate dates BC
Sargon	2334–2279
Rimush	2278–2270
Manishtushu	2269–2255
Naram-Sin	2254–2218
Sharkalisharri	2217–2193
Collapse and fragmentation	
Dudu	2189–2169
Shu-Turul	2168–2154
The Ur III dynasty	
Ur-Namma	2112–2095
Shulgi	2094–2047
Amar-Suen	2046–2038
Shu-Sin	2037–2029
Ibbi-Sin	2028–2004

Source: Van De Mieroop, M. (2007). *A History of the Ancient Near East, ca. 3000–323 BC*. Oxford: Blackwell, pp. 302–303.

widely to create his empire, both north into Assyria, perhaps even into Anatolia, west as far as the Mediterranean, and south into Sumeria, meeting strong resistance from local rulers who valued their independence. The Sumerian cities of southern Mesopotamia, led by Lugalzagesi of Umma, later king of Uruk, formed a coalition against him, but Sargon defeated it, boasting that he captured 'fifty governors ... and the king of Uruk'. Militarism, violence, and the aggrandisement of the king were hallmarks of Sargon's fifty-year rule and of the imperial Akkadian dynasty he founded. His title, king of Kish, came to mean 'king of the world', playing on the Akkadian word *kishatum*, which meant 'the entire inhabited world'.[4]

Why did this vigorous dynasty and its empire collapse after such a short time? Both the nature and the causes of the Akkadian collapse, and of the collapse of the subsequent Ur III dynasty (*c.* 2100 – *c.* 2000 BC), continue to be debated within the community of Mesopotamian specialists, among primarily text-based historians, archaeologists, and, increasingly, hard scientists. One view that has been championed in recent decades is related to climate change and migration, and it is this explanation that we shall look at first.

TELL LEILAN AND CATASTROPHIC COLLAPSE

The case for a catastrophic collapse caused by an abrupt climate change event has been put forward and maintained by the Near Eastern archaeologist Harvey Weiss over the last twenty or more years.[5] Weiss and colleagues make their case based on work done at Tell Leilan (a 'tell' or 'tel' is a mound formed by continuous occupation of a site), a city in the Habur River plains of northeastern Syria, a region known as Subir, where he has worked since 1978, as well as combining their views with scientific data gathered elsewhere; others have supported their hypothesis with their own evidence.[6]

Northern Mesopotamia had traditionally been seen as less developed than the south, which has long been known as the cradle of urban civilisation, but this northern fertile rain fed dry-farming region, 'one of the bread baskets of Asia', which is strategically placed to link communities north and south, east and west, is now known to have developed urban settlements as at Tell Brak early on, in the fifth millennium BC.[7] Weiss's excavations showed that Tell Leilan, and other sites, which had been small agricultural settlements, also developed into urban sites and small states between 2600 and 2400 BC; Tell Leilan grew from a 15 hectare site based on an acropolis to a 100 hectare urban area with a lower town.[8]

In their reconstruction of events, Sargon invaded the region, conquering its cities and concentrating the population into a few sites, such as Tell Brak and Tell Leilan, through which they controlled the region to their own benefit. The Akkadians imposed strong direct control in the region through the site of Tell Brak, which controlled Tell Leilan and Tell Mozan, with military outposts to repress periodic local rebellions. Tight control of the region allowed, in this view, the Akkadian dynasty to appropriate the grain produced in the region, upon which it came to rely, perhaps in part to feed an army or to redistribute to key people or groups whose support Sargon and his heirs wanted. One source on Sargon recorded that 'daily 5400 men ate at his presence' – a hugely expensive feat that would have required control of significant resources in order to keep his followers on side.[9]

Then, around 2200 BC, Tell Leilan and Tell Brak, and a host of other sites in the Habur and Assyrian plains region, were suddenly abandoned, and no pottery of the period appeared in surface surveys – it seemed that this once prosperous region had been deserted.[10] This abandonment and desertion are marked in excavations by layers of deposited material that indicated a long period of aridification and cooling lasting three centuries, between 2200 and 1900 BC, in which the region turned to desert – occupation at Tell Leilan began again only when moister climatic conditions returned a few centuries later.

What had brought on this abrupt climate change? Weiss and his colleagues, including soil specialist Marie Agnes-Courty, thought that a volcanic eruption may have been the cause – there was a thin layer of volcanic ash under a thick layer of sand – but whatever the cause, the result seemed to be reduced rainfall, drought, and increased windstorms blowing around the desiccated topsoil; even earthworms seemed to be less active.[11] Then, in 2000, another team of researchers reported that they had found supporting evidence for a climate event, now known as the 4.2 kya (kya = thousands of years ago) climate event, in a sediment core drilled in the Gulf of Oman.[12] Dating samples from the core, they suggested that greatly increased deposits of windborne dust, dolomite, and calcite, had been deposited that indicated a period of massive drying.

This flip to a dry period, it is claimed, reduced rainfall by some 20–30 per cent, and the hypothesis is that this had a devastating effect on the rain fed agriculture in the Habur region. This had a number of consequences. Since the Akkadian dynasty was dependent on this grain, produced in an 'imperialised landscape', the collapse of its unified state was an inevitable result of grain shortages. But in addition to the collapse of the imperial system that bound the region together, the human response was a region-wide abandonment, leading to a drastically reduced number of inhabited sites and of total inhabited area. This set in motion southwards migrations of Hurrians and Gutians, as well as, later on, the semi-nomadic Amorites, whom the Ur III king Shulgi (2094–2047 BC) sought to repel by constructing a wall – 'the repeller of the Amorites'.

The hypothesis is an attractive one; the evidence seems persuasive and the conclusions seem to make sense, and some other archaeologists, like Roger Matthews, suggest that Weiss's case becomes more compelling as more supporting evidence is found, yet other specialists are much less certain of the truth of this narrative.[13]

CLIMATE CRITICS

Karl Butzer, an archaeologist with a long interest in environmental history and human ecology in the Near East, rejects the 'megadrought' explanation of the Akkadian and region-wide collapse, mass abandonment of the region, and migrations. He suggests that the case for a megadrought or a massive and global 4.2 kya event is not proved by the evidence. Palaeoclimatic data always comes with chronological imprecision, which varies depending on the type of proxy being used,[14] and Butzer notes a 'non-trivial spread of 400' years in the accumulated reports for the onset of the arid period.[15] In fact, Marie-Agnes Courty also revised her interpretations of events at Tell Leilan, suggesting that the soil record resulted from the effects of an explosive extraterrestrial impact event during 2600–2300 BC – a long period of some three hundred years, and possibly earlier than the Akkadian Empire.[16]

Weiss has suggested that 'the strongest evidence for abrupt climate change comes from cores of dust sediment on the floor of the Gulf of Oman'.[17] But it is not certain that the dust record from the Gulf of Oman really reflects what was happening in far off northern Syria. Archaeologist Tony Wilkinson thinks that this evidence is much more likely to reflect the situation in nearby Arabia, where a moister phase ended around 5,000 years ago; this resulted in a dryer dustier local environment.[18] Wilkinson also notes that in the Habur region population shrank in some areas but actually increased in others; population mobility may have been primarily regional, without a massive southwards migration. Also, further west, there seems to have been an increase in small settlements – deurbanisation may have fuelled a repopulation of the countryside, which would be harder for archaeologists to spot on the ground.

Arne Wossink, in his 2009 book, has reviewed the evidence and is similarly cautious; he noted that there is as yet little direct evidence of climate change, and that 'the lack of local well-dated palaeoclimatic proxy records is unlikely to be resolved in the near future'.[19] Given the uncertainty attached to dating climate events rather than long-term trends (and he too identifies increased drying), he recommends that the 'drawing of correlations between unique climate events and unique historical events should be avoided'. Regardless of whether or not there were climate events, he notes in any case that population growth and urbanisation were more important factors than aridification in determining how human–environment interaction played out.

Gojko Barjamovic, in his more recent discussion of Mesopotamian empires, does not mention climate change at all in his treatment of the end of the Akkadian Empire; he notes that 'the imperial elite' inspired 'opposition among the ancient cities. It had upset the traditional balance of local political leadership and the conventional patterns of land use'.[20] In her 2014 chapter on Mesopotamia, Joan Oates has discussed evidence, based on her own work in northern Mesopotamia, that there was a period of heavy rainfall at the end of the Akkadian period.[21]

Coupled with the ambiguity of dating climatic events, whatever the effects of such events might have been, is the lack of precision in the historical chronology itself – as Marc Van De Mieroop explains: 'the absolute chronology of Near Eastern history is a vexing and controversial problem'.[22] While Weiss's date of 2200 BC is based on carbon dating, the dating of Mesopotamian dynasties is based on lists of kings tied to much later astronomical events, and there is much disagreement about the actual dates of kings and of the duration of breaks between kings and dynasties. For Sargon's accession, the 'middle chronology', often used for convenience, gives 2334 BC, with collapse in the reign of Sharkalisharri in *c.* 2200, which seems to tie in well with Weiss's date. But those arguing for a lower chronology have provided various other dates for Sargon's accession, which can be placed in 2250 BC, 2200 BC, or even 2180 BC. We might have to concede that Sargon's empire was actually founded when an arid period was already in full swing.

Tate Paulette rightly points out that 'whatever the eventual verdict in this debate, it is certain that drought posed a significant and recurring threat to the people of Bronze Age Mesopotamia'.[23] In some areas of northern Mesopotamia rainfall is as little as 25 mm per year, and 36 per cent of years have no harvest; the potential for disaster is clear. But farmers and complex societies in such areas tend to adapt themselves to their environments – whether by storing up food for hard times, moving flocks, moving surplus between areas, or planting various crops rather than just one. Famine was thus often avoided in bad years. Interestingly, Paulette writes, 'in Mesopotamia, surprisingly little documentary evidence directly links drought with famine'.[24]

THE CURSE OF AKKAD

As with Egypt, there is textual evidence from Mesopotamia that suggests to some that there really was a climate change event that brought down the Akkadian Empire. This is a text known as *The Curse of Akkad*, and it describes the downfall of the Akkadian Empire.[25] It is a 'lamentation', and is one of several such texts that describe the fate of Mesopotamian cities and kingdoms, and the passing of kingship from one city and dynasty to another.

Weiss prefaces his 1996 article 'Desert Storm' with part of the text, which describes what seem to be the effects of a climate change event:

The large fields and acres produced no grain, the flooded fields produced no fish, the watered gardens produced no honey and wine, the heavy clouds did not rain ... On its plain where grew fine plants, 'lamentation reeds' now grew.[26]

Like the *Dialogue of Ipuwer* and the biographical texts we saw in First Intermediate Period Egypt, the *Curse of Akkad* describes a time of water and food shortages, of want and despair. But, as we asked with the Egyptian texts, should we take this story literally as reflecting an eyewitness account of climate change? Some scholars and journalists certainly do, believing it correlates well with the scientific evidence.[27]

But there is much more to the *Curse of Akkad* than a few excerpts that seem to relate to the climate.[28] For example, before relating the downfall of Akkad, the poem provides a long description of an ideal capital city – well organised, with far-flung connections, and rich with tribute. There follows a section describing the withdrawal of divine support for Akkad, as the gods withdrew themselves and their attributes from the city – Enki and wisdom, Utu and counsel. The symbols of royalty were also removed, which can be taken as a sign that the city's right to rule was gone. After that, the king, Naram-Sin, Sargon's grandson, dreamed the city's destruction and fell into a paralysing seven-year depression. Failing to receive any positive omens from the gods, Naram-Sin set about despoiling and destroying the god Enlil's temple, and 'as the goods are removed from the city, so is the good sense of Akkad removed'.

How did the gods wreak their revenge on Naram-Sin? By setting in motion an invasion by Gutians, tribespeople 'who know no inhibition, with human instincts but canine intelligence and with monkey features'.[29] The Gutians laid waste to the land, no one travelled, there was no trade, some people took to nomadism while others planted crops within cities. The poem ends – 'Akkad is destroyed – hail to Innana'. The tone of the poem and the list of disasters it enumerates are very like the *Dialogue of Ipuwer*.

Although some see this as a contemporary account of climate change, drought, and woe, the poem was actually composed much later, and it is, again, as stressed by text specialists like Piotr Michalowski, not a historical text at all.[30] Gwendolyn Leick suggests that it was composed during the next period of Mesopotamian unity, the Ur III dynasty, and that the story served 'to suit the political agenda of the Ur III kings, who glorified their own achievements and ... presented the ruler of an earlier 'empire' as hubristic in comparison'.[31] She also notes that there is no evidence for Naram-Sin destroying Enlil's temple – rather the statues of him there continued to be worshipped – and also that the Gutian invasion happened much later.

The cause of destruction in *The Curse* was not climate change but rather the transgressions of a ruler against right behaviour – 'the good sense of Akkad had turned to folly' and the world turned upside down – even in ancient Mesopotamia collapse literature had a lesson to teach. Like *Ipuwer*, it expresses comment on the nature of kingship and right rule: "The Curse of Agade' exposes an ideological concern for the right relationship between the gods and the absolute ruler'.[32]

But in the Sumerian king lists, after the death of Sharkalisharri we do see a sign of instability and the fragmentation of the Akkadian Empire – the king lists announce: 'then who was king, who was not king?' followed by the rule of four kings in three years.[33] As in Egypt (and the Roman Empire), fragmentation and weakness meant the proliferation of rulers. If *The Curse* does not provide reliable evidence for the climate change narrative, and some doubt the hard evidence, what other factors might have driven this powerful military empire to collapse suddenly under Sargon's great-grandson Sharkalisharri?

THE SOCIAL AND POLITICAL SIDE OF AKKADIAN COLLAPSE

The Weiss hypothesis suggests that the Akkadian collapse happened because of climate change that affected grain production in northern Mesopotamia, which was essential to the empire. But how deep and stable was Akkadian imperial rule in the north anyway; can the Habur be described as an imperialised region that was essential to the survival of the Akkadian Empire? Jason Ur points out that 'the only indisputable physical manifestation of Akkadian imperial control in northern Mesopotamia remains the massive Naram-Sin palace at Tell-Brak'.[34] The bricks of the palace are stamped with his name. But while the palace is certainly an imperial foundation and reflects a strong interest in the region, it is unclear both how long it functioned and how far its reach extended.

The evidence of conquest from written texts and royal inscriptions – neither of which are proper 'historical' records – do not elaborate on the administration and control of conquered areas. And while there are texts in the Akkadian script from Tell Leilan and elsewhere, these may show no more than contact and the spread of literacy practices within an area that had strong commercial and cultural links (much like the use of Latin as a *lingua franca* in later Europe). The marriage of Taram-Akkad, Naram-Sin's daughter, to the ruler of Tell Mozan also does not necessarily indicate Akkadian control or subordination of the area – diplomatic marriages are a common political tool and 'soft power' could be used instead of more direct and coercive methods.[35] It is not at all clear that the Habur region was securely incorporated into the Akkadian Empire from Sargon's reign onwards, and unlikely that the dynasty was reliant on it for the survival of their empire.

What of the nature of the empire? Sargon's rule was punctuated by 'rebellions' and campaigning, as were those of his sons Rimush and Manishtashu, and of his grandson Naram-Sin, all of whom evidently had to follow up Sargon's initial 'conquests'. Rebellions were brutally crushed.[36] On coming to the throne (possibly by murdering his brother), Rimush immediately faced a rebellion led by the elite classes Sargon had displaced. Westenholz sums it up as 'a desperate, all-out effort to shake off the Akkadian yoke once and for all' – tens of thousands may have died.[37]

It might have been impossible for the Akkadians to form a permanent territorial empire; the imperial strategy may not even have been to set up such an empire but rather to influence and to benefit from influence in key areas. Augusta McMahon notes that while there are many 'imperial' looking features "the 'empire' was patchy and acted more like a commercial enterprise aimed at access to raw materials rather

than accumulation of land and subjects'.[38] However we conceive of the
imperial project, repeated fighting was necessary to impose Akkadian
authority throughout the empire's existence. Van De Mieroop suggests
that opposition to Akkadian rule might have been the major cause of
its collapse; 'that even the region near the capital participated in the
opposition to Akkad is a sign that the idea of centralized rule was intolerable everywhere'.[39] Rimush was eventually murdered.

Sargon and Naram-Sin became especially famous in Mesopotamian
culture. They gained their reputations for 'greatness' because of
their far-reaching military clout, but they were also remembered for
their arrogance.[40] One reason for Naram-Sin's reputation is that, as
mentioned earlier, he was forced to deal with uprisings against the
empire, which he did so harshly, and in the aftermath, perhaps in an
attempt to promote unity, or less sympathetically because of the great
power he wielded, he declared himself a god – his name was written
preceded by a star symbol, and he is portrayed wearing a horned
crown, both being symbols of divinity.[41] He visibly dominates the
scene on his famous Victory Stele (Figure 3.2).

Naram-Sin's self-deification may have backfired. Akkadian rulers
all faced the constant challenge of maintaining their pre-eminence,
and this meant relying on an intermediary elite that could run things
on a more local level and keeping them loyal. Parcels of land were
taken from conquered states and given as rewards to loyal followers,
something that would provoke simmering resentment in the cities.[42]
Reinhard Bernbeck suggests that Naram-Sin's boosting of his own
position as a divine king increased the distance between him and the
Akkadian elite and made relations between them more unequal and
unpredictable, which would have destabilised the empire.[43] Simply
trying to run the empire created potential fracture points in it.

That the other Mesopotamian cities still had the capacity for
organising concerted military action suggests that Akkadian rule,
whatever exactly that was, had neither overcome the other cities'
desire for independence or their ability to fight for it, even after
decades of Akkadian dominance. Marc Van De Mieroop observes
that the Akkadian phase 'had not radically altered the fundamental
political and economic organization of the area'.[44]

In 1952, E. A. Speiser, in his discussion, focussed on the relationship of the Akkadian dynasty with its neighbours. Speiser thought

FIGURE 3.2. Naram-Sin's Victory Stele.
Courtesy of Getty Images.

that a long period of cultural interaction between Akkad and other dynasties and peoples had something to do with its end: 'The agents responsible for the end were many, some known and others as yet obscure, but all influenced in some degree by prolonged contact with Akkadian culture'.[45] Contact drove political and military change but also brought people into conflict, and while Akkad could face off individual enemies, the eventual formation of coalitions was a different matter. Speiser also stressed the ambiguity over the Gutian migration – both about when it happened and what its effects were – did it affect the empire or bring it to its end, or were the Gutians drawn into a post-imperial vacuum?

Altogether the Akkadian enterprise seems bound to have failed eventually; it continued its existence based on its abilities to assert military might as and when needed and be supported with a degree of consensus at different levels of society, from local rulers to the general population. Such frequent warring, as well as the reported deportations of thousands of defeated enemies, must have created turmoil and instability throughout northern and southern Mesopotamia, and this in itself would have had a damaging effect on agricultural production, the economy, and day-to-day life – and the regime would hardly have endeared itself to many of its subjects.

We cannot be certain about what caused the collapse of the Akkadian Empire, nor exactly, given the problems with assigning a secure chronology, when it happened. But the Akkadian collapse, regardless of whether or not there was a climatic drying trend, seems best understood not as a catastrophic collapse but as a political collapse in which the attempt to create and maintain a unified empire from competing independent city-states was ultimately defeated by those peoples' desire for independence.[46] As Jean-Jacques Glassner, who blamed the collapse on political problems and civil wars, has pointed out, 'man is the essential factor' not climate change.[47] The Akkadian collapse may well have been welcomed by many.

AFTER THE AKKADIAN EMPIRE

Did the Akkadian collapse bring about a dark age? No. The usual interpretation of the phrase from the Sumerian kings list 'who was king who was not king?' is as a sign of disorder and fragmentation, but, in fact, the situation of having many kings was a return to the normal situation of city-state independence. The short-lived unity imposed by the Akkadian dynasty was itself an anomaly in the usually fragmented political organisation of Mesopotamia.[48] Other research shows that the extent of site abandonment in northern Mesopotamia is much less than Weiss and colleagues had supposed, and there was continued settlement at most major urban sites.[49] Also, further research on the chronology from study of pottery shows that the timing of changes to urban life, still 'urban collapse,' in Ur's words, varied across sites, and it was not as sudden or universal as sometimes presented.[50]

The Akkadians too did not disappear; in the aftermath of the imperial collapse, kings continued to rule Akkad, as one state among many – Dudu and Shu-Durul reigned thirty-six years in total.[51] Cities continued to thrive. Then, soon after the Akkadian collapse, Ur-Namma founded a dynasty based at the city of Ur in southern Mesopotamia.[52] This dynasty also laid claim to an imperial state, governing Sumer and Akkad, and expanding towards the eastern mountains rather than the west.[53] This state, known as the Ur III dynasty (*c.* 2100–2000 BC), presumably learning from its Akkadian predecessor, appears to have been very centralised, with a single administrative and tax system, a standing army, and a new system of weights and measures, a calendar, and a law code.

The Ur III dynasty is often mentioned in environmental histories, with its collapse apparently caused by food shortages and famine caused by increasing soil salinity due to the intensive irrigation agriculture on which the state's initial success was based. The landmark article on this theory by Thorkild Jacobsen and Robert M. Adams was published in *Science* in 1958.[54] In their paper, Jacobsen and Adams observed that temple records showed declining wheat yields over time and an increase in the cultivation of barley, which is a more salt tolerant crop than wheat. They trace this trend over seven centuries from 2400 BC to 1700 BC. Paulette cautions, however, that 'direct evidence for salinization in Bronze Age Mesopotamia comes largely from cuneiform documents' rather than from physical evidence.[55]

At the same time, while irrigation was common in the south, northern sites, which did not use irrigation agriculture, and therefore were not prone to increased salinity, also increased the proportion of barley grown, implying that this choice was not simply a response to decreasing wheat yields. Andrew Cohen suggests that barley in fact became a key symbol for Mesopotamian people, that is, it was not only of practical use but also of symbolic value (we might think of 'beer countries' and 'wine countries', where the drinks have a cultural value), and this may be an important consideration in evaluating agricultural change.[56] In addition, environmental and other histories tend not to cite a 1985 paper by Powell that questioned the salinity narrative; in it, he noted that the Mesopotamians could have mitigated salinisation by 'flushing' the soil and also that the salt tolerance of wheat and barley is almost the same.[57] Powell's critique has in turn been disputed by others such as Michal Artzy and Daniel Hillel.[58] Recent research has attempted to model progressive salinisation and has emphasised the strategies used by farmers to solve the problem.[59]

Norman Yoffee states that the collapse did not happen because of salinisation, and notes that 'at the capital of Ur life for most citizens went on much as before after one ruling dynasty was toppled, and, after a short time, a new dynasty came into power'.[60] This is slightly more optimistic than Gwendolyn Leick's reconstruction, which involves the destruction of the city by enemies (but such things were normal) – but even so, she notes that the city soon revived, probably in part due to its importance as a centre of religious cult, and it thrived for centuries 'until the end of the Mesopotamian era'.[61] The second major centralising dynasty had again failed to impose a lasting unity on a world of independent-minded cities and regions. Mark Chavalas notes that far from being either apocalyptic or terribly sudden, the

collapse of the Ur III state was gradual in that governors of outlying provinces began to assert their autonomy from the central administration. By the end, these governors had set up their own dynasties, which denied supplies to the capital.[62]

Barjamovic does not mention salinisation at all and simply notes that 'following the collapse of the Ur III state, Mesopotamia reverted to a political landscape of city-states and tribal groups tied into networks of changing political alliances'.[63] These could 'intermittently attain a character of loose imperial states'. This again sounds like the fragmentation of the Egyptian Old Kingdom, with its local governors gaining power at the expense of the pharaoh, although in the Mesopotamian case the 'fragments' were much stronger.

The later literature about the fall of Ur III gives a prominent role to invading Amorites and the Elamites. But this is to some extent a literary construct, one that echoed treatment of the Gutians in the fall of Akkad – Amorites had already been living in the cities and rural areas of Babylonia before the end of the Ur III state, where 'they were already integrated in all levels of society'.[64] The Elamites, however, did take advantage of Ur III's weakening power – they conquered and occupied the city of Ur for seven years, deporting the king, Ibbi-Sin, to Susa.

Mario Liverani makes it clear that we have to see collapse – that is the fragmentation and reformation of political units like the Akkadian Empire and the Ur III dynasty – as part of an entirely normal ebb and flow of power between participants in the Mesopotamian culture area. As he makes clear, the Mesopotamian conception of dominance or power was one of fleetingness or ephemerality, with dynasties referred to in Sumerian and Akkadian by words indicating temporary offices or positions. Anyone who looks at the Sumerian kings list will see that it creates, in its present form, an unbroken and connected history, in which dominance passes from one city and dynasty to another. The list states that

Ur was indeed given kingship [but] it was not given an eternal reign. From time immemorial, since the land was founded, until the population multiplied, who has ever seen a reign of kingship that would take precedence [forever]? The reign of the kingship had been long indeed but had to exhaust itself.[65]

Surrounded by physical remains of earlier cities and states, the notion of temporariness, and the inevitable rise and fall of dynasties and cities, change must have suffused the region. The past, real or imagined, could serve as a moral example – past rulers failed and the world fell into chaos – and at the same time help current rulers advertise the rightness of the present and of their own rule.

THE GUTIANS

We know very little about the Gutians, who are often associated with the Akkadian collapse – they left no archaeological or other record; it is not even certain that the term Gutian refers to a single people rather than a number of different 'barbarian' people from different places. Even so, many modern scholars place their origins in the Zagros mountains, east of Mesopotamia. The Gutians seem to have been a tribal people who raided the cities and countryside of Mesopotamia. Sources first mention the Gutians in Akkadian times, and mostly they are represented in a very negative fashion – as 'monkey faced', for example.

It seems unlikely that the Gutians actually caused the Akkadian collapse, but rather that they benefited from it; as Marc Van De Mieroop states: 'More likely Gutians took advantage of the political difficulties of the Akkadian kings to gain a political foothold in some cities'.[67] At some cities, Gutian dynasties were founded, and they may have ruled for fifty or even a hundred years, though native dynasties also continued. While one Gutian king, Erridu-pizir, left three inscribed statues at Nippur, the Gutians as a whole left little or no impression on the cities and culture of Mesopotamia. The Gutian dynasty at Babylonia was eventually ousted by a native king of Uruk Utu-hegel, who defeated a king called Tirigan.

FINAL THOUGHTS

The collapse of the Akkadian Empire was a political one, in which an empire, one that had never been particularly cohesive or stable, fragmented into constituent parts that had previously been independent. What role climate change might have played in this is still uncertain. Even if the Akkadian Empire was destabilised by climate change and agricultural problems, its collapse was surely driven by the desire for independence amongst Mesopotamian city-states. The collapse brought about a return to local autonomy. But the empire set a precedent for other dynasties to seek to extend their power, as the Ur III dynasty did shortly after the Akkadian collapse. Its collapse too by no means marked the end of Mesopotamian civilisation. Both Akkad and Ur continued to exist, and, at Akkad, Sargon's dynasty continued to rule for a while. Mesopotamia continued to experience periods of unification and fragmentation until the whole region was eventually incorporated into a Hellenistic empire, in the aftermath of Alexander the Great's conquests in the fourth century BC.

The stories of climate change and salinisation presented in Mesopotamian collapses are of obvious contemporary interest – salinisation is a threat to modern agriculture too. Contemporary scientists are seeking ways to develop increasingly salt tolerant cereal crops that can be grown in areas that suffer from salinisation.[66] Environmental histories such as Clive Ponting's work stress the deleterious effects of salinisation on Mesopotamian society, but they do not consider the wider nature and patterns of Mesopotamian history; they present apocalyptic descriptions that leave no place for the continuity that we can identify. We do not need history to tell us that causing salinisation is bad for agriculture – we know this for ourselves. In judging the Akkadian and Ur III collapses, it is the human relationships, the politics, the motivations, and the ideologies that provide more satisfactory accounts, even when environmental stressors may well be a factor.

4

The Indus Valley: A Truly Lost Civilisation?

Indra stands accused ...

Mortimer Wheeler[1]

THE INDUS VALLEY CIVILISATION

The Indus Valley civilisation is still best known through the cities of
Harappa and Mohenjo-Daro, the latter of which, as Greg Possehl says,
can be regarded as the best preserved Bronze Age city in the world
(Figure 4.1).[2] Famous images of the civilisation include the Great
Bath at Mohenjo-Daro, statues like the Dancing Girl and the Priest
King (Figure 4.2), and the many seal stones inscribed with animals
real and mythological, accompanied by lines written in the still undeciphered Harappan script. This Bronze Age urban civilisation and
all clear memory of it seemingly disappeared completely, although
its ruins remained. The ancient Greek geographer Strabo recorded a
description of the ancient Indus region from the time of Alexander
the Great, citing Aristobulos, who said:

> he saw a country of more than a thousand cities, together with villages, that
> had been deserted because the Indus had abandoned its proper bed, and had
> turned aside into the other bed on the left that was much deeper, and flowed
> with precipitous descent like a cataract, so that the Indus no longer watered
> by its overflows the abandoned country on the right, since that country was
> now above the level, not only of the new stream, but also of its overflows.[3]

The Harappan civilisation began to come to light when British engi-
neers John and William Brunton, driving the East Indian Railway from

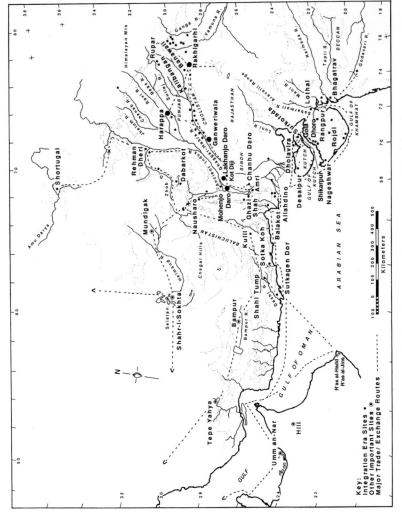

FIGURE 4.1. Map of the Indus Valley (Harappan) culture area and major sites.
Source: Courtesy of J. M. Kenoyer.

FIGURE 4.2. 'Priest king', from Mohenjo-Daro.
Source: Courtesy of Getty Images.

Karachi to Lahore, needed more ballast to support the tracks, which were to be laid over the sandy local soil. John Brunton had heard rumours of an ancient brick-built city called Brahminabad, located in the desert of Sind, and, finding the ruins, he used its ancient bricks for the railway; meanwhile, his brother mined out Harappa to the north for the bricks to support his stretch of the track for almost 100 miles.[4] Besides finding and plundering these cities, John Brunton did record some observations and excavated objects, including stone seals, which came to generate archaeological interest in the region later on. Some objects appeared in *The Illustrated London News* in 21 February 1857, labelled 'Relics from the buried city of Brahmunabad, in Sind'.

Even so, that the 'Harappan' remains were those of a 'new' civilisation was not recognised until much later, after organised investigations began in the early 1920s, and Sir John Marshall of the Archaeological Survey of India, who had trained with Arthur Evans at Knossos, and others began to recognise the similarities between the distant sites of Harappa and Mohenjo-Daro – 'though these two cities are some 400 miles apart, their monuments and antiquities are to all intents and purposes identical'.[5] On his retirement, Marshall, because of his contribution to its archaeology, was said to have left India two thousand years older.

Continuing investigations revealed an entire world that stretched north to south from Afghanistan to Gujarat and from the Makran in the west to the area between the Indus and Ganges Rivers in the east, in a range of environmental settings from the coast, to river plains, and mountain valleys. In the Harappan phase, also known as the urban phase, the seven centuries between around 2600 and 1900 BC (Table 4.1), the culture area covered an area of around 500,000 square miles, an area several times larger than that of Great Britain.[6] There were several major cities: Harappa and Mohenjo-Daro, Ganweriwala, Dholavira, and Rakhigarhi, but some 1,500 or more Harappan sites are known in total.[7]

The Indus Tradition developed into its best-known form from indigenous beginnings, with large walled settlements with streets appearing in the later Early Harappan phase.[8] Sites such as Kot Diji and Rehman Deri were early grid planned cities, and aspects of the Kot Diji ceramic tradition continued through Harappan history. Harappa itself shows a long development and the early appearance of many 'classic' Harappan features.[9] The urban Harappan phase gave way to

TABLE 4.1 *Eras and phases of the Indus Tradition*

Era	Phase	Approximate dates (BC)
Regionalisation Era	Early Harappan	5500–2600
Integration Era	Harappan (urban)	2600–1900
Localisation Era	Late Harappan	1900–1300

Source: Page 5, Kenoyer, J. M. (2015). 'The archaeological heritage of Pakistan: From the Palaeolithic to the Indus civilization.' In Long, R. D. (ed.). *A History of Pakistan*. Oxford: Oxford University Press, pp. 1–90.

the Localisation Era, the Late Harappan phase, from around 1900 BC[10]; it is this transformation, the breakdown of the urban culture, which has been identified as the Indus Valley collapse. The collapse involved the abandonment of the old urban centres around or after 1900 BC; while some classes of artefact disappear or become rare – 'stamp seals, triangular cakes, miniature cart-frames and wheels, perforated pottery, cubical weights, fired bricks, and instances of script become obsolete or extremely rare', others continue into the next phase, including 'worked shell, semiprecious stone, metal, and faience'.[11]

In this chapter, let us first consider what we know about the Harappan culture before looking at how the collapse has been portrayed and explained and questioning whether collapse is a good term to use in this case. Finally we shall look at the idea of a 'global' Old World collapse at the end of the Early Bronze Age.

A PEACEFUL CIVILISATION WITHOUT STATES?

The image of classic Harappan culture is one of a sophisticated and pacificist urban society with large well-built cities and sanitation facilities – baths and drains, long-distance trade, fine art objects, and seals inscribed with a mysterious writing.[12] But beyond that, there is much we do not know about the specifics of Harappan society. It has even been labelled 'faceless' in comparison to other past cultures where human and other figures loom large in the archaeological record.[13] 'Sameness' and a lack of change across centuries and vast distances is an oft-noted characteristic of Harappan civilisation, leading to charges of 'stagnation' or 'complacency' amongst its inhabitants.[14]

Some early European archaeologists interpreted this apparent uniformity as a possible result of an oppressive 'oriental' system, perhaps with a theocratic element, where people, places, and life were planned, marshalled, and regimented, and strong rulers and a priestly class co-opted, through force or religious ideology, the labour of the masses for their grandiose building schemes. Now archaeologists argue that there is evidence for status differentiation and the presence of elites.[15] But rulers have proved hard to find. Unlike many societies, the Harappans did not emphasise individual rulers and elites in iconography (this is similar, though, to the Minoans, Mycenaeans, and Teotihuanacos), conspicuous burials, or clearly differentiated (to us, at least) palace-type buildings. There is no clear evidence for kings (though Dholavira's (in Kutch) architecture might suggest a single ruler, or a governor) or priest-kings or a distinct ruling class; though the layout of cities like Mohenjo-Daro and Harappa, with multiple walled compounds, suggests that they may have been occupied by different elite family groups (Figure 4.3).[16] Before we dismiss the existence of kings, a note of caution should be sounded – the Spartan kingdom in Archaic and Classical Greece had a long-lived (dual) monarchy, but the kings 'enjoyed no outward sign of their position, such as palaces or crowns, but they possessed exalted status'; power is not always archaeologically visible and may be deliberately hidden in material terms.[17]

This (apparent) invisibility of rulers has created a difficulty in conceptualising how Harappan society worked and how the area as a whole was organised. Stuart Piggott saw the cities of Harappa and Mohenjo-Daro as northern and southern capitals of a single kingdom, each with a ruler's citadel and a lower town for the urban middle class, although for Mortimer Wheeler it was unclear how some areas like Saurashtra, south of Kutch, would fit into such a state.[18] But the idea that there was a single Harappan kingdom or state is no longer accepted.[19] Some even doubt that Harappan society had states – but partly this is a problem of satisfactorily defining what a state is.[20] The general consensus now seems to be that the large cities represent state-level societies that controlled their immediate environs (and possibly sometimes smaller 'cities'), and that other

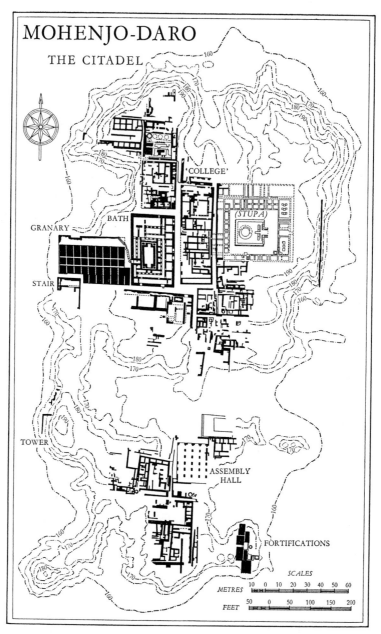

FIGURE 4.3. Mohenjo-Daro citadel.
Source: From Wheeler, M. (1968). *The Indus Civilization*. Third edition. CUP, p. 39, figure 7.

sites elsewhere may have been the focal points of chiefdoms. The city-states may have been ruled by hereditary or appointed kings or councils of some kind; Kenoyer points out that there was probably diversity and change over the centuries of the Harappan phase, and this makes sense, though changes are not visible to us as they are in some other societies.[21] In the Harappan phase, we should probably think of 'major regional polities' that were integrated into a 'larger ... economic, political and ideological system' – adding up to what we think of as the Indus Valley or Harappan civilisation.[22]

Trade is emphasised as a feature of Harappan society, and one of the most notable aspects of this is the presence of a standardised set of weights and measures in use across the Indus region, the first traces of which are from the Early Harappan (the Kot Dijian phase).[23] Trade was carried out within the region and also internationally as far afield as Mesopotamia. Harappan seals have been found at Ur in Mesopotamia, and the Indus Valley region is thought to be the land of Meluhha recorded in Mesopotamian texts; Sargon of Akkad boasted that ships from Dilmun, Magan, and Meluhha came to Akkad.[24] Merchants and translators from Meluhha even lived in Mesopotamia; the Indus Valley region was far from isolated, but was part of what Greg Possehl has called the Middle Asian Interaction Sphere.[25]

Seals, which acted as identifiers and ownership marks on traded goods, also first appeared then; these were often decorated with figured motifs and Harappan script.[26] Writing developed possibly as early as 3500 BC, and came to be more common from 2600 BC; it was employed on a variety of media including as 'graffiti' on pottery, on seals, and on copper tablets.[27] Symbols may also have been used on perishable materials such as textiles and wood, and possibly on the body as tattoos.[28] Also beads, blades, tools, and ceramics became increasingly standardised, and there was a standard size of brick, with a 1-2-4 ratio. Even urban areas seem to have shared a fairly standard plan, with raised citadels in the west and a lower town in the east.[29]

In the absence of clear rulers, there has been a focus on the role of ideology in Harappan society as a way of explaining the breadth and depth of the civilisation and its means of enrolling people in it. Robin Coningham and Mark Manuel have written of 'willing subordination'.[30] Another reason for this focus is the absence of evidence for warfare. Just as the Maya and Minoans have been thought of as 'peaceful' and 'priestly', so too have the Harappans been excused from the violent habits of many complex human societies; and from the work of Marshall onward, the 'acceptance of 'peaceful Harappans'' 'has coloured ... discussions of Harappan warfare' and society.[31] There is little evidence of warfare or destructions in Harappan society, and the constructions identified as 'fortification' walls may have had other primary functions.[32]

That said, there are swords and arrowheads, and Edward Cork has suggested we might have fewer weapons in contrast to other societies because in those other cases the evidence comes primarily from burials; Harappan archaeology is based on investigation of settlements.[33] There is also evidence of a degree of interpersonal violence, which may be status differentiated.[34] Some archaeologists, such as Keir Strickland, note a general difficulty with finding archaeological evidence for warfare in south Asia – even when we know from historical sources that it was happening.[35]

A society that de-emphasised differences materially does not mean there were no differences in the lived experience of people. The cities would have provided a venue for a range of activities and interactions, and these no doubt differed according to such factors as age, gender, status, and so on – there was music and entertainment, we know. Evidently, there were craft specialists, farmers, merchants, and others. Some people travelled long distances, but most probably stayed close to home. The city-dwellers did not exist in a vacuum either and were part of a settlement hierarchy that included a range of smaller 'towns' and non-urban sites; only a few of the urban centres were very large, with populations of tens of thousands; they must have been bustling and lively places.[36]

We know enough now to move on to examine some of the theories put forward to explain the Indus Valley collapse. First of all, let us look at an old favourite – the Aryan invasion.

INVADING ARYANS

Harappan civilisation has often thought to have been ended by barbarian invasions, much like the Western Roman Empire or even Mycenaean Greece. Most associated with this view is probably

Mortimer Wheeler, who thought, probably on the advice of his col-
league at Harappa, V. S. Agrawala, that the ancient Indian Rig Veda
texts could contain clues to real historical events.[37] The Vedas
describe destructions by Aryan (Indo-European) invaders of the
walled cities of the indigenous *Dasa* people, and it seemed to
Wheeler that such an invasion might represent the arrival of Indo-
Aryan speaking peoples – 'Indra stands accused', he famously wrote.
Wheeler suggested that while other factors – climate, economy,
politics – might have been involved, destruction at human hands,
'deliberate and large scale destruction', was the most plausible immediate cause, and as part of his argument he noted evidence of a massacre at Mohenjo-Daro.[38]

Although most archaeologists are now sceptical about the role or
even reality of many ancient migrations and invasions described in
myths, these ideas are still to be found in modern literature. A recent
handbook on warfare takes seriously these myths of Aryan superior-
ity and adds further detail.[39] In this view, handfuls of Aryan invaders
on chariots were able to defeat much larger Harappan infantry forces
(of 30,000 to 100,000) in open battle. When Harappans decided to
stay inside their 'earth-and-timber-walled citadels', the Aryans used
rams and fire arrows against them. In this way, India was invaded and
conquered in the period 1500–1000 BC and the native Harappans
became the 'outcasts' in the Hindu caste system. James Wellard
thought that Aryan barbarians could only have defeated the sophisticated Harappans if the social order was already fragmenting; he
notes deteriorating building standards and physical infrastructure
that could suggest just such a 'decline'.[40]

Wheeler based his view at least in part on human remains found at
Mohenjo-Daro. Of the remains, he argued that 'we have here in fact
the vestiges of a final massacre, after which Mohenjo-Daro ceased to
exist'.[41] Another pillar of the theory was the appearance of new pottery styles. But even in the mid-1960s, George Dale was questioning
the idea that the human remains represented a massacre; he suggested that there was no evidence they were contemporary or even
that they represented a single event.[42] Neither could he find any evidence that the cities had been attacked or destroyed. On the appearance of a new material culture, Coningham and Young quote Indian

archaeologist H. D. Sankalia, who in 1962 wrote that after a hundred years of research 'we have not found anything 'Aryan' on the ruins of the Indus Valley Civilisation'.[43] The Rig Veda itself may well date to 1000 BC, almost a millennium after the collapse, and can hardly be expected to be a reliable record of what happened hundreds of years earlier.[44] There is also no biological evidence for migration or invasion.[45]

The invasion theory, a modern myth, has been completely discredited – Kenoyer calls it an 'absurd theory ... entrenched in the popular literature'.[46] Even Wheeler himself later retreated from what he insisted had only been a 'light-hearted' hypothesis 'enlarged or decried beyond warrant' – he knew collapse was a complex issue.[47] But it evidently retains an appeal, in part because it is simple, seems plausible, and also because of the attractiveness of the theory that languages spread through the migration of population groups.[48]

CLIMATE CHANGE

Early researchers such as Marshall, Sir Aurel Stein, and V. Gordon Childe believed that the climate of the Indus Valley region must once have been wetter in order to afford the development of cities with clay bricks and drainage, and thus climate change to a more arid environment has been frequently cited as a cause of Harappan collapse.[49] As we saw in the first chapter, climate change theories have been in the news: *The Times of India*'s 2012 headline proclaimed that 'Climate killed Harappan civilization'.[50] This story was based on a paper by Liviu Giosan and colleagues, in which they argued that there was a reduction in monsoon rainfall, which affected the flow of the Indus basin river system.[51] But rather than 'killing' a civilisation, the authors suggested that from around 1900 BC there was a decline in settlement, a process of site abandonment, and a shift in population and population density to the east (Figures 4.4a and b). A more recent paper by Yama Dixit and colleagues based on isotope analysis of lake sediment cores also suggests a 200-year failing of the monsoons around 4,100 years ago, though the date is somewhat uncertain and may be out by a century.[52]

A number of researchers suggest that climate change had a direct impact on the Harappans.[53] The evidence for this comes from core

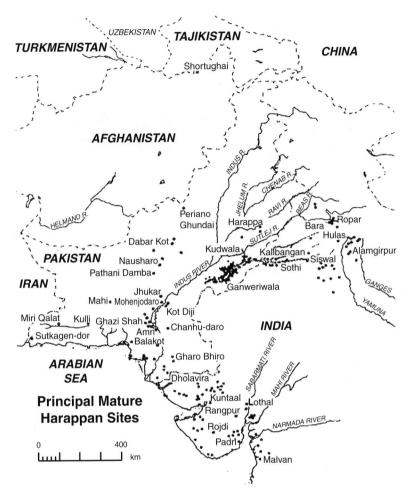

FIGURES 4.4A AND B. Sites of the Harappan and post-urban Late Harappan. *Source*: With kind permission from Springer Science and Business Media.

samples drilled in the Arabian Sea, which indicate a reduced discharge of water and reduced river flow, around 2200 to 2100 BC, which could indicate drought. This might have led to experimentation in agriculture as the Harappans began to plant different crops. Others argue that climate change had an indirect bearing on the Indus collapse. They claim that it was in fact the climate-caused collapses in Egypt and Mesopotamia that disrupted trade with the Indus

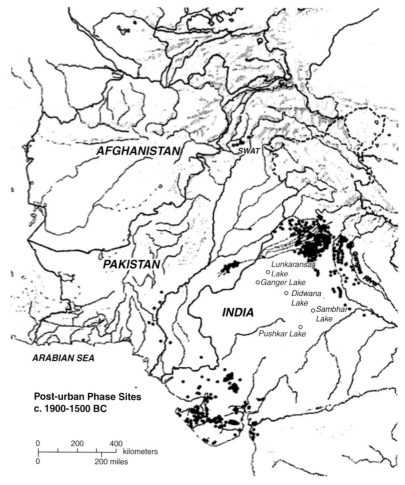

FIGURES 4.4A AND B (*continued*)

Valley area, causing decline. This might place too much weight on the importance of foreign trade, which was almost certainly negligible to the survival of the Harappan zone as a whole.[54]

Some believe that the supposedly global 4.2 kya climate event was responsible for causing the Harappan collapse, for bringing about the First Intermediate Period in Egypt, the collapse of the Akkadian Empire, and for an Early Bronze Age collapse in Greece and the Levant in the late third millennium BC.[55] As Michael Staubwasser and colleagues pithily state: 'The 4.2 ka event is coherent with the termination of urban Harappan civilization in the Indus valley'.[56] But it is notable that much of Harappan society did not collapse at that time, rather the deurbanisation of the western areas happened later. If there was a drying of the climate, and even a reduced river flow, the Indus Valley communities may have continued in existence supported by glacier fed rather than rain fed systems, which would have ensured a continuing supply of water to some rivers.[57]

In 2006, Marco Madella and Dorian Fuller observed that archaeologists tended not to put much faith in climate change arguments for the collapse, in contrast to scientists.[58] Reviewing the evidence, they suggested that, in fact, 'urbanism emerged on the face of a prolonged trend towards declining rainfall,' and that 'no climatic event can be blamed for a precipitous end' of Harappan civilisation. They argue that changes in agricultural practices, possibly in response to climate change, could have contributed to the social changes that took place over time. It should also be remembered that the Indus civilisation covered a vast area with a range of different environmental conditions – climate change cannot explain everything everywhere. Greg Possehl has stated that 'we should stop thinking about the physical world and start looking at the fabric of society'.[59]

COLLAPSE OR TRANSFORMATION?

Here we have to step back and consider that what we think of as an abrupt Indus collapse was really a much longer transformation that saw different kinds of changes in different areas at different times – Giosan and colleagues rightly stress this. Areas like Kutch (Gujarat) seem to have continued straight through *c.* 1900 BC into later times without a blip; at Rojdi, the site expanded.[60] Kenoyer writes of the Localisation Era that it saw a splitting of the Integration Era system into three areas: the Punjab Phase in the north, including Harappa; the Jhukar Phase in the south (Sindh and Baluchistan); and the Rangpur Phase in Gujarat. The regions produced 'new painted motifs and ceramic styles, seals with geometric designs and new burial customs'.[61] Despite the novelties, there were also many

continuities, and Kenoyer stresses the continued presence of urban
societies – Harappa was occupied for a further five centuries – some
possibly at a state level.[62] In the northeast of the region the number of sites increased rather than decreased. It seems that what we
are dealing with is not an abrupt collapse at all but a longer-term
process – transformation (rather than decline) is perhaps a more
appropriate term for what was happening.

RIVERS AND CIVILISATION

Climate change and changes in rainfall may have affected Harappan
society, but that society was one especially based on rivers rather than
rain fed irrigation. As we saw earlier, Strabo noted that the rivers of
the Indus area sometimes changed their courses, and he suggested
that villages were abandoned because of it. This river change theory
has proved attractive to archaeologists over the years.[63] Although in
modern times the river has been 'trained' to follow a particular regular course, in the nineteenth and early twentieth centuries the Indus
was well known to shift its course.

Several archaeologists, going back to Ernest Mackay in the 1940s,
have argued that an avulsion of the Indus could have led to the
abandonment of Mohenjo-Daro. In one view, first suggested by M. R.
Sahni in 1952, a dam formed of alluvium down-river caused flooding up-river.[64] This behaviour had been observed after an earthquake in 1819, which created the Allah Bund, a ridge that damned
some of the eastern Indus streams, causing 2,000 square miles of
flooding.[65] Tectonic uplift in coastal areas was identified by George
Dales in 1960/1961; and it was proposed by Robert L. Raikes in 1964
that earthquakes and flooding could have caused the destruction of
sites and might explain 'how at least part of the Harappa culture met
its end'.[66] Raikes suggested that communications and trade would
have been interrupted. This view came in for criticism in 1967 by
H. T. Lambrick, who instead suggested, like Aristobulos, that the
Indus changed its course upriver of Mohenjo-Daro, leaving the city
'starved of water', which caused its abandonment.[67] Both could have
caused some of the gradual eastern shift of population – floods or
shortages.

But could a collapse at Mohenjo-Daro (or a more gradual abandonment) have caused the wider changes? Probably not. As Greg Possehl points out, the Indus Valley civilisation was far more than just one urban site, however grand it may have been, and it is very doubtful that the abandonment of one centre could have a very significant effect on the Harappan culture zone as a whole.[68] Could it be though that the Mohenjo-Daro state, if there was one, did collapse because of issues with riverine changes?

The research mentioned earlier by Liviu Giosan and colleagues posited a reduction in monsoon rainfall; this they argue affected the course and flow of river systems of the Indus region, especially the Ghaggar-Hakra River.[69] But they state that while 'the unprecedented scale of hydroclimatic stresses must have increased the vulnerability of Harappan society, [it] does not provide a simple, deterministic explanation for the transformations in site size, distribution, and interrelationships across the whole civilization area'. It is likely that, over time, as the nature of the rivers changed, people experimented with growing different crops, and generally the balance of population shifted eastward into better-watered areas. These theories of shifting river courses seem to have superseded the tectonic uplift flood theories.[70]

Some of the biggest effects might have come from the drying of the Saraswati River, along which settlement and population seem to have been fairly dense.[71] Changes to the river courses and systems of the region seem very likely to have affected the patterns of settlement, promoting a general eastern shift of habitation and the partial abandonment of many of the western urban centres over time, as Kenoyer states:

Shifting river patterns and the eventual drying up of the Saraswati–Ghaggar–Hakra River resulted in the abandonment of many sites and migration into the Indus valley, Gujarat or to the Ganga–Yamuna valley. The disruption of agriculture and the eventual breakdown of trade and political networks led to the decline of urbanism and the disappearance of many distinctive features of the Indus culture.[72]

However, recent work seems to show that there were many more sites not concentrated along the river channel, and this has led to doubt about the date of the drying of the river. It may be the case that the

river dried up long before the Harappan culture took off, and thus
that it played no role in the Indus transformation.[73]

OTHER IDEAS

Of the three theories examined so far, changes in the courses of
rivers seems to be the one favoured by experts for influencing the
trajectory of Late Harappan society, but this may turn out to be
wrong, depending on the dating of the dried up river beds in the
area. There are other ideas that can be considered though. For
example, there is increasing evidence for disease and violence.
Jane McIntosh has suggested that poor health could have caused a
decline in population at Mohenjo-Daro.[74] Examination of human
remains has shown signs that individuals suffered from malaria;
they may also have suffered from cholera caused by contaminated
drinking water. Gwen Robbins Schug and her team have found evidence that at Harappa people increasingly suffered from infection
and infectious diseases.[75] Both diseases must have been a threat
throughout the life of the city, and it is unclear why they would
have had such a devastating effect at the end of the Harappan
phase, but they certainly may have encouraged people to leave the
cities.[76] Additional evidence from human remains at Harappa suggests that violence existed in Indus Valley communities, and that
it was 'structured along lines of gender and community membership'.[77] Given that this forces us to reconsider the idea of 'peaceful
Harrapans', we might give more weight to social and ideological
factors, for example, inter-group conflict and the withdrawal of
'support', in Indus de-urbanisation.

Changes in trade have been touched upon earlier; it is widely
agreed that international trade does seem to reduce, but it is unclear
whether this might have been a cause or a consequence of the other
changes that took place. It has to be noted too that the ports of
Gujarat remained in contact with the Persian Gulf region.[78] Within
the Indus zone, trade continued but was fragmented into the three
Localisation Era areas.[79] Interruption in the trade of luxury materials or items into the Indus region could have undermined the position of traders or urban elites if they relied on these materials to
exchange or to boost their status; equally, as mentioned earlier, social

and economic changes in the Indus region could have reduced the trade in such items and materials.[80]

Two other environmental arguments involve the degradation of the landscape, salinisation, and deforestation.[81] Wheeler suggested thus in 1968:

Impoverishment of the surrounding farmlands by over-cultivation, by the destruction or neglect of irrigation-channels, by over-grazing, has been postulated. The untiring consumption of major vegetation implied by the firing, age after age, of millions of bricks may, even with the aid of hill-timbers, have helped to bare the land and may possibly ... have reduced the transpiration of moisture. I have suggested that Mohenjo-Daro was wearing out its landscape.[82]

Wheeler admitted that 'all this is conjecture', but Coningham and Young agree that these factors could have caused problems in some local areas.[83] Farmers may, over time, have sought to grow more salt tolerant crops in some areas, though barley might have been grown because it makes softer straw for animals – was there a change to the agricultural economy and a social change because of (or as a result of) it? We could also easily imagine that deforestation could have played a role in driving change, but Possehl has argued that only a relatively small amount of forest (400 acres) would have been needed to rebuild the city every century and a half.[84] These theories have not found wide acceptance.

CONTINUITY, CHANGE, AND HARAPPAN HERITAGE

The image that Harappan civilisation inspires is often one of surprise at their apparent modernity – particularly at their urban architecture and plumbing, which contrasts with the archaeology of later times, of urban abandonment around and after 1900 BC. The Harappans seem to lack clear and conscious cultural heirs, and their fairly recent rediscovery through archaeology distances them from historical Indian civilisation. But this does not mean that the civilisation, the lives, traditions, and memories that were lived and experienced by people, was simply cut off or changed overnight – as Mark Manuel says of our modern division of Harappan civilisation into phases, they are 'arbitrary points along a continual line of social and political development'.[85]

The six or seven centuries of widespread Harappan urbanism, whatever we can see through what remains, cannot have been without history or events, however static it may seem. In fact, the transition from Early to Harappan seems accompanied by deliberate burning at many sites, which is perhaps indicative of political changes, maybe even the formation of regional states.[86] Many Harappan features are really more associated with the last half of that phase – so it was not really static at all. Wheeler, painting a picture of decline followed by collapse, based mainly on Mohenjo-Daro, suggested that the 'shoddy' houses that replaced the old ordered look of the city indicated a loss of 'civic pride', and that the new 'hovels which huddle together in a rabbit-warren of buildings' housed 'a swarming lower-grade population'.[87] The constant rebuilding of the cities, and the changes to their architecture in later times, is often seen as decline, which to some extent reveals our bias and values, but these changes presumably reflect transformations in lifestyle, society, and probably in people's ideas of what a city should be; they testify to a long and busy life. The transition from Harappan, the Integration Era, to the post urban Localisation Era should not be seen as an instantaneous or apocalyptic change.

Possehl has discussed the nature of the transformation of the Harappan, and even though he talks of the 'failure' of Harappan civilisation as a 'fleeting moment of Bronze Age urbanization' (rather too long to be 'fleeting', perhaps), he also questions the notion of any simple collapse, eclipse, or end; others too refer to 'transformation' or 'restructuring' rather than an ending.[88] Although a number of cities were abandoned over time, there is continuity in local non-urban sites, and also in sites further east and south in the Sorath Harappan area. The city of Pirak in Baluchistan continued to thrive from around 1850 BC into the Hellenistic period some 1,500 years later.[89] In the Punjab, there is continuity through this post urban phase to around 1000 BC, and overlap between Bronze Age ceramics and the Painted Grey Ware, which develops out of it. Possehl suggests that despite a real ideological change most notable in the end of urbanism, 'the descendants of the Indus Civilization in northern India flow gracefully into the peoples of the Early Historic there'.[90] Jim Shaffer also explains that there was no South Asian dark age, while Kenoyer suggests that 'current studies of the transition between the two early

12: M-304 A

FIGURE 4.5. A seal from Mohenjo-Daro showing a seated deity, sometimes interpreted as Shiva or a 'proto-Shiva'.
Source: Courtesy of Ute Franke.

urban civilizations claim that there was no significant break or hiatus'.[91] Bridget and Raymond Allchin also note that the Harappan 'personality contributed a major element to the life and culture of the Indian people long after the first cities had disappeared'.[92]

Some of the later Indus seals show scenes familiar to Hindu traditions, a possible three-headed Shiva in a yogic posture, for example (Figure 4.5). Other Harappan traditions of henna painted cattle, tandoori ovens, and oxcarts pulled by water buffalo connect present-day society with the ancient past. While the urban Harappan societies did not continue unchanged, and cities were abandoned, 'the descendants of the peoples of the Mature Harappan pursued their lives as farmers, herders, and many types of craftsmen'.[93]

One of the key changes was the 'arrival' of Indo-Aryan speakers, which is often related to the migrations of Indo-European peoples – the Aryans discussed earlier. Although it is contentious, some archaeologists and linguists suggest that the Harappans spoke a Dravidian language, or range of languages, and that one of these is represented by the Indus script.[94] A Dravidian language called Brahui is still spoken in some parts of the Indus region, with others spoken elsewhere in both northern and especially southern India. But there is no archaeological evidence of any invasion. The adoption of the horse, often associated with the spread of Aryans, need not indicate migration or new people at all – evidence for horses begins to appear around 2000 BC, possibly several hundred years later.[95] Kenoyer suggests that 'Indo-Aryans are a modern construct' and that some of the peoples mentioned in the Vedas were living or passing through the Harappan area in Harappan and Late Harappan times.[96] Strictly speaking, it is not necessary to suggest that the kind of violent migrations found in Indian myths, which are not historical texts, really happened, although people certainly moved around and were, to some extent, mobile; 'arrival' may not be the best way to think about such a complex issue as culture or language change.

Later Indian writing systems show little or no continuity with the Indus script, but as in Greece, where the syllabic Linear B script fell out of use and was eventually replaced by the alphabet, script change does not indicate that there was any population replacement, migration, or even language change.

A GLOBAL 4.2 KYA COLLAPSE?

What about the supposed Early Bronze Age collapse? Was there a 'global' mega-collapse around a 4.2 kya climate event? In my view, no. It is still rather unclear what caused the Akkadian collapse, as we have seen, but Mesopotamian society and states continued to exist. In Egypt, the First Intermediate Period was a lively and in many ways flourishing period – not one in which complexity was reduced – and the Middle Kingdom built on its culture. Recent work on radiocarbon dating by Johanna Regev and Felix Hoflmayer suggests that Early Bronze Age collapse, or deurbanisation, in the Levant happened significantly earlier than the First Intermediate Period in Egypt, weakening the case that a global climate change caused widespread collapse.[97] The collapse identified in Early Bronze Age Greece is also now seen much more as a gradual change in material culture. Jeanette Forsen has studied the evidence for the Early Bronze Age period in Greece in depth.[98] In a study of some eighty-nine sites, she concluded that when site-wide destruction levels could be well dated, they are not clumped together in space or time at the end of the EBA but occur over a long period of time. Harappan urban culture also, as we have seen, did not end suddenly, but people shifted eastward over decades and centuries. While some cities were eventually abandoned, others continued, blending eventually into a new cultural package. It seems better, on balance, to look at and clarify what happened in each case, rather than packing together 'collapses'; different things were happening in different places at different times, no doubt for different reasons. This should not surprise us.

FINAL THOUGHTS

Many archaeologists recognise that it is unlikely that there was a single cause for the transformation of Harappan culture in the years around 1900 BC and after, just as there is no single cause for its appearance. Monocausal explanations are unlikely to provide a complete explanation of what was a long term process (or set of processes) – Wheeler, once a strong proponent of an invasion hypothesis, mentioned that war, climate, malaria, geomorphological change, and invasion could all be involved, stating:

any one of these, or other causes are likely to be fallacious in isolation. The fall, like the rise of a civilization is a highly complex operation which can only be distorted by oversimplification. It may be taken as axiomatic that there was no one cause of cultural collapse.[99]

Complexity is difficult to imagine and very difficult to reconstruct. Even where there are environmental issues, people choose (within their cultural and experiential frameworks) how to respond. Coningham and Young state that 'scholars do need to look beyond the more usually accepted archaeological explanations and interrogate those that allow the ordinary people of the Indus Civilisation a conscious will and agency'.[100] It is the human factors that are at the heart of every collapse or cultural transformation.

THE INDUS VALLEY SCRIPT

The Indus Valley civilisation was a literate one, but unfortunately, despite the efforts of many scholars, no one has yet been able to decipher its script or even to agree on what language it may represent.[101] There is a corpus of over 3,000 inscriptions from around the Indus culture area, which are found in a variety of media: on seals, steatite, marble, ivory, silver, terracotta, bone, ceramics, axes, bangles, and ladles.[102] Many inscribed seals carry a picture of a single animal, but some appear to be narrative scenes. The longest inscription is made up of twenty-six characters, though most are shorter; some consist of only a single sign. Of the number of characters, different scholars come up with different totals, which range from around 150 to more than 500. What does seem agreed upon is that some signs are pictographs representing things (such as fish), which also have syllabic values, while others represent words; the system is described as logo-syllabic.

While it is not known which language the inscriptions represent, or even if they represent a single language, many believe it to be a Dravidian rather than an Indo-European language such as Sanskrit. Indo-European languages are thought to have displaced or replaced in the north Dravidian languages that still exist in southern India (and a northern pocket of the Dravidian language Brahui in Baluchistan), owing to supposed migrations of Indo-European speakers in late or post-Harappan times.

Although the Indus pictographs bear some similarity to Sumerian, and the also as yet undeciphered Proto-Elamite script, this has not helped matters. Unfortunately for scholars and would-be decipherers of the Indus script, no bilingual texts have (yet) been recovered, so we are, unfortunately, a long way off recovering a historical Harappan civilisation.

5

The End of Minoan Crete

Minoan civilization was at the height of its prosperity when disaster struck all the palaces, towns, and villas, with the exception of Knossos. Devastating fires brought destruction to the majority of sites and they were abandoned for many years.

Ken Wardle[1]

PALATIAL CRETE

Knossos, explored by the famous British archaeologist Arthur Evans, is the place where Crete's history began; it is where the island was first settled, and it was to play a profound role throughout the island's prehistory (Figure 5.1). In the Old Palace period (Table 5.1), people around Crete, at sites such as Mallia and Phaistos, seem to have imitated the 'palace' that was constructed at Knossos, adopting its architectural schemes, sharing types of rooms usually considered to be shrines, and copying details including the use and themes of fresco painting. Even the architects of much later Mycenaean palaces on the mainland may have drawn inspiration from this symbolic language, their central megarons with thrones situated on the right, as in the throne room at Knossos. Not only in architecture was Knossian style valued, Knossian artifacts were also prized, acquired, and copied locally – pottery, seal stones, ivory figurines, and stone vases.

Jeffrey Soles explains this 'Knossos effect' visible in material culture by identifying Knossos as a cosmological centre, a location with a special meaning as the original home of people and culture on Crete.[2] This 'palatial' culture need not have been organised or ruled by kings or queens – in the archaeology of Crete, palace means 'a substantial

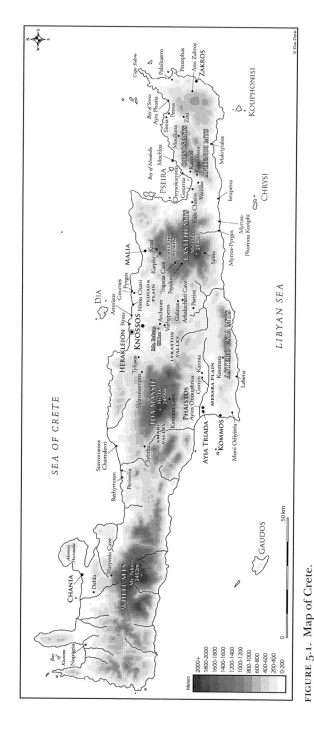

FIGURE 5.1. Map of Crete.

Source: From Shelmerdine, C. W. (ed.). (2008). *The Cambridge Companion to The Aegean Bronze Age.* Cambridge: Cambridge University Press, xxxiii (Map 4).

TABLE 5.1 *Chronology of later Minoan Crete*

Cultural period	Pottery phase	Approximate date (BC)
Neopalatial (New Palace) period	Middle Minoan (MM) III	1750–1700
	Late Minoan (LM) IA	1700–1580
	LM IB	1580–1490
Final Palatial	LM II	1490–1430
	LM IIIA1	1430–1370
	LM IIIA2	1370–1320
Postpalatial	LM IIIB	1320–1200
	LM IIIC	1200–1100

Source: Page 99, Rehak, P. and Younger, J. G. (1998). 'Review of Aegean prehistory VII: Neopalatial, Final Palatial, and Postpalatial Crete.' *American Journal of Archaeology* 102(1): 91–173.

architectural complex, with spacious public rooms, prestigious building materials, and provisions for large scale food storage', which are often associated with luxury finished goods.[3] Palaces were centres of redistribution, with storage space and records of goods going in and out, implying a political authority of some sort. They were also centres of production and consumption and a focus of community life at the heart of surrounding settlements; a courtyard for social/ritual activities and gatherings is a notable feature of Cretan palaces.

Crowds will have gathered at the palaces, as is depicted in some of the fresco paintings, and no doubt individuals participated in palace occasions and festivities in ways that mirrored and displayed their place in society. Feasting and dancing, sports and bull-leaping may have taken place. Knossos and the other palaces had a significant effect on Cretan society, both in material and ideological terms.

What type of rulership was present on Crete remains unclear, since there are no obvious signs (paintings, statues, etc.) of very powerful individuals, and it may have differed in any case by location and over time. The influential archaeologist Arthur Evans, responsible for uncovering and (re)constructing much of Minoan society, envisioned priest-kings and pacifist-imperialists, similar to influential early interpretations of the Maya or the Harappans. Apparently he even suppressed data he had collected on Minoan military installations.[4] But we need not assume that the Cretan polities were all the same, or that the people were unusually egalitarian, peaceful, or religious, as they have often been presented. Rather, like other people, they were political, took an interest in production and trade, and in all probability engaged in conflict and warfare, even if they did not use much militaristic imagery in their self-representation.[5]

Crete had contacts at some level as far north as Samothrace and Troy, in the northern Aegean, and as far afield as Egypt, where at Avaris, Tell el-Dab'a in the Nile delta, Minoan-type frescoes with scenes of bull-leaping have been found (Late Minoan (LM) I). The latter have led to speculation that there may have been a royal marriage, perhaps between a Cretan princess and an Egyptian prince, or that a Knossian colony may have existed – certainly artists from Crete were responsible for the work.[6] It was not uncommon for rulers in the eastern Mediterranean to share skilled craftsmen. People on Cyprus were also in touch with Crete, as a Cypriot script owing something to Cretan Linear A writing was developed on the island. And, as is well-known, the Bronze Age community on the Aegean island of Thera were also influenced by Cretan culture – they formed part of the same world.[7]

The Old Palace period ended in widespread destructions at palaces and towns around the island in the Middle Minoan (MM) II period.[8] These are often attributed, rightly or wrongly, to earthquakes. But rather than causing a collapse, the sites were rebuilt afterwards 'on the same scale and with as much magnificence'; this next period is therefore known as the Neopalatial period (MM III – LM IB).[9] So far, Neopalatial palaces have been excavated at Knossos, Phaistos, Malia, Zakros, and Galatas, and archaeologists suspect that as yet undiscovered palaces may exist at Chania and near Rethymnon in western Crete.[10] These palaces did not exist in isolation, there were towns too, and also rural sites known as villas, often with accompanying settlements. Neopalatial Crete is often regarded as the high point of the island's Minoan culture, yet the end of this period was marked by real and significant change.

NEOPALATIAL COLLAPSE

The Neopalatial period came to an end at the end of the LM IB pottery phase, in the fifteenth century BC.[11] Aegean archaeologist Ken Wardle summarised the Neopalatial collapse as a devastating blow to the island, with palaces, villas, and towns destroyed – only Knossos

FIGURE 5.2. Part of the Knossos palace, as reconstructed in concrete by
Arthur Evans.
Source: Courtesy of the Ashmolean Museum.

seems to have survived for longer (Figure 5.2). Others believe that
Knossos too may have been damaged at the same time, but that it
recovered quickly.[12] In some places, buildings had been abandoned
already, for example, at the southern harbour town of Kommos, at
Galatas, and at Sissi.[13] John Younger and Paul Rehak note that 'many
art forms did not survive the Neopalatial period, and the period that
follows was so different in character that there was probably a significant change in culture'.[14] Laura Preston points out the appearance
of many cultural elements from the Mycenaean Greek mainland at
this time.[15] Unlike the previous series of destructions that had ended
the Old Palace period, there was no similar rebuilding, though many
major sites were later reoccupied. These are what define the Minoan
collapse.

What could have caused such widespread and violent destructions
and culture change? Some have suggested invasion by the Hyksos,
who came to power in the Egyptian Nile Delta, or the supposedly
'warlike' Mycenaeans from mainland Greece, which would explain
the 'Mycenaeanisation' of material culture and the appearance

of Linear B writing, used to write Greek, which replaced Cretan Linear A.[16] The first of these can be dismissed as total conjecture and the second we shall consider in more detail below. Also, the people of Knossos have been blamed for the LM IB destructions, and we shall return to this idea too.[17]

After experiencing a serious quake in Crete in 1926, Arthur Evans began to think that Old Palace period Knossos, at least, was probably destroyed by earthquakes.[18] In part, this view was encouraged by his notion that the peaceful Minoans should have come and gone 'on their own terms'. In Evans' conception of Minoan civilisation, it 'progressed without interruption through successive stages of infancy, maturity, and decay and at the end of its Golden Age collapsed abruptly as a result of a natural phenomenon. No other civilization ever gained hegemony over the Cretans'.[19] As John Papadopoulos points out, this narrative of 'an eternal, idealized, peace-loving realm on an island girt by sea and on which the sun always shone', such a contrast to a Europe shattered by the first world war, could not allow any mainland 'enemy' the role of destroyer.[20] Instead, natural forces, forces that were certainly real and known, could take on the role of destroyer, rendering the whole story of the Minoans even more mythical, as they were divorced from regular human affairs such as politics and war.

C. Monaco and L. Tortorici have, in a recent paper in the journal *Tectonophysics*, suggested that several large earthquakes could indeed have brought about the Old Palace period destructions and the Neopalatial collapse, a proposal similar to the earthquake storm hypothesis of Mycenaean collapse that we shall see in the next chapter.[21] However, the earthquake hypothesis fails to explain why the Neopalatial palaces, unlike the Old Palace period palaces, were not rebuilt. But others too have seen a role for natural catastrophes in Crete's prehistory and in the Neopalatial collapse, in particular related to the eruption of the Thera volcano.

CRETE AND THE THERA ERUPTION

In 1939, the Greek archaeologist Spyridon Marinatos put forward probably the most famous hypothesis to explain the Cretan destructions, one that in some form many will have encountered, for example, on television documentaries.[22] Marinatos argued that invasions seemed unlikely, either from the Greek mainland or elsewhere, and that Knossians could not have been responsible for the island-wide destructions because Knossos and nearby Amnisos were also damaged (which of course could have been from fighting that they were involved in). But he thought Evans' earthquake theory was along the right lines. The destructions, Marinatos argued from pottery styles, were contemporaneous, and he thought therefore that 'the only remaining explanation of the disaster is one of "natural causes" '.[23] But it seemed to many unlikely that a single earthquake could have caused so much damage over a very wide area. Given the varied geology of Crete, when earthquakes occurred, sites could suffer a lot of damage or very little, even within a limited area. Rather, Marinatos suspected that 'the disaster in Crete must be attributed to a tremendous eruption of the volcano on the neighbouring island of Thera'.[24]

Thera (Santorini) is now famous for the well-preserved remains of the Late Bronze Age town of Akrotiri, with its frescoes providing some of the most well-known images of the Late Bronze Age Aegean – a naval flotilla, boys boxing, a fisherman with his catch, a pair of swallows, scenes of goddesses, soldiers, and of town life. The Thera volcano too is now famous, and the LBA eruption is reckoned to be the greatest volcanic eruption of the last ten thousand years; some 15 billion tons (60 km³) of matter was pumped into the air.[25] But when Marinatos first developed his theory, this was not the case; he began the modern excavations himself in 1967.

One source of inspiration for Marinatos was the 1879 book *Santorin et des eruptions* by French scholar Fouque, who had begun studying Thera after a series of eruptions that began in 1866 and went on until 1870. A summary article of Fouque's work was published in *The Popular Science Monthly* in 1880, revealing the prehistoric origins of Thera's volcanic form, and some early archaeological evidence for its prehistoric population:

The bay itself was created by a catastrophe which was anterior to history, for no writer of antiquity mentions it. Yet remains of habitations have been discovered in the lava, with numerous objects and domestic utensils, which lead to the conclusion that a civilized population, who had already developed artistic tastes, were its witnesses and victims. Judiciously conducted excavations and microscopic examinations of their potteries have furnished much information concerning these ancient people.

They were laborers and fishermen; they had flocks of goats and sheep, cultivated grain, made meal, extracted the oil from olives, wove cloths, fished with nets, and lived in houses with walls of squared stone and wooden beams.[26]

On Crete, excavating a building near the north shore at Amnisos, Marinatos had found significant quantities of small rounded pumice stones in a square pit, which he originally thought might have been a trader's store. Pumice was known to come from Thera in antiquity, and it was traded and used to polish marble; it was also seen as ejected material that floated and washed around the Aegean Sea. Later, associating the pumice with the Theran eruption, he suspected that a tsunami wave must have destroyed the building and covered it with pumice – a building further inland, the 'Villa of the Frescoes', had no pumice, but the walls were deformed, perhaps from the action of a powerful wave, yet the building seemed to have been burnt.

The apparently contradictory evidence seemed to fit the events of other known eruptions, in particular, the powerful eruption of Krakatau in 1883 that captured the world's imagination.[27] When Krakatau erupted, one record reported houses on the coast at Tjaringin being overturned and swept away by waves, and the ruins being burned by overturned lamps; where eruptions happened at night or caused darkness, and people lit oil lamps, fires could easily result. In Greece and the eastern Mediterranean, tsunamis are a well-known hazard, recorded throughout history; the late Roman historian Ammianus Marcellinus wrote a vivid account of a disaster in Alexandria from AD 365, which is worth quoting in full:

While this usurper [Procopius] yet lived, whose various deeds and whose death I have described, on 21 July in the year in which Valentinian was consul for the first time with his brother [A.D. 365], fearsome terrors suddenly strode through the whole circle of the world, the like of which neither legends nor truthful ancient histories tell us.

Slightly after daybreak, and heralded by a thick succession of fiercely shaken thunderbolts, the solidity of the whole earth was made to shake and shudder, and the sea was driven away, its waves were rolled back, and it disappeared, so that the abyss of the depths was uncovered and many-shaped varieties of sea-creatures were seen stuck in the slime; the great wastes of those valleys and mountains, which the very creation had dismissed beneath the vast whirlpools, at that moment, as it was given to be believed, looked up at the sun's rays. Many ships, then, were stranded as if on dry land, and people wandered at will about the paltry remains of the waters to collect fish and the like in their hands; then the roaring sea as if insulted by its repulse rises back in turn, and through the teeming shoals dashed itself violently on islands and extensive tracts of the mainland, and flattened innumerable buildings in towns or wherever they were found. Thus in the raging conflict of the elements, the face of the earth was changed to reveal wondrous sights. For the mass of waters returning when least expected killed many thousands by drowning, and with the tides whipped up to a height as they rushed back, some ships, after the anger of the watery element had grown old, were seen to have sunk, and the bodies of people killed in shipwrecks lay there, faces up or down. Other huge ships, thrust out by the mad blasts, perched on the roofs of houses, as happened at Alexandria, and others were hurled nearly two miles from the shore, like the Laconian vessel near the town of Methone which I saw when I passed by, yawning apart from long decay.[28]

The Alexandria tsunami was devastating, but not enough to cause the city to fail or be abandoned. The Thera eruption itself and the tsunami waves that would have accompanied it also could not have destroyed all the palaces and towns on Crete – not all were on or near the north coast, facing the Aegean Sea and Thera, around 100 km across the sea to the north. Marinatos therefore conjectured that a series of violent earthquakes was responsible for much of the destruction. Quakes had been noted as occurring before and after the Krakatau eruption and a theory of seismic activity associated with volcanic eruptions had been proposed by a seismologist at the University of Athens in 1926. Professor Kretikos had noted that earthquakes occurred around the region before and after every eruption of Thera. Marinatos noted that the 1926 earthquake on Crete, the one that Arthur Evans had experienced, was probably to be associated with an eruption earlier that year. It had caused fatalities and damage on other islands, including thousands of homes lost on Rhodes and in Turkey, and he even associated it with damage in Alexandria and Cairo in Egypt, supporting this with historical examples.[29]

Marinatos' model of Minoan collapse remains popular and well known – earthquake, volcano, and tsunami. Geologists like Floyd McCoy and Grant Heiken have popularised the story in the mass media, and people continue to search for evidence to support it.[30] McCoy and Heiken examined coastal and marine deposits possibly laid down by a tsunami caused by the collapse of Thera's caldera and pyroclastic flows, which suggest a wave of 7–12 m in height struck the coast. Colin McDonald notes that pumice appears at a height of 15 m above the Villa of Lilies at Amnisos.[31] Others have suggested that agriculture could have been seriously harmed either directly by ash, gases, or by climate change events caused by the eruption and the injection of dust into the atmosphere.

Apart from the physical effects, however, Marinatos also emphasised some of the psychological effects of such a catastrophe and their social impacts, and plausibly so, since they rested on eyewitness accounts of the Krakatau eruption by Dutchman Rogier Verbeek, who was 150 km away in Java.[32] Verbeek reported a roar from the mountain that prevented people from sleeping, accompanied by flashes and vibrations that moved loose objects and rattled buildings, which was followed by absolute silence. In the morning, more movement threw doors and windows open and brought down plaster and house fittings, followed by darkness, cold damp mists, and sulphurous yellow-grey smoke. Animals and people alike were terrified and in anguish.

It was calculated by Dutch authorities that the over 36,000 people died, with 90 per cent killed by tsunamis.[33] Others downwind of the volcano were killed by clouds of hot volcanic ash. The destruction was immense, and its after-effects terrible. At Tjaringin, a fortnight after the disaster, a newspaper reporter wrote:

Thousands of corpses of human beings and also carcasses of animals still await burial, and make their presence apparent by an indescribable stench. They lie in knots and entangled masses impossible to unravel, and often jammed along with cocoanut stems among all that had served these thousands as dwellings, furniture, farming implements, and adornments for houses and compounds.[34]

Ammianus Marcellinus' description from the ancient world also makes clear how shocking and terrifying earthquakes and tsunamis could be.

DATES AND DECLINE

But the volcanic knockout argument has weaknesses, since, as was pointed out by Hans Pichler and Wolfgang Schiering in 1977, and, as is now widely accepted, the Thera eruption actually took place in the LM

IA pottery phase, decades before the Neopalatial collapse at the end of the LM IB phase.[35] Thera had no Minoan pottery later than LM IA, but the destructions on Crete were in LM IB; there was no good reason why Thera should not have LM IB too if the destructions were in that phase, though some argued that its inhabitants abandoned the island earlier due to earthquakes. The absolute date of the eruption is still debated by experts, split between those who support the scientific dating and those who follow the 'traditional' archaeological correlations.[36] Even McCoy and Heiken point out that collapse took place only 'in the aftermath of the eruption, both the Cycladic and Minoan cultures were replaced about two centuries after …' – and two centuries is a long time.[37]

To make the scenario make sense, a picture of 'decline' and weakness is often projected onto the Neopalatial Minoans, suggesting that after natural disaster they became ripe for the picking by the now stronger (and supposedly 'warlike') Mycenaean people of the mainland. But such a picture is unduly simplistic, since life evidently went on until the Neopalatial collapse decades later; Jan Driessen and Colin McDonald note that 'in most cases, rebuilding activities or repairs follow the ash fall, and many argue that Crete really witnessed its greatest days after the eruption'.[38]

Even so, a disaster of such proportions as has been suggested could well have sparked social, political, and religious changes in Cretan society, just as thousands of years later the Black Death had a profound impact on many aspects of European culture.

HUMAN AGENTS AND SOCIAL CHANGE

In their recent work on the LM IB collapse and the Thera eruption, Driessen and McDonald have further modified the disaster and decline scenario. They propose that:

the combined effect of an earthquake and the Santorini eruption in LM IA did indeed cause the eventual demise of Minoan civilization in the sense that these natural catastrophes caused serious crises on the island early in the succeeding Late Minoan IB period, producing a snowball effect that culminated in the destruction of the Minoan palace states.[39]

In their view, the collapse may have been ultimately triggered by natural disasters, but it was social in nature, built upon an already troubled situation, and took years to play out.[40]

In the aftermath of disasters, there are responses at a number of levels – from 'official' to personal and individual actions, and from co-operation and rescue to opportunism and looting. A desire to get away from the disaster-struck area, whether for emotional, psychological, or economic reasons, could result in problems for the continuity of local life, affecting agriculture and industry – the local and regional economy and society. In ancient disasters we should remember that there would be a lack of rescue experts, sniffer dogs and the like, of medical and sanitary facilities, of rescue equipment, and rapid response capability, which would make for very difficult post-disaster conditions; even in the modern world response to disaster depends heavily on local political and economic factors and international interest. Two years after the Haiti earthquake of 2010, thousands of people were still living in parlous conditions in a tent city.[41] We might expect the effects of disasters to have been much worse in ancient times, with shock, dislocation, and disease being common.

When disasters such as earthquakes hit the Roman Empire, with its overarching organisation, emperors, responding to requests from disaster-struck regions, could organise relief in the form of appointed officials to oversee rebuilding, sending supplies, and instituting tax relief to facilitate the immediate and long-term recovery of a city.[42] Tax relief was a practical measure that allowed local areas to keep more of their own wealth and invest it in regeneration. Local people, in the tradition of classical urban life, would also contribute to rebuilding public buildings. There was continuity, but the after effects, in health, psychology, and outlook, could have profound and longer-term effects.

Following Marinatos' lead in noting psychological and anthropological effects of disaster, increases in stress and illness, and accepting the likelihood of effects to infrastructure and resources (agriculture, fresh water supply, ships, etc.), Driessen and McDonald argue that features of post-eruption Crete can be explained within a context of societal stress. For example, in LM IB, access to palaces and mansions becomes physically more restricted and many buildings were repaired with spolia (building materials robbed from other buildings) and appeared less grand than before, big rooms were subdivided and often given over to storage. New, sometimes massive, wells were dug, and in towns enclosures were built, perhaps to protect animals or for protection from other people.

Such 'crisis architecture' seems likely to reflect a new and less stable situation, one in which there was a physical need to control access to particular places and to devote space to storage and production of food and goods. In this situation, it is possible that local mansions became more important but also more independent from palaces, and localisation became one response to disaster. In addition, there is evidence that traditional religious activity also seems to have changed – some peak sanctuaries, sacred mountain top sites used for centuries and connected in Neopalatial times with palaces and towns, may have gone out of use; there is little trace of LM IB activity at Mount Iuktas in central Crete, for example.[43] People's faith in tradition, the authorities, and the world order may have been shaken, and this could lead to the rejection of a dominant ideology.

Driessen has argued that the Minoan collapse in LM IB requires human agents to explain the archaeological evidence, rather than just natural causes.[44] He notes that destruction was selective, with particular buildings destroyed when others were only abandoned without damage, and that prestige items were smashed; the lack of valuables found indicates plunder and malice. Burning is the only certain means of destruction identified. Fires can be caused by earthquakes, but the best evidence of earthquake, deposits of rubbish from clearing out debris to reuse the building, is not found after the LM IB destructions. There was also a lack of reoccupation after the LM IB collapse. In addition, pre-destruction features such as securing of access, water supplies, livestock, and the hiding of valuables may represent preparations made during a time of instability. All considered, the destructions were the deliberate acts of people, and, in Driessen's view, were 'especially directed towards symbols of authority, of a class or an elite'.

In this scenario it seems best to return to the idea of conflict during unstable times. As Rehak and Younger say:

while it is fair to say that, architecturally, Crete reaches its greatest degree of complexity in the Neopalatial period, it is also clear that our general assessment of developments during this period has been simplistic. Neopalatial Crete is not a monolithic, entity that rises uniformly in MM II/LM I and falls at the end of LM IB: rather the period is punctuated by a series of destructions and rebuildings at almost all sites, and these may have occurred at different times in different places, and perhaps for different reasons.[45]

Although the destructions of the collapse seem contemporaneous, in view of pottery styles, they may really have happened over some decades, and so destructions were not unusual events in the Neopalatial period. Some think that those in the east of the island may have happened sometime after those in the west and centre.[46] Given this stretching of destructions from roughly contemporaneous to a much longer time frame, it makes sense that they could have had different causes, as Rehak and Younger pointed out. Earthquakes may have destroyed some sites, people, others. Elites at one site could have taken advantage of weakness elsewhere. Under certain circumstances, non-elite people may have withdrawn support for elites and their ideology, also effecting change in Minoan society and resulting in what we find in the archaeological record.

It is not clear whether the palaces of Crete were in some way subordinate to Knossos during the Neopalatial period, but it could also be the case that Knossos was trying to create or defend a hegemony over a larger part of the island. This could explain a range of factors – competing palace centres, periodic and selective destructions, and instability that led to the eventual collapse of the system.

But although we can make a number of plausible suggestions about what could have been happening, we should also remember the danger of trying to pin too precise and simple a narrative on undoubtedly complex events in a period where nothing was really standing still – a period that was full of events and personalities that will forever remain invisible to us.

CRETE AFTER THE COLLAPSE – MYCENAEAN TAKEOVER?

Laura Preston has remarked that after the Neopalatial period on Crete, attention often shifts to mainland Greece and to the developing Mycenaean culture, with its handful of palace states and other centres.[47] Indeed the Mycenaeans seem to have taken over as the regional Aegean power, politically and economically, with their international connections indicated primarily by export of pottery, which seem to peak in the thirteenth century BC. But life in Crete did not simply come to an end; there was no abandonment of the island and neither culture nor people disappeared.[48] Evidently there were no environmental issues that prevented people or complex societies from existing. What seems to have disappeared at the end of Late Minoan IB was the island wide system that had existed in Neopalatial times, often regarded as the cultural 'climax' of the Minoans, but it was replaced by a new and very different material and political landscape and a partly transformed culture with new elements drawn from mainland Greece integrated with Cretan traditions.

The Minoan collapse and Mycenaean expansion are often seen as going hand in hand. The mainland Mycenaeans are often reckoned to be aggressive and warlike in comparison to the 'peaceful Minoans', but this is undoubtedly a gross oversimplification – a modern myth.[49] But many have seen them as taking advantage of the weakened state of Minoan society, weakened because agriculture suffered, or the navy was destroyed, or because of a lack of 'confidence' or the transformation of the social order caused by the natural catastrophes. In the aftermath of disaster, Mycenaean invaders were able to gain a foothold and to impose a more mainland lifestyle on the peaceful and sophisticated Minoans, thus beginning the long process of Cretan hellenisation. Sometimes this is also seen as a shift from a Minoan thalassocracy (rule of the sea or dominance either militarily and/or in trade) to a Mycenaean one, with Mycenaeans taking over the position of the Minoans in long distance trade.

To imagine a simple transition from a Minoan to a 'Mycenaean Crete' is an oversimplification.[50] The picture of what happened is very unclear, and undoubtedly it is much more complex than we can ever reconstruct, but it is not entirely dark. The confusion is partly reflected in the variety of modern names that archaeologists have for the period: Postpalatial, because of the palatial destructions at the end of LM IB, but also the Final, Mono, or Third Palatial, because of the continuity of a palace at Knossos. The Knossos palace continues later than the others, but the date of its final destruction by fire is still uncertain – perhaps 1325–1300 BC, so the term 'Postpalatial' is quite misleading.[51] In terms of the pottery chronology, used by Preston and others because it is more neutral, it covers LM II to LM IIIB, possibly a period of around 170 years or so – the duration of about thirteen Egyptian pharaohs' rule.[52]

In this Final Palatial period, the Knossos palace continued to be in use, and in the aftermath of the Neopalatial collapse, it seems to have dominated most of central and western Crete, but the written script of the palace administration changed from the non-Greek Linear A to Greek Linear B. The tablets themselves seem to indicate that a number of former Neopalatial centres were subordinate to Knossos: *ku-do-ni-ja, pa-i-to, se-to-i-ja, da-*22-to, ku-ta-to*, and *a-mi-ni-so* – Kydonia (*ku-do-ni-ja*), modern Chania, is in western Crete, and some Linear B tablets are known from there (dating to the end of LM IIIB, about 1250 BC), Phaistos (*pa-i-to*) is in the south, while Amnisos (*a-mi-ni-so*) was a cult centre near Knossos. People called 'Collectors' in the tablets seem to have played an important intermediary role between Knossos and other centres, managing flocks and production; they may have been local aristocrats, members of the royal family, or palace elite, who were entitled to a part of the resources they managed for the palace.[53] That they are mentioned more at Kydonia is taken to imply that it had greater autonomy from Knossos than other places – it may have been the last functioning palace on Crete. What the exact nature of the relationships was is difficult to say, but we need not imagine a total population or even elite replacement by Mycenaeans – whichever 'Mycenaeans' these are reckoned to be.

The Knossos palace was reconfigured, although not on such a grand scale as earlier changes; new Mycenaean themes now figured in the frescos.[54] In tombs too, a new 'warrior style' burial became evident around Knossos, containing more militarised paraphernalia, and the tomb types themselves, tholos tombs and chamber tombs, are often thought of as being of mainland inspiration (though Crete had earlier 'warrior style' burials); fine Mycenaean pottery also appears. Preston states that 'the most ostentatious tombs at Knossos combined mainland ideas with traditional Minoan elite symbols in their architecture and assemblages in innovative ways'.[55] At secondary sites, there is little evidence of much building or of wealthy burials, perhaps indicating that local elites were subordinate to Knossos.[56] The accumulated evidence has often been interpreted as indicating a Mycenaean takeover, possibly by a small group based at Knossos.

Some have supposed that the wealth of the early Mycenaean grave circle B, found by Schliemann, indicates that they served as mercenaries for Minoan leaders, and that, in a scenario something like the barbarians and Romans, or Saxons and Britons models, or in a palace coup, they may have inserted themselves at the top of Minoan society.[57] It is possible that some Mycenaeans may have served as mercenaries in Egypt – soldiers with Egyptian kilts and (possibly) Mycenaean boar's tusk helmets appear pictured – but whether they are actual 'Mycenaeans' is not clear. Could a group of invading or mercenary Mycenaeans have taken over or have organised a palace coup at Knossos, sponsoring a leader of their choice? Could something like the Norman takeover of England have happened, with its elite replacement and suppression of rebellious natives going on for decades? Quite possibly, but it is not certain that anything like this did actually happen.

What is important to remember is that all of these high status Mycenaean elements existed alongside or were integrated with Cretan traditions.[58] Rather than a clear transplantation of Mycenaean culture, there is a selective use of aspects of high status mainland culture and symbols – something of a hybridisation. Colin McDonald explains that, while there are novelties, 'there are also many aspects of continuity, so much so that we might be tempted to put the "Mycenaean Greek" language into the mouths of "Minoans"'.[59] Contacts between Crete and the mainland were nothing new; the inspiration for mainland states is usually seen as reflecting earlier state formation on Crete, even though this was not simply 'diffused' from one to the other.[60] We can expect that the people of Crete, the mainland, and the Aegean islands were part of the same world, and could borrow from and mix freely with other traditions when it suited their purpose.

Rather than a Mycenaean takeover, it is also possible to imagine that in the aftermath of conflict in LM IB, existing rulers or new ones sponsored a new ideology at Knossos to replace the one that had clearly lost its value and was abandoned.[61] They may even have been responsible for (some of) the earlier conflicts and destructions. This new ideology employed imagery and symbols developed by mainland Mycenaean elites, perhaps reinforcing and advertising a real connection with a mainland centre, or adopting them as exotic symbols that they imbued with a new high status meaning at Knossos. It may seem odd to us that a Cretan elite would change from Linear A to Linear B, but Greek speakers may already have been on Crete, a linguistically, and quite possibly ethnically, mixed island; there may well have been Greek speaking 'Minoans' (but we need not imagine conflicts as necessarily arising along ethnic lines). Linear B was derived from Linear A anyway. Using an administrative language that differed from the regular spoken language has not been uncommon throughout history.

During LM IIIA, things changed, and Knossos' apparent monopoly began to break down. As time passed, pottery styles became more regional, and monumental buildings were again erected at local centres, some with apparently more Mycenaean features like megarons, halls with porches and side corridors, but with variation between sites – hybrids again, but without high status Neopalatial Minoan features like 'lustral basins'.[62] Members of local elites began to use more visible and ostentatious burials to display themselves (or for their families to display them) more prominently. The type of tholos burial pioneered at Knossos became much more widespread, though often not associated with known centres, which may point to a rise of local elite power. Conversely, at Knossos this kind of display tailed off, and this is taken to indicate the probable collapse of the Knossos regime.[63] Crete at this time looks very much like a patchwork of small states and non-states, with people at different levels seeking to claim and display an elite status.

Possibly at the end of LM IIIA (though the date of this event is again disputed), the palace at Knossos was burnt and subsequently little used, though evidence of the later period may have been lost during Evans' early excavation. Colin McDonald explains:

the tablets document a rather frenetic final economic year but give no hint of the disaster to come. If earthquake was the cause, why did the Knossians not rebuild and repair as they had done countless times before? Other factors undoubtedly caused the abandonment of the palace as an institution that had lasted more than half a millennium.[64]

In LM IIIB the shifting pattern of communities changed again. Though Knossos was destroyed, Linear B was still in use at Chania/ Kydonia, which also is notable at this time for its more extravagant burials – it was clearly involved in regional trade, since stirrup jars from there have been found around the Aegean and Crete. No palace has been found yet at Kydonia, though it may be just a matter of time before one is found (it could be at Vlasaki),[65] but it seems likely that an equivalent type of 'Mycenaean' state with a *wanax* existed – Crete may therefore still have been palatial in the west, in a very minimal sense, albeit nothing comparable to what it had been a couple of centuries earlier in the Minoan heyday.

FINAL THOUGHTS

In conclusion, the Minoan collapse at the end of the Neopalatial period remains mysterious, but it was undoubtedly a process that involved human action, response, and decision making, perhaps against a backdrop of natural disaster that transformed attitudes and outlooks over several decades. Jan Driessen recently quoted the apposite words of fellow Aegeanist Jerry Rutter, who stated:

the collapse of Neopalatial Minoan civilization is an enormously complicated phenomenon. The more finely tuned our ceramically based relative chronologies are becoming, the more complex the situation is turning out to be, not only across the entire island but even within its comparatively small regions. It is perhaps time at long last to give up overly simplistic approaches, such as invocations of single natural disasters, whether these be volcanic eruptions, earthquakes, tidal waves, or combinations thereof, and to acknowledge that we need to build up a more complete data bank of actual events through fuller publication before we launch into the process of interpretation.[66]

Did post-Neopalatial Crete become Mycenaean? Our ideas of this transition too have become more complex and nuanced; we need to look and think beyond a simple Minoans versus Mycenaeans scenario – neither of these were ethnic groups as such, both are modern constructs that no doubt oversimplify. It is quite possible that a Cretan group, or a Knossian faction, developed Final Palatial Knossos and attempted to control much of the island, and that this group actively integrated aspects of 'Minoan' and 'Mycenaean' material culture and symbols. Thus while it is fair to see a Neopalatial collapse, the real 'Minoan' collapse may have happened in the Final Palatial period – it depends on how we interpret the evidence and the way we want to tell the story.

Ongoing study will reveal more about the Neopalatial and Final Palatial periods, but it will not necessarily furnish us with a straightforward explanation of the Neopalatial collapse or the longer term transition – if anything, it will become even more complex.

AFTER COLLAPSE ON CRETE – THE YEARS C.1200 BC

Although it is overly simplistic to refer to thirteenth-century Crete as Mycenaean, the Linear B using states of Crete also collapsed in *c.* 1250 – 1200 BC. One of the most notable features of this collapse is the changing pattern of settlement on the island. Many scholars have noted the abandonment of low-lying and coastal sites and the increased occupation, in Late Minoan IIIC (after *c.* 1250 BC), of remote and inaccessible sites in the mountains, which have come to be known as 'refuge' sites. It is often thought that these new sites were founded away from the sea because of the threat of raids or attacks, perhaps from the Sea Peoples or from pirates.[67] Was there a mad scramble away from danger? Not exactly, or at least not so suddenly. New sites, such as Karphi, began to be built in the Late Minoan IIIB, so the change was not as sudden as once thought. Saro Wallace argues rather that later thirteenth century Crete experienced a 'planned collapse' and that the changing pattern of habitation indicates 'well-joined up local decision-making' and an 'exceptionally controlled and deliberate response to the unstable and threatening circumstances of the late thirteenth-century Aegean'.[68] Whatever the circumstances that brought about these new patterns, local people reacted and adapted positively to them as best they could.

6

The Kingdoms of Mycenaean Greece

[The collapse] was one of history's most frightful turning points. For those who experienced it, it was a calamity ... the twelfth century ushered in a dark age, which in Greece and Anatolia was not to lift for more than four hundred years ... Altogether the end of the Bronze Age was arguably the worst disaster in ancient history, even more calamitous than the collapse of the Western Roman Empire.

Robert Drews[1]

MYCENAEAN GREECE

By the thirteenth century BC, Late Bronze Age (LBA) Greece was divided up among a patchwork of states with kings and palaces, important centres, and regions that had central places but no palaces (Figure 6.1; Table 6.1). Most of society was probably at a village level, but it is the major centres at Mycenae, Tiryns, Thebes, and Pylos and now a recently found palace at Ayios Vasileios, near Sparta, and elsewhere, and the Linear B texts found at Pylos and Knossos in particular, that command the most attention.

Scholars like Klaus Kilian and James Wright argue that the palaces were bound up with the figure and ideology of the *wanax*, the king, a figure known from the Linear B documents.[2] While palaces formed the architectural focus of some sites, the focus of the palace itself (or at least some of them) was a particular kind of construction called a megaron. Architecturally, a megaron was simply a rectangular

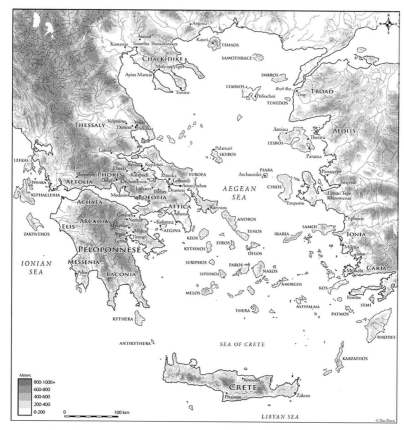

FIGURE 6.1. Map of the Late Bronze Age Aegean.
Source: Shelmerdine, C. W. (ed.). (2008). *The Cambridge Companion to The Aegean Bronze Age*. Cambridge: Cambridge University Press, xxxi (Map 2).

building with four columns surrounding a large central hearth and a throne on the right hand wall; the long walls extended beyond the entrance to make a porch. These central megarons, and other buildings and courtyards, seem to have played a key role in creating and reinforcing the ideology of rulership through communal activities such as drinking, feasting, and ritual – palaces were equipped with thousands of wine cups or *kylikes*, for the use of guests; symbolic miniature *kylikes* have even been found throughout the Pylos palace.[3] We can imagine that the ruling palace elite orchestrated social occasions at which people gathered, and where a few of the most important

TABLE 6.1 *Mycenaean (low) chronology*

Cultural period	Pottery phase	Approximate date (BC)
	Late Helladic (LH) I	1600–1510/1500
Early Palatial	LH IIA	1510/1500–1440
	LH IIB	1440–1390
Palatial	LH IIIA1	1390–1370/1360
	LH IIIA2	1370/1360–1340/1330
	LH IIIB	1340/1330–1185/1180
Postpalatial	LH IIIC	1185/1180–1065

Source: Page 540, Shelmerdine, C. W. (1997). 'Review of Aegean Prehistory VI: The Palatial Bronze Age of the southern and central Greek mainland.' *American Journal of Archaeology* 101(3): 537–585.

people were allowed into the megaron, with others allowed into various courtyards, whilst access to different kinds of food and drink, service, and tableware elaborated and constructed social differences.

But the Mycenaean world – the area that is identified by what we see as Mycenaean material culture – was not all the same, and people used variations of their common cultural repertoire to create meanings appropriate to their goals. Dhimini, the most northerly of the 'palace' centres, did have megaron complexes, but it does not look like the other 'classic' palaces; Teikhos Dymaion was a major fortified centre in the northwest Peloponnese, a fully 'Mycenaean' area, where as yet there is no trace of a palace. Not all areas developed state societies with palaces and a literate bureaucracy; some areas may have been more akin to chiefdoms – such variation was found even in Classical Greece, and should come as no surprise. Some people have argued that non-palace areas may have been dependent on, or controlled by, palaces, but we can imagine a range of contacts, not all of which need have been exploitative, and that circumstances varied from place to place and changed over time. Throughout the Late Bronze Age world in the Aegean and further east, state societies co-existed with non-state societies.

The material culture we call Mycenaean had been in development on the mainland over the preceding few centuries, from the end of the Middle Helladic period, while the political landscape was transformed over time by the competitive politics and interaction of local and regional elites throughout mainland Greece and in connection with Crete, where state-like societies had been around for

FIGURE 6.2. The Lion Gate at Mycenae.
Source: From Schliemann, H. (1880). *Mycenae: A Narrative of Researches and Discoveries at Mycenae and Tiryns*. New York: Scribner, Plate III.

centuries.[4] Some elite groups in mainland Greece seem to have created or emphasised their position, and gained some of their wealth, through the control or manipulation of access to mainland resources to outsiders from Crete or the Cyclades, and possibly by their use of material and cultural 'exotica', as well as by conflict (Figure 6.2). Over time, a number of bigger polities were created, put together by local people, and so some places increased in regional importance and overshadowed other formerly important local sites.

John Bennet has mapped this process of expansion for the palace at Pylos, in Messenia, where a combination of Linear B texts recording place names, archaeological survey, and excavation have enabled the most detailed hypothetical reconstruction.[5] From being one of several locally important sites by the end of the Middle Helladic (*c.* 1700 BC) period, the elites of Pylos expanded their influence so that, possibly by *c.* 1400 BC, the site had expanded and become the administrative centre of a territory of 2000 km², split into two provinces – the 'hither' and 'further' provinces (Figure 6.3). We can imagine influence being extended through alliances, conflict, diplomacy, and opportunism. The state based at Thebes probably

FIGURE 6.3. Reconstruction of the throne room of the Pylos palace.
Source: Courtesy of the Department of Classics, University of Cincinnati.

expanded in a similar way, extending its influence to communities as far away as the island of Euboia.

INDICATORS OF COLLAPSE

The Mycenaean collapse is identified by several types of evidence.[6] The most conspicuous is a series of destructions of major centres and palaces taking place over perhaps a few decades around *c.* 1200 BC, the end of the Late Helladic IIIB (LH IIIB) period, after which the palaces were not rebuilt. Many smaller sites seem to have been abandoned, especially in the southwest Peloponnese, the kingdom of Pylos. An indication of the changes is given in Mervyn Popham's (1994) maps of sites and cemeteries, which shows a dramatic reduction in sites in the period after the *c.* 1200 destructions.[7] With any maps of this kind it is important to remember that the distributions indicated do not necessarily mean that all the sites shown for one period were in use at the same time, and to recall that dots can indicate cemeteries with no known settlements (as at Perati in the Postpalatial period) – not everyone may be visible in the archaeological record. It is clear, nevertheless, that some major changes took place.

These features are usually taken to indicate the end of the existence of the Mycenaean states, and there is no evidence that monumental architecture continued to be erected or that Linear B writing continued to be used, both of which were characteristic of the palaces. Most of the visible changes, such as the discontinuation of writing, fresco painting, ivory working, the making of precious goods, and seal stone use, clearly relate to the elite culture of the palaces. Although non-elites would have been affected by the collapse, perhaps in some areas more than others, there is no reason to suppose the general population was wiped out; the Greek language continued in use, for example, some gods continued to be worshipped (for example Poseidon, Athena, and Dionysus), and aspects of Mycenaean culture, such as pottery, continued for more than a century.[8] The period is often said to be one typified by population movements; but while there may have been increased mobility, it is doubtful that the kind of mythological migrations of peoples, such as 'the Dorian invasion', actually took place – these stories were very much a product of later times and used to construct, express, and mediate the interrelationships of later Greek 'tribes' and peoples.[9] Despite the collapse, local and overseas trade and contact appear to continue. Although there were, undoubtedly, rulers in the Postpalatial period, their distinction from their subjects was not so conspicuously marked.[10] What could have caused the palace states to collapse?

CLIMATE CHANGE

The climate change theory of Mycenaean collapse has been around since Rhys Carpenter first proposed it in 1966.[11] Carpenter suggested that the climate became drier for some three centuries owing to a change in the prevailing winds. In his view the changes primarily affected the southern Peloponnese, Boeotia, Euboea, Phocis, and the Argolid, while other areas in Greece, Attica, the north-west Peloponnese, Thessaly, and the Dodecanese were little affected. In his view, this explained the changing population levels in different parts of Greece, while the destructions themselves could be attributed to raids by hungry people looking for food stores.

Carpenter's argument was not based on any hard evidence, but in 1974 a team of climatologists led by Reid Bryson sought to show that his reconstruction was plausible.[12] They identified a period in 1954–1955 in which the weather patterns matched Carpenter's hypothesis. However, some archaeologists did not agree with Carpenter's reconstruction of the apparent population changes and dismissed the hypothesis.[13] Continued research has shown that, while the southwestern Peloponnese in particular does seem to have experienced a sharp drop in population (or at least in visible signs of habitation), this seems not to have been the case in other areas such as the Argolid, where Tiryns actually expanded; habitation continued in the northwestern Peloponnese, the Euboean Gulf region and Phokis.[14]

However, in subsequent years, more researchers have gathered evidence from around the eastern Mediterranean to support the climate change hypothesis, and the theory has been given wide public attention, for example, in Michael Marshall's 2012 *New Scientist* article.[15] That article was based on a study by Brandon Drake, published in the *Journal of Archaeological Science* in 2012.[16] Relying on an array of climate proxies, such as oxygen-isotope speleothem records from Israel, pollen cores from Lake Voulkouria in western Greece, and sediment cores from the Mediterranean, Drake identified a prolonged arid period lasting from the end of the Late Bronze Age, before 1190 BC, to Roman times (350 BC), which he thinks would have put 'a continual stress' on the palace states.[17] He believes the palace states were very densely populated and that the climatic shift rendered them unsustainable – one result of this confluence of factors was 'population migration', specifically the movements of the Sea Peoples (or some of them) out of Greece. The Sea Peoples have attracted a lot of scholarly attention – they are best known from inscriptions at the mortuary temple of Ramesses III at Medinet Habu, Egypt. The inscription shows a naval battle, and the text describes how they destroyed various major eastern Mediterranean centres. They are usually interpreted as violent migrant populations coming from various locations (including Sardinia, Sicily, and Greece), though the whole story is somewhat less certain and more complicated than often admitted.[18] We will meet them again in the next chapter.

David Kaniewski and colleagues made a similar argument to Drake in 2013, based on evidence from core samples taken at Larnaka Salt Lake (Hala Sultan Tekke) in Cyprus.[19] They compared this to other data, for example, from Gibala in Syria. They too linked this climate change with migrations into and around the eastern Mediterranean and with the Sea Peoples. In another recent study, in the southern Levant, Dafna Langgut and colleagues also found evidence of a Late Bronze Age drought in their analysis of pollen from a core taken from the Sea of Galilee.[20] They 'believe the domino effect ... cold spells, droughts and famine in the north, causing groups to invade sedentary lands in the south – explains the Late Bronze collapse' – essentially the same conclusion as J. Neumann had reached in 1993.[21] In an even more recent paper, Kaniewski has reiterated his faith in the old idea of climate change > collapse > migration domino effect, with northern invaders driven south into Greece and Anatolia, and assigns a significant role in the Late Bronze Age/Early Iron Age transition to the Sea Peoples.[22]

There are various problems raised by the studies mentioned earlier. For one thing, it is guesswork that the populations of the Mycenaean kingdoms was especially dense, so we do not know that any climatic changes would have caused problems in food supply for the general population or pressure on the rulers. The Linear B records from Greek centres do not seem to indicate any problems in food production, distribution, or in agriculture. It is true that there are fewer visible sites in the Postpalatial period, but as mentioned earlier, some central palatial areas, such as Tiryns, continued or even expanded. Farms were still working and food could still be produced.

Also, the chronology of the proposed climate changes is uncertain. The dates for the start of climate change range from 1250 BC to 1190 BC, a spread of some six decades, which surely affects our confidence in whether climate change can have been a causal factor in collapse. If an early date is correct, we would have to admit that the palace states adapted and thrived even as climatic change was happening. Each team also gives a different duration for the changed climate – why does the evidence not allow agreement on the dates? Drake's arid phase lasts more than eight centuries; Kaniewski's, three centuries; and Langgut's, a century and a half. As Drake points out,

Archaic and Classical Greek culture develops, and the population of Greece increases, during the arid phase; why then would a change in climate have had such a terrible effect on LBA Greece, whose population probably was no bigger (and quite possibly smaller) than that of Classical Greece? Clearly, even if there was climate change, it was not the main factor in the Late Bronze Age collapse.

Finally, the idea of mass migrations from north to south into the Mediterranean area, and out of Greece into the east, and the idea that some of the Sea People's, in particular the Philistines, were Greek, are speculation, although these are often still repeated as fact.[23] There is no evidence for new populations invading or migrating to Greece – this harks back to the old and discredited idea of a Dorian migration – an invasion of 'Dorian Greeks' into Greece, which pushed out 'Achaean Greeks', Mycenaeans.[24] Even if we accept the idea of migrations (even of mass migrations, which are, for practical reasons alone, very unlikely), we ought to wonder why 'northern peoples' would have gone south into regions also affected by strife – and the same goes for the notion that Greeks and others went east. If the whole eastern Mediterranean was affected by droughts and famine, surely people would not have headed into troubled areas but would have gone elsewhere away from them. As Mervyn Popham stated some years ago, 'if they were refugees from trouble at home, they chose unlikely havens'.[25]

So while, on the face of it, there would seem to be a reasonable amount of evidence for a role for climate change in the Mycenaean collapse, and this is a theory in vogue once again, on closer examination the stories are less convincing. But Aegean archaeologists are not climate sceptics. Many believe that climate could have played a role in collapse, but, as Eric Cline states, 'climate change, droughts, and famines ... are not enough to have caused the end of the Late Bronze Age without other mitigating factors having been involved'.[26] We might do better to wonder not about climate changes but rather the less visible bad weather events – bad years could, as we know from historical evidence and contemporary experience, cause societies real and potentially very serious problems; a run of bad years could possibly be fatal. It is no surprise that a prime duty of Roman emperors and governors was to keep their population fed, because when, for whatever reason, food ran short, riots and civil strife would ensue.

POSEIDON'S HORSES

Anyone who has been to Greece has probably experienced an earth tremor, if not a full-blown earthquake. Greece, the Aegean, and Turkey are known areas of high seismic activity – Poseidon the 'earth-shaker' was a god for Bronze Age and Classical Greeks alike. Visitors to Greece seeing ruins such as the Temple of Zeus at Olympia, with its vast stone column drums fallen and flowing over the ground, can immediately envision how such sites could be destroyed by earthquakes.[27] Indeed the wider region is littered with ruined cities – as Amos Nur notes – 'from Egypt to Israel, and from Turkey to Greece and Italy, ruined cities and shattered buildings litter the Mediterranean countryside'. He doubts that people alone could have been so destructive and reckons that 'earthquakes [are] the best explanation for many, if not most, of these cases of wholesale destruction'.[28] In particular, destructions by earthquake have come to play a much bigger role not only in accounting for physical destructions, which are a normal and regular part of life, but for the collapse of the palatial societies of the Late Bronze Age.

We saw that Arthur Evans thought Knossos may have fallen to earthquakes. Similarly, a number of archaeologists blame earthquakes for the destruction of the mainland palaces. Klaus Kilian, who worked at Tiryns, thought that earthquakes were responsible for destructions that could be aligned with changes in pottery style.[29] He later came to blame earthquakes for the other destructions that mark the collapse. More recently, Elizabeth French and Philip Stockhammer have also seen earthquakes as the cause of destruction at Mycenae in mid-LH IIIB and later at the end of LH IIIB, the time of the collapse, and also later in the Postpalatial period.[30] However, it has always seemed unlikely that one earthquake could have been responsible for the apparently simultaneous collapse of entire states *c.* 1200 BC. But considering that these states probably collapsed over some decades, rather than in an instant, Nur and Cline suggested in their 2000 paper 'Poseidon's horses …' that an earthquake storm, a series of interlinked earthquakes that can occur over a span of years, could have played a role in the collapse.[31]

It is easy to understand that an earthquake could destroy a site, even a whole city, but how could they destroy a state? A possible example comes from later in Greek history. In Classical Greece, in the decades leading up to the Peloponnesian War fought between Athens and Sparta, a major earthquake struck the Peloponnese. According to Diodorus Siculus, the earthquake in 465/464 BC killed some 20,000 Spartans, a huge number, and enabled an opportunistic revolt of Sparta's subjugated class of Greek serfs, the Messenian Helots, who massively outnumbered actual Spartans. Sparta could have been, but was not destroyed, due to the support of other states. But if the Spartan state had collapsed, would the earthquake have been to blame, or would the cause lie in the inherent fragility of the structure of the Spartan state?

The cases of Pompeii and Herculaneum are well-known volcanic destructions, though these towns were only small parts of a big empire. Tacitus also records widespread disaster in eastern Anatolia in AD 17 when night time earthquakes destroyed twelve cities.[32] Because they were not independent city-states but part of a greater imperial system, it is inappropriate to consider these as collapses. The state could offer some measure of support and disaster-relief, and the devastated cities and their affected populations subsequently received aid from the emperor Tiberius. Ancient people were not simply victims of natural disaster – they sought to recover from disasters quite as much as modern people do – but disasters could have serious social and political effects, as the case of Sparta shows.

Earthquakes may account for some of the physical destructions. But even so, everyone living in the Aegean area must have been relatively used to earthquakes, and in the LBA, sites were usually rebuilt after apparent earthquake destructions earlier on. Some buildings from the LBA are still standing, like the tomb known as the Treasury of Atreus. But if earthquakes or earthquake storms did destroy the palaces, why were they not rebuilt by survivors?

UNCERTAINTY ABOUT THE EARTHQUAKE HYPOTHESIS

Nicholas Ambraseys, a civil engineer with expertise in seismology, has voiced a consistent note of caution in debates about the effects of earthquakes on ancient societies.[33] Detecting past earthquakes, he suggests, is much less clear cut than often admitted. Archaeologists may hypothesise earthquakes, which are then regarded as fact by seismologists and others – but this becomes a circular argument, not necessarily a true one. Architectural evidence often associated with earthquakes, including leaning, displaced, collapsed walls, and so on, can have multiple causes. Earthquakes can destroy, and although they can seem an attractive explanation for collapse, especially where it is difficult to find any other clear reason, this alone is not sufficient to believe in them. Ambraseys cautions:

> The problem with neo-catastrophe theories is that their propounders do not seem to pay attention to the evidence presented by others or data from outside their own field of expertise. It seems easier to ascribe the ruins found in an excavation to earthquakes. If the solution to a problem is not immediately obvious, amateurs eagerly consider a catastrophe theory, which the pioneers of this discipline developed, for example, to account for the collapse of the Aegean Bronze Age.

He further observes that 'perhaps it is one of the most interesting findings that the lasting effects of major earthquakes over the last 25 centuries in the eastern Mediterranean region would not seem to have been significant'.[34] Ultimately the idea that earthquakes could have caused the Mycenaean collapse is still treated with caution by many archaeologists, even those who agree that particular sites could have been affected by such catastrophic events. As with all collapses, environmental circumstances cannot explain everything – there must be some human factors involved.

DECLINE AND FALL?

A recent theory proposed in 2009 by Joseph Maran, who has done much interesting work at the site of Tiryns, discusses the collapse first through the idea of decline and fall.[35] Many scholars have inferred, from a range of evidence, a period of crisis in thirteenth century before the collapse at its end.[36] Maran notes that the many architectural changes made to the citadels and palaces, including increased fortification and securing access to water sources, have often been interpreted as indicating increased warfare – the need arising for better protected fortified centres – and he suggests that this could be regarded as 'decline' of a sort. But he argues that it would be wrong to see these changes as responses to crisis alone: 'seemingly the motives of the building programs carried out around 1250 BC comprised just as much precautions for the case of war as such for festivities in a peaceful time'.[37] The constant maintenance and rebuilding can be read rather as indicating a thriving culture on the eve of an unpredictable collapse, in Maran's words:

I would therefore doubt that on the eve of the catastrophe the political dignitaries felt they were living under the shadow of a crisis. On the contrary, they enjoyed extensive international contacts, they may have profited from vassals over-sea, they conceived impressive, even visionary, building programs thus possibly fulfilling what was expected from the elite, and they made plans for a bright future.[38]

So what, in Maran's view, caused the collapse? Possibly, he suggests, the cost of so much building, the maintenance of a military, and the number of people working for the palace caused something like a labour crisis, with the villages and agricultural communities that ultimately supported the palace economies strained to breaking point, and with fewer people being able to work the land. In this context, palace infrastructures could have been undermined and their elites no longer able to protect villages, all of which may have caused an increase in warfare, which would have caused further economic dislocation. Maran suggests, in his economic and military collapse theory, that this violence and warfare may ultimately have spread – local warlords and factions may also have emerged to vie for power with the central kings. It even seems possible in this scenario that the general population could have revolted or taken sides.

In this view, kings perhaps became too ambitious, putting unsustainable strains on their state systems, which had a knock on effect through which these societies unwound and became prey to opportunistic factions and neighbours. Even so, the evidence which for some implies crisis or decline then fall can be read as one of 'business as usual', followed by sudden collapse.

TRADE AND COLLAPSE

Others have proposed economics-based collapse theories of a different kind. In a recent book *Archaic State Interaction: The Eastern Mediterranean in the Bronze Age*, edited by William Parkinson and Michael Galaty, contributors have applied world-systems theory to the eastern Mediterranean and to the period of collapse.[39] They, like others, see the eastern Mediterranean region as a world-system, in which states and diverse peoples and areas were connected to each other through trade and contact – with a kind of 'globalised' economy.[40]

In this system, Robert Schon argues, Mycenaean royal elites manipulated and monopolised access to exotic goods and types of craft production, which they used to shore up their political and cultural power.[41] Such a system is called 'wealth finance' – contrasted with 'staple finance', which refers to staples such as agricultural produce. As Schon says, 'by distributing to secondary elites the items made in palatial workshops from imported raw materials, as well as finished imports, the palaces were better able to secure their loyalty'.[42] This can be thought of as something like the potlatch of some Native Americans in the Pacific northwest. Walter Donlan explains the role of gift giving in archaic societies thus:

Among the elite particularly, the complicated etiquette of the gift – who gives, who takes, and under what circumstances – is enlisted as a major competitive strategy, to demonstrate, and even to establish, gradations in status and authority.[43]

In this context, Galaty, Parkinson, and the other contributors to *Archaic State Interaction* suggest that different palace centres seem to have had special connections with different regions overseas. Mycenae seems to have had an Egyptian connection, Tiryns, a Cypriot one, and Thebes was more closely linked to Mesopotamia. The operation of the palace-based social system depended on these relationships to maintain a flow of prestige goods and raw materials to be used by the royal elites. As for the collapse, they suggest that it was the breaking down of these international relations that caused the end of the palace states – Pylos, on the western edge of the Mycenaean world, suffered the worst collapse because it was more distant from trade routes east, Mycenae collapsed because 'Mycenae traded with Egypt and paid the price when Egypt, once again, descended into chaos (sometime after 1200 BC)'.[44] Tiryns survived the collapse better, because Cyprus also did.

The hypothesis is an interesting one, and is not entirely new. In the 1960s, Aegean archaeologist Emily Vermeule suggested that the Sea Peoples, known primarily from several Egyptian sources, were responsible for disrupting peaceful trade.[45] In the 1970s, Nancy Sandars characterised the Sea Peoples as Viking-like raiders, responsible for violent and destructive naval raids and migrations.[46] Both Vermeule and Sandars thought that disruption to trade by the Sea Peoples, some of whom might have been from Sicily and Sardinia, with others from coastal Anatolia, could have brought about collapse. Mervyn Popham later suggested that some Mycenaeans themselves may have joined the Sea Peoples, who he saw as 'aggressive, well-armed, efficient and ruthless raiders'.[47] The image has stuck, and the Sea Peoples are often implicated in the events around 1200 BC all over the eastern Mediterranean, from Greece to Egypt.

Sue Sherratt has also suggested a collapse scenario based on trade, but she has put forward a different kind of argument.[48] She has a 'minimalist' view of Greek palaces and states, seeing the palace culture as 'clumsily grafted' onto what were basically warrior societies; these focused on controlling trade routes rather than territories. This trade was largely in the hands of Cypriot traders rather than the Greeks themselves. In the later palatial period, Sherratt argues, trade routes began to shift and Cypriot ships began to operate routes that bypassed the Greek mainland; this could have 'increased the edginess of the palatial authorities', which might have been cut out of the loop by new markets and mechanisms for the movement of goods.[49]

In her view, the Mycenaean palaces eventually lost out to competitors. Although doing well initially and exporting vast amounts of pottery to the east in the thirteenth and fourteenth centuries, Cypriot traders increasingly began to market their own similar pottery and to bypass the palaces.[50] In addition to this, local areas in the Aegean, Anatolia, and the Levant started to produce their own versions of Mycenaean pottery – import substitution.[51]

So, if palaces depended on foreign trade, particularly the receipt of 'exotic' goods and materials, to maintain their political economies, they would indeed have been vulnerable to changed or disrupted trade routes, or to changes in the economies of distant trade partners.

But such dependency is not certain; take Thebes, for example. The most impressive Near Eastern import is a cache of precious carved seal stones. Konstantinos Kopanias, who has recently restudied these, suggests that the Theban sealings could have had a variety of uses to the Theban king: as raw materials (many were lapis lazuli) for jewellery, as gifts to other kings or nobles, as trade items or gifts to other subjects, and to advertise the king's exotic connections.[52] This would fit them into the context of palatial wealth finance. But the cache itself, which could have been contained in a single shipment, is not good evidence of a Theban dependency on trade with Mesopotamia. Indeed the seals had mixed origins, one was Hittite, some Cypriot, and some Mycenaean. Dakouri-Hild notes that some were reworked on Cyprus, before arriving in Thebes, where Theban artisans also refashioned and reused them.[53] In reality, there is not much evidence for a dependency on Near Eastern trade. Thebes, inland in northern Greece, was perhaps only indirectly connected with international trade routes.

We can equally wonder whether Mycenae was really dependent on trade with Egypt. While it is true that many Mycenaean pots have been found in Egypt, suggesting trade, and there are Egyptian artefacts, such as plaques bearing the names of Amenophis III and IV, at Mycenae, there is little to suggest a dependent relationship. Egypt also did not fall into its next intermediate period around 1200 BC, but over a century later. And if Tiryns was Mycenae's port town, then trade from both Egypt and Cyprus must have gone through there, which makes it difficult to explain why Tiryns would have weathered the collapse better than its neighbour.

Palatial Pylos, meanwhile, was plugged into the Aegean, as we can see from the Linear B tablets that record Anatolian workers on the palace staff. It was also ideally located for contact with the central Mediterranean and the Adriatic, and in the Postpalatial period the northwestern Peloponnese and the Ionian islands were thriving. It is difficult to explain the destruction of Pylos and the huge reduction in visible sites in Messenia as simply due to a lack of foreign connections or trade in eastern exotica.

The manipulation of exotica was very likely one of the strategies of kingship; as Bryan Burns points out, 'it is difficult not to view Mycenaean arts as reflecting the needs and expectations of the political elite'.[54] But establishing a strategy dependent on imports over which rulers had little or no control meant that certainly one strand of kingly ideology was vulnerable to a change in the system. The issue here is whether there was such a dependence.

Although we may imagine relatively stable kingdoms that suddenly collapsed, this is largely because we lack literary evidence that tells us otherwise, as it does for the Romans, Hittites, and others where rivals for power can be identified. It is better to imagine, as Burns reminds us, that "the palace' was not a monolithic whole and that each region's king acted in the company of potential rivals to economic and social power'.

If disruptions to trade were a factor in collapse, we must guess further to suggest that when royal elites were not able to come up with suitable ways of manipulating social capital, the system broke down violently – for it is violent destruction followed by rejection of the palace system that marks the collapse. Such an argument perhaps implies that it would be local elites opting out of the palace-based system that might have caused its demise.

PLAGUES AND EPIDEMICS

The Mycenaean collapse sees the abandonment of many sites around *c.* 1200 BC, a pattern which is especially noticeable in the southwest – the kingdom of Pylos. One possible explanation for this, and for long-term population decline and the adoption of cremation, is the occurrence of plague or serious epidemics of some kind.[55] This is plausible because we know of outbreaks elsewhere, in Hittite Anatolia and Cyprus, for example, in the Late Bronze Age. Two scholars, Lars Walloe and E. Watson Williams, have proposed that plagues affected the Mycenaeans in the late thirteenth century, bringing about collapse and population decline over several centuries.[56]

Both scholars point at the effects of known historical plagues. The Justinianic plague recurred episodically for two centuries, from AD 541 to AD 761; it killed 40 per cent of the population of Constantinople, some 200,000 people. The later Black Death is reckoned to have killed a third of Europe's population in three years, and possibly half of Britain's population in fourteen years, between AD 1348 and 1362. Infectious diseases brought by Europeans to the Americas were also deadly killers on a massive scale. Apart from causing death directly, plagues can also cause famines, population mobility, conflict, and changes in settlement patterns. Of particular note is the abandonment of some 1,300 villages in England between AD 1350 and 1500, which was, in part at least, due to the ravages of disease. In Italy, during the Justinianic plague, one response was the movement of people to hill tops or more defensible locations. It is at least plausible that similar changes in Greece happened due to the effects of plague.

If there was a plague, it would have affected the rulers and elites more than the general population, since there were fewer of them. This could potentially explain why palaces were not rebuilt later along the same lines, as well as the loss of literacy, which was extremely restricted. The common people would also have been affected, though, and this could have caused famines and general crisis and instability, which would certainly have affected the successful operation of a kingdom. Plague may have also affected the military ability of rulers, rendering states vulnerable to attack or internal conflict. The population may have been reduced and kept to a low level through repeated outbreaks.

Whilst the occurrence of plagues may potentially explain many factors of the Mycenaean collapse, the key problem is a lack of positive evidence; we just do not know whether there was or was not any plague in late Mycenaean Greece. Even if there was, we should not imagine a simple knockout scenario. The Black Death in Europe may have caused mass depopulation and significant social change, but it did not cause the collapse of any states. Classical Athens also experienced plague during the Peloponnesian war and retained its strength and ability to act for some years. The plague hypothesis remains an intriguing idea – and, as archaeologists say, absence of evidence is not evidence of absence.

MILITARY TACTICS AND CHANGES IN WARFARE

One of the most coherent explanations of the Mycenaean collapse, and of collapses elsewhere in the eastern Mediterranean, has been proposed by Robert Drews.[57] His hypothesis is based on the idea of changes in military equipment and tactics by 'barbarians' at the fringes of LBA states. As Drews states:

The Catastrophe came about when men in 'barbarian' lands awoke to a truth that had been with them for some time: the chariot-based forces on which the Great Kingdoms relied could be overwhelmed by swarming infantries, the infantrymen being equipped with javelins, long swords, and a few essential pieces of defensive armor.[58]

In Greece, Drews envisions land raiders from Locris, Phokis, and inland Thessaly destroying the Boeotian palaces at Orchomenos and Thebes (perhaps also Gla), and sea raiders from coastal Thessaly attacking elsewhere.[59]

However, Drews theory has not met with widespread acceptance.[60] The key point is perhaps his idea that LBA kingdoms in Greece and elsewhere relied heavily on chariots crewed with archers for warfare. Given the topography of Greece, it is unlikely that chariots were ever the mainstay of the military, even though we know from Linear B tablets and painted pottery that chariots were used. Early Mycenaean representations of warfare, whilst chariots are present, often show warriors on foot, and early and later graves contain hand-to-hand weapons. It is possible that Mycenaean elites used chariots symbolically as part of the way they defined their identity as members of the elite, rather than relying on them practically as the main instrument of war.

Drews also underplays the role of infantry in LBA warfare. The Amarna Letters, diplomatic correspondence sent between Egypt and other Near Eastern states in the fourteenth century BC, contain requests for archers and infantry forces. In Greece the famous Pylos Battle Scene fresco depicts 'Mycenaean' warriors, dressed in boar's tusk helmets and armed with spears and swords, fighting skin-clad barbarians on foot. Another fragment of the fresco appears to show other warriors and a chariot. In the Hittite Empire, one letter from Masat refers to the use of chariots and foot soldiers against the Kaska. Surely we should accept that Mycenaean forces were mixed and rulers would field forces suited to the campaign. In addition, it is unclear how the sea-borne raiders that Drews also imagines would suddenly have an advantage over the Mycenaean states.

It is unlikely that the LBA states relied near exclusively on chariot-borne archers, and it is far from certain that a sudden tactical revolution took place amongst the populations outside them. Given that the collapse most likely took place over several decades, it is difficult to imagine that LBA states would have been unable to respond had there been a change in tactics. There is also no evidence to suggest large populations of barbarians that would have been sufficient to 'swarm' over LBA state forces. Thus, while Drews' theory is an interesting one, and his review of other explanations is important, the military theory remains an unlikely explanation of the Mycenaean collapse.

POSTPALATIAL GREECE

Whatever caused the palace states to disappear, the collapse did not mean the end of Mycenaean civilisation, or the disappearance of people from Greece – Mycenaean style pottery, for example, continued to be made for more than a century, and it influenced the earliest 'Greek' styles. Pictorial pottery of the Postpalatial LH IIIC Middle period provided an expressive medium for artists in an age where there were no palaces and no opportunities for fresco painting. There were other continuities besides. Late Bronze Age sword types continued in use for centuries, and it seems likely that ship types and technology continued too. Invisible continuities include the Greek language and religion – many gods and goddesses known in Classical Greece were worshipped already in Mycenaean times, and some sanctuaries that were in use for centuries were founded in the immediate aftermath of collapse. Eva Rystedt has also pointed out a number of cultural similarities between LBA and later Greece, visible in figured pottery, where we can see depicted similar death and mourning rituals, chariot scenes, and athletics competitions.[61] In this vein, Jeremy Rutter has stated that 'the Aegean world weathered the actual palatial collapse of *ca.* 1200 BC well enough'.[62]

Some building activities also happened after *c.* 1200 at Tiryns, and possibly also at Mycenae, and elsewhere. At both sites it is possible that there could actually be Postpalatial 'palaces', although without Linear B texts. Joseph Maran has identified a very different kind of 'megaron' at Tiryns, known as Building T (Figure 6.4). The walls of this building partially overlie those of the earlier megaron and include the throne emplacement, but this new narrower megaron, with its central row of columns, has no central hearth as a main feature. All traces of earlier frescoes were removed and no new frescoes were created. In front of the entrance, the former round 'altar' in the courtyard was modified to a square altar, while the residue from the destruction of the palace was cleared away. What had been the palace area seems to have been left deliberately as a quite empty space apart from Building T and the altar.[63]

At Mycenae, the picture is less clear, partly because the remains of what might be a Postpalatial palace, Palace IV, a building on a different orientation (part of the artificial terrace supporting the old palace fell away into the ravine below), were removed in 1920 to get at the remains underneath, and the process was not well recorded. But it has been thought more plausible since the identification and dating of Building T at Tiryns, along with the fact that several other new buildings were constructed within the citadel, including the Granary,

FIGURE 6.4. Tiryns: A reconstruction of the Postpalatial (LH IIIC) acropolis. *Source*: Courtesy of Joseph Maran.

which was in use throughout LH IIIC until it too was destroyed by fire.[64] In other places, such as Midea, there is building similar to Tiryns, and at a few places in the Aegean there are also new small, but potentially 'central', sites. Although some of these, for example, at Koukounaries on Paros, have been seen as temporary sites made by fleeing Mycenaean elites, we might equally think of them as being built by locals who were expressing or claiming status using symbols derived from the mainland culture when mainland power had been curtailed.

At other sites too, especially in the northwest Peloponnese and Ionian islands, but also at Kynos, Mitrou, Lefkandi, and Perati, there is continued activity in the Postpalatial period and the continued presence of foreign material, showing continued international contacts. At Aigeira, recent research has revealed settlement activity throughout the Postpalatial period and later; a new fortification wall was built on the acropolis after a destructive fire.[65] There is also now clear evidence of a lower town.

At some sites there is evidence from figured pottery of an ideology of seaborne warfare, overseas military ventures, or raiding that develops particularly in the Postpalatial period pottery.[66] But even though such scenes seem to become more popular after *c.* 1200, this does not mean that we can simply conclude that they are an index of what was going on – that actual naval escapades were infrequent in Palatial times or increased in frequency or intensity later on. The scenes may represent generic scenes, myths, or may have simply become popular themes with those who used the pottery in their drinking parties, representing something of an idealised elite way of life.

In Greece and the Aegean there is no direct evidence of invasion or attack from the sea – although a Linear B tablet from Pylos mentions the setting up of coastguards, we do not know whether this was normal or not. In any case, destructions on the Greek mainland were not simultaneous. Andreas Vlachopoulos, an expert in the archaeology of the Aegean islands, has also argued that there is a 'lack of evidence for simultaneous catastrophes' in the Aegean; rather, he suggests that the evidence 'strongly suggests that LH IIIC was a peaceful period for the Aegean and that no common external threat existed'.[67]

So, there were still people, buildings, settlements, and Mycenaean pottery in the period after the collapse of the palace states. The changes to Tiryns in particular, but also Mycenae and Midea, suggest that the old palatial system had been rejected – people chose not to rebuild in the 'classic' palatial style. There were still contacts between the mainland and elsewhere in the eastern and central Mediterranean, even if these were on a reduced, or at least less visible, scale. Decorated pottery – probably made for a market of drinking elites – increasingly shows ships and military scenes, and a spate of 'warrior burials' were performed in certain areas. Tiryns grew in size, and it seems to continue as a site vested with importance for another hundred years or so, before it too was almost completely abandoned. But at Pylos, on the other hand, as Jack Davis explains, 'the destruction ... ca. 1180 BC was so devastating that neither the palace nor the community subsequently recovered', and there are only bits and pieces from LH IIIC.[68]

AN AGE OF MIGRATIONS?

Many researchers have suggested that Mycenaeans, either rulers and their followers or common people, migrated from Greece after the collapse, perhaps first to the Aegean, then to Cyprus, and eventually to Canaan, and that there may have been Greeks amongst the Sea Peoples (as mentioned earlier – more on them in the next chapter).[69] Some even believe that the Biblical Philistines were descended from Mycenaean migrants. Apart from the Medinet Habu reliefs of Ramesses III, this idea is mainly based on the appearance of Mycenaean-looking pottery and other features that appear post-1200 BC. Rather than importing pottery, it began to be made locally, suggesting migrants maintaining their traditions and culture. This view, though, is increasingly criticised, and the picture admitted as being more complex.[70]

For one thing, pottery does not simply represent an ethnic or linguistic group – does wearing jeans make us American, does having a Japanese television make us Japanese, does having a wok make us Chinese? Discussing the Cypriot archaeology of the Late Bronze Age and Early Iron Age, the pottery and other aspects of material, Ioannis Voskos and Bernard Knapp make it very clear that the supposed Mycenaean features are thoroughly mixed with Cypriot and Levantine features.[71] It is a similar case with the supposedly Mycenaean culture of the Philistines. The material does not tell us about ethnicity at all, but rather it can be explained as people choosing the type of material they wanted to make and use – imported Mycenaean pottery had been around for many years.

Some Greeks did migrate, of course. Kingdoms developed on Cyprus, and the island became increasingly part of the Greek world as time went on. In the eleventh century, at Palaepaphos-Skales, one man with a Greek name, Opheltas, was buried with a bronze spit bearing his name in syllabic script. But as has been pointed out, to inscribe such an object was a very 'eastern' practice – not a LBA Greek one.[72] And the grave goods do not differ from other Cypriot burials; the only thing that marks Opheltas out as 'Greek' is his name. We can only guess at what was going on, but for some reason some people on Cyprus came to value Greek culture – perhaps

Cypriot elites were using 'exotic' culture to build up their positions at home, as Mycenaean kings had in Greece. Anyway, it must indicate continued contact post-1200 BC and a degree of population mobility, but we need not envision a massive exodus from Greece or a replacement of the Cypriot population.[73]

Crete and the western coast of Anatolia, and the Aegean islands themselves, also became increasingly Greek over time. Yet in the Homeric poems, probably representing the period several centuries after the end of the LBA, Crete is referred to as a multi-ethnic island (*Odyssey* 19.172–180):

There is a land called Crete in the middle of the wine-blue sea, a handsome country and fertile, seagirt, and there are many people in it, innumerable; there are ninety cities. Language with language mix there together. There are Achaians, there are great-hearted Eteocretans, there are Kydonians, and Dorians ...

The processes that led to Hellenisation are no doubt complex and played out over a long time. The practice of being 'Greek' was an ongoing project of people forging identities in contact with each other, myths were developed that expressed commonalities and differences.[74]

FINAL THOUGHTS

The Mycenaean collapse saw the end of the palace kingdoms of Greece, but not the end of Mycenaean culture, or life in Greece. Non-palatial areas, such as the northwest Peloponnese, thrived, as did the Aegean and Ionian islands, and also some former palace sites such as Tiryns. Some areas that had once been part of kingdoms, such as Lefkandi, also took on more importance. What happened in the Pylos kingdom, which seems to have become seriously depopulated, if site counts are anything to go by, is uncertain. Greece remained involved in international trade and contacts, and there may have been an increase in mobility for individuals and groups – people often flee unstable areas. Eventually what was left of the Postpalatial Mycenaean pottery types transformed in stages into Protogeometric style; other continuities existed in religion and the gods worshipped, in ship and weapons technology, in funerary rites, and possibly in the importance of athletic games. The Homeric epics, not a straight-forward representation of LBA Greece at all, most likely incorporate elements from the Postpalatial period, perhaps in the importance of gifts and the blurred line between traders and pirates, as well as the importance of being 'a man of action' in order to win power and renown.

In the next chapter, we shall look at the Mycenaeans much bigger and more powerful neighbours in Anatolia – the Hittites – and we shall also look some more at the Sea Peoples.

HOMER, THE MYCENAEANS, AND THE TROJAN WAR

The Homeric poems, the *Iliad* and the *Odyssey*, describe incidents during and after the Trojan War, and it has long been debated whether they represent a real historical war. There is agreement that the poems in their current form date to around the middle of the eighth century BC, but many have thought that the stories originated much earlier. For some, the poems record a partial history of Mycenaean Greece, and an adventure undertaken under the leadership of Mycenae, which may well have been the pre-eminent Mycenaean site. For others, the poems are much more a product of the Postpalatial Early Iron Age, around the twelfth century and after, recalling a heroic past. Equally, they could be influenced by society in later 'dark age' times. What is certain about the poems is that they contain fragments of detail from each period; they were being continuously developed in an oral tradition, over time, until they were finally preserved in one form in writing.

While the poems contain fragments of the different pasts, mentioning artifacts from the Late Bronze Age and later times (weapons, for example), this does not mean that any of the narrative itself is true; the matter of whether there was 'a Trojan War' between a coalition of Greeks and Trojans in Asia Minor is still debated. Research on oral traditions and the composition of epic 'heroic' poetry shows that in a relatively short time details can be changed, episodes invented, and characters conflated.[75] A story which begins as, or is based on, a factual account can quickly be transformed beyond recognition. So the poems are unreliable as historical sources.

Much recent discussion, rather than being based on analysis and interpretation of the poems themselves, hinges on possible clues from Hittite texts of the Late Bronze Age.[76] Some mention a land called Ahhiyawa, which is now mostly taken to match 'Achaea', a Homeric term for Greece. Others mention a land called Wilusa, which could be an early form of Ilios, another name for Troy. A character named Alaksandu, similar to Alexander, another name of Paris from the *Iliad*, was for a time king of Wilusa. Some read the texts to imply a conflict between Ahhiyawans and Wilusa, in which the Hittites aided Wilusa – could this be evidence of a real Trojan war?[77]

7

The Hittites and the Eastern Mediterranean

The cataclysmic upheavals that came with the twelfth century completely changed the political and social landscape of western Asia, sweeping away the Bronze Age world. The Hittite empire collapsed, and Hattusha was sacked and abandoned by marauding barbarians from the Black Sea coast.

Christopher Edens[1]

THE HITTITES

In the eastern Mediterranean of the Late Bronze Age (LBA), the Hittites, based in Anatolia, were one of the great powers, along with Egypt; the two famously came to blows in the battle of Kadesh, near the Orontes River in Syria, in 1274 BC, afterwards making the first known international peace treaty (Figure 7.1).[2] Rulers of the two states, both 'great kings', remained in diplomatic contact over several decades at least. After Kadesh, a Hittite princess married Ramesses II and a Hittite prince, Heshmi-Sharruuma, visited Egypt to oversee grain shipments back to the land of Hatti.

Hittite history presents us with an unbroken chain of kings from the little known Labarna in the seventeenth century BC to Suppiluliuma II who ruled around 1200 BC (Table 7.1). Similar to Egypt, Hittite history is usually subdivided into an Old Kingdom (c. 1650–1500) and the New Kingdom or Empire (c. 1400–1200 BC), with an intervening Middle Kingdom, or intermediate period (c. 1500–1400), noted for weakness, retreat from empire, and

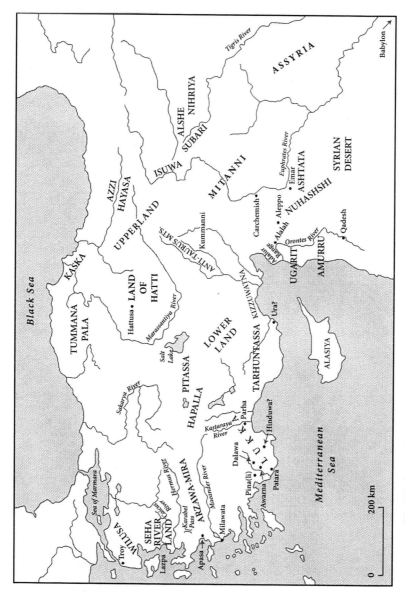

FIGURE 7.1. The Hittite world.
Source: Courtesy of Trevor Bryce.

156

TABLE 7.1 *Hittite 'New Kingdom' kings*

Kings	Dates (BC)
Suppiluliuma I	1350–1322
Arnuwanda II	1322–1321
Mursili II	1321–1295
Muwattalli II	1295–1272
Urhi-Teshub	1272–1267
Hattusili III	1267–1237
Tudhaliya IV	1237–1209
Arnuwanda III	1209–1207
Suppiluliuma II	1207–????

Source: Page xv, Bryce, T. (2005). *The Kingdom of the Hittites.*
New edition. Oxford: Oxford University Press.

instability. Because we have a vast number of tablets from the Hittite capital Hattusa (Boghazkoy) and elsewhere, as well as various inscriptions, we know much more about the doings of the Hittite state, its royals, and society generally than we do about their Aegean neighbours the Minoans, whose Linear A script remains undeciphered (we do not even know the language represented), and the Mycenaeans, whose Linear B texts are very limited in scope.

For much of their history, the Hittite kings tried to extend and maintain their sway; they waged wars against a range of enemies in western and northern Anatolia and in the northern Levant – as well as Egypt. They annexed the important cities of Ugarit, an important port city on the Mediterranean coast, which they made a vassal state, and Carchemish in northern Syria, which became a viceregal kingdom within their empire. Periodically, they also claimed dominion over Cyprus too, although this is hard to see in the archaeology. It is likely that they were in contact with LBA Greece; although there is little evidence of trade, there are Hittite letters to the king of Ahhiyawa, which many read as being a form of a Homeric word for Greeks – Achaeans.[3] They may have come to blows over the city of Millawata (later Miletus) on the western Anatolia/Aegean coast.

The Hittite Empire in Anatolia collapsed during the reign of the Suppiluliuma II, sometime after 1207 BC. This is indicated by the destruction and abandonment of the grand capital Hattusa, in north central Anatolia, in the curve of the Halys River, and the end of the rule and records of its Great Kings. There was also an abandonment of urban living in central Anatolia. In addition, Ugarit was destroyed and there were destructions in Cyprus too. These widespread destructions are often attributed to the 'Sea Peoples', commonly portrayed as the Vikings of the LBA.

In this chapter, we shall look at the causes proposed for the collapse of the Hittite Empire and state, as well as examine what happened at Ugarit and in Cyprus. We shall also look at some of the other peoples and states of Anatolia to find out what happened to them around *c.* 1200 BC. And we shall also consider what happened next – the transition from Late Bronze Age to Early Iron Age (EIA).

THE SEA PEOPLES – BRINGERS OF DOOM?

Pride of place in explanations of the end of the LBA in the eastern Mediterranean must be given to the Sea Peoples, for they tend to dominate accounts of this period and are seen both as a cause and effect of collapse, and as bringers of change in material culture.[4] But who were the Sea Peoples, where did they come from, and what did they do?

The prime evidence for the Sea Peoples comes from Egypt, from the Medinet Habu complex of Ramesses III, which attribute to him a naval victory over an invading Sea Peoples 'armada' and a land victory over Sea Peoples migrants, represented by fighting men as well as women and children in oxcarts (Figure 7.2). The famous Medinet Habu text reads thus:

The foreign countries made a conspiracy in their islands. All at once the lands were removed and scattered in the fray. No land could stand before their arms, from Hatti, Kode, Carchemish, Arzawa, and Alashiya on, being cut off at [one time]. A camp [was set up] in one place in Amurru. They desolated its people, and its land was like that which had never come into being. They were coming forward toward Egypt, while the flame was prepared for them. Their confederation was the Peleset, Tjeker, Shekelesh, Denyen, and Weshesh, lands united. They laid their hands upon the lands as far as the circuit of the earth, their hearts were confident and trusting: 'our plans will succeed!'[5]

Other peoples, mentioned in a few other texts, are also associated with the Sea Peoples – the Lukka, for example, and the Ekwesh and

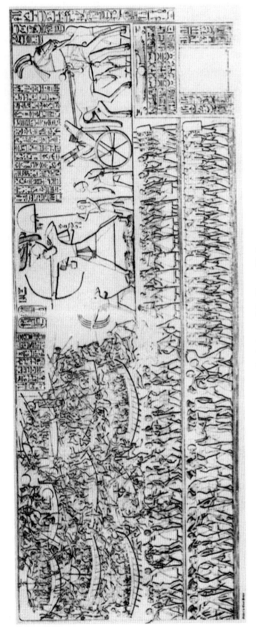

FIGURE 7.2. Ramesses III defeating the 'Sea Peoples', from Medinet Habu.
Source: Courtesy of the Oriental Institute of the University of Chicago.

Sherden. The Lukka we know came from southern Anatolia, and had a history of raiding, but where did the others come from? The most truthful answer is that we do not really know. On the basis of similarities in names, scholars claim the Sherden were Sardinian, the Shekelesh Sicilian, the Ekwesh Achaean and Denyen Danaan (both Greek), and most famously the Philistines, who are widely thought to have been Greek migrants who settled in what became Palestine.[6] However, it is unclear whether these equations are correct – it is possible that, if some of them are, that the names could have been given to destinations rather than points of origin – Shekelesh could have gone to Sicily from the eastern Mediterranean, not arrived from it. Robert Drews has also pointed out that 'islands' can be translated as 'coastal areas'; it is quite possible that these were peoples already in the eastern Mediterranean – why could the Philistines not have come from Palestine?[7] We also do not know their numbers or that they represented discrete ethnic groups, or that they were the violent migrant peoples they are often made out to be.[8]

What did the Sea Peoples do? Migration and destruction are the two activities most associated with them, with the addition of generally disrupting established eastern Mediterranean trade and intercommunications. As the list in the Medinet Habu text indicates, many destructions around the eastern Mediterranean were assigned, by the Egyptians, to the Sea Peoples. Some archaeologists have attributed destructions in the area of Ugarit and northern Syria to the Sea Peoples.[9] Most recently a group of researchers led by David Kaniewski has resurrected an old theory that climate change and famines spurred the violent migrations, population movements, and invasions, and they attribute the destruction of the Ugaritic port city of Gibala specifically to the Sea Peoples; they argue that the destruction dates to 1192/1190 BC.[10]

As for migration, the most important evidence comes from the appearance of locally made Mycenaean or Aegean style pottery in the eastern Mediterranean, along with some other new features. This is most often associated with the Philistines, whom Assaf Yasur-Landau, the latest in a line of scholars, which includes Moshe and Trude Dothan, and Lawrence Stager, claims to be Mycenaean or Aegean migrants.[11]

Could the Sea Peoples have caused the widespread eastern Mediterranean collapses and destructions? Did they include Mycenaean migrants among their number?

Louise Hitchcock and Aren Maeir characterise the Sea Peoples as pirates, and as pirates they could have affected trade.[12] Cyprus expert Bernard Knapp notes too of the period 1250–1150 BC that 'communications were disrupted severely, while brigandage on land and piracy at sea complicated international trade'.[13] Both he and Hittitologist Trevor Bryce point out that textual sources record raiding as early as the fourteenth century BC, when Lukka and Ahhiyawa people raided ports in Anatolia, Cyprus, Egypt, and the Levant.[14] It is safe to say that such activities were well-known in the ancient eastern Mediterranean. We might well expect that piracy and raiding would grow up alongside well-trod and lucrative trade routes, as it did in Roman times when the pirates of Cilicia became an serious menace that required massive intervention by the Romans to quell.[15]

Additional evidence from the Levant suggests that cities were experiencing problems from the sea in the LBA. A letter from the king of Ugarit (which traditionally provided the land-based Hittites' navy) to the king of Alashiya (a kingdom based on Cyprus) suggests destructive raids around *c.* 1200 BC.[16] After the customary royal greetings, it says:

Father, the ships of the enemy have been coming. They have been burning down my villages and have done evil things to the country. Does my father not know that all my troops [and chariots] are in Hatti and that all my ships are in Lukka? They have not yet reached me, and so the country is undefended. May my father be informed of this. Now the seven ships of the enemy that came have done evil things. If other enemy ships appear, send me a message so that I know.

A possible reply about the actions and location of these enemy ships from the king of Alashiya states:

Now, the twenty ships that the enemies earlier left in the mountainous areas, have not stayed behind. They left suddenly and we do not know where they are. I write to you to inform you so that you can guard yourself. Be informed!

It is certainly possible that towards the end of the LBA there were troubles from the sea – but we know that these troubles were nothing new. There is nothing explicit in the Hittite or Levantine texts to associate these troubles with the Sea Peoples of the Egyptian texts; who were 'the enemy'? Nor is it possible to associate specific destructions, for example, at Gibala, or in Cyprus, with the Sea Peoples. Amelie Kuhrt soberly observes that 'the only sources for the role of the "sea-peoples" in the crisis [in Anatolia and the Levant] are the accounts of two Egyptian campaigns'.[17]

Egyptologists know that such pharaonic pronouncements as the Medinet Habu texts must be taken with a pinch of salt – their purpose was not to record history as we understand it, but to present the pharaoh (to the gods) in a suitable light, performing deeds which are appropriate for him, such as saving the country and defeating enemies.[18] Toby Wilkinson puts it thus: 'the Egyptians were adept at recording things as they wished them to be seen, not as they actually were'.[19] It is not uncommon to find pharaohs lifting texts and deeds from their predecessors, and the various 'Sea Peoples' had been around, mentioned in Egyptian texts, for some time – they did not suddenly appear around 1200 BC. Marc Van De Mieroop notes that 'the Egyptian picture of a coordinated and sudden attack is refuted by the fact that two kings living several decades apart told essentially the same story and that long-known people were involved'.[20]

We also know that the list of destructions is wrong in some details. The city of Carchemish was not destroyed at this time, for example.[21] After the collapse of the Hittite state in Anatolia, the empire continued to exist at Carchemish, rather like the Eastern Roman Empire with its capital at Constantinople that continued well beyond the fifth century AD western collapse. Members of the Hittite royal family based at Carchemish claimed the title of Great King in the years after 1200 BC.[22] In addition, if the important city of Ugarit was destroyed by the Sea Peoples, why was this not mentioned in the text? Given the problems with the evidence, can we really believe that the Hittite Empire, with its still extant military might and with its capital far inland, was brought low by the Sea Peoples, or did this grandiose rhetoric simply suit Ramesses III? Hittitologist Hermann Genz and others think not.[23]

Equally, the archaeological record does not prove that there was any migration of Sea Peoples.[24] Although it is often claimed that the Philistines were Greek migrants, this is based on a simplistic claim that material culture, especially pottery, represents distinct ethnic groups. It is true that the early Philistine pottery looks somewhat like Mycenaean pottery, but Philistine material culture shows mixed features from the beginning – the pottery has features that originated in Greece, but were modified in Cyprus, and also included Canaanite elements. Mycenaean pottery had long been known in the east, and could easily have inspired people to copy it, as they did elsewhere. Eastern Mediterranean specialist Ann Killebrew thinks that the Philistines were new to the southern Levant but doubts they were Mycenaeans or even that there was any direct contact between Greece and the Levant around 1200 BC and after. Another curious aspect of this argument is the names. Denyen and Ekwesh Sea Peoples are identified with Greeks through the old names for Greeks Danaans, and Achaeans, but no name for Greeks related to Peleset or Philistines is known. The migration narrative is a modern one.

Putting this all in context, we can see that coastal sites and presumably vessels moving around the eastern Mediterranean were vulnerable to attack from 'pirates' or raiders. But we know also that this was no novelty in the years around 1200 BC; presumably this kind of activity was a normal hazard throughout the LBA. If a city's ships or military were in action elsewhere, they would of course be more vulnerable to attack, even from a relatively small number of ships. We cannot trust the story the Medinet Habu reliefs tell us. So then can we conclude that 'the Sea Peoples' destroyed the Hittites? The answer must also be no. The 'Sea Peoples' narrative, with all its problems, is regarded by some as a largely modern invention. As for Ugarit, it is quite possible that seaborne attackers did destroy the city, but that does not explain why it was not refounded or why it did not continue to play the same important role it had done for centuries (and some cities to the south were not torched and did continue through into the Iron Age), nor need we associate its destruction with the Sea Peoples of the Egyptian texts.

GRAIN SUPPLY AND FOOD SHORTAGES IN HATTI

There is some evidence that refers to food shortages in the latter years of the Hittite kingdom, and this has sometimes been related to climate change.[25] In this context, Bryce has suggested that the Land of Hatti may have become more dependent on imported grain from Egypt and the Levant after the reign of Hattusili III (1267–1237 BC). A draft letter written by his wife, the Hittite queen Pudehepa, to Ramesses II refers to a shortage of grain; as mentioned earlier, Hittite princes were sometimes active in Egypt organising and overseeing grain shipments. Whatever was going on, it was important enough to be overseen at the highest levels. A letter sent from the Hittite court to the king of Ugarit, dated to the reign of Tudhaliya IV, refers to the delay of a 450 ton cargo of grain as a matter of life and death ('My Sun' refers to the Hittite king):

And so (the city) Ura (acted(?)) in such a way … and for My Sun the food they had saved. My Sun has shown them 2000 *kor* of grain coming from Mukish. You must furnish them with a large ship and crew, and they must transport the grain to their country. They will carry it in one or two shipments. You must not detain their ship![26]

In Egypt, the Karnak stele of Merneptah (*c.* 1213–1203 BC) also referred to shipments of grain sent to 'keep alive the Land of Hatti'. In Hattusa, archaeologists have discovered two large grain storage silos, which may be of late Hittite date. These could store enough grain to feed 20–30,000 people for a year.[27] Summarising the relevant textual evidence and arguing that the Hittites could no longer feed themselves, David Kaniewski states:

The invested efforts to procure grain emphasize the severity of the situation in the Hittite Kingdom. Similar conditions of food shortage occurred quite frequently on the Anatolian plateau at this time, leaving little doubt regarding the unprecedented proportions of this famine.[28]

What could have caused such concern over grain supplies? As an imperial capital, Hattusa was probably well enough populated so that its immediate hinterland alone could not support it (like imperial Rome). It is possible that the Hittite royals came to depend on supplies of grain from abroad to sustain the city. It is certain that the Hittites, as with all agriculturally based societies, would have been vulnerable to bad years, whether caused by drought, pests, or too much rain, and central storage facilities would have reduced the risk of many going hungry.

Ronald Gorny has made a case for environmental changes that might have sparked such shortages.[29] Gorny suggests that the climate became warmer and drier around 1200 BC, following a cooler and moister phase from around 1500 BC. This, he suggests, would have affected agricultural production on the Anatolian plateau, as well as the steppe vegetation that nomads depended on. These effects could have included drought and crop failure, which would have resulted in famine, malnutrition, and disease. A situation like this could have a range of results – the general population may have revolted, or become less satisfied (and less co-operative) with the ruling classes, while steppe nomads could have been forced to relocate to more favourable areas, putting pressure on Hittite lands. Thus, Gorny links environmental changes to socio-political factors.

Gorny admitted that his was a speculative hypothesis, writing that 'we lack reliable climate and chronological data for central Anatolia'.[30] But more recently Kaniewski and team proposed that there was a 300-year drought beginning later in the thirteenth century BC; they base their data on palaeoclimatic reconstructions drawn from the analysis of lake sediment cores.[31]

Whatever conclusions one draws about the climatic reconstructions, there is little to suggest that the Hittite kingdom was unable to function in its later days – certainly kings were still able to campaign far and wide. Hattusa too became most grand in its last days, under Tudhaliya IV, who more than doubled the urban area, constructed many new temples, and built massive new fortifications.[32] We should not underestimate the resources that were evidently at the disposal of the Hittite kings of the second half of the thirteenth century BC.

Campaigning, however, could have brought about problems. Warfare could directly affect food supply, and this could have prompted the Hittite rulers to import grain from overseas, or to depend on it more. Warfare requires manpower, which means fewer people working the land, and it also reduces the areas available to cultivate, and can result directly in the destruction of crops (or the failure to plant or harvest) and agricultural equipment. We know that the Hittites were almost constantly at war with their western neighbours, the Lukka and Arzawa people, or campaigning to the south east, and their heartlands were regularly raided by their northern ('barbarian') neighbours, the Kaska. It is possible that a dependency on imports could have grown up, and that this would have placed the Hittite state at great risk; if something upset the balance – whether pirates at sea or wars on land – famine, disorder, and collapse could have followed as the state found itself unable to cope.

However, the problem in this line of explanation is that we do not actually know the purpose of these grain imports, or how reliant on them the state, that is the ruler, was. It would suit the Egyptian mentality to see their actions as keeping alive the Land of Hatti (just as FIP regional leaders boasted of their ability to keep alive their own people and give grain to neighbours). Was the grain distributed to the general population of Hattusa, much as a corn dole was given out in Rome, or was it distributed to the Hittite elite, or was it to feed the armies of the king or the construction workers of Hattusa? We do not know. Whatever the answers to these questions, it is possible that, regardless of whether or not there was a shift in climate, a failure of grain supplies could indeed have caused or contributed to the collapse of the Hittite kingdom by affecting some key relationship between the ruler and those who received the grain. It does not tell us who the agents of destruction were, though we might suggest a hungry mass of (urban?) population, discontented troops, noble factions, royal relations, enemies taking advantage of a weakened state, or a combination of some or all of these. But if this was the cause of the Hittite collapse, it does not seem to explain the destruction of Ugarit. Also, given the scale of the last Suppiluliuma's military escapades, we should be wary of thinking that the Hittite state was particularly weakened before it collapsed.

CONFLICT WITHOUT AND WITHIN

The Hittites were, more often than not, at war. They fought their southern rivals the Egyptians, before making peace with them after Kadesh, they fought the Kaska to the north and in their own lands, they fought Arzawa and Lukka to the west and south, they fought with Alashiya (Cyprus), and the Assyrians to the east. The constant attacks, raids, rebellions, and punitive reprisals and mass relocations of people show their empire to have been profoundly unstable, with territories constantly having to be re-won or pacified – its long existence is more surprising than its collapse. The texts show that towards the end of the thirteenth century the last Hittite king, Suppiluliuma II, was at war, and that the war zone extended across western and southern Anatolia and over the sea to Cyprus.

FIGURE 7.3. Hieroglyphic reliefs from Room 2 at Hattusa, which record a sea battle between Suppiluliuma II and Alashiya.
Source: Courtesy of Thalia Lysen

The extent of these wars is recorded at Hattusa in 'Room 2' of an underground cult complex (Figure 7.3).[33] Its walls are decorated with reliefs of gods, of Suppiluliuma, and are inscribed with hierogylphic texts. They mention that Suppiluliuma fought at sea off Alashiya, which probably would have required Ugarit's help, as the Hittites seem to have had no navy of their own: 'the ships of Alashiya met me in the sea three times for battle, and I smote them,' the king recorded. He then engaged on land with 'enemies from Alashiya', though we do not know if this was on Cyprus or in Anatolia, or whether the enemies were Alashiyans or others on the island.[34] It may be that the Hittites' regional pre-eminence was coming under increasing challenge from all sides.

Suppiluliuma apparently won these encounters, although he would not have been likely to record failures, but the cost in resources and manpower, even if he was victorious, would have been immense. Hittite warfare, though, had gone on for centuries, but the empire had coped before – why should it collapse now? Grain shortages could have been part of the story. But, equally, problems in the royal house itself may have played a role.

There were, evidently, problems in the succession – the royal family had grown so big over the years that there could be many rival lines and claimants to the throne. Tudhaliya IV issued the following proclamation in an attempt to secure his own position and that of his direct descendants:

My Sun has many brothers and there are many sons of his father. The Land of Hatti is full of the royal line: in Hatti the descendants of Suppiluliuma, the descendants of Mursili, the descendants of Muwatalli, the descendants of Hattusili are very numerous. With regard to kingship, you must acknowledge no other person (but me, Tudhaliya), and protect only the grandson and great grandson and descendants of Tudhaliya. And if at any time (?) evil is done to My Sun – (for) My Sun has many brothers – and someone approaches another person and speaks thus: 'Whomever we select for ourselves need not even be a son of our lord!' – these words must not be (permitted). With regard to kingship, you must protect only My Sun and the descendants of My Sun. You must approach no other person.[35]

As Bryce comments, 'these are the words of a king who recognized that his throne was far from secure, and that the greatest danger to it came from possible rival claimants within his own family'.[36]

There were other problems too. A coup by Hattusili III earlier in the thirteenth century had created a dangerous division in the royal house, which destabilised the state for years to come.[37] Hattusili rebelled against the rightful heir, his nephew Urhi-Teshub, defeating him in open war; Urhi-Teshub was exiled to northern Syria. But Urhi-Teshub, his brother, and descendants continued to fight for the throne against Hattusili and his descendants. Both parties had their supporters. Urhi-Teshub's brother Kurunta claimed the throne and was at some time also recorded as 'Great King' at Hattusa, as well as in the south at Konya, and on seals, but Bryce suggests he was probably never king there; he may have been king in Tarhuntassa in the south.[38] Hattusili's son Tudhaliya continued to rule as Great King from Hattusa, and it is very likely that war between these rivals and their supporters continued.[39] It is possible that the wars fought by Suppiluliuma II around 1200 BC were wars against a coalition led by his rivals in Tarhuntassa.[40] Conflict among members of the royal family were serious threats to peace and unity.

In such circumstances, parts of the Hittite Empire, not necessarily willing ones, could take advantage of instability at the centre to assert themselves.[41] One vassal, King Ibiranu of Ugarit, failed to 'check in' properly with the new king Suppiluliuma, as the following letter shows:

Since you have assumed royal power at Ugarit, why have you not come before My Sun? And why have you not sent messengers? This has made My Sun very angry.[42]

Later on, Ammurapi of Ugarit even divorced a Hittite princess – quite a slight to the Anatolian Hittites; he was perhaps turning towards the Hittite rulers of Carchemish as the Hatti-based empire became increasingly unstable. Ugarit itself was not to last long though.

The empire of the Hittites was fragile indeed, constantly beset by the desire for independence of regions forced into it, and attacked by enemies. It is quite possible that Suppiluliuma and his empire collapsed in the flames of battle, fighting enemies both external and internal. Why it collapsed at this point in time may be down to chance, to the specific constellation of events and choices. However, according to Jurgen Seeher, the capital seems to have been evacuated in an organised fashion, emptied of its valuables and abandoned – was this done by Suppiluliuma?[43] Did he and his court, and the people of the city, up sticks and settle elsewhere, perhaps even in and around Carchemish, possibly meaning to return one day?

THE KASKA: NORTHERN 'BARBARIANS'

Like the Roman Empire, a major theme in the history of the Hittite Empire is their interaction with 'barbarians', in this case the Kaska peoples, who lived to the north of the Hittite homeland. Claudia Glatz and Roger Matthews have studied this long-standing and defining relationship, which reveals that the Hittites and Romans, and their neighbours, found themselves in quite similar situations.[44] The nature of Hittite-Kaska relations are described in texts from Hattusa and from an archive in the fairly small and remote frontier town of Masat Hoyuk, east of Hattusa, which contained letters from the king to various officials, and demonstrate the level of concern with defence that the Hittites had.

The texts record Kaska raids, Hittite military campaigns, and also diplomatic treaties. Kaska populations could be wiped out or forcibly moved, with areas being repopulated by Hittites or by people transported in hundreds or thousands from imperial conquests elsewhere.[45] Some Kaska were in this way recruited into the Hittite military. Punitive follow-up campaigns against the Kaska by the Hittites seem, like Roman campaigns, designed to provide a show of strength in order to deter future raids. The treaties agreed on terms of interaction, such as Hittite access to towns for religious reasons, Kaska grazing rights and occasional settlement within Hittite areas, and the recruitment of Kaska as soldiers. People from both sides, when captured by the other, were subject to harsh treatments – blinding, forced labour, and enslavement.

Roger Matthews conducted an archaeological survey of the Paphlagonia region, around 100 km northwest of Hattusa, and a disputed area between Hittites and Kaska.[46] The survey revealed a network of strategically located Hittite fortified sites spread throughout the area, along with lookout posts that probably also functioned as signalling stations, as at Eldivan – defence in depth. Roads or tracks that facilitated more rapid military movements linked this network. The archaeology suggests that the Hittites developed a 'landscape of terror and control,' or at least of attempted control.

But relations should not be thought of purely in terms of conflict. Scholars suggest that, across a broad swath of time and space, we should imagine a range of political, social, and economic contacts at different levels between the two peoples, including intermarriage and cohabitation.[47] Kaska individuals could hold positions of authority in the Hittite military while some Hittites went to live with the Kaska. Kaska could adopt and adapt Hittite ways, as when one leader called Pihhuniya, who uniquely fought open battles with the Hittites, was said to have ruled 'like a king' – the Kaska seem normally not to have been ruled by individuals; Pihhuniya may have adopted some techniques of power from his southern neighbours to boost his own position and status.

Nevertheless, the Kaska, whose history is intimately bound up with that of the Hittites, may have been the ones responsible for the final destruction of Hattusa (they did destroy it in earlier times). They repeatedly attacked and even occupied territory claimed by the Hittites, always posing a threat. Years before the final collapse, they had pressed the Hittite rulers so hard that they were forced to relocate their capital from Hattusa further south to the safer location of Tarhuntassa, although the rulers' strategic interest in northern Syria were probably also a factor in this move.[48] In the words of king Hattusili III:

> When, however, my brother Muwattalli at the command of his (patron) deity went down to the Lower Land, leaving the city of Hattusa, he took the gods and the ancestral spirits of Hatti ... and he brought them down to the city of Tarhuntassa and made it his place of residence.[49]

The Kaska probably had many motivations for their raids; quite possibly raiding was an integral part of their culture. Their raids were more than just an annoyance for the Hittites – they provoked a major defensive response, which influenced the functioning and structure of the state. Their attacks could be very damaging, especially if the Hittites were occupied in fighting elsewhere. The Kaska are archaeologically invisible, so it is difficult to tell their side of the story. If they moved into former Hittite territory, as seems probable (they were encountered by Assyrians as far as the Euphrates), it may provide us with one reason why urban society disappeared from the Anatolian plateau at the time of the Hittite collapse.[50]

MOVING THE CENTRE, SPLITTING THE EMPIRE

As described earlier, the Kaska posed a real and constant threat to the Hittites, and were a drain on resources too; when the king's attention was directed elsewhere, Hatti and Hattusa were always vulnerable. A landscape in which conflict is normal can become depopulated and unproductive, and this seems to have been the case in early thirteenth century BC Hatti.[51] Also, only around twenty years earlier a plague had broken out in Hatti, in the final years of king Suppiluliuma I. While it is not possible to quantify the demographic effects of this plague, the Plague Prayers of Mursili, recorded on clay tablets, suggest it was serious enough to encourage attacks by neighbouring peoples and vassal territories, who took the opportunity to weaken the Hittites or throw off Hittite rule:

> What is this, o gods that you have done? A plague you have let into the land. The land of Hatti, all of it, is dying; so no-one prepares sacrificial loaves and libations for you. The ploughmen who used to work the fields are dead ...

To mankind, our wisdom has been lost, and whatever we do right comes to nothing.[52]

The kingdom survived then, owing much to the abilities of the charismatic king Mursili.[53] But it is in the aftermath of this troubled time that king Muwatalli moved the capital from Hattusa, maybe around 1280 BC, south to Tarhuntassa, taking 'the gods and ancestral spirits of Hatti,' to a less vulnerable region that was also closer to other regional powers in Syria, Egypt, and Cyprus. This was probably intended as a permanent move, and as Bryce points out, 'Muwatalli's decision ... had the effect of virtually partitioning the Hittite kingdom, with the northern part ... including much of the homeland, now directly ruled by his brother Hattusili'.[54] Just as the Roman emperors would eventually realise, the effective running of a large empire could require the division of power on a grand scale. Hattusa was not abandoned though, and Urhi-Teshub later brought the gods back, making it again the capital. But Tarhuntassa, as we saw, became the seat of a rival Hittite royal dynasty, and again, in parallel with the division into Western and Eastern Roman empires, this may have laid the foundations for new conflicts and further instability.

The Hittite state, for all the ability of its rulers to wage wars in distant lands, and to engage in international diplomacy as a member of the club of great states, was indeed characterised by chronic instability. In the words of Glatz and Matthews:

The Hittite state is characterized throughout its existence by dramatic swings in its fortunes, with the total territory under its control fluctuating wildly in extent within sometimes brief time-spans. The empire appears to teeter on the brink of collapse at several points in its history before a total, irrevocable collapse at the end of the Late Bronze Age, around 1200–1180 BC.[55]

NEW PEOPLES?

After *c.* 1200 BC, in the Iron Age, a new culture appeared in Anatolia – that of the Phrygians. It has been widely thought that the Phrygians as a people migrated into Anatolia from Macedonia or Thrace around the end of the LBA.[56] Some modern scholars believe that this migration happened as a result of climate change and famines, which forced people south and east – possibly causing the collapse of the

Hittites, as well as generating the Sea Peoples phenomenon.[57] The evidence for the migration comes from the fifth century BC Greek historian Herodotus, and from other Greek sources:

This people [the Phrygians], according to the Macedonian account, were known as Briges during the period when they were Europeans and lived in Macedonia, and changed their name at the same time as, by migrating to Asia, they changed their country.[58]

Lynn Roller notes that the Greek sources disagree on the date of this migration, with Homer mentioning the Phrygians as allies of the Trojans in the Trojan War and Xanthos of Lydia putting their migration into Anatolia after the Trojan War.[59] In addition to the mythic tradition, linguistic evidence is also put forward to support a migration from the Macedonia area – the Indo-European Phrygian language is more similar to Greek than to the Anatolian family of Indo-European languages, which includes Hittite and Luwian; furthermore, it does not occur in inscriptions before the Iron Age.[60] Roller also cites evidence that, at Gordion, significantly different handmade pottery appears in the EIA, after the LBA levels, which is similar to Thracian handmade pottery.[61]

Examining Gordion in central Anatolia, one of the best known Phrygian sites, one that had continuity of occupation through the LBA/EIA boundary, Mary Voigt emphasises that 'there are changes in virtually every aspect of material culture between these periods from form and construction of houses to the way that people dug their storage pits and made their pots'.[62] In her view the LBA Hittite-related population moved out and a new population – of immigrants from Thrace – moved in. The move may have been peaceful. New research since 2000 at Hattusa has also revealed continuity of occupation, rather than a gap between LBA and EIA; the occupation was on a massively reduced scale, however.[63] In the EIA there was initially some continuity in pottery forms, though this soon changed.

Did a Phrygian migration cause the collapse of the Hittites? First we must consider that the received wisdom on the origin of the Phrygians is not necessarily correct. The Homeric evidence is unreliable as to LBA or EIA political geography – what it contains is likely to have been tainted with retelling over time, the performing poet making the story relevant for each generation/audience by mentioning current peoples and powers. Furthermore, Homer and Xanthos disagree on dates, which is not surprising; but which do we choose to believe and why? The value of Xanthos and Herodotus as sources on Phrygian origins, on events that supposedly took place more than five centuries earlier, is anyway negligible – their 'evidence' can fairly be discounted as not straightforward historical memory. The linguistic evidence does not rule out Phrygian being spoken in the LBA (Lydian, which was of the Anatolian Indo-European family, was first written only in the fifth century BC, though it is widely thought to descend from LBA 'Lydian' within Anatolia), and that might explain its later wide dispersal in Anatolia.

With the very early period of the EIA there is really very little evidence to go on. Kealhofer and colleagues note that in central Anatolia there are only three sites that have revealed architectural remains, mostly domestic.[64] And for the POTTERY, even Voigt suggests that the similarities with Thracian ceramics are 'admittedly vague'.[65] She also suggests that the 'new people' arrived at Gordion 'near the beginning of the second millennium BCE', which is long after the Hittite collapse. Antonio Sagona and Paul Zimansky state that 'the linguistic evidence is not incompatible with a European origin, although it does not prove it either'.[66] They also note that the migration or European origin 'cannot be demonstrated archaeologically'. Genz argues that the changes we see result from internal breakdown rather than population movements.[67]

So while we may be seeing new cultures appear in Anatolia in the EIA, it is not certain that this was the result of migrations, peaceful or otherwise. It seems highly improbable that the Phrygians had anything to do with the Hittite collapse.

THE HITTITE LEGACY

It is quite possible that what destroyed the Hittite Empire was a combination of food shortages, warfare, internal faction, and invasion or raiding by the Kaska. We do not know what happened to Suppiluliuma II, but it is quite possible he was eventually defeated in war or that he fled into exile. Hattusa may have already been abandoned by the time it was destroyed by fire, and it is possible that

Suppiluliuma ruled from elsewhere – as Trevor Bryce has said, there may be an archive as yet undiscovered.[68]

But just as Romans and Roman culture outlived the fall of the western empire, locally and in the continuing Eastern Roman Empire, so the Hittites and their culture outlived the fall of Hattusa and their Anatolian empire, and their centre shifted permanently south and east, especially to northern Syria. The kingdom of Tarhuntassa, that had been part of the Hittite Empire in the south, may well have survived past *c.* 1200 BC.[69] The so-called Neo-Hittite kingdoms of the EIA are those that remained familiar to the western world through the Old Testament.[70] Members of the royal family, that sprawling and divided gang descended from successive generations of Hittite kings, also survived. At Carchemish a Hittite royal had been in charge since the fourteenth century BC, and 'Great Kings' continued to rule there (one was called Tudhaliya).[71] 'In the key centres of Hittite power, such as Karkamish, Hittite imperial control appears to have survived in the form of diminished 'rump' states ruled by dynastic lines with direct ancestral links with the royal family in Hattusa'.[72]

Carchemish had been governed by a viceroy during the Hittite Empire. The last viceroy, Talmi-Teshub, was the son of Ini-Teshub, a cousin of Tudhaliya IV; he was the great-great-grandson of Suppiluliuma I.[73] His son, Kuzi-Teshub, inherited the throne of Carchemish and was styled 'Great King'. His descendants ruled a kingdom called Melid. Bryce suggests that Carchemish might have been a place of refuge for displaced people, elites especially, from Hattusa and the old Hittite lands: thus 'the establishment of a Hittite viceregal seat there with its accompanying social and administrative infrastructure must have created an environment not unlike that of the palace society at Hattusa'.[74] However, after attempts to consolidate its power – resettling cities and building roads – the kingdom of Carchemish fragmented over time into smaller units.[75]

At Tell Tayinat, Timothy Harrison has charted the rise of a Neo-Hittite kingdom in the EIA.[76] The city had Hittite style buildings and Luwian hieroglyphic inscriptions (the Neo-Hittite rulers used a hieroglyphic script that had been used in late Hittite times rather than cuneiform). Some of its kings bore the same names as the earlier Hittite Great Kings; in the ninth century BC there was a Lubarna and a Suppiluliuma.[77] Other ruling families of

Neo-Hittite states sought to demonstrate a link with the past too. In eastern Anatolia, the kingdom of Kummuh, there were kings called Hattusili, Suppiluliuma, and Muwatalli.[78] Nearby at Gurgum there were three kings called Muwatalli.[79] Bryce suggests that the Gurgum dynasty and state also may have been founded by a branch of the old Hittite royal family.[80] Several other Neo-Hittite kings styled themselves 'Great King'.[81]

The Hittite kingdom of Anatolia was gone, but it and its rulers were not forgotten. 'The imperial symbols of Hittite prestige and wealth were revived even though effective Hittite power had been destroyed, and a Hittite legacy was created anew in the Iron Age'.[82]

WHAT HAPPENED IN THE REST OF ANATOLIA?

The Hittites and their Kaska neighbours were not the only peoples in Anatolia in the LBA; western Anatolia was home to other kingdoms in the land of Arzawa.[83] Arzawa was made up of five kingdoms.[84] The most important is referred to as Arzawa Proper, which had its capital at Apasa (near Ephesus in southwestern Turkey). One Arzawan king, Tarhundaradu, was even courted as an ally by the Egyptian pharaoh Amenhotep III.[85] There were also Mira, Seha River Land, Wilusa, and Hapalla, along the Aegean coast.[86] The kingdoms sometimes acted in concert, forming federations with each other and with others, often to fight their powerful eastern neighbours, the Hittites.[87]

First mentioned by the Hittites in the seventeenth century BC, the Hittites raided Arzawa, who then, along with many others, rose up against them. Arzawa was apparently conquered by Tudhaliya I/II around 1400 BC, but fighting continued for decades; then, around 1400–1350 BC, in the reign of Tudhaliya III, the Arzawans invaded and occupied the Hittite Lower Land up to the Hittite homeland border. At the same time, the Hittites were beset by other invading forces. It is at this point that Amenhotep III made his overtures to the Arzawan king Tarhundaradu. Although they were eventually driven out, the Arzawans continued to make trouble for the Hittites, even destroying one of their expeditionary forces. But with a concerted effort, the Hittites, under Mursili II, destroyed the kingdom of

Arzawa Proper and transported, so he claimed, 65,000 of its population to the Hittite homeland. The Arzawan king Uhhaziti fled overseas. After the destruction of Arzawa Proper, the four other Arzawan kingdoms continued to exist, though they became Hittite vassal states, and treaties were made between their rulers and Mursili and his son Muwattalli II.[88]

Additionally, in western Anatolia there were two polities independent of the Hittites – Masa and Karkisa.[89] Both of these were governed by councils of community elders and were occasionally in conflict with the Hittites. Masa was apparently conquered by the last Hittite king, Suppiluliuma II, at the end of the thirteenth century BC, but it must soon have regained its independence after the Hittite collapse.

Another people present in southwestern Anatolia in the LBA were the Lukka. The Lukka, like the Kaska, do not seem to have formed a state, but they may have come together in occasional confederations – they also raided (by sea) and fought with and alongside others. Because there was no Lukka state, they proved hard for the Hittites to deal with. They are mysterious in the sense that we know from historical sources that they existed, but as yet they are archaeologically invisible (again much like the Kaska).[90] The earliest known settlements in Lycia (as it became known to the Classical Greeks), what had been the Lukka Lands, are from the eighth century BC, although there may now be some evidence of LBA settlement at Patara.[91] So we know that the Lukka continued to inhabit the regions associated with them in the LBA into later times, eventually becoming the Lycians of Lycia in Archaic and Classical times. Their language was related to LBA Luwian and their culture retained elements from the LBA, for example, in the names of a number of the gods they worshipped.[92]

The period of transition from LBA to EIA is not well known archaeologically. But we should neither imagine that Anatolia or northern Syria were devoid of people nor that there was a complete break with the past, whatever the cultural developments and differences of later times (the rise of the Phrygian and Lydian states). The stories of the Kaska and the Lukka show continuity – that is, the non-state areas may have fared well enough (as in Mycenaean Greece). But the rise of the Neo-Hittite kingdoms demonstrates the importance of the grand imperial past for new regimes.

CYPRUS

The Medinet Habu text claims that the Sea Peoples destroyed Alashiya, Cyprus. Several important sites on Cyprus were indeed destroyed or abandoned around 1200 BC, during the LC II/III transition: Enkomi, Kition, Maa-Palaeokastro, and others; some inland centres were also abandoned.[93] Were these destructions caused by the Hittites or the Sea Peoples? As we have seen, Suppiluliuma II fought people from Alashiya. It is not quite certain whether he fought non-Alashiyan enemies on and off Alashiya or whether this refers to a follow-up conquest of Cyprus (though there is, as yet, no archaeological evidence for a Hittite occupation). New elements of material culture and practices that appeared in LC IIIA have been associated with the Sea Peoples and with people from the Aegean, and a degree of mobility between Greece and Cyprus must have existed. Some see this new cultural expression as defining newly formed pirate bands that appeared in the wake of the regional collapse.[94]

However, there was a great deal of continuity on top of the destructions and the new features that appear. Louise Steel also notes that 'overall … there was no substantial change in the pattern of settlement. For the most part the LC IIIA inhabitants rebuilt the towns of LC IIC and continued to bury their dead in the same locales …'.[95] She places the major cultural transition on Cyprus later on, in the twelfth and eleventh centuries. Indeed, rather than a period of collapse and decline, the LC IIIA period is noted as 'the culmination of urbanisation on Cyprus and a period of great economic and cultural prosperity'.[96] Cities such as Enkomi, Kition, Palaepaphos, and Hala Sultan Tekke were thriving, with grand construction projects being undertaken, and they were still internationally connected – some of the building techniques may have been brought by specialists from Greece or even Anatolia. Thus Cyprus seems to have weathered whatever fortune threw at it at the end of the thirteenth century in the years around *c.* 1200 BC.

Some see twelfth century Cyprus as a regional cultural and economic powerhouse, influencing the eastern Mediterranean areas of Cilicia, and the northern and southern Levant, which to some extent shared in a new package of material culture once thought to represent émigré Mycenaeans.[97] This is more plausible than mass migrations from Mycenaean Greece.

A SOCIAL REVOLUTION?

A final explanation of collapse, and perhaps more of why some states were not reconstructed, should be mentioned, not least because it reveals something about some scholars' notions about the character of the states of the eastern Mediterranean in the LBA. This is the idea of a social revolution of some kind. Marc Van De Mieroop in his study of the region in the thirteenth century BC highlights the vast differences between the wealthy elites and everyone else.[98] For him, the palaces and their ruling elites were a burden on the general population, monopolising aspects of production and redistribution, mobilising labour for the army and for 'public' projects, and separating themselves physically and socially from the general population. He notes especially at Ugarit that a relatively small population of farmers would have supported the 'lavish circumstances' of the urban elite. For some, the pressure and burden was so great it caused them to up sticks and flee. One treaty between a Hittite king and the local ruler from the fifteenth century BC demonstrates this – Van De Mieroop quotes it thus:

> If the people of a settlement of the Great King with its women, its goods, and its large and small cattle gets up and goes into the land of Kizzuwatna, Paddatissu will seize them and return them to the Great King. And if the people of a settlement of the Paddatissu with its women, its goods, and its large and small cattle gets up and goes into the land of Hatti, [the Great King] will seize them and return them to Paddatissu.

The general population could (try to) vote with their feet, but international treaties were set up to prevent this. Is pent-up dissatisfaction amongst the people the reason why Ugarit was never rebuilt? Could the selective destructions at Hattusa represent attack by a disaffected population?

This explanation may be part of the story. Certainly some of the palace states may have been burdensome on their population and this may well have stored up resentment (there are arguments for this in the Mycenaean world too). Revolts could have happened when the elite's attention was engaged elsewhere or when natural disaster struck.

FINAL THOUGHTS

Are we any closer to understanding the Hittite collapse and what happened in the eastern Mediterranean more widely? I think we have a fair indication that a number of trends and events came to a head in the reign of Suppiluliuma II (although the sense of impending crisis may come from modern hindsight) – possible grain shortages, rebellions and wars, conflict with the Kaska, disgruntlement of the population at large, and factions in the royal family and possibly amongst the elite. The extent of the military action alone may well have been enough to destabilise the state, and it could well have used up too many people and created conditions in which it was hard to practise agriculture. And what happened to Suppiluliuma himself? Was he killed in action, did he flee – was there a loss of leadership that meant things fell apart?

The role of the Sea Peoples in the Hittite collapse (and indeed in the history of this period in the eastern Mediterranean generally) is far from clear, and on the face of it, it seems unlikely that sea raiders could have destroyed Hattusa and the empire, although they could have been responsible for the destruction of Ugarit. The destructions on Cyprus, whether caused by Sea Peoples, pirates, or the Hittites, were soon overcome and a period of prosperity followed – the events and circumstances of the period resulted in different outcomes in different places. It is also possible that sea raiders could have disrupted shipping and the grain supply. We are on surer ground with the Kaska tribes to the north, who we know were a constant thorn in the side of the Hittite kings and their state. Plagues, famines, the revolt of vassals, problems with the succession, are all recorded in the Hittite texts, and give us a picture of how difficult it was to maintain a functioning empire. We might bear these factors in mind when looking at other collapses, perhaps especially imperial ones. But the legacy of the Hittites lived on, as did descendants of the Hittite royal family, some ruling the Neo-Hittite kingdoms of eastern Anatolia and the northern Levant. The names of the Hittite Great Kings continued to have meaning through later times.

ECHOES OF THE PAST

The Hittites are known to many from their appearance in the Old Testament of the Bible; this is where their modern name comes from – they referred to themselves as people of the Land of Hatti. The Bible places them as a tribe of Canaan, rather than an Anatolian people, and this is due to the survival of Hittite, or Neo-Hittite, kingdoms in northern Syria and Canaan. But this is not the only echo of the Bronze Age Hittites, their kingdom, and empire. Much later, Greek writers such as Alcaeus and Herodotus recorded the name of Myrsilos as the Greek name for Candaules, king of Sardis in western Anatolia. Yet another Myrsilos was the tyrant of the Greek island state of Lesbos in the sixth century BC.[99] This is interesting because Lesbos (Lazpa) had probably been part of one of the Arzawa kingdoms rather than being controlled by the Hittites.

Myrsilos, or Mursilis, was the name of several Hittite kings. Mursilis II took a particular interest in western Anatolia during his reign, and it seems that he even gave his name to several locations there. The name seems to have been preserved through the end of the LBA and into historical times, even when there was little or no accurate memory of the Anatolian Hittite kingdom. Presumably the name was initially retained and reused by rulers seeking to link themselves with a Hittite past and a former Great King – this is particularly interesting given its survival in areas that had not been strictly Hittite. There are other cases where Neo-Hittite rulers echoed the past by reusing the names of Great Kings – at Commagene there was a Suppiluliumas and a Hattusilis, and in Konya, central Anatolia, there was another Mursilis. The Greek Myrsilos of Lesbos, living more than five centuries after the Hittite king of the same name, may have been descended from the island's non-Greek population, though we can also detect here the mixing of cultures and peoples.[100]

8

The Fall of the Western Roman Empire

As is well known, historians are not in agreement on the manner in which the transformation took place: some have taken the revisionism so far that they question the very fall of Rome, while at the opposite extreme, others have theorized a radical break between the period of the Roman Empire and the history of the modern west. In reality, both positions constitute two sides of the same coin: both those who believe in continuity and those who believe in discontinuity use the sources in an impressionistic manner with the intent of demonstrating their own theories.

Giusto Traina[1]

INTRODUCTION

Historian Andre Demandt has compiled a list of some 210 suggested reasons for the fall of the Western Roman Empire (WRE), which came into existence under Octavian Caesar, the emperor Augustus, in the late first century BC (Figure 8.1).[2] These range through both external explanations, such as climate change, earthquakes, and invasions, and internal explanations like celibacy, corruption, and civil war; and economic reasons, such as the reduction in tax flowing into imperial coffers, and the flow of wealth into the hands of the super elite. The incursions of barbarians into the empire and religious (and social) change from paganism to Christianity have been key themes in explaining the fall of the WRE since Edward Gibbon's *Decline and Fall* appeared in the late eighteenth century. Scholars still

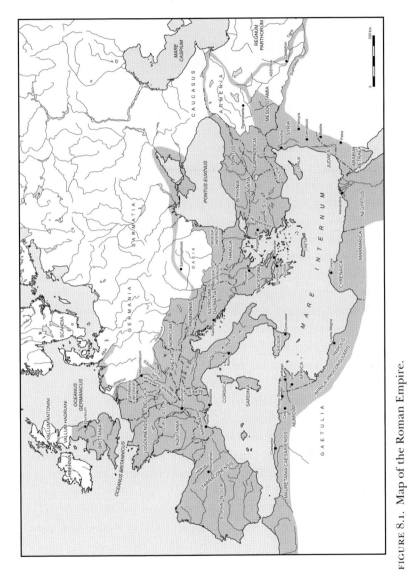

FIGURE 8.1. Map of the Roman Empire.

Source: From Snodgrass, A. (2014). 'The classical world.' In Renfrew, C. and Bahn, P. (eds.). *Cambridge World Prehistory. Volume III.* Cambridge: Cambridge University Press, 1971 (Map 3.28.5).

disagree on causes, and this is in part because people conceptualise what happened in very different ways. In a 2004 episode of BBC
Radio 4's *In Our Time* on the collapse of the WRE, the three Roman
scholars each had a different vision of what happened and different
ways of explaining the changes.[3]

One put forward the idea that nothing lasts forever, that collapse
itself is unsurprising, a view that Gibbon also had:

> The story of its ruin is simple and obvious; and instead of inquiring *why*
> the Roman empire was destroyed, we should rather be surprised that it had
> subsisted so long.[4]

Even if it is unsurprising, collapse must still have direct causes – things
happened. Another saw the barbarian invasions of the fifth century
AD as a primary cause of collapse; the barbarians literally carved up
the western half of the empire for themselves. Apart from physically
reducing the area of the WRE, this also reduced its tax revenues, lim-
iting its capacity for action – a vicious circle. 'Barbarisation' also got
a mention – in this view the empire was changed for the worse by the
barbarians who had come to occupy it prior to its collapse. It has also
been used to explain the poor performance of later Roman armies,
diluted by barbarian recruits, which were then unable to cope with
the invasions of yet more barbarians. And then there was the idea
that Christianisation and the growth of the church caused decline
and contributed to eventual collapse. The new religious culture
diverted manpower from the armies and changed people's outlook
from the worldly to the spiritual; classical aesthetics and culture were
given up and change was inevitable.

But of course the Christian Roman Empire did survive in the east.
Neither a transformation to Christianity nor an influx of barbarians
brought about the eastern Roman collapse. The Roman Empire as
such did not really fall until AD 1453, when Constantinople was conquered by the Ottoman Turks; it endured for more than 1,500 years
and was eventually ended by direct military conflict, which had also
been responsible for its reduction in size, and therefore also its power,
over the many years of its existence (Table 8.1).

It is impossible here to describe and evaluate each of the 210
reasons listed by Demandt, and others have already provided useful discussions.[5] Instead, we shall examine some of the themes and

TABLE 8.1 *Some key dates for the Roman Empire*

Event/person	Date
Augustus – first emperor	31 BC – AD 14
Year of four emperors	AD 69
The Antonines (inc. Trajan, Hadrian, Marcus	AD 96–192
Aurelius)	AD 167+
Plague	AD 167+
Germanic invasions and wars	
Period of crisis – many emperors, short reigns	AD 235–285
Diocletian and the Tetrarchy (four-emperor system)	AD 284–305+
Constantine	AD 307–337
Julian, the last pagan emperor	AD 360–363
Goths seek sanctuary in the empire	AD 376
Gothic wars	AD 378–382
Theodosius I, last emperor of a unified empire	AD 379–395
Honorius (western emperor)	AD 395–423
Germanic invasions	AD 406/407
Sack of Rome	AD 410
Visigoth capital at Tolosa	AD 418
The Vandals take Carthage	AD 439
Romulus Augustus	AD 475–476
Justinian (eastern emperor; reconquest of some western territories)	AD 527–565
Capture of Constantinople and end of eastern Roman (Byzantine) Empire	AD 1453

explanations given. What we can note first off is that in this instance of collapse, unlike many others, a degree of narrative is possible, owing to the textual sources, including histories, that we have. First, since they play such a large part in the WRE collapse, we should look at the role of 'barbarians' at the end of empire.

THE BARBARIANS COME TO ROME

The story of Rome and 'the barbarians' (a shorthand for many different groups of Germanic peoples who lived to the north of the Roman borders) is usually characterised by violence and animosity. A recurring theme on Roman military gravestones and on legionary distance slabs is the image of a Roman soldier smiting a bearded barbarian – Roman identity for some was created in contrast to the stereotypical barbarian[6]. But the relationship was a long and complex one that began long before Rome's fall. There is no space to tell that history here; instead we shall much more briefly look at the events of the late fourth century AD onwards.

In AD 376 a group of Goths, the Tervingi, sought and were granted sanctuary in the Roman Empire. They were fleeing from their lands northeast of the Danube because of the incursions of the Huns, who were harassing them from the east. The late Roman historian Ammianus Marcellinus tells the story and gives this description of the Huns:

a hitherto unknown race of men [who] had appeared from some remote corner of the earth, uprooting and destroying everything in its path like a whirlwind descending from high mountains.[7]

Rome had only recently been at war with the Goths, and the outcome had been indecisive – certainly there was no great Roman victory, and the memory of this must have been very fresh in the minds of all concerned. The number of Goths allowed in was perhaps fifteen to twenty thousand (although these figures could be too high), consisting of warriors and their families; although they were supposed to be disarmed, this probably was not effectively carried out.[8] Why would a Roman emperor allow a large enemy force a free pass into the empire?

The policy of resettling barbarians in different ways within the borders was not new.[9] The empire could at once offset the danger caused by potentially 'rogue' groups within its borders and benefit from them populating and farming underpopulated areas, paying tax, and serving in the Roman armies. For the emperor Valens, who agreed to allow the Tervingi entry, the idea of turning a possible threat to his advantage probably seemed sensible. Unfortunately for Valens, the job of resettlement was completely botched by the two commanders put in charge, Lupicinus and Maximus – Ammianus states that 'their sinister greed was the source of all our troubles'.[10] He recounts that the two commanders failed to provide the promised supplies to the refugees and that instead the starving Tervingi were coerced into giving up hostages in exchange for dogs to eat. At the same time, while the Roman army was dealing with the Tervingi, another Gothic group, the Greuthungi, snuck across the river into Roman territory.

As a result of their mistreatment, the Goths joined forces and rose up and defeated Lupicinus' forces; they then went on to plunder the Balkans.[11] It took some time for the empire to roll a response into action; Valens eventually brought an army from Persia back west, where it was defeated at the battle of Adrianople in AD 378. He had decided not to wait for his nephew Gratian, with his army, to come east. Valens was killed and his eastern army slaughtered. But over the next few years the Goths were ground down by Gratian (those that were already inside the empire were massacred) and the newly appointed Theodosius; it seems that some kind of treaty was made in AD 382 in which the Goths possibly surrendered.[12] After that, the Goths were allowed to settle, to farm, and again to join the army, possibly in Gothic units.[13] The whole incident, so damaging in human and economic terms, and no doubt traumatic for many, could have been avoided if the empire had been able to manage its policy of Gothic resettlement effectively.

What happened clearly demonstrates that individual decisions and actions can and do shape wider and sometimes very profound events – in many cases of collapse, especially those known primarily through archaeology, these historical particularities are lost to us. It also shows that empires or states as actors are fallible in executing policies (even good ones), can be very slow to respond to events, and may not always respond in the 'best' way.

Forty years after the Gothic settlement, in the winter of AD 406 or 407, the Roman border was again breached by barbarian groups, but this time without the permission of the emperor; these people also sought to settle within the empire.[14] What caused the migrations is unclear; northern Gaul and Britain could already have been militarily and structurally weak, so that people saw and took opportunities to settle. There is a tradition that saw the emperor Maximus, a 'usurper', as the last true western emperor in Gaul and Britain; he was killed by Theodosius in AD 388.[15] The presence of a usurper suggests a positive local response to crisis as much as a man with personal ambition, and several others were to rise to power in the early AD 400s.

At any rate, the empire was unable to prevent the various sovereign rogue groups of Vandals, Alans, and Suebi from dismembering the western empire and annexing parts of it for themselves.[16] By mid-century there were new and independent kingdoms in what had formerly been Roman territory. The Vandals, for example, eventually took the whole of Roman North Africa and turned it into a Vandal kingdom, though their leaders and elite took on the trappings of a Roman lifestyle. In AD 410 Rome itself was sacked by Alaric and the Goths – the authorities had still not learned to deal more effectively with the 'barbarians' – this fate was destined to be repeated forty-five years later when the city was sacked by the Vandals.[17] Ironically, Attila's Hunnic Empire that had caused so much trouble collapsed after his death – Huns were then permitted to settle within the Eastern Empire.[18]

Our very quick narrative would seem to show clearly that the barbarians played a decisive role in the fall of the Western Empire – but even this conclusion forces us to think whether the collapse was inevitable. Could the Romans have halted the fragmentation of the west by adopting different policies? Could their military have been deployed to better effect? Could better crisis management (as in choice of commanders, etc.) have resulted in different outcomes such as a peaceful and successful (to both parties) Gothic settlement that would have resulted in a stronger and more unified empire and military? In turn, this forces us to think not only of external pressures but also of internal structural issues, of the choices of individuals, and of historical chance and coincidence.

But next, let us look at how some of our characterisations of the end of empire have developed up to the present – and decide whether we should think of what happened as decline, collapse, transformation, or all three. We shall start by looking at the influence of Edward Gibbon's now classic model of decline and fall.

DECLINE OR TRANSFORMATION?

Ever since Gibbon, it has been commonplace to identify a Roman decline and fall, epitomised in the title of his *Decline and Fall of the Roman Empire*; the collapse followed by a grim dark age. The cultural influence of his history, penned in the late eighteenth century and published in six volumes between 1776–1788, and immediately a bestseller, cannot be underestimated: 'it was very influential in communicating images of empire and decline to contemporaries' and has provided an enduring image of change and collapse beyond just the fall of Rome.[19] In the 1960s, the work even inspired an epic Hollywood film directed by Anthony Mann: *The Fall of the Roman Empire.*

Many historians, though, are unhappy with the terms 'decline', or 'decay' because they are quite vague in meaning. Both decline and decay suggest 'worsening', say, of architecture, art, literature, and so on, or a reduction in the amount of something produced, but this is a subjective value judgement based on the view from hindsight and on the comparison of a less-favoured period with another more favoured one (hence we have in the past seen so-called 'dark ages' as less valuable, less worthy of attention than other periods). They can also mean anything from a reduction of power or effectiveness, say in the military sphere, to territorial fragmentation and loss over time.

The medieval poet Petrarch and historian Flavio Biondo saw a golden age of antiquity, followed by a dark age, and then their own renaissance of classical culture – modern historian Theodor Mommsen noted that Petrarch thought of the post-Roman period as dark 'because it was worthless not because it was little known'.[20] A rhetoric of decline is a persistent feature of western culture, from Homer to the present; it continues to exist alongside narratives of progress – it being oddly possible to hold the two perspectives simultaneously.[21]

In writing about Rome, Gibbon too identified a golden age of peace and plenty when the Roman world fell under the governorship of a few beneficent emperors – Nerva, Trajan, Hadrian, Antoninus Pius, and Marcus Aurelius (during AD 96–180) (Figure 8.2).[22] In formulating this view, Gibbon owed something to a panegyric of Aelius Aristides, a Graeco-Roman aristocrat who delivered a speech in praise of Rome to the emperor Antoninus Pius. The speech extolled the virtues of empire in the mid-second century AD.[23] But identifying a golden age of some kind inevitably means that other periods will be regarded as lesser – it encourages us to think of decline and decay. We are likely to make such judgements based on our own tastes, preferences, and interests.

But, as Bennett Bronson observes, 'the symptoms of decline are rarely easy to recognize, in spite of the folklore that tells us that things get worse as the end approaches'.[24] As he rightly suggests, if

FIGURE 8.2. Five 'good' emperors of the golden age: Nerva, Trajan, Hadrian, Antoninus Pius, and Marcus Aurelius, followed by the 'bad' emperor Commodus. *Source*: Courtesy of David Potter.

we pick a random year in the history of a state, we will probably find many of the features commonly associated with decline – civil disorder, corruption, faction, inefficient government; these, though, are also to be found in states increasing in power and not about to collapse. Corruption, the exchange of favours 'against the rules', can sometimes be regarded as a sign of stability, a successful system in itself embedded within a wider system.[25]

Gibbon was also interested in and influenced by the physical remains of the Roman Empire. His inspiration was, after all, the ruins of the city of Rome itself, and Roman ruins were to be found all over Europe, of interest to the educated class. In Gibbon's day these were attracting increasing interest as objects of antiquarian and eventually archaeological investigation; investigations at Pompeii had begun earlier in the century. Artists like Piranesi produced and published images of Rome's ruined glory (Figure 8.3). For Gibbon, buildings, monuments, and remains were an index of moral and physical decline from the ideal. Roman ruins and archaeological remains sharpened the view of a rupture between the days of empire and the present.

Gibbon's work influenced the work of pioneering British archaeologist Francis Haverfield.[26] Haverfield published his influential *The*

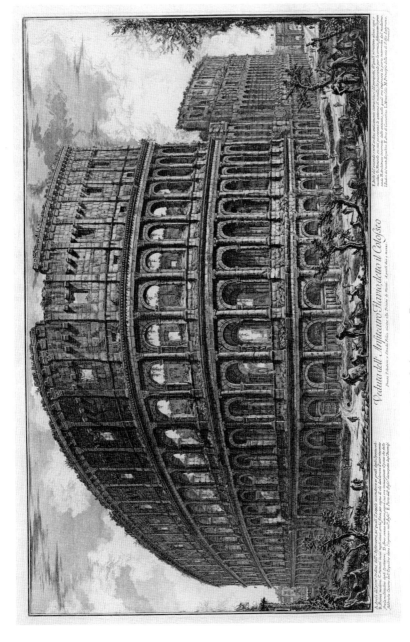

Veduta dell' Anfiteatro Flavio, detto il Colosseo

FIGURE 8.3. Piranesi's AD 1757 etching of the Colosseum, Rome.

191

Romanization of Roman Britain in 1906. This was the first modern
account of Roman Britain and made use of both archaeological and
epigraphic data. For Haverfield 'the most potent single factor in the
Romanization was the town'.[27] Adopting Gibbon's ideas, he saw the
growth of towns and cities and their amenities as part of the civilising
of the Britons and others. And, just as urbanisation could be equated
with civilisation, so could de-urbanisation, or the physical decaying
of urban areas, be equated with its loss.

This idea of decline reflects an inherently appealing conception of states and empires as living entities – a basically biological
metaphor; as Philip Parker recently stated, 'In the end ... all the
countless pages of speculation about why the border collapsed, particularly in the west, amount to one simple fact: the empire grew
old'.[28] Even Adrian Goldsworthy resorted in the end of his 2009
book on the fall of Rome to metaphor – the empire losing strength
like the body of an aging athlete.[29] But empires and states are not
biological organisms.

Nowadays, rather than decline, the later history of the Roman
Empire is often characterised as an age of transformation (perhaps
'Transformation'). The period of third and fourth centuries AD and
after is now referred to as 'Late Antiquity', and many scholars, taking a lead from Peter Brown, who published the seminal *The World
of Late Antiquity* in 1971, are keen to show it as a positive, rich, and
active period in its own right, rather than a time of collapse, poverty,
and weakness. This seems both better and more accurate than simply
seeing a 'decline', but it should not mask the fact that the WRE did
disappear as a political and social entity and that that was in and of
itself a significant change.

Brown's book spanned the period when the empire in the west
fell, but it largely ignored the fall itself. Instead it painted a well-
illustrated picture of a vibrant and rich cultural milieu that predated
the fall and lasted well beyond it. Brown's version was shaped by
his readings of earlier historians like Rostovtzeff, who in his *Social
and Economic History of the Roman Empire* (1926) presented numerous
forms of change as decline – barbarians reaching positions of power,
Christianity and a religious mentality promoting anti-intellectualism,
economic simplification causing urban decay and preventing cities

from generating the Hellenising or Romanising spirit of classical culture. With a palpable class bias, Rostovtzeff wrote in terms of barbarisation, 'a gradual absorption of the higher classes by the lower, accompanied by a gradual levelling down of standards'.[30] Brown was also influenced by the times – the post-war period, especially the 1960s, was a period of imperial decline for Britain (meaning specifically fragmentation, loss of territory, and a reduction in political and military 'clout') and other European colonial powers, yet it was clearly culturally vibrant, global, and interconnected, a time of change and transformation rather than mere decline.[31]

The school of Late Antiquity has taken up Brown's position, defining a new period that in the words of Glen Bowersock, Brown, and Oleg Grabar is 'a distinctive and quite decisive period that stands on its own,' stretching from the middle of the third to the end of the ninth century AD. No longer did Rome decline from a golden age, or fall, ushering in a dark age, and even the dismemberment of the Western Empire has come to be regarded by some as a largely peaceful process, a process of accommodation rather than violent invasion.

Such changes in scholarly views did not come from nothing. In fact, a work earlier than Brown's, *The Myth of Rome's Fall* (1960) by Richard Mansfield Haywood, reflected such changes already permeating scholarship, the author noting of the so-called decline of empire that 'little by little scholarly opinion has swung to the view that change is not necessarily decay. The changes that took place are better understood than they used to be, and are less apt to be regarded as signs that something was wrong'.[32] Haywood retained the narrative of invasions and of an imperial collapse in the west, but noted a great degree of continuity and heritage too, albeit in recognisably different circumstances. The seventh century, with the entry of the Slavs into the Balkans and the Islamic expansion, marked a more significant and irreversible change, he suggested. A collection of essays entitled *The Transformation of the Roman World* published in 1966 also promoted the new paradigm, and this has been followed more recently by a European Science Foundation project with the same title.[33] If Late Antiquity spanned this long period, when can we place the western Roman collapse?

DATING COLLAPSE – THE SACK OF ROME IN AD 410

Collapses tend to be seen as events, and are often reckoned to be rapid (measuring in decades, usually), if not always sudden; so can we say when the Roman west collapsed? A date commonly given is that of the sack of Rome by Alaric in AD 410. And if we follow Procopius, the sixth century eastern Roman historian who documented the wars of the emperor Justinian, we might indeed date the collapse of the west to the reign of Honorius (AD 395–423), and the initial loss of land to the northern peoples: 'Now while Honorius was holding the imperial power in the West, barbarians took possession of his land' (Figure 8.4).[34] But, despite the attack on the city, there was no overnight change, and what we see in the collapse of the West is a story of fragmenting power and the creation of new more localised powers and identities that built on Roman heritage; in Peter Heather's words, the 'destruction of central Romanness' and its replacement with 'local Romanness'.[35]

Power at the time clearly did not lie with Honorius, but rather with Stilicho, a military man of Vandal birth, who had been favoured by Theodosius I, whose niece he had married. Stilicho, who can fairly be described as a warlord, dominated the WRE in the last decade of the fourth century. He was not the first 'over-mighty general' – Merobaudes and Arbogast too had arguably been more powerful than the emperors they nominally served.[36] There is some similarity here with the situation in historical Japan, where emperors lost power to become only titular heads of state, secluded in Kyoto – real power came to be held by the shoguns.[37]

J. B. Bury, describing Stilicho's fall in rather partisan terms, laid much of the blame for collapse, somewhat unfairly, at his feet:

> For thirteen and a half years this half-Romanised German had been master of western Europe, and he had signally failed in the task of defending the inhabitants and the civilisation of the provinces against the greedy barbarians who infested its frontiers ... [he] cannot be absolved from responsibility for the misfortunes which befell the Roman state in his own lifetime and for the dismemberment of the western realm which soon followed his death.[38]

Stilicho, in a spectacular fall from grace, had been declared a public enemy in Constantinople and was beheaded in Ravenna in AD 408. Gaul again had its own emperor, another Constantine, fighting

FIGURE 8.4. The emperor Honorius.
Source: From Ludwig von Sybel, L. (1909). *Christliche Antike, vol. 2*. Marburg.

its battles against the barbarians. This was a time when 'the driving political force came not from the youthful rulers, but from the men who dominated their courts and controlled their armies'.[39]

The date of Rome's sack in AD 410 has such a cache – the first sack of the city in centuries – that when its 1600th anniversary was marked in 2010 it was compared with the 11 September terrorist attacks on New York's World Trade Centre; in Britain it was also remembered as the end of Roman Britain – 'Roman's go home'.[40] But AD 410, a real disaster and a psychological blow, was not the end, or even the beginning of the end – the sack was the result of events stretching back three decades, and there were still emperors in the west until AD 476.[41]

OTHER DATES FOR COLLAPSE

Deciding exactly what we mean by either the decline or the fall of Rome can change our dating of it, and historians offer various versions. This is a problem in understanding several other collapses too. In the history of early Chinese states, for example, we find a similar tension in descriptions. Feng Li, writing on the Western Zhou, suggests that the dynasty collapsed in 771 BC for two reasons, firstly because of the king's adoption of a military strategy which led directly to defeat, but also, 'at a fundamental level, the fall was the result of the long process of Zhou's gradual weakening' – there was both decline and defeat in this view.[42] At the same time, Edward Shaughnessy notes how normal 771 BC would have seemed, and presents the Western Zhou period as something other than just an 'unremitting series of crises'.[43] This parallels the situation in studies of the later Roman Empire, and the tension between those who take a 'decline and fall' or 'late Roman' approach and others who see a continuous world of Late Antiquity stretching from the second or third centuries AD to well beyond the fifth century.[44]

   In his recent book on Rome, David Potter suggests three ways that we can consider dating the fall of the empire.[45] We could think of it, firstly, as an empire that has shrunk from its maximum extent, achieved under Septimius Severus (AD 193–211); secondly, as no longer being the most powerful state in the Mediterranean; or thirdly, as no longer ruling Italy, the 'home ground' of the empire. These alternatives bring up dates either side of AD 410 and AD 476. But while western Europe in AD 400 and AD 500 looked very different, if we zoom in on any individual dates around this time, as Giusto Traiano observes in his exploration of the year AD 428, we also tend to find business as usual, people getting on in the prevailing circumstances.[46] The first category we shall deal with below, but first let us look at Rome as a Mediterranean and Italian power.

   Potter suggests that it was the loss of Syria and Alexandria in AD 636 and 642, under the emperors Heraclius and Constans II,

to Islamic armies that reduced the power of the remaining Eastern
Empire and rendered it a local power only; this is a reminder that the
empire did continue to exist without the western parts that modern
westerners regard as central to their idea of 'Rome'.[47] As for the loss
of Italy, this raises other problems, for the emperor Justinian's wars
of reconquest (AD 533–554) put an end to some of the barbarian
kingdoms founded inside the western regions in the fifth century; he
again extended imperial Roman rule through areas of former Roman
territory, including north Africa and Italy; parts of the Italian peninsula then remained attached to the Eastern Empire for a further 500
years (Figure 8.5).[48] Do we see this as the continued existence of the
empire in the west?

Reconquest and reincorporation was not necessarily a welcome
prospect, even for those who still called themselves Romans – being
part of the empire meant the resumption of heavy taxation to fuel it,
and many 'Romans' were loyal to their new non-Roman rulers rather
than the eastern invader Justinian. During his wars in Italy, the city of
Rome itself suffered much more than it had in AD 410, resulting in the
end of the ancient senate, the destruction of physical infrastructure
such as aqueducts, plague, and depopulation. As Walter Pohl explains:

The reintroduction of direct Byzantine rule and the arrival of tax officials
provoked such opposition that within a year or two Italy flared up in rebellion, and the new Gothic king Totila successfully recaptured most of the
peninsula … Procopius portrays the gradual collapse of the ancient landscape in the old heartland of empire. Destruction of the infrastructure, the
decimation of the population, hunger, and the plague affected region after
region …[49]

Just a few years after Justinian's death, most of Italy fell to invaders again, this time to the Lombards in AD 568 – Justinian himself
had encouraged them to enter the empire, where they could act as
a buffer for the east against the Franks. Self-interest could see eastern emperors manipulating politics in the west for their own ends.
Historians note that Justinian's Roman reconquest possibly did more
to ruin Italy than any barbarian actions.[50]

An alternative way to think about the end of empire, though again
one without a precise date, is to consider the end of that key state
institution – the Roman army in the west. The army seems to have

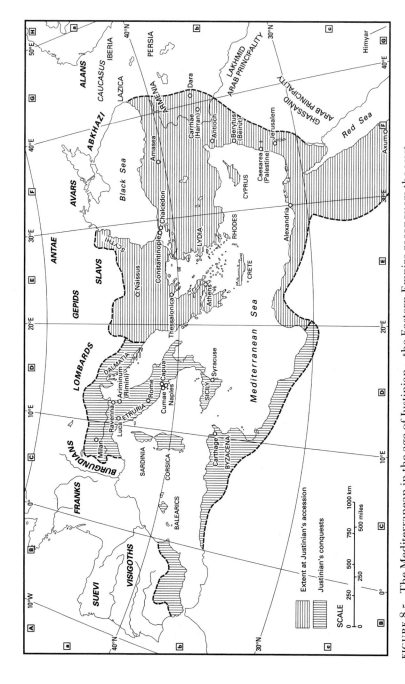

FIGURE 8.5. The Mediterranean in the age of Justinian – the Eastern Empire reconquers the west.
Source: Cameron, A. 'Justin I and Justinian.' In Cameron, A., Ward-Perkins, B., and Whitby, M. (eds.). *The Cambridge Ancient History. Volume XIV. Late Antiquity: Empire and Successors, AD 425–600.* Pp. 63–85, p. 68, Map 2.

fragmented from the late fourth century onward, along with the loss of the territory that ultimately paid for it, and in some places, surviving soldiers were left without an empire to serve – they turned either to local warlords or landlords – barbarian or otherwise, or became local powers themselves. Brown suggests a drop of some 50 per cent in western imperial tax revenues by AD 431, the government was particularly hard hit by the loss of Africa in AD 430.[51]

Eugippius' biography of St Severinus describes how soldiers were once stationed around the empire 'at public expense', and also how this custom came to an end in the fifth century.[52] He suggests that these forces were wiped out bit by bit, and describes how pay stopped coming to those who survived; we can easily imagine a chaotic and perhaps, depending on the locality, a sometimes banal scenario of the end of imperial armed might. Border soldiers seemingly survived in some places for some time – in Africa such hereditary guards may have survived the Vandals to become 'imperial' once more under Justinian.

Though Rome and the senate survived, by the end of the fifth century, there was neither army nor emperor, nor the infrastructure that went with them – not in what had been the Western Empire, at least; instead, there were a number of new kingdoms governed by people that had ultimately originated outside the empire.

THE LAST EMPEROR?

The emperor usually noted as the last one in the west, Romulus Augustus (often known as 'Augustulus'), was put on the throne by his father Orestes, the latest of the western warlords, and was soon after 'retired' by Odoacer. Odoacer, a barbarian whose career had been somewhat like Stilicho's, and whose armies were mixed forces of Romans and barbarians, worked in and outside the previously conventional structures of empire, and eventually became king in Italy.[53] In a recent biography of Romulus Augustus, this shadowy yet famous young emperor, Adrian Murdoch has argued for the importance of AD 476 as a point of no return, a tipping point after which things were, and were felt to be, different.[54] A contemporary writer in the Eastern Empire, Malchus, recorded Romulus' fate:

(Romulus) Augustus, the son of Orestes, hearing that Zeno once again held the imperial power in the East, having driven out Basiliscus, he forced the senate to send an embassy to Zeno saying that there was no need for their own emperor, and that one emperor would be enough for both regions. (They added that) they had chosen Odoacer as a suitable person to look after their affairs, as he had political and military experience, and asked Zeno to appoint him a patrician and grant him the government of Italy . . .[55]

Both AD 410 and AD 476, three or four lifetimes apart for the average Roman, are noted as turning points, even if they are widely recognised as manufactured by ancient and modern writers, they were of little importance in themselves.[56] The name of Romulus Augustulus, echoing both Romulus and Augustus, two founding figures in Roman history, has certainly added to the AD 476 effect – it is sometimes regarded as the 'official' end of the empire, purely for convenience of marking periods. In fact another man, Julius Nepos, was still the legitimate western ruler, still recognised by Zeno in the east and ruling in Dalmatia – the real 'last emperor', he died in AD 480, but his name has no poetic effect.

Romulus was a pretender and Odoacer, safe in the knowledge of Romulus' irrelevance and the irrelevance of the office of western emperor, put him into quiet retirement; and why should the emperor in the east have minded when neither half really required the other? Yet, after this date, the new powerful figures in the west, Odoacer in Italy, and later Clovis, king of the Franks in Gaul, still recognised the authority of the eastern emperor in some sense, though he lacked any direct control over them and no longer could harvest what wealth could be squeezed from them; contacts were maintained, east and west still shared a world and a religion, and 'a polite fiction' of imperial power or approval could still have value.[57]

LOOKING BACK FROM THE EAST

Procopius and others, writing in the surviving Eastern Empire in the late fifth and sixth centuries, clearly did recognise an end of sorts, an end that could clearly justify reconquest. Zosimus, a pagan historian in a Christian world, recognised 'the present destruction of the state', and traced its causes, Christianity and the barbarisation of the army, back to Constantine.[58] In Walter Goffart's view, Zosimus began the decline and fall narrative that is so well known from Edward Gibbon's work – his programmatic statement announcing: 'For just as Polybius narrated how the Romans acquired their sovereignty within a brief period of time, so I am going to tell how they lost it through their own blind folly within no long period of time'.[59] Jordanes too, an eastern Roman of Gothic descent, stated:

The western Empire of the Roman race, which Octavianus Augustus the first of the Augusti, began to govern in the seven hundred and ninth year from the founding of the City, perished with this Augustulus in the five hundred and twenty second year from the beginning of the rule of his predecessors and those before them, and from this time onward kings of the Goths held Rome and Italy.[60]

Saint Jerome, writing in Jerusalem, was contemporary with the sack of Rome in AD 410, and described it in horrific terms, but, as Stefan Rebenich has shown, Jerome's writing is rhetorical more than historical – 'he was not interested in any precise historical information'.[61] He wove together a narrative of recent events to present the idea of a unified and global thirty-year catastrophe. In this way, he sought to make sense of contemporary events for himself and his community of readers. Jerome's understanding and his characterisation of this troubled time was eschatological, concerned with 'last things', and was influenced by both his religious mentality and his classical education. His use of biblical and classical stories, which shape his narratives, is clear, as this extract from *Letter* 127 shows (the sources of his quotations have been added):

While these things were happening in Jebus [Jerusalem], a dreadful rumour came from the West. Rome had been besieged and its citizens had been forced to buy their lives with gold. Then, thus despoiled, they had been besieged again, so as to lose not their substance only but their lives. My voice sticks in my throat; and, as I dictate, sobs choke my utterance. The City which had taken the whole world was itself taken; nay more famine was beforehand with the sword and but few citizens were left to be made captives. In their frenzy, the starving people had recourse to hideous food; and tore each other limb from limb that they might have flesh to eat. Even the mother did not spare the babe at her breast. In the night was Moab taken, in the night did her wall fall down [Isaiah 15.1]. 'O God, the heathen have come into thine inheritance; they holy temple have they defiled; they have made Jerusalem an orchard [Psalms 79.1.70]. The dead bodies of thy servants have they given to be meat unto the fowls of the heaven, the flesh of thy saints unto the beasts of the earth. Their blood have they shed like water round about Jerusalem; and there was none to bury them [Psalms 79.1–3.].'

Who could describe the horror of that night, and all its carnage? What tears are equal to such suffering? An ancient city, for so many years a queen, now falls in ruin, while through its streets lie countless corpses, motionless and still ... death in ten thousand forms [Virgil *Aeneid* 2.361].[62]

POINT OR PROCESS?

In fact, and not really surprisingly, it is not possible to pin the fall of the Western Roman Empire down to a single moment in time, or to a single cause or event; it was a long and bumpy ride through a world of events, personalities, and processes, and at some point that western empire and its army were gone. In bare terms, the western empire, the territories controlled at least nominally by an emperor, and from which taxes and troops could be drawn, reduced massively from AD 376 to the 440s, when only Italy and part of southern Gaul remained really imperial. Contingent events, as Bury said, would seem to make this an unpredictable and not inevitable collapse that happened over something like a century in time.[63]

In more recent times, and perhaps a conceptually helpful parallel, is the collapse of the British Empire. Of course there was no invasion and settlement of Britain from outside, though there has been immigration from former colonies, but like Rome, the British Empire experienced piecemeal fragmentation over a similar span of time. It shrank in fits and starts from a territorial peak around 1920, losing India in 1947, many other colonies through the 1960s, and handing Hong Kong back to China in 1997. For many modern day British people, despite the fact that British imperial collapse happened recently, it is perhaps of little or no direct relevance or psychological or economic significance. Nevertheless, the map of the world and its powers changed dramatically; new countries and new political and social values and identities emerged, economic connections also changed. For some, Anglo-Indians, for example, the changed world rendered their identity anachronistic, yet still it was relevant to them.

RECENT VIEWS ON THE COLLAPSE

Until the beginning of the twenty-first century, the fall of Rome seemed to be receding into the background as Late Antiquity was revalued more positively. Decline and fall, and violent invasions and migrations were less relevant – the paradigm that no longer spoke to anyone.[64] But the notion that Bowersock mooted in the mid-1990s, that 'it is probably fair to say that no responsible historian of the ancient or medieval world would want to address or acknowledge the fall of Rome as either fact or paradigm', went too far, and since then yet more arguments have appeared, with scholars reasserting that there was both a real end and that it was accompanied by violence and uncertainty and followed by a less pleasant world.[65]

A number of British scholars in particular have followed more or less 'traditional' interpretations of the fall, based on the barbarian invasions. Peter Heather has presented his case that it was ultimately fairly sizeable Germanic invasions of the fifth century that drove imperial collapse. These movements were triggered by the Huns far outside the empire, but the problems facing the west were exacerbated by the sudden collapse of the Hunnic Empire, with which Rome had achieved a balance of power, even coming to rely on Hunnic soldiers in its own armies. In Heather's words: 'the Roman empire had sown the seeds of its own destruction, therefore, not because of internal weaknesses that had evolved over the centuries, nor because of new ones evolved, but as a consequence of its relationship with the Germanic world ... [which] had responded to its power in ways that the Romans could never have foreseen'.[66] The presence of empire changed the world around it unpredictably, external events and individual choices ended it in the west. But it was the collapse of the Hunnic Empire that Heather sees as the real cause.

Both Heather and Guy Halsall see collapse as something embedded in the relationships that existed within the empire, and would agree that 'the key factor in the break-up of the Empire was the exposure of a critical fault-line between the imperial government and the interests of the regional elites'.[67] Yet Halsall offers a very different theory to Heather's, albeit one which incorporates the same events: 'while Heather sees the appearance of the Huns as decisive in exposing this fault-line, the thesis proposed here is that the reasons for the Huns' profound effects on barbarian politics are themselves to be sought in the processes, originating *inside* the Empire, that uncovered the weaknesses of the ties binding the empire together'.[68] Migrations and the formation of new states in the west were made possible by western collapse, by changes in the nature of imperial rule around AD 400 – they were an effect of collapse, not its cause.[69]

These arguments oppose internal and external causes of imperial collapse in the west, a typical situation in any example of collapse. Even when external events are clearly apparent, the effect that they have is not certain but depends on the state of what is being affected – hence the appeal of decline, which can explain the collapse of something that once seemed strong. This is debatable in the case of the Roman Empire, even given that we have a lot more evidence, textual and archaeological, than in many other cases of collapse. The empire could have collapsed at numerous points; before it actually did so; it had fragmented numerous times, territorially and politically, had suffered the crisis of invasions in the third and fourth centuries, but people had pulled it through, with luck and chance, as well as policy and strategy. Barbarians had even settled 'unofficially' within its borders in the fourth century – encountered by Julian in Gaul – although they had not formed states they did stake a territorial claim to their new homes:

His [Julian's] first objective was the Franks, those specifically called the Salii; they had had the temerity in the past to settle themselves on Roman soil at Toxiandria. When he arrived at Tongres he was met by a deputation from this people ... They offered peace on the condition that they should be left undisturbed and unmolested in what they regarded as their own territory ...

A like fate befell the Chamavi, who had dared to behave in a similar way ... They prostrated themselves in Julian's presence and were granted peace and permission to return home in safety.[70]

Bryan Ward-Perkins also offers a strong defence of the traditional barbarian invasion and collapse scenario – rejecting the idea of transformation as unduly positive: 'the Germanic invaders of the western empire seized or extorted through the threat of force the vast majority of the territories in which they settled without any formal agreement on how to share resources with their new Roman subjects'.[71] He emphasises the unpleasantness of the fall of Rome, the fragmentation of empire, noting the anxiety that comes through in the sources, the constant threat of violence in the barbarian settlement carried out through force and extortion. In addition, he demonstrates that the archaeological evidence suggests 'a startling decline in western standards of living during the fifth to seventh centuries'.[72]

This 'disappearance of comfort' that Ward-Perkins identifies is apparent, with different patterns present across the region, in the loss of general literacy, the end of the production and circulation of mass produced pottery, flimsier and smaller buildings, even as high status constructions, reduction in the use of coined money, all of which seem to indicate the breakdown of a complex economy that had connected the west. Although others see in these changes a transformation in meaning and values – new high status buildings, for example, may have been different in construction and size, but they nevertheless retained their position as high status buildings – Ward-Perkins sees the change as a collapse to a level of economic complexity perhaps lower than in pre-Roman times; old systems that had been intensified during Roman times unravelled.[73] In his view there was a very real and, for many, a very unpleasant collapse.

For Ward-Perkins, a Late Antiquity that focuses on religious figures and the east misses the reality of what happened in the west. Interestingly, he associates this transformationist school primarily with American scholarship, with 'charismatic ascetics and intellectuals, in isolation or in small communities, finding their path to God in a highly individualistic … way', even with influence from 'new-age' spirituality.[74] C. R. Whittaker, on the other hand, argues well for distrusting a host of sources on 'the barbarian invasions', citing 'the perversions of modern historiography, the distortions of ancient historiography and the problems specific to individual authors'. This echoes the conclusions of A. H. M. Jones, who thought the later, weaker, empire faced more and possibly better organised barbarians.[75]

There are also environmental hypotheses. In a 2011 paper in *Science*, Ulf Buntgen and colleagues modeled the ancient European climate through the study of tree rings; they identified increased climate variability during AD 250–600, bracketed by warmer, wetter, and more prosperous conditions.[76] They associate this variability with population movements that brought about the end of empire. But this is a wide span of time and it is the case that Romans and barbarians had been in conflict long before AD 250 and the WRE survived until long after – why did it collapse when it did? An earlier climate change explanation was put forward almost a century ago, in 1917, by

Ellsworth Huntington, but he argued that climate change, detected in tree rings, had undermined the agricultural base of the empire.[77] He was writing in response to another position put forth by Vladimir Simkhovitch, who suggested that Roman agriculture declined because of the exhaustion of the soil.[78] But an environmental explanation of the collapse is completely insufficient to explain the complex inter-linked events and processed experienced by the Roman Empire from the late fourth century onwards. This should caution us against accepting simplistic environmental explanations in other contexts.

A TENDENCY TO DIVISION

The Roman Empire was big, and impossible for one man to govern, so power was always shared in one way or another in a vast pyramid with the emperor at the top. In the early days of empire, with the memory of the republican system still fresh, the emperor still relied on the senatorial aristocracy as well as on his own household. Over the course of empire the bureaucracy constantly increased in an effort to cope with its administration. But when the central insti-tutions of power failed to function to the satisfaction of interested parties, new leaders were sought. This could lead to armies and prov-inces creating their own emperors. Peter Brown notes the comments of a traveller from the eastern empire in the mid-fourth century who wrote of Gaul:

It is a very great province, and for that reason always needs an emperor pres-ent. It produces an emperor of its own.[79]

In the third century – and later the fourth and fifth – there were many emperors and pretenders, usually military men sponsored by their troops. The period is known as one of a crisis of empire – even sometimes called 'the third century collapse'.[80] It was quite possible that the empire could have collapsed and fragmented permanently much earlier than it actually did had it not been for the actions of emperors such as Aurelian.

In Gaul, a Gallic Empire was formed by Postumus in AD 260. In the east, Palmyra had grown its own empire within the Roman Empire, and it became independent under its queen, Zenobia. The 'real' Roman emperor Aurelian managed, in his short reign, to end (or postpone) this fragmentation. But in the 270s and after, two men, Firmus and Achilleus, proclaimed independence in Egypt. In the 280s and 290s Britain created its own emperors Carausius and Allectus. In the early fourth century, Domitius Alexander, the prefect of Africa, declared himself an independent ruler. There were plenty of others, such as the British Maximus, mentioned earlier.[81]

The empire was perennially prone to fragmentation and division – simply because no one could rule it alone – no emperor could be everywhere at once or respond to everything that was happening. Rome had started as a kingdom and been developed into a republic with a power-sharing nobility, only to fall back into individual rule – which was, over the long term, untenable in practice. There existed always an unhappy tension between the psychological draw of a unified empire, the different powers within the empire, and the need to deal with general and local problems, crises in succession, and external and internal conflict, as they occurred. Such problems have beset most kingdoms and empires, the Akkadian and Hittite, for example, and have been drivers of instability, change, adaptation, and collapse.

Brown explains that 'the Roman empire in the west had always been a federation of regions'.[82] After all, the empire was a mechanism welded together from small parts and peoples. In the fourth century, the necessity for the division of power was formalised by Diocletian, who created the tetrarchy.[83] Under this system, the empire was formally divided into east and west, each side having two emperors: a senior Augustus and a junior Caesar. Diocletian's reorganisation of empire staved off collapse, but the fight for power at the top continued, and civil war – war between competing factions of 'Romans' and their armies, often now with 'barbarian' soldiers – was a feature of the fourth century too, with internal peace and unity established only occasionally. Under Diocletian, power had already moved away from Rome closer to the edges of empire, where emperors and armies were needed to fight the barbarians. Under Constantine, this power shifted east to Constantinople – Rome did not become a total backwater, but real power resided elsewhere.[84]

The Eastern and Western Empires were again unified for a time under Theodosius, though his reign was not without its own pretenders, but on his death, in AD 395, it was divided between his sons, the teenage Arcadius in the east, and the ten-year-old Honorius in the west. As Stephen Mitchell explains, 'the year 395 is sometimes seen as the moment when the eastern and western empires parted ways. However, this would probably not have been apparent to contemporaries, who were aware that this was a division of responsibilities precisely as favoured by Valentinian and Valens in 364'.[85] In other words, nobody knew this would be a final separation.

In Honorius' reign, as we have seen, Alaric and the Goths sacked Rome after years of conflict and political machinations involving Arcadius and his successor Theodosius II; Alaric had sought a reasonable settlement with the establishment, but the emperors, faced with a multitude of threats, prevaricated, seeking to play the various parties off against each other. The youthful Honorius, in the capital of Ravenna (late western emperors were not based in Rome), when he heard the news of the sack, apparently thought that it was his chicken 'Roma' that had perished – a story symbolising at once both his ineptitude and irrelevance.[86]

THE ETERNAL CITY AND OTHER PLACES

Collapse is often associated with site abandonment, but of course Rome the city was not abandoned, at least not completely. The division of power and the founding of Constantinople, a new capital run along the lines of Rome itself, drew off power, people, and even monuments from Rome, diverting trade eastwards; the new city also ransacked the eastern Mediterranean for classical monuments, just as Rome itself had robbed the region centuries earlier, but Rome retained its special, venerable, and ancient position.[87] 'With no emperor, and a population in decline, the city nevertheless continued to be generally regarded as the capital of the world'; in the years after the emperors the Catholic popes made it their capital, and so it remains.[88]

Cities in the west, such as Trier and Milan, had also benefitted at Rome's expense as they became imperial capitals, and Ravenna grew to three times its former size in the early fifth century. As barbarian settlement and state formation proceeded, in Gaul, for example, towns maintained their importance in the new kingdoms as seats of church and state, but in Britain, urbanism disappeared sometime in the fifth century, as government 'devolved onto a non-urban tribal basis'.[89] The size and population of a city was not simply a function of its natural environment, but of its political and social importance, and of the threats posed to it.

The fifth century saw a significant reduction in Rome's population from a stable fourth century level of perhaps 800,000 to 60,000 by AD 530.[90] Rome was looted for a fortnight by the Vandals raiding from Africa in AD 455, and in AD 472 it was besieged again in a civil war, with Romans and their barbarian allies fighting on both sides. In AD 536 Rome was taken by Justinian's general Belisarius, in a settlement that did not long outlast the emperor. People and wealth flooded away from the city; some aristocrats, whose landed wealth might be spread through the empire, travelled east to Constantinople; poorer people may have gone where they could, and the remaining population concentrated mostly in the loop of the Tiber.

The danger and instability created by conflict, then as now (as we are seeing in 2015 with refugees fleeing Syria in vast numbers), caused people to flee their homes, and changes to the *annona*, free food distributions, suggest that the population dropped by 300,000 between AD 408 and AD 419.[91] The *annona* had begun in the Republic as a highly politicised supply of subsidised and then free grain, which gained would-be politicians, and later emperors, popular support. It became more complex and expensive to organise, as extras were added, oil, wine, pork; some 200,000 citizens were entitled in the fourth century. The *annona* was a mechanism of supplying the city and keeping its people happy, but it was also, like the army itself, an economic stimulus that bound far-flung provinces together. The loss of provinces such as North Africa to the Vandals in AD 429–439 made supply more difficult, although the *annona* was maintained for the smaller populations of Rome by the kings of Italy after AD 476, with wheat coming from Sicily and wine and oil from northern and southern Italy. In the sixth century the church took over the *annona*, with supplies from estates in Africa and Gaul, as well as Italy, Sardinia, and Sicily, but the free dole was ended by pope Sabinianus, who opted for selling the wheat rather than giving it away. At Constantinople, emperors continued to organise an *annona* supplied from Egypt.[92]

After AD 410, many great houses in Rome, the residences of the noble families, were abandoned, but not all, and they could still be the subject of legal disputes. In Italy, nobles of the southern cities stopped investing in their cities, an ancient classical tradition which ended with the Vandal invasion in North Africa, but this had tailed off much earlier in other parts of the west.[93] This 'decline of the *curiae*' was both a symptom and a cause of the political and social changes in the empire, and of the physical transformation of Roman cities. Rome had been changing for years, and for years competing forces battled over its heritage and its future. The increasing influence and social value of Christianity was one such change. The city transformed, but as Bertrand Lancon points out, this suggests that it remained symbolically important and wealthy enough to be worth fighting over. Many European cities have Roman foundations, testifying to significant continuity through collapse.

ROME'S FINAL VICTORY?

The western tradition of Rome's dismemberment by barbarians is ambivalent. On the one hand, barbarians were agents of destruction and collapse; John Lemprière, the English classicist, described the Goths thus in his classical dictionary of 1792: 'From becoming the enemies of the Romans, the Goths gradually became their mercenaries, and as soon as they were powerful and united, they soon dictated to their imperial masters, and introduced disorder, anarchy, and revolutions in the west of Europe'.[94] But on the other, they have also been seen as an 'invigorating' and necessary force for European development. As Gibbon explained: 'This diminutive stature of mankind ... was daily sinking below the old standard, and the Roman world was indeed peopled by a race of pigmies, when the fierce giants of the north broke in and mended the puny breed. They restored a manly spirit of freedom; and, after the revolution of ten centuries, freedom became the happy parent of taste and science'.[95]

Walter Goffart offers an interesting characterisation of the fall of Rome, suggesting that the barbarians were in fact conquered by Rome, much as Greece had (culturally) captured the Romans centuries earlier.[96] People wanted in on the idea of Rome and made use of the rich heritage it provided, and even though the Western Empire in an institutional sense vanished, this heritage did not disappear. Romans and barbarians occupied the same space, barbarians were drawn into the empire across its history, and those who had settled inside early on, or their descendants, became citizens in AD 212.[97]

In other lands, where barbarians destroyed and took over, we can also find them being colonised by the experience. In China, Jurchens 'became' Chinese and there was continuity of Chinese ways of life.[98] 'Barbarians' could become Chinese by participating in its culture. Rome had since the very beginning been a mixed population and Romanness (or Romannesses) could transcend or go alongside other identities – people could become Roman by how they lived. Even as the Roman west fragmented, barbarians continued to be Romanised.

FINAL THOUGHTS

The lesson of Rome is often taken as a warning about collapse that could happen to us, whether it is blamed on barbarians, climate change, economic policies, lead poisoning, or any of the hundreds of other causes suggested. But Rome is a useful example of collapse because it teaches us that while historical change happens, modern attempts to explain it can involve seriously different interpretations of the same evidence. Even with textual history and contemporary sources commenting on what was happening, in addition to archaeological evidence, Rome's collapse is still debated in terms of whether it even happened, whether there was a clean break, or whether we should think instead of a period and process of transition and transformation. Having more evidence does not necessarily make it any easier to understand a collapse – it can make it much harder. The way we interpret the evidence and the stories we tell with it are also very much affected by our current concerns.

It should be obvious that, across such a large territory, change took many forms and that many people, processes, and events were responsible. In examining other collapses, recalling the complexity of what happened in the WRE should caution us against simple or simplistic explanations and characterisations of what was happening. Seeing as there was no apocalyptic collapse of empire that wiped the slate clean or killed everyone off, a great degree of continuity is assured, but that does not mean there was no imperial collapse, or that such a collapse was insignificant historically, even if it was a steady erosion of imperial power that took place in the west over a century. The archaeology too, particularly in areas like Britain, demonstrates significant changes that indicate a real social collapse in some parts of the empire. Although we are culturally programmed to mourn the loss of the empire that we often associate ourselves with, culturally and intecllectually, we can wonder whether the collapse of a vast military autocracy, often at war with itself and its neighbours, really was such a bad thing after all.

THE PIRENNE THESIS

Henri Pirenne was a Belgian historian who attempted to explain the decline of the Classical world and the transition to the Middle Ages.[99] In a series of papers and a book, *Mohammed and Charlemagne*, which was published in 1939, after his death, he developed a theory that the Classical world of the western Mediterranean did not end with the Germanic invasions, but effectively continued until the seventh century. He proposed that it was in the mid-seventh century that urban life in the west collapsed. In his view, the Germanic invaders of western Europe had tried to preserve what they could of their Classical inheritance. It was conflict with the expanding Arab world that put an end to Mediterranean trade links and, as a result, western urbanism.

Critics of Pirenne, who was writing before much archaeological work was done, such as Chris Wickham, argue that Pirenne placed too much importance on long-distance trade between the eastern and western Mediterranean, and also that he focussed mainly on luxury goods.[100] Wickham explains that the western Mediterranean already had a much lower volume of trade, and also that we now know that luxury goods continued to be traded east-west even after the Arab conquests. Richard Hodges and David Whitehall, marshalling the archaeological evidence, suggest that commercial life continued in the west in such places as Rome and Carthage, though on a declining scale, until the sixth century.[101] They see the Arab expansion as a consequence of change, rather than a cause. The Muslim expansion into the Mediterranean world was not responsible for the changes we see in western Europe.

9

Collapse and Revolution in Mesoamerica

Monarchy first changes into tyranny; and next, the abolition of both gives birth to aristocracy. Aristocracy ... degenerates into oligarchy; and when the commons ... take vengeance on this government for its unjust rule, democracy comes into being; and in due course ... mob rule ...

Polybius[1]

INTRODUCTION

Polybius was an ancient Greek historian of the second century BC who sought to explain the great changes that had led to the emergence of Rome as the great power of the Mediterranean. Through his researches, he identified an apparently recurring pattern of political change, from monarchy through to mob rule. Rome had passed through monarchical and tyrannical phases, before passing into an aristocratic republican system, which in turn transformed into an oligarchy (rule of the few) and then a monarchy again. Such social and political changes – revolutions – were well known to Polybius from Greek history, where citizens had periodically changed the way their states were organised.

For Machiavelli, who observed the perennial disturbances in Italian states more than a thousand years later, revolution was also something to be expected, as communities cycled through different forms of political constitution.[2] He thought of this as a positive renewal, periodically necessary, and he describes how the rulers of

Florence in the fifteenth century found it necessary to 'take back the state' every five years. This meant 'striking the same terror and fear into the hearts of men that they had instilled upon first taking power, when they struck down those who had, according to that way of life, governed badly'.

History tends to be dominated by stories of kings and kingdoms, even when it is reconstructed from archaeology rather than texts. This is partly because high elites are simply more visible, but it also reflects a tendency to see these people and their stories as more important. We also often assume that monarchy must have been the norm for past societies. Clearly, though, other systems of political organisation were present throughout history, but even after acknowledging this, there has been a tendency in western scholarship to see republican or oligarchical systems as something distinctly European.[3] This view undoubtedly owes something to western ideas of 'the other' that stretch back to classical Greek times – the slavish orientals and their despotic monarchs who were compared to the active, rational, and independent minded Greeks. Increasingly such assumptions are being challenged. In a recent paper, Lane Fargher and colleagues have identified two Postclassic Mesoamerican cities, Tlaxcallan and Tizatlan, as probable republics.[4] They note evidence suggesting that, in fact, republican systems of one kind or another can be found around the world and far back in time. The real picture, then, is one of diversity and change in political systems.

In this chapter, we will look at collapse as a form of revolution using two examples from Mesoamerica: Rio Viejo and Teotihuacan (though we could choose others; Figure 9.1). First, though, it will help set the discussion in context by looking at some of the material aspects of revolutions and how these might be interpreted as collapse.

REVOLUTION AND COLLAPSE

In modern times, as in the past, revolutionary change has been a norm. The French Revolution, for example, did not just oust a king, or even a dynasty, but overturned a whole social system and an ancient and deep-rooted ideology. One feature of the revolution was iconoclasm – the destruction of images. The revolutionaries recognised the power of symbols to manipulate society and people's thinking and decided that those associated with the old regime were to be

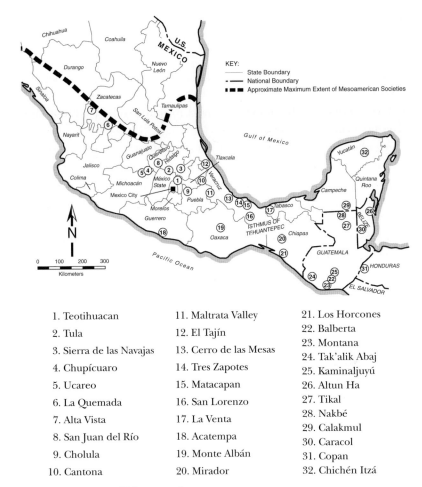

FIGURE 9.1. Map of Mesoamerica.
Source: From Cowgill, G. L. (2015). *Ancient Teotihuacan: Early Urbanism in Central America*. Cambridge: Cambridge University Press, 3 (figure 1.2 by S. Vaughn).

1. Teotihuacan
2. Tula
3. Sierra de las Navajas
4. Chupícuaro
5. Ucareo
6. La Quemada
7. Alta Vista
8. San Juan del Río
9. Cholula
10. Cantona
11. Maltrata Valley
12. El Tajín
13. Cerro de las Mesas
14. Tres Zapotes
15. Matacapan
16. San Lorenzo
17. La Venta
18. Acatempa
19. Monte Albán
20. Mirador
21. Los Horcones
22. Balberta
23. Montana
24. Tak'alik Abaj
25. Kaminaljuyú
26. Altun Ha
27. Tikal
28. Nakbé
29. Calakmul
30. Caracol
31. Copan
32. Chichén Itzá

obliterated. On August 11th 1792 a law was passed which decreed 'that all statues in Paris 'erected in honor of despotism' be destroyed'.[5] A law that would sanction widespread destruction and change the visual landscape of France, it stated:

Whereas, the sacred principles of liberty and equality will not permit the existence of monuments raised to ostentation, prejudice, and tyranny to continue to offend the eyes of the French people ... it is decreed; I. All statues, bas reliefs, inscriptions, and other monuments made of bronze or other metals, which exist in public squares, gardens, parks, public buildings ... will be removed by the communes ... III. All monuments containing traces of feudalism, of whatever nature, that still remain in churches, or other public places, and even those in private homes, shall, without the slightest delay, be destroyed by the communes.

The reclaimed bronze was to be used to manufacture cannons for use in the national interest.

Another important symbol of the revolution was the notorious Bastille prison.[6] It became to the revolutionaries the ultimate symbol of monarchical oppression, of royal despotism, and the storming of the Bastille on 14th July 1789 represented their revolt against all it stood for. Capturing the Bastille was not enough, though, the revolutionaries sought to destroy it completely, and so the whole complex was taken down and demolished by November 1789. Stones and chains were kept as mementoes of tyranny, some carved into miniature Bastilles to be sold as relics, some set up as a memorial in what would become the Place de la Bastille, an open public square, which continued to attract republicans and activists well into the twentieth century. The French still celebrate Bastille Day more than two centuries later.

The revolutionaries did not just destroy, they attempted to create a new France, with new slogans and symbols to rally people. One such symbol was the Tricolore, often worn as a cockade; clothing and personal fashion changed too, mirroring the new social mores; the new regime even sought to rebrand time by developing a new calendar, something which would deeply affect everyone's life.[7] The new rulers sought also to undermine the traditional power and place of the church – exercising a policy of 'dechristianisation'.[8] People growing up in the new regime would have had no experience of life before, they would grow up with a whole different worldview compared to earlier generations – significant social change would thus have been effected fairly rapidly over a few decades.

We could also trace similar political, social, and ideological changes brought about in the Russian revolutions and the rise and fall of communism in eastern Europe, the Chinese and Iranian revolutions, the fall of Saddam Hussein in Iraq – and the rise of Islamic State. The long twentieth century is marked by almost unbelievable degrees of revolutionary change – measured in terms of the number of people affected and the ways in which they were affected. Some of the changes associated with revolutions involved the end of royal and aristocratic power, increased and decreased levels of democracy, military and despotic or charismatic rule (and its end), radical changes to social status and property and other rights, the appropriation and redistribution of land, and changes in the status of religion from being officially discouraged to the creation of theocracies, to mention a few. Many will remember news stories showing acts of iconoclasm like that of the French revolution, with statues of Lenin, Stalin, Ceaucescu, and Hussein, amongst others, being toppled and defaced. Such acts of destruction mark beginnings as well as endings.

It seems very clear that sometimes rapid revolutionary change would look to an archaeologist like collapse. Revolutions, with their destruction and transformation of symbols of elite power, including objects, art, and locations, seem likely to leave clear indicators in the material record. It is also clear that revolutionary changes are fundamentally and actively driven by people rather than by natural disasters or environmental change, although these might create reasons or opportunities for revolutions or challenges to the status quo to be initiated.

So far in this book, our examples of collapse have been drawn from the Old World, but many of the best-known examples of collapse in the archaeological record come from the New World. Of course, there are the historical cases of Aztec and Inka collapse, which are clearly linked to the Spanish invasions of the late fifteenth and sixteenth centuries, and a wider population collapse because of the diseases brought by the newcomers, but in this chapter we shall examine two prehistoric cases of collapse that may be related to revolutionary change – one case involving communities in Oaxaca, southern Mexico, and the other involving the important and influential city and state of Teotihuacan. An important reason for looking at these collapses is that archaeologists now place human agency and choice as central to their stories.

COMMONER POWER IN OAXACA

Arthur Joyce, Laura Arnaud Bustamente, and Marc Levine have noted that in discussions of collapse, at least in Mesoamerican contexts, common people have tended to be forgotten; if they are thought of at all, it is usually as the passive victims of environmental changes of various kinds, caught up in interstate warfare organised by elites, or subject to change imposed by invaders or migrants.[9] Rarely, if ever, do they play an active role in the changes that were happening around them. However, historical texts from Mesoamerica do mention resentment of common people towards elites. In the Maya *Book of Chilam Balam of Chumayel*, for example, 'people are said to lament the hardships that a warlike leader imposes on subjects because of military drafts, famine, and strife resulting from frequent warfare'.[10] In addition, Joyce and Errin Weller suggest that all complex societies that have 'institutionalized power differentials' have probably included 'expressions of resistance to political domination'.[11] These expressions may be largely hidden by the dominant ideologies of the time, as expressed through the material culture that is available for archaeologists to study, but as Joyce and Weller argue, the changes we can see in collapse and post-collapse periods may allow us to identify earlier 'hidden' elements of resistance.[12]

In their investigation of the Rio Viejo state in the southern Rio Verde Valley, Oaxaca, Joyce and colleagues discard the passive view of common people, and reject the argument that the collapse of the Rio Viejo state was brought about by an influx of new people, as some have believed. Instead they build a case for local agency in transforming local society.

The Rio Viejo State

The Rio Viejo state, located on the Pacific coast of Oaxaca, Mexico, was created some time in the Terminal Formative Period, that is, between 100 BC and AD 250, and the city of Rio Viejo itself eventually reached some 250 ha in size in the Late Classic period. The Classic period city-centre was made up of a number of platform mounds raised above the floodplain of the river. Grey ware pottery was made on Mound 4, Mounds 2 to 4 and 6 to 14 were residential areas, and Mounds 2, 8, 9, and 11 probably contained some large public buildings. Mound 1 seems to have been the main ceremonial centre and ruler's residence, with a platform measuring 350 m by 200 m, raised 5 m above the floodplain, and evidence for two structures on top. Three carved stone monuments of rulers were found here.

This area would have been visibly conspicuous and also demonstrated the power and ability of a ruler to marshal the resources necessary to undertake such a project. In addition, there was a sunken patio, probably for activities restricted to certain privileged participants, and a plaza for more public displays. The high status domestic pottery also suggests elite residence.

Joyce and colleagues describe the Rio Viejo state as quite similar to other Late Classic Mesoamerican states, with 'urbanism, monumental art and architecture, writing, the institution of kingship, craft specialization, and a settlement hierarchy with at least four levels'.[13] Most of the population were farmers who were spread throughout the landscape and lived in houses of wattle and daub. Rulers and nobles proclaimed their ideology through the urban programme and through stone statues located not only at Rio Viejo itself, but at other sites in the valley, which showed rulers in elaborate dress, some with a calendrical name glyph, others with glyphs that probably refer to ritual bloodletting and sacrifice. Late Classic Rio Viejo was in all likelihood one of the main regional powers, with influence east and west, and with far flung trading connections. But this situation was not to last, and the state appears to have collapsed around AD 800.[14]

Postclassic Transition

Early Postclassic Rio Viejo after AD 800 was still an important site, but the city and the whole landscape had changed significantly from the earlier period (Figure 9.2a and b).[15] There was no monumental architecture being built anymore and the city shrank in size to 140 ha. Another major shift is reflected in the rise of a new rival regional site, nearby San Marquitos, which grew from its Late Classic size of 6.8 ha to 190.9 ha in the Early Postclassic. Rio Viejo's power was presumably fragmented. Throughout the valley itself the total number of sites decreased by more than half, from fifty to twenty-two, but individual sites actually increased in size and many more sites were built on the lower slopes of hills than during the Late Classic. The total population may not have shrunk, rather people may have left the former centre and come together in larger communities for protection or for other reasons perhaps related to their agricultural practices or to the rejection of the former dominant ideology.

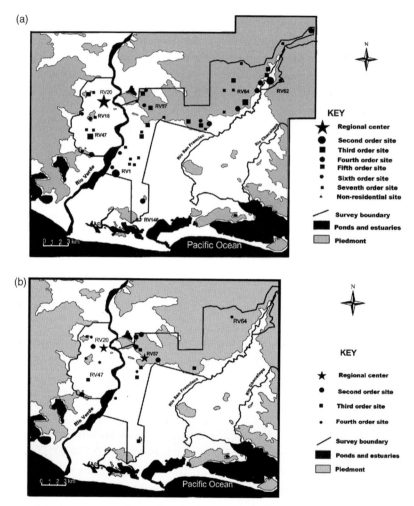

FIGURES 9.2A AND B. Late Classic (a) and Early Postclassic (b) settlement hierarchies in the Rio Verde Valley.
Source: With kind permission from Springer Science and Business Media.

Representations of rulers also changed or were no longer made at all – only three examples, statues rather than carved reliefs, may date to the Early Postclassic; these were positioned on a natural hill rather than on a mound.[16] Mound 1 was no longer a ceremonial mound occupied by the elite. Instead, excavation revealed that in the Early Postclassic period, Mound 1, Structure 2, was overbuilt by small houses on five new low platforms, which suggests that the area, once a distinct and separate space, had been occupied by commoners for whom the value of such spatial boundaries had changed. Fragments and monuments of former rulers were also used as building materials in Early Postclassic houses; one piece had even been used as a *metate*, a corn grinder, before being reused again.

Several rather enigmatic carved flat boulders were also found, one on the surface of a patio space of Mound 1, another from Mound 8. These contained deeper and shallow hollows ground and pecked out from the rock. Several interpretations of these have been offered, including that they represent the eye or face of the sun god, and relate to rain rituals, or that the hollows were containers for blood and water from autosacrifice; it is also possible that they were used in processing of some kind. In fact, stones in different areas may have been used differently – some associated with burials perhaps having a ritual function. Does this evidence indicate a revolution?

People Redraw the Boundaries

Clearly life at Rio Viejo changed from Classic to Postclassic, and the use of once valued symbols and uses of space that reified a particular set of social arrangements were ultimately rejected and lost their earlier value for the people at Rio Viejo, even as life went on in the region. The mechanisms of change, as so often in collapse, remain unclear, perhaps unknowable; as Joyce, Arnaud Bustamente, and Levine admit, it is difficult to know whether there was any kind of 'commoner rebellion' or a social revolution as such, although it is quite possible.[17] The move into the piedmont, more defensible than valley land, and the fragmentation of power between two first-order centres may indicate conflicts of some kind, which might have promoted a rejection of traditional rulers and their system, who could not provide peace and stability. Knowledge of social changes and the rejection of traditional rulers and systems at other sites may also have inspired local people to drive change.

One of the most interesting suggestions that Joyce and colleagues make about the social changes at Rio Viejo is that they also reflect the reconstruction of gender ideologies, with women and female images playing a much more prominent role in the Postclassic.[18] This is a rare approach in collapse studies. As they note, the Postclassic statues are possibly all females, rather than male rulers.

More durable and decorated spindle whorls became more common, replacing the less permanent Classic ones, which may suggest an increased social importance for women and their work, and perhaps their economic position. Reuse of the ruler monument as a *metate* may also indicate that women played a key role in subverting earlier symbols of power.

Even though it is not possible to construct a narrative with named actors and groups, the redrawing of boundaries in Rio Verde is clear enough, and commoners in the Postclassic seem to have prospered. It was the power, institutions, and ideologies of the nobles that collapsed. Some might think the end of elite culture would indicate a 'dark age', but evidently the elite rulers were not really so necessary to the success of the community after all, and the negotiated consensus of earlier times, however stable or unstable it was, broke down. If we continue to focus on external causes of collapse, such as climate change, we neglect the fact that societies can and do transform radically through the actions of their citizens.

Now let us move on to the story of a Mesoamerican mega-state: Teotihuacan.

TEOTIHUACAN

Teotihuacan, situated some fifteen km from Lake Texcoco in central Mexico (near present day Mexico City; Figure 9.3), became one of the largest and most culturally influential of the Mesoamerican cities during *c.* AD 0–650, and its cultural legacy lasted long after its collapse, as we shall see (Table 9.1).[19] The site was surveyed and mapped by Rene Millon and colleagues, and at its greatest extent (AD 350–550) it covered an area of 20 km².[20] The city had, at its height, a very large population, estimated, from the number of apartment compounds occupied, at between eighty and one hundred and fifty thousand; like other cities and central places elsewhere, people were drawn in from the surrounding areas, leaving them comparatively depopulated, although people continued to live in smaller sites in the Basin of Mexico such as Axotlan, thirty-five km to the west.[21] It also possessed one of the grandest monumental cores of any Mesoamerican city, with 'public' buildings arranged around the five km long Street of the Dead, which ran approximately

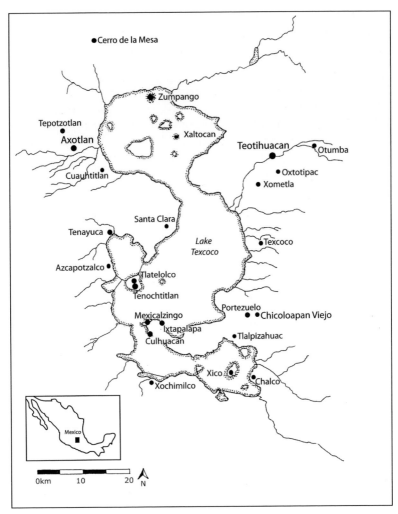

FIGURE 9.3. Map of the Basin of Mexico showing Teotihuacan.
Source: Courtesy of Sarah Clayton.

north-south through the city, and created an axis for the city's development (Figure 9.4).

It is generally agreed that Classic Teo, to adopt George Cowgill's nickname for the city, was the centre of a regional state, and that its authority extended to a distance of some sixty to ninety km around the city. It may have controlled specific sites and routes outside this

TABLE 9.1 *Teotihuacan periods, phases, and dates*

Periods	Phases	Dates	'Events'
Terminal Formative	Patlachique	100–1 BC	Moon Pyramid
	Tzacualli	AD 1–100	Sun Pyramid
	Miccaotli	AD 100–150	Ciudadela/ Feathered Serpent Pyramid
Classic	Early Tlamimilolpa	AD 150–250	Xalla complex + urban reorganisation
	Late Tlamimilolpa	AD 250–350	Adosada Street of the Dead complex
	Early Xolalpan	AD 350–450	
	Late Xolalpan	AD 450–550	Reduced foreign interactions + political and economic problems
		c. 550	
			Burning and collapse?
	Metepec	AD 550–650	Burning and collapse (AD 600/650)?Drop in population and possible temporary abandonment of city
Late Classic/ Epiclassic	Early Epiclassic/ Oxtotipac Coyotlatelco	AD?600–700 AD 650–900	

Source: Page 10, Cowgill, G. L. (2015). *Ancient Teotihuacan: Early Urbanism in Central Mexico*. Cambridge: Cambridge University Press; Nichols, D. L. (2015). 'Teotihuacan.' *Journal of Archaeological Research*. DOI 10.10007/s10814-015-9085-0.

area too. Teo developed a much wider cultural influence throughout Mesoamerica, even in the very distant Maya lowlands at sites like Tikal. It seems possible, though this is disputed, that some individuals from Teo (or individuals who proclaimed a Teo or exotic identity through material culture) even became rulers of sites elsewhere, or were otherwise directly involved in the politics of other states (see Box below).[22] This attests to the existence of contacts throughout the wider region, which moved people, resources, and ideas, and to the active use and reuse of shared and exotic symbols and material

FIGURE 9.4. The central area of Teotihuacan, looking south along the Street of the Dead, with the Moon Pyramid in the foreground and the Sun Pyramid behind.
Source: Courtesy of Michael E. Smith.

culture rather than a simple 'imperial style' dominance (although it is not out of the question that Teo may have interfered in and even sought to control distant locations, regardless of whether or not it built a large territorially contiguous empire).[23]

Teo was cosmopolitan, though whether the inhabitants spoke an early form of Nahuatl, the language of the Aztecs, or another language or languages is not known and remains a highly controversial issue, which, through the idea of migrations of groups of people, is connected to the collapse.[24] Probably many languages could be heard on the streets of the city. Indicative of Teo's cosmopolitanism is the variety of finds, architecture, burial, and decoration, in some of the residential compounds, *barrios*, which are interpreted as the homes of foreigners from Oaxaca and the Gulf Coast, the Maya lowlands, and elsewhere, perhaps in Teo in a diplomatic, trade, or craft role.[25] Strontium isotope analysis suggests a non-local origin for burials in such areas.[26] These enclaves may also have served symbolic as well as practical functions, incorporating distant exotic locations and groups into the fabric of Teo itself. The city may have been something of an 'international' phenomenon from early on, exerting the pull of a major cultural and population centre, and attracting people from farther afield than the Basin of Mexico to swell its population.

Around 2,200 residential compounds with multiple apartments and commonly a courtyard have been identified at Teo. These vary between spacious, luxurious palaces, and cramped compounds, which were home to several families, perhaps housing up to a hundred people. Each unit was walled and private, with rooms arranged around a central courtyard. According to studies by Rene Millon and Ian Robertson, most areas seem to have been mixed in terms of the relative status of inhabitants, although there does seem to have been a bias towards higher status occupants nearer the centre, and, over time, individual neighbourhoods seem to have become less diverse.[27]

The centre of the city came to be dominated by suites of civic-ceremonial architecture that combined politics and religion and promoted the ideologies of some of Teo's elite inhabitants. As in other capitals and centres of power in ancient and modern times, this was done through the use of architecture, images, and space, and through participation in orchestrated events that involved doing, watching, and listening within the spaces created for groups to assemble. Such social acts created bonds and distinctions, identities, within society by the selective use of participants and proximity. Power was both expressed and created in and by these spaces.

Any individual or group seeking to increase its power would have needed to court the wider population to ensure their continued participation in the community. As in Rome, the city is likely to have experienced shifting balances of power between elite families and factions, and between these and the people, and also perhaps to have produced particularly charismatic and powerful individuals, but all rulers, as everywhere, required a degree of 'consent' or legitimation from the general population.[28]

Monuments continued to be constructed over time. The Ciudadela and the Pyramid of the Feathered Serpent at its south end were built in the Miccaotli-Early Tlamimilolpa phase, and probably completed by AD 250. In the Early Classic period the Xalla complex, which included pyramids of its own, was constructed and the city's residential areas were reorganised around a grid plan following the north-south orientation of the Street of the Dead.

Palaces and Monuments – Power through Time

When thinking about the past, it is easy enough to tend to view cultures or societies as static and unchanging, rather than dynamic and complex social arenas, even when common sense tells us otherwise. This is especially true if our information is reconstructed primarily from archaeology and objects, which might be seen 'at once' on display (or in a book), rather than told through texts that reveal a series of characters and events through time. At Teo, though, archaeologists have reconstructed a dynamic picture which explains material change as a result of changing social and political relations between motivated, if unidentifiable, individuals and groups. These relationships may also offer a key to understanding the Teo state's eventual collapse, now dated to the mid-sixth or mid-seventh century, and the transition to the Epiclassic period. Over some six or seven centuries, it would be surprising if Teo's systems of governance had not changed – think of the massive changes to Rome and its empire from 350 BC to AD 350, or for that matter the history of the British Isles from AD 1000 to 1600 – and archaeologists tend to think broadly in terms of a Teo history that pays attention to this dynamism, and which is reflected in the changing civic-ceremonial and elite architectural aspects of the city. William Sanders and Susan Toby Evans break down Teo's classical history into three stages.[29]

Teo may have initially risen to importance within an environment of regional competition and conflict in the first century BC, and it already had a sizeable population before any monumental construction took place (in the Patlachique pottery phase). Its success, possibly military (possibly also ideological), may have drawn people in. Work on major monuments then began early in the first millennium AD, with the development of the Street of the Dead, with the Pyramid and Plaza of the Moon at the north end, the Pyramid of the Sun to the east; these may have been completed by around AD 150 (though they continued to be developed and modified later; Figure 9.5).[30]

What drove these changes at Teotihuacan – what was the stimulus for the increasing social complexity suggested by the archaeology?

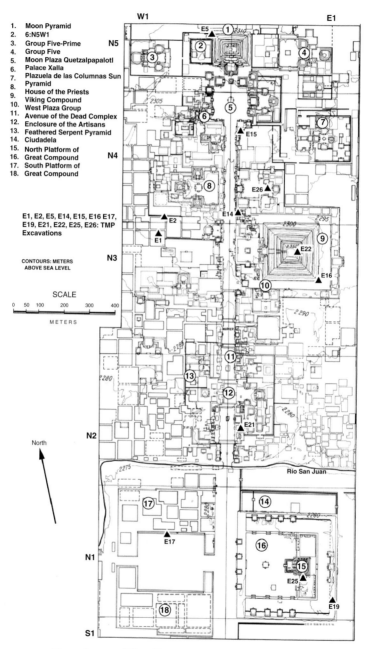

1. Moon Pyramid
2. 6:N5W1
3. Group Five-Prime
4. Group Five
5. Moon Plaza Quetzalpapalotl
6. Palace Xalla
7. Plazuela de las Columnas Sun Pyramid
8. House of the Priests
9. Viking Compound
10. West Plaza Group
11. Avenue of the Dead Complex
12. Enclosure of the Artisans
13. Feathered Serpent Pyramid
14. Ciudadela
15. North Platform of Great Compound
16. Great Compound
17. South Platform of Great Compound
18. Great Compound

E1, E2, E5, E14, E15, E16 E17, E19, E21, E22, E25, E26: TMP Excavations

CONTOURS: METERS ABOVE SEA LEVEL

SCALE

0   50 100   200   300   400

METERS

North

FIGURE 9.5. Plan of central Teotihuacan.
Source: After Millon, R. (1973). *The Teotihuacan Map. Part I: Text.* Austin: University of Texas Press.

This remains unclear; we do not know how the early state was organised – there is no obvious ruler symbolism or cult of the personality, unless this is to be inferred from the creation of the monuments themselves.[31] It may be that the monuments were created communally, but early Teo could equally have been more oligarchical in character, possibly governed by a council of some kind with members drawn from the most powerful families.[32] However, one compound, the Xalla complex, has been pointed out as perhaps being palatial in character, and thus is possibly indicative of a single ruler or ruling family or lineage group; Cowgill notes that it 'is unlike anything else at Teotihuacan'.[33]

The Xalla complex was about ten times the size of a regular residential compound, and perhaps significantly it was located between the Pyramid of the Moon and the Pyramid of the Sun. It had eight ceremonial courtyards, including a large central patio 30 m across, which unusually had five small temples – one at each cardinal point and another in the centre. Lopez and Manzanilla point out that various motifs from the courtyard and Xalla, plumed felines, for example, generally match up with those from the Pyramid of the Sun, perhaps pointing to a connected programme of construction.[34]. Some archaeologists suggest that there were royal tombs associated with both the Sun and Moon Pyramids.[35]

However, recent research seems to indicate that the Xalla compound is later in date than was previously thought – it may thus echo, no doubt deliberately, aspects of the Pyramid of the Sun rather than being contemporary with it.[36] It could have been a palace, but later than was thought, but Cowgill has suggested instead that, due to its unique features, it might rather have housed a 'distinctive religious cult'.[37] Whatever its function, the Xalla compound remained in use into the sixth century AD.

A second political phase is thought to be marked by the development of the Ciudadela complex. This bounded area, located far to the south of the Pyramid of the Moon and to the east of the Street of the Dead, was big enough to hold the entire gathered population of Teo. The earlier buildings on the site were destroyed to make way for it, which to Cowgill suggests that this novel complex indicates 'a sharp break with what went before' and represents 'new religious and political ideas and practices'.[38] Pasztory has also noted that the earlier pyramids are hard or impossible to see from the Ciudadela, and are certainly peripheral to it; he states that 'the Ciudadela seems to be the architectural representation of a major change in the social and political structure of Teotihuacan … A powerful leader may have literally redesigned the city, putting the palace – and thus rulership – at its center'.[39] There is a persistent belief that the Ciudadela may have been a royal compound.

Along with the Ciudadela went the construction of the Pyramid of the Feathered Serpent. The pyramid is decorated with sculptures of the Feathered Serpent, hence the name, but also with the Fire Serpent, which (in Aztec times) represented warfare.[40] The pyramid-temple could be connected with warfare and the military aspect of Teo society. This notion is supported by the presence of around 200 human sacrifices, in mass graves, made when the pyramid was being constructed.[41] Stable isotope analysis of the remains suggests that many of the individuals originally came from outside Teo. They were generally in good physical condition at death, were wearing military regalia, and were buried with weapons. They had had their hands tied behind their back and their ankles tied together and may have been buried alive. The sacrifices seem to have accompanied the burial of an individual, who could have been Teo's ruler and the mastermind of the Ciudadela (or perhaps his successor built the complex capitalising on the reputation of his predecessor). The Pyramid of the Feathered Serpent can be interpreted at least in part as a funerary monument to a strong ruler.[42] The sacrificial victims could have been elite royal guards, the interpretation Cowgill favours, or defeated captives (but captives would normally have been stripped, not buried clothed).

So the evidence from the Pyramid of the Feathered Serpent could be taken to suggest the presence of a strong ruler who stamped his mark on the city. But also inside the Ciudadela, north and south of the pyramid, were two identical apartment compounds, called the north and south palaces.[43] These had five sets of rooms around a courtyard area.[44] The presence of dual 'palace' suites in the Ciudadela has lead some to suggest that there may have been a period of joint rule of some kind.[45] If this idea of two equally powerful rulers sounds odd to modern ears, we can recall that in ancient Greece the Spartan kingdom was ruled by two kings, one each from the two royal families, the Agiads and the Eurypontids. These Spartan kings fulfilled priestly as well as political and military functions. Republican Rome was also governed by two consuls, usually drawn from the 'best' families, who essentially retained the powers of earlier kings but on a temporary basis.

However, modern terminology may lead us astray – the north and south palaces may not have been palaces at all. Sanders and Evans point out that they only superficially resemble residential compounds – the courtyards were much bigger, but actual residential units, which would have housed the royal families, their court, followers, staff, and hangers on, and which would have been used, in various ways, for administrating the state, are lacking – 'decidedly odd' in their words.[46] The rigid symmetry and layout of the compounds suggest to them a more ritual or even military feel, but they admit that the actual royal residences could have been located elsewhere, with the north and south palaces serving specific functions connected to the cults of the two ruling families (if such there were). Saburo Sugiyama also doubts that the Ciudadela was a royal residence – he thinks that they housed the priests of the Pyramid of the Feathered Serpent. But Cowgill returns to the unique nature of the Ciudadela, suspecting it was 'built and first occupied by persons who held unprecedented kinds of political office …'.[47]

Whatever the original meaning and function of the Ciudadela complex, later Teotihuanacos seem later to have rejected it. In the fourth century, the Pyramid of the Feathered Serpent and the temple built on top of it were defaced and burned, and parts of the debris, moulded clay motifs, were thrown into the fill of a new stepped platform monument, the Adosada, which was constructed directly in front of it. Susan Toby Evans calls this 'a very expensive act of ritual termination'.[48] The new monument preserved some of the burnt remains of the pyramid and also left its ruins exposed to view. Tunnels were dug into it and the contents of its inner burial pits removed. Cowgill has suggested that this change could represent a reaction to an overly ambitious ruler, or a revolt against a later less strong ruler.[49]

The locus of power may have shifted again, this time to the new Street of the Dead complex.[50] This was situated in the centre of the city on the Street of the Dead between the Ciudadela and the Pyramid of the Sun. Rather than monumental, it was simply a large complex of buildings with enough space for residential and administrative functions. But within the complex, the large Viking Group area had uniquely large rooms and courtyards – perhaps the suite of a ruler.

At the same time the city was spectacularly reorganised into regular apartment compounds. The Street of the Dead complex was clearly important and its location straddling the Street of the Dead allowed its users to control movement, processions, and display between the Ciudadela area and the Pyramids of the Sun and Moon.

It is likely that the Street of the Dead complex was the core of rulership in later Teotihuacan. It could be that a strong ruler imposed these changes on Teo, and then governed from the Viking Group and the Street of the Dead complex. The changes could represent a turning away from the lineage or (possibly militaristic or autocratic) style of rulership of the Ciudadela and Pyramid of the Feathered Serpent era. Just because the complex is not as 'showy' does not mean there could not have been a single ruler, but rather that power was being expressed differently. Of course, it could also be the case that the sub-royal elites had come together to end the tradition of single rule and began to govern by council, or that they elected rulers from among their number.[51]

One issue with this interpretation is the construction date of the Street of the Dead complex. Cowgill now thinks it may have been built whilst the Feathered Serpent Pyramid was in use.[52] The two could be complementary, rather than successive, and it may be that rulers ruled from the Street of the Dead complex while priests used the Ciudadela. But this is just one possible interpretation.

Before moving on, something should be said of the apparent lack of clear ruler iconography, in comparison to, say, the Roman Empire (but similar to Harappa, Minoan Crete, and Mycenaean Greece). Powerful rulers may have felt little need to advertise themselves or may not have showed off their position iconographically. We could consider the various building projects as evidence of strong government, even of single rule, but this is just one interpretation. Perhaps the Ciudadela complex supports this view the most. Cowgill suggests that we may have ruler iconography, but have just not understood it.[53] For example, there is a carving of a massive (50 cm across) clenched fist, of uncertain date, which could alone be a symbol of power or could have been part of a monumental statue of a ruler. Disembodied hands appear on other media too – perhaps these signified the ruler or royal power.

There is another statue, unfinished, from south of Teo; it is over seven metres tall and weighs about 180 tons – the 'colossus'. It may date to the period when the Adosada was built over the Pyramid of the Feathered Serpent. Cowgill thinks that it clearly represents an important figure, but not a divinity; he speculates that it could have represented the ruler associated with the Pyramid of the Feathered Serpent (or its destruction).[54] Further he posits that work on it might have remained unfinished because of that ruler's excess or hubris – perhaps there was a revolt against him and so the statue was abandoned in the quarry where it was being made.

What can we conclude? It seems safe to say that Teo went through significant political, social, and ideological changes over time – something which should not really surprise us. The people of Teotihuacan evidently competed for power, and at times strong rulers, lineages, or corporations were able to effect significant changes to the fabric of the city, rejecting earlier models and replacing them with new ones. This does not mean that Teo was particularly unstable, or any more unstable than other polities, but it does mean that a whole complex, and for the most part hidden, history lies behind the archaeological evidence we have.

The Collapse

The Teotihuacan collapse is associated both with the end of the city's regional dominance, and with evidence of burning and destruction – smashed buildings and images – in the city, the rejection of an existing rulership and/or elite, and with its possible abandonment. The dating of the collapse is not entirely clear and there is some disagreement about the order of events. Laura Beramendi-Orosco and Linda Manzanilla and their team have dated the burning and destruction events to around AD 550, the beginning of the Metepec pottery phase, and Linda Manzanilla also follows this date.[55] However, George Cowgill dates the collapse to the end of the Metepec phase, around AD 600/650, because of the typical Metepec pottery he has found in destruction deposits.[56] Saburo Sugiyama is less certain. He states that 'we still do not know exactly when this happened in absolute years'.[57]

Researchers do seem to agree that, before the collapse, Teo's regional influence was declining, that there were signs of problems within the city, and also that the population was falling.[58] Cowgill suggests that during the Metepec pottery phase the population of the city shrank by a half or two-thirds, especially in the outskirts of the city; at the same time, disparities in wealth were increasing, which is indicated by the deposition of grave goods.[59] The urban landscape was changing too; there was reduced diversity of groups in neighbourhoods, and communications between areas, such as La Ventilla, was blocked by the construction of gates; rubbish also began to accumulate in the city.[60]

There are of course a range of theories to explain the collapse, and we shall examine these below, dividing them roughly into environmental, external, and internal explanations.

Climate Change

Matthew Lachniet and his team used speleothem data to reconstruct a rainfall record for the Basin of Mexico over the last 2,400 years.[61] They see a peak in dry conditions from AD 620 to 770, a megadrought that followed centuries of drying. Drying and drought would have put pressure on the ability of Teo's hinterland to provide enough food for Teo's large population and could have caused the population of the city to decline, with people moving out to secure their own provisions more directly. They suggest that the smashed Storm God artifacts could be significant: the population might have believed that the god had abandoned them. Equally, they might have abandoned that particular cult if it no longer seemed to 'work'. Faith in leaders who played an intermediate role between the population and the Storm God could have been undermined, causing civil strife.

But this explanation has not found favour with specialists. Emily McClung de Tapia too finds no evidence for any changes caused by drought in the Teotihuacan Valley.[62] Some have cited evidence for drought in western Mexico, but Michelle Elliot's study, which also finds no evidence of climate change earlier than the AD 1500s, contradicts this.[63] The evidence from western Mexico is ambiguous, but in any case it is distant from Teotihuacan and perhaps of limited relevance.

It is interesting to note that Lachniet's team does not associate the later Toltec collapse (*c.* AD 1150) with drought, although a team led by Stahle does.[64] Stahle and colleagues' data also point to a very severe drought in Mesoamerica during the late fourteenth century, and they note that the Aztec historical record mentions the worst drought as happening in AD 1454. Clearly neither of these impeded the growth of the Aztec state or caused its collapse, which was caused by the Spanish invaders. There is no simple relationship between climate and collapse here.

Environmental Damage

As Teotihuacan grew in influence and population, it would have undoubtedly had a major impact on the natural environment with the need for food and water and firewood for domestic and industrial use. Barba has calculated that to produce enough lime for plaster with which to plaster the buildings an area four times the size of the valley floor would have been needed (though this need would have been over time).[65] Manzanilla claims there was 'large-scale environmental degradation due to deforestation and a long-lasting drought'.[66] According to Emily McClung de Tapia, the population of Teo would early on have outstripped the carrying capacity of the Basin of Mexico, even on low population estimates, and in order to supply the Teo megacity with food, 'economic control of adjacent regions was fundamental to the urban support system'.[67] Environmental damage was clearly a potential hazard but carrying capacity was linked to the control of other areas.

Sanders has found Manzanilla's claims wanting – he thinks lime would have been processed elsewhere, as it was in later times, rather than bringing stone to the valley to be processed there; thus deforestation may have been less than suggested.[68] McClung de Tapia also notes that Teo's environment was able to sustain the impact of the Classic period polity over five to six centuries – that is, the Teotihuanacos were able to manage themselves in their environment very successfully over a very long period of time. Why would collapse have happened when it did? Political instability or military conflicts could have upset the system, though, perhaps interrupting supply networks and reducing the resources available by putting some land out of use or access or reducing the territory of the state.

There was eventually environmental collapse in the valley, but this took place in the late Postclassic and early colonial period, much later on. The reasons for this were that local systems were disrupted by the incoming Spanish, who brought different agricultural practices and pressures to bear on the landscape – it was their system that was unsustainable.[69]

Competition

Some suspect that Teo's decline and collapse may be related to the rise of polities elsewhere. It has been thought that cities such as Xochichalco (Morelos) and Cacaxtla-Xochitecatl (Tlaxcala), which became more powerful in the Epiclassic, might have become rivals of Teo and that this may have contributed in some way to the Teo collapse.[70] Cholula, Tula Chico, and El Tajin might also have been rivals. Their increasing power may have cast doubt over Teo's charismatic draw, governance, and leaders, and it is not at all impossible that there were military conflicts between these states. However, archaeologists at Xochichalco have suggested that the city grew only after Teo's collapse, which might make it a result of Teo's collapse, rather than a cause.[71] But then again, if we recall Sugiyama's ambivalence over the exact chronology of Teo and its collapse, as well as the chronological issues at the other sites, it is still possible that there is a connection – this remains unclear.[72] It is likely that some of the population of Teo migrated outwards to other regions, either because of instability or dissatisfaction, or the prospect of a better situation elsewhere, and these neighbouring cities, as well as the countryside, may have attracted people from Teo.

New People – Migration and Invasion

As in many explanations of collapse, and equally controversially, there are scholars who suggest that it might have been caused by the arrival of new people, specifically Nahua speakers, and the possible replacement of earlier populations.[73] In the case of Teo, these new people are associated with Coyotlatelco pottery tradition. This was in use all over the Basin of Mexico area in the Epiclassic, the area which had been part of the Teo state; settlement and population in the area shifted to a decentralised landscape no longer dominated by a single massive urban centre, where smaller and possibly hostile local centres divided the Basin between them.[74]

The Coyotlatelco pottery includes types associated with cooking, serving, and storing food. A few archaeologists believe that some of its features derive from earlier Teo pottery, and that there is some visible transition, indicating that the people who made this pottery were living in Teo alongside its local inhabitants. However, most see it as a tradition associated with, and brought to Teo by, people from the north and west, but via some very different mechanisms.[75] Evelyn Rattray, for example, imagines an intrusion by a warlike population from the Tula area, perhaps Toltec-Chichimec, who lived in several villages in Teo, indicated by concentrations of pottery, and who formed a new post-Teo elite distributed around the Basin of Mexico.[76]

Manzanilla, whose excavations suggest continuous use from Classic to Epiclassic of quarry tunnels for domestic and ritual purposes, and also Epiclassic reuse of Classic ritual areas, suggests, based on bioarchaeological evidence, that Coyotlatelco users included people of local and non-local origin.[77] New people may have been moving to the city before its collapse, making their role in the collapse itself uncertain.

In a recent summary of the migration debate and evidence, Cowgill analyses a range of evidence, pottery, figurines, stone spear points, and language change, and does conclude that new people were present in Epiclassic Teo, but he notes that there was no simple destruction, takeover, or replacement, these people 'interacted in complex ways with Teotihuacan survivors, leading to ceramic complexes that included both emulation and inheritance from multiple antecedents'.[78] He believes it likely that a Teo weakened by internal problems would have been an attractive target for invaders from western Mexico.

A military confrontation (with or without any significant population movement) could have resulted in the selective burning and destruction of buildings at Teo. As Sugiyama points out, 'it was a long-standing tradition in Mesoamerica to set fire to the temples of conquered areas'.[79] The Epiclassic period does seem to have been one of increased conflict and it seems possible that Teo's destruction could be an early sign of this trend.[80] Militaristic imagery has been thought to have become more prominent in later Teo society, although the military must have played a role in earlier times, as shown by the warrior burials.[81] Sugiyama also refers to 'a wide, deep canal system and high platforms' which 'may have functioned as defensive facilities'

and to the building of thick walls to control access to neighbourhoods – were these built to deter Teotihuanacos or outsiders?[82]

Others also doubt the reality of large-scale population movement
or ethnic migrations – pottery styles do not necessarily indicate ethnic groups.[83] Coyotlatelco ceramics could represent an innovative
use of a non-local material culture in circumstances that rendered
established Teo traditions inappropriate (and this could be what happens in other instances of collapse too). Both local people and non-
locals may have been responsible for this, without having to think in
terms of one dominating the other. Doubtless, movements of people,
which had always happened anyway, continued out of Teo and into
the Basin of Mexico, and also into and out of the region itself. DNA
and isotope analysis on their own tell us little about culture or the
conscious self-identifications of individuals and groups. As Cowgill
notes: 'ethnic identities probably shifted and may have been rapidly
redefined'.[84]

Revolt and Revolution

Internal explanations for collapse seem to be those most favoured
by Teo specialists at the moment. Rene Millon described how sites
around the Street of the Dead were systematically targeted in an
'organized, planned campaign of ritual destruction', whilst in
other parts of the city, public buildings, temples, and pyramids,
rather than residential blocks, were burnt.[85] More than 150 buildings, and almost all of the buildings around the Street of the Dead,
have evidence of burning. Individuals were also killed and dis-
membered in the palaces and images of deities were smashed. As
with the French revolution, he states that 'iconoclasm does seem
to have formed part of the process of destruction represented
by the systematic smashing, dismantling, and burning of central
Teotihuacan'.[86] Manzanilla has studied the destructions at Teo
closely and agrees that structures were dismantled and objects
ritually killed.[87]

Millon believed that only Teotihuanacos themselves would have
been motivated to carry out such a programme of sustained destruction, and, surely correctly, that the target was both the ruling class

and the system it represented, embodied in the ceremonial fabric of the city.[88] The actions represented more than just a change of leadership. He is admittedly uncertain about what could have caused such a situation, but he speculates that Teotihuacan society was, or became, overly rigid, without the flexibility to allow change, so that internal pressures built up. We can only guess at the make-up of the group that were responsible – elites, the military, commoners, outsiders, or a combination.

Manzanilla too writes of 'inherent contradictions' in the operation of Teotihuacan society.[89] She has suggested that intermediate elites – people of status and wealth independent of the state (that is, their position and wealth was not derived from the state) – were increasing their own power and diverting wealth from the state. They, in addition to the ruling elite, were responsible for systems that brought in raw materials and workers from outside Teotihuacan. There may have been tensions between intermediate and ruling elites, between different intermediate elite groups, and also possibly tensions connected with the multiple ethnic groups present, which could have increased over time in a competitive spiral or in response to rigid or attempted control. She concludes:

no traces of foreign invasion are visible … We interpret this event [the burning and destruction event] as a revolt against the ruling elite, perhaps a response to a late intervention on the part of the state to control the entrepreneurial movements of the intermediate elite.[90]

It is possible that the thick walls Sugiyama mentions could reflect spiralling inter-neighbourhood (group or family) competition and conflict.

Cowgill notes that it is possible that there was factional strife within the ruling elite itself.[91] This would not be surprising, but it is unclear why a faction trying to take over would destroy so much without rebuilding its own replacement complexes. It is possible that things got out of hand. Millon has stated that what could have started as a coup 'once underway, may have changed its character. Once set in motion, it may have taken on a life of its own, with consequences not foreseen or intended'.[92]

Religious and Ideological Change

Could religious change have undercut the social systems of Teotihuacan and led to collapse? Millon has noted one category of evidence that could support such a theory: small ceramic vessels called *candeleros* became more common in households before the collapse, which could indicate a growth in domestic and personal cult at the expense of state-sponsored religious practices.[93] He adds, though, that they could simply indicate an increased religiosity or a change in existing systems of cult practice. At Teotihuacan, and across Mesoamerica, some scholars have suggested the spread of a new world religion based on the Feathered Serpent, which may have shared a common set of symbols.[94]

Profound religious changes of course happened in the ancient world, and some involved significant changes in behaviour, world-view, and material culture. The growth of Christianity led to shifting attitudes to the built environment, the disposal of the dead, the abandonment of temples, and to the violent destruction of pagan statues and monuments, which were often considered the abode of evil spirits; the destruction of the temples of Alexandria by order of Theophilus, AD 391, is a good example.[95] Not only was there physical destruction of property, but the act of destruction by locals itself signified the rejection and termination of the authority, social institutions, and networks that they had embodied, as well as their accumulated store of knowledge.

Abandonment?

After the burning, Teo's population dropped, but by how much is disputed. Evelyn Rattray and some others argue that Teotihuacan was largely abandoned at this time, perhaps for a few decades, before the Coyotlatelco pottery users arrived.[96] We have seen some of the problems in interpreting the significance of the Coyotlatelco pottery. Jeffrey Parsons and Yoko Sugiura call this the 'small site' theory, in which Teo was reduced to a few scattered villages and hamlets.[97] The 'large site' theorists, on the other hand, do not see evidence of large-scale abandonment, and they believe Teotihuacan remained influential (though never as influential as it had been) and the major site in the Basin of Mexico, retaining a population of perhaps 35,000 and a spread of ten square kilometres.[98] Nichols, in her recent review, thinks it remained one of the largest sites in the area, but she makes it clear that 'we do not have an adequate understanding of this phase of Teotihuacan's history'.[99]

Teo and Its Influence Later On

The reasons for Teo's collapse will remain uncertain, but continued occupation of the city and the region, albeit in a different pattern, would seem to rule out any complete environmental collapse, or that circumstances prevented people from continuing to subsist.[100]

Despite all the transformations that played out in and around Teotihuacan, in the centuries after the collapse the city was still substantial, with an estimated population of between 20 and 40,000.[101] Although the Classic Teo state did not survive, the city did become an independent city state in the Postclassic. Its cultural legacy was important to the Toltecs of Tula.[102] Later the Aztecs regarded Teo as important too – according to them it was created by the gods.[103] The Aztecs carried out ceremonies in the centre of Teo and there were a few settlements scattered around the periphery; some Teotihuacan objects, presumably dug up, have been found at Tenochtitlan. Teo was still there when the Spanish arrived in Mexico in AD 1519. At that time, as one of perhaps up to fifty city-states, or *altapetl* in the Basin of Mexico, it was a small town with an estimated urban population of up to 5,000.[104]

Archaeology also reveals that some cultural features, such as *talud-tablero* architecture, continued to be adopted at sites in the Epiclassic after the collapse of Teo. As with classical architectural language in the west after Rome, and Hittite symbology in the eastern Mediterranean, these remained an important option in the cultural armoury of local people.

FINAL THOUGHTS

In the absence of written evidence, archaeologists do their best to interpret what, as indicated by the material evidence, happened over time in Mesoamerican states such as the Rio Viejo state and Teotihuacan. Literary and textual evidence, such as we have for the Hittites and Rome, can provide narratives and characters to a story that otherwise remains without names and clear motivations, but for Rio Viejo and Teotihuacan we lack these. But it is at least clear that these states experienced change over time, expressed through changing architectural plans and population levels. We might be seeing changes in rulers, dominant lineages, and systems of governance. For states to succeed, a degree of consensus between its 'citizens' and factions at different social levels is required. At Rio Viejo and Teotihuacan, groups of people rejected ideologies of their forebears, and it looks like it was elite or ruling ideologies that were being erased. Especially at Teotihuacan, the evidence suggests a serious and violent revolution, though we do not know what the causes were or the identity of the protagonists. Revolutions often come about because parts of the population feel disenfranchised, excluded, or downtrodden – the evidence of these collapses might give us a clue to what it was like for many people living in Classic Mesoamerica.[105]

TEOTIHUACAN AND THE MAYA

Teotihuacan had a wide influence in Mesoamerica, although the form of Teo's relationships with other sites remains generally unclear.[106] However, it is becoming increasingly recognised that Teo had a direct relationship with several Maya cities during their formative years in the Maya Early Classic period (AD 250–600). Take Tikal, for example. There are a number of lines of evidence, including stone stelae and decorated pottery, as well as glyphic inscriptions, which show the relationship between Tikal and its rulers and Teotihuacan. So what was going on?

In AD 378, the Maya king of Tikal, Chak Tok Ich'aak I ('Jaguar Paw'), disappeared. In the same year 'strangers from the west' came to Tikal, possibly from Teotihuacan, as is shown on a decorated pottery vessel from the city and recorded in Stela 31. A year later, in AD 379, a new king came to the throne, called Yax Nuun Ayiin, or 'Curl Snout'. He seems to have been aided by a party of Teotihuanacos led by Siyaj K'ak ('Smoking Frog'). Yax Nuun Ayiin belonged not to the Maya dynasty, but was the son of one Spearthrower Owl, who seems to have been an important ruler, and who may have been the king of Teotihuacan itself. Thus Teotihuacan, its rulers or members of elite factions, may have interfered directly in Maya politics, quite possibly using violence to achieve their ends.

In addition to the historical record, there are other indications of a Teotihuacan presence (or at least 'influence') at Tikal. The pottery vessel mentioned earlier also shows Teo style *talud-tablero* architecture on a Teotihuacan style temple and a *talud-tablero* platform topped by a Maya temple. Teo people are also shown, indicated by their spearthrowers and tassled headdress. Some are shown carrying ceramic gifts to a seated Maya figure. It seems sure that there were relations of some kind between the two sites.

Teotihuacan influence was not restricted to Tikal alone – many other sites, Maya and otherwise, may have had a relationship of some kind with Teotihuacan or its people, or may have claimed a relationship by adopting symbols of Teo. Undoubtedly the nature of these relationships varied between direct interference, diplomacy, violence, and trade (direct or indirect).

10

The Classic Maya Collapse

The evidence shows that the Classic droughts were of an intensity and duration that the Maya had never before experienced ... They were devastating,
obliterating droughts in the face of which no political system, no agricultural practices, no population density, no religious rituals had any effects or
could have had any effects. There was nothing they could do or could have
done. In the end, the food and water ran out – and they died.

Richardson Gill[1]

THE MYSTERIOUS MAYA

In collapse studies, perhaps only the Classic Maya collapse can rival
the fall of the Western Roman Empire in its fame, a position which
fuels both continued academic research and debate from the natural
sciences as well as archaeology, and is widely discussed in popular
writing and television documentaries (Figure 10.1). In archaeology,
there are literally hundreds of studies on, or relating to, the Maya
collapse – James Aimers counted over 200 published during 1997–
2007.[2] And yet, as Maya specialist David Webster points out of the
more public side of the discussion, people always seem to prefer the
simple or weird version.[3]

Indeed, the versions of Maya collapse that do get popularised on
television, and either discussed or mentioned in many books, but
also 'explained' in hard science journals, often do a disservice to the
attitudes and research of the wider archaeological community. They

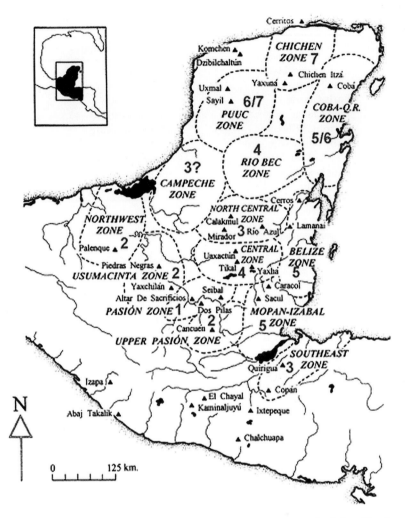

FIGURE 10.1. The varied beginnings of collapses at the end of the Classic
and Terminal Classic periods.
Source: From Demarest A. A. (2004). *Ancient Maya: The Rise and Fall of
a Rainforest Civilization*. Cambridge: Cambridge University Press, 227
(figure 9.10).

tend to emphasise the more apocalyptic, dramatic, and 'silver bullet'
theories, which form a minority opinion in the diverse archaeological literature; present new theories as revealed truths that eclipse
other ideas; and underplay the fact that change, collapse, and their

TABLE 10.1 *Periods and dates for the Maya culture*

Periods	Approximate dates
Middle Preclassic	1000–400 BC
Late Preclassic	400 BC-AD 300
Early Classic	AD 300–600
Late Classic	AD 600–800
Terminal Classic	AD 800–1000
Early Postclassic	AD 900–1150
Middle Postclassic	AD 1150–1350
Late Postclassic	AD1350–1500
Colonial	AD 1500+

Source: Pages 12–17, Demarest, A. A. (2004). *Ancient Maya: The Rise and Fall of a Rainforest Civilization*. Cambridge: Cambridge University Press.

causes and processes are complex. By doing so they help to create and maintain some of the key myths of collapse in society, such as the idea that climate change wiped out the Maya people and civilisation sometime before AD 1000 (Table 10.1).

DISCOVERING THE ANCIENT MAYA

One of the reasons we imagine the Classic Maya collapse as an all-encompassing disaster, which annihilated the Maya people and culture, is because this is the way their story is often repeated – they rose, they fell, millions died, and the cities vanished into the forest. The few Maya that survived became less 'civilised', returning to the rainforest to become 'noble savages' living amongst the ruins of their own past. Collapse comes to the fore partly because it is an episode embedded in and created by other stories that are more about ourselves than the Maya. Unlike the Romans and the classical heritage, so key to western identity and culture, the ancient Maya, their monuments and (real or imagined) heritage, are psychologically distant enough, and our knowledge of them precarious enough, for them to be cast in whatever role modern people with powerful voices choose.

In modern Western society, the ancient Maya have been exotic 'others' since the nineteenth century, mysterious and mystical, a long vanished American Indian people who built pyramids in the unlikely environments of the central American rainforests, who devised calendars of fantastic intricacy, and who bequeathed us their fascinating art and writing, and prophecies about the world's end. This Maya mystique, as Webster calls it, guarantees that 'the Maya' are a popular 'topic', and while this kind of attention can increase interest in archaeology and the serious study of the past, it also means that many other interest groups can make claims on the Maya past, or the past Maya, and that misconceptions about them abound. Collapse looms large in this; as Webster says: 'The one thing most people think they know about the Maya is that their civilization came to an abrupt and dramatic end'.[4]

The story of the Maya collapse has often been subordinated to a tale of western intrepidity, adventure, and discovery, whose heroes are the Anglo-American pair John Lloyd Stephens and Frederick Catherwood – nowadays the heroes of Maya research are modern scientists who purport to explain the collapse. Stephens had made his name as a travel writer, publishing accounts of Europe and the Near East in the 1830s, while Catherwood had trained as an architect and had studied, sketched, and painted ancient ruins in Egypt, Turkey, Greece, and elsewhere. The two met in 1836, in London, and read reports by Juan Galindo, who had published a description of Palenque in 1831, the Usmacinta River in 1833, and Copan in 1834.[5] In 1839 and 1840 Stephens and Catherwood travelled through Central America and in 1841 published their discoveries in *Incidents of Travel in Central America, Chiapas, and Yucatan*, followed by another volume *Incidents of Travel in Yucatan* in 1843.[6]

Galindo, who was for a time the governor of Peten, had already made a connection between the local Indians and the monuments he encountered, and suggested linguistic continuity between the ancient and modern people of the area. He also rightly suggested that there was ancient writing and had ventured a guess as to the monuments' age, believing them older than central Mexican or Peruvian ruins:

I have seen sufficient to ascertain the high civilization of the former inhabitants, and that they possessed the art of representing sounds by signs, with which I hitherto believed that no Americans, previous to the conquest, were acquainted ...

Everything bears testimony that these surprising people were not physically dissimilar from the present Indians ... I would say, that this nation was destroyed by an irruption of barbarians from the north-west ... I also presume, that the Maya language is derived from them; it is still spoken by all the Indians.[7]

But Stephens and Catherwood gave a different perspective, and one
that reached a much wider audience:

We sat down on the very edge of the wall and strove in vain to penetrate the
mystery by which we were surrounded. Who were the people that built this
city? In the ruined cities of Egypt, even in the long-lost Petra, the stranger
knows the story of the people whose vestiges are around him. America, say
historians, was peopled by savages; but savages never carved these stones. We
asked the Indians who made them, and their dull answer was 'Quien sabe?'
'who knows?'

There were no associations connected with the place; none of those stir-
ring recollections which hallow Rome, Athens, and 'the world's greatest
mistress on the Egyptian plain;' but architecture, sculpture, and painting,
all the arts which embellish life, had flourished in this overgrown forest;
orators, warriors, and statesmen, beauty, ambition, and glory, had lived and
passed away, and none knew that such things had been, or could tell of their
past existence. Books, the records of knowledge, are silent on this theme.
The city was desolate. No remnant of this race hangs round the ruins, with
traditions handed down from father to son, and from generation to generation. It lay before us like a shattered bark in the midst of the ocean, her masts
gone, her name effaced, her crew perished, and none to tell whence she
came, to whom she belonged, how long on her voyage, or what caused her
destruction; her lost people to be traced only by some fancied resemblance
in the construction of the vessel, and, perhaps, never to be known at all.[8]

In their strikingly illustrated bestsellers, great travel writing and still
fascinating to read today, Stephens and Catherwood, while stressing
the complexity of the ancient society, dwelled dramatically on how
the monuments seemed utterly forgotten, and on the disconnections
and disjunctions between the monuments and the modern-day local
people and culture. There was no continuity of knowledge as with
ancient Rome, and no books to help us. We have to recall, though,
that Stephens was not writing straightforward academic history, he
was writing for effect – stressing the exotic and mysterious for his
Anglophone audience of armchair explorers; the 'Maya mystique'
narrative was born before serious archaeological work began.

In characterising the ignorance of the locals, who answered their
question about the identity of the builders of the monuments 'dully',
I wonder if Stephens and Catherwood considered that it may have
seemed as strange and irrelevant a question as it would be to ask local
English people who built Stonehenge – and that one is unanswerable

still. The Maya books that might have shed more light on the matter had of course been burned by the Spanish friar Diego de Landa
in 1562. In William Gates' words: 'if ninety-nine hundredths of our
present knowledge is at base derived from what he [de Landa] told
us, it is an equally safe statement that at the Auto de fe of '62, he
burned ninety-nine times as much knowledge of Maya history and
sciences as he has given us in his book'.[9] By burning these books,
erasing a chunk of Maya culture, colonial Europeans helped set the
stage for the genesis of later ideas of a collapse.

Unlike the Romans and their empire, which are part of the narrative of Western collective identity, the Classic Maya lie outside of
biblical and classical tradition. For the non-Maya western archaeologists who have studied them, their remains have provided something
like a psychologist's Rorschach test, a test in which subjects respond
to an abstract figure they are shown, revealing something about
themselves in the process. For a long while, the ancient Maya were
regarded as a peaceful and religious people, concerned with star-
gazing, calendars, and rituals, and who gathered in ceremonial centres that were not to be regarded true cities; as William Fash explains:

This myth of the Classic Maya became so pervasive that the civilization came
to be thought of as unique in the annals of human history: flourishing in the
jungle, with intelligentsia devoted to the arts and sciences ... all the while
removed from the plights of war, over-crowded cities, and despotic rulers, as
the common people devoted themselves to the cult of their rain gods and
peacefully tilled their fields (*milpa*) with corn, beans, and squash.[10]

As research continued and especially as Maya writing was deciphered
in the 1980s and after, allowing histories of individual kingdoms to be
written from stone stelae and monuments, the ancient Maya became
much less mysterious and much more like ancient peoples and states
elsewhere. Kings advertised and claimed their status by building elaborate monuments at which they would conduct public rituals, and they
recorded their exploits in a true writing system, just like the Egyptian
pharaohs and Roman emperors, society was complex (as Stephens
had suggested), warfare was normal, and the relationships between
the many Maya towns and cities spread through Yucatan were highly
political, complex, and competitive (Figure 10.2).[11] But although we
now know much more about the Maya, more 'facts', we continue to

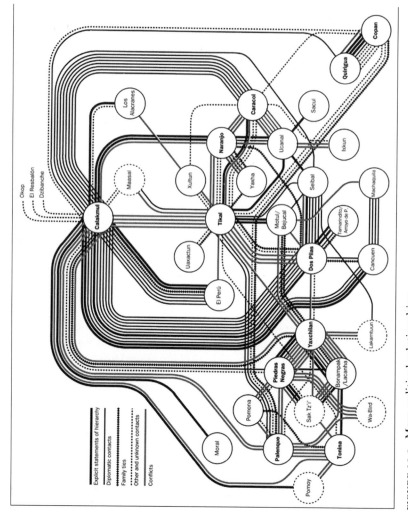

FIGURE 10.2. Maya political relationships.
Source: Image by Simon Martin.

construct 'the Maya' through study and story-telling: 'Maya civilization is an abstract concept created by 150 years of study', and as we change, it changes with us.[12]

CONSTRUCTING THE MAYA COLLAPSE

'Huge cities were swallowed up by the jungle, and Mayan wisdom and knowledge was lost to mankind for centuries. What brought down this thriving society, which had survived and prospered for millennia?' – so runs one summary of the Maya collapse[13] The monuments themselves have always been an important part of the Maya collapse story – explorers encountering those uninhabited stone cities in their jungle setting conjure up something of the feel of that old English poem *The Ruin*, in which Anglo-Saxons encountered the ruins of Roman towns in England, or remind us of Horace Smith's nineteenth century poetic musings on London's post-collapse future.[14] It was self-explanatory that the presence of such monuments in a wild jungle peopled by a few undeveloped locals required explanation – Galindo, in the spirit of the time he lived in, had thought barbarian invasions from the northwest that had happened in precolonial times had brought about collapse.

As major sites came to be investigated by archaeologists, it also became clear that the carved monuments, especially stelae and altars, contained calendrical data, which provided a chronological scheme for fitting Maya history together. In 1946, Sylvanus Morley compiled and studied the available 'Long Count' dates.[15] His chart showed the number of cities that recorded long count dates, which increased to a peak around AD 800, fell sharply after that, but continued at a low level for more than a century after. It seemed that there was a clear 'rise' over more than four centuries, an eighth century florescence, and a rapid 'fall' of the Maya system. The end of the long count records was taken as an index of Classic Maya history.

Thomas Gann and J. E. S. Thompson thought in 1931 that 'the entire population of all the cities deserted their homes in the south, with the enormous investment which these represented in temples, palaces, monoliths, and private houses, and migrated into the peninsula of Yucatan ...'.[16] In 1946, Tatiana Proskouriakoff stated that 'the catastrophically sudden extinction of the arts can be explained only in terms of some widespread and unforeseen disaster that affected most Maya cities soon after AD 800'.[17] As Webster explains, for many people this basic construction of the Maya collapse remains valid today.[18]

But there are problems with this view. As Morley's chart showed, though the number of cities with long count dates fell, they did not disappear suddenly, there was clearly something more complex happening. In focussing on this one type of evidence, he also did not consider major sites that had no inscriptions. In 1997, Fraser Neiman compiled a table of the last dated monuments at sixty-nine sites; the final dates have a range of some 178 years, the earliest found at Tortuguero (AD 711) and the latest at Tonina (AD 909).[19] Also, while early researchers tended to stress the uniformity of Maya civilisation, it has become increasingly clear that Maya cities and states were much more varied and individualistic, forming part of a complex and interconnected zone that shared aspects of culture and lifestyle but were not simply integrated parts of a single empire or unity.

Further research has revealed that there was no simple rise and fall of the Maya that can be provided by long count dates. Many sites have 'gaps', sometimes quite lengthy ones, in their recorded dates. At Tikal, for example, there is a gap of 130 years between AD 562 and AD 692, where no long count date was recorded.[20] These gaps have been regarded as a mini-collapse, called the Hiatus, but it may be more accurate to see Maya states individually as always having more or less successful periods in relation to each other. Evidently they were affected by conflict and warfare with rival states, and also suffered from internal political problems when kings became less powerful or when there were dynastic problems. But even when there were no long count dates recorded, kings might still be active – indicated by the burial of Animal Skull at Tikal and substantial monumental construction during the 'hiatus', and by references to kings recorded at sites other than their own.[21] There may also have been times in the Classic period when some sites did not have single strong rulers.

Beyond the kings and elites, and their literate advertising and memorialising habits, what of the rest of society? Even before Morley compiled his chart, some archaeologists disputed the idea that the southern Maya lowlands had been deserted, or that there had been any widespread abandonment or outmigration based on such evidence – these inscriptions related to the super-elite but did not reveal anything about the majority of the population. Later on Thompson stated that 'the interval spanned by inscriptions on monuments bears no relation to the actual occupation of a site'; ceramic evidence often suggested some continued settlement even when the central complexes of major sites had been abandoned.[22]

The Classic Maya collapse has continued to be debated in much the same terms amongst archaeologists, and others without an archaeological background. The combination of the romantic story of nineteenth century rediscovery of a lost world, with its implications of mystery and a vanished population, supported by some of the well-known presentations of collapse, dovetail neatly with the idea of an apocalyptic disaster, and one of the most prevalent stories of Maya collapse in recent years, with a clearly contemporary cache, is that they were unwitting and helpless victims of climate change.

THE MEGADROUGHT MODEL OF MAYA COLLAPSE

The story we saw at the beginning of Chapter 1 is just one of the latest additions to the idea that the Classic Maya collapse was an apocalyptic event caused by massive droughts. In fact, climate change and droughts have been part of the story of the Maya collapse since the early twentieth century – Ellsworth Huntington advanced such a theory in 1917, but it was not widely taken up because of the cultural and racial determinism that such theories evoked (he proposed climate change theories for the collapse of the Western Roman Empire too).[23] But interest in climate studies did continue; in the 1970s studies began to appear which presented new kinds of data that enabled researchers to begin reconstructing the climate in ancient Maya times.[24] An early study carried out by Alan Covich and Minze Stuiver, for example, analysed isotopes in the shells of freshwater snails from a lake in northern Yucatan, which suggested climate change. Since then, climatology has played an important role in Maya studies.

That droughts and excessive rains affected the Maya region was known from the time of initial Spanish arrival and settlement, and there were records of these events in the Maya books of the Chilam Balams, as Gunn and colleagues describe.[25] According to de Landa, who lived in northern Yucatan in the sixteenth century, famine and scarcity of water were a major cause of conflict; famine could also lead to the abandonment of towns. In the nineteenth century too, droughts could create high death tolls of up to 50 per cent amongst Maya; famine could happen even when foreign grain could have been imported to offset local shortages – famines are often caused or exacerbated by individual human and social and political factors, rather than simply being natural disasters. Droughts and bad years were serious hazards, but could they really be responsible for the collapse of a whole cultural and political system?

The most well-known proponent of the megadrought hypothesis of Maya collapse, and from whose work the chapter epigraph is taken, is Richardson Gill, a banker turned archaeologist in the spirit of Heinrich Schliemann. Gill's theories, put forward in his book *The Great Maya Droughts*, are now widely known to Maya specialists and to the public, and were appealing and dramatic enough to be incorporated into the BBC's documentary *Ancient Apocalypse: The Maya Collapse*; they also remain on the Maya pages of their educational website, from which they gain a degree of authority and acceptance.[26]

These popular programmes present Gill's work as an intrepid journey in which we sympathise with his transformation from businessman to archaeologist, itself caused by the collapse of his family business. His ideas and process of research and deduction are presented as a heroic, almost religious, story of revelation, an emotional journey in which, as an outsider to the archaeological community, he searches for a hidden truth that archaeologists, the gatekeepers of historical knowledge, had not been able to uncover. In the end, he finds 'conclusive proof' and reaches a personal understanding – 'his quest was over'.[27]

Gill's theories are presented as narratives calculated to appeal to a non-specialist audience – part of the appeal is that he comes off as a problem-solving maverick in comparison to the stuffy and reactionary archaeologists, who have failed to find an explanation for the collapse. But Gill's work does not exist in isolation, nor did his ideas on climate come from nothing. However, it is important because in both his book and in a number of academic papers in archaeological journals, he proposes an apocalyptic Maya collapse, which was a catastrophic climatic and demographic disaster that the

Maya were powerless to overcome. If Jared Diamond wondered why societies choose to fail or succeed, Gill was assured that the Maya had no choice in the matter.

Gill and others have developed an argument that explains the Classic Maya collapse (Terminal Classic period *c.* AD 750–1050) as a demographic collapse in which millions of Maya people died because of agricultural failure caused by a series of unusually severe and prolonged droughts.[28] The evidence for the droughts is found in lake sediment cores from Lake Chichancanab and Punta Laguna in northern Yucatan and titanium deposition in the Carioco Basin off northern Venezuela, and has been linked with solar and volcanic activity.[29] Recently, evidence from cave deposits at Yok Balum, Belize, has also been used to chart rainfall, and to suggest a wet period in which the population grew, and a drier period that caused increased warfare during AD 660–1000, followed between AD 1020 and AD 1100 by population collapse caused by prolonged drought.[30]

Many dates are available for the apparent climate changes. Curtis and colleagues proposed that droughts occurred in AD 585, 862, 986, and 1051, suggesting that those of 585 and 862 'coincide with major changes in Maya cultural evolution' and with the ninth century collapse.[31] Hodell and colleagues identified an early dry phase (AD 770–870) and a late phase (AD 920–1100) punctuated by relatively moister periods.[32] Gill and colleagues assemble evidence for the dates of proposed drought events connected (between AD 760 and 930) with cultural change, and argue that the Classic collapse took place in four phases of abandonment (AD 760, 810, 860, and 910).[33] They emphasise that the collapse was unavoidable, catastrophic, and due directly to climatic factors killing off the population.

There is an additional theme to this argument. For many decades, some researchers, including T. Patrick Culbert, have suspected that the Maya lands became increasingly densely populated, with more areas brought under cultivation, changing the landscape.[34] The collapse of the Classic Maya is thus often made into a typical overshoot argument, where a population supposedly grew too much, overused the land, and societies became much less able to tolerate even slight environmental changes. But the endurance of the Maya through centuries punctuated by climatic or severe weather events really suggests a high level of cultural and biological resilience, as we shall see.

THE RETURN OF CATASTROPHISM?

Many archaeologists are certainly willing to see climate change and drought events as affecting Maya society and possibly implicated in collapse, especially in some specific areas such as Quintana Roo and northern Yucatan, which were much drier than the river-watered southern Maya lowlands.[35] But few, if any, accept the megadrought hypothesis, with its overtones of apocalyptic collapse that wiped out the Maya or their culture *en masse*, as a silver bullet explanation of the long and complex 'collapse' of the Classic Maya. Arthur Demarest, for example, has strongly critiqued Gill's work for being selective with data and for failing to match up with collapse chronologies. In his words:

> Gill relies on a crazy quilt of disarticulated bits and pieces of materialist theory from Leslie White, Betty Meggars, Jared Diamond, Carol Crumley, and Richard N. Adams, patched together with elements from chaos theory and complex systems theory as presented in physics and the hard sciences. The overall effect is to awe the reader with the hard-science foundations for the interpretations in the subsequent chapters. This discussion includes extraneous references to the degrees and Nobel prizes of various experts cited. What is absent, however, is a coherent theoretical structure that could be subjected to skeptical critique.[36]

There are several reasons why archaeologists are sceptical about the megadrought hypothesis as a whole. Two problems come from the evidence of the droughts. The sediment cores come from Lake Chichancanab and Punta Laguna in northern Yucatan, but the northern Maya cities, much closer to where the sediments were actually laid down, did not collapse, but rather experienced 'a time of great activity' during AD 750–1050.[37] Rainfall in the dryer north is approximately half what it is further south, yet it was southern cities, including those located near rivers and lakes, Copan, Quiriga, and others, that were collapsing early on.[38] Some inland sites without permanent water supplies, Tikal, Calakmul, and Caracol, outlasted those with such supplies. Evidence from the Carioco Basin, off the Venezuelan coast, is even further distant from the Maya lands, and since droughts and climate conditions can be very localised even during global events, it may not be a reliable indicator of anything to do with the Maya. Drought or reduced rainfall can be no simple cause of the events of the Maya collapse even if droughts did punctuate the period, which they most likely did.

Another problem exists, this time with the dating of the droughts. As Larry Peterson and Gerald Haug point out, giving 'point' dates is misleading, as there is a range of thirty-years error above and below the given dates.[39] In the north, at the time of the supposed droughts in the Terminal Classic period, sites such as Uxmal in the Puuc hills of northwest Yucatan were actually growing in size, probably in part because of people moving from southern areas. Conflicts seem to have increased between local centres, which were eventually unified by the king of Uxmal. In northeastern Yucatan a rival confederacy based at Coba may have collapsed because of conflict with Uxmal and with Chichen Itza – as in the Petexbatun a century or more earlier, sites became increasingly surrounded by defensive works.[40]

Demarest notes that in Petexbatun, in the wetter southern lowlands, the problems that lead to political collapse appeared in the late seventh century; and rather than being sudden, it took over a century to play out as endemic warfare between competing sites took over the region.[41] This created conditions of violence and instability in which demographic decline would take place through outmigration and subsistence problems – war always affects agriculture. He also notes that local palaeoecological and palaeopathological evidence does not indicate climatic change, drought, or famine in the region at the time.[42] David Wahl recently presented evidence from the Peten region that actually indicates that relatively dry conditions, represented by a peak of oxygen isotope values, prevailed up until about AD 900, when isotope values drop dramatically.[43] But pollen evidence indicates that agriculture and settlements were not abandoned until the apparent shift to a wetter climate. He suggests that dry conditions may have been those favoured for Maya agriculture. For Demarest, collapse happens in different places at different times over a long period, and for reasons that need not be the same in each case.

The prominence of the megadrought hypothesis has inspired a considered response from Maya archaeologists and other climate specialists in the form of a 2014 volume edited by Gyles Iannone, entitled *The Great Maya Droughts in Cultural Context: Case Studies in Resilience and Vulnerability*.[44] The contributors to the volume recognise that droughts did happen at various times, but argue that there was no simple uniform final collapse. At different sites and in different regions, each of which was embedded in a particular ecological niche, there were different responses and trajectories. The volume and its conclusions are unlikely to receive as much airtime as the popular model, or to replace it in common knowledge anytime soon. But the volume demonstrates a maturing of ideas on the Maya collapse, and a willingness of scholars to work constructively across disciplinary boundaries.

There most likely were droughts during the Classic and Terminal Classic periods, and, depending on other circumstances, they may have caused serious problems for rulers and for the integrity and functioning of Maya states. But what the evidence shows is not a single sudden termination of the Classic Maya world as a whole. Rather it shows a pattern of state collapses taking place over two to three centuries. If there were droughts in the north, the northern Maya weathered them well enough. In the south, other factors probably played a more important role than climatic fluctuations or multi-year droughts.

Despite the profundity of some of the events and processes of the Terminal Classic and after, the Maya and their culture survived.

WHAT MAYA COLLAPSE?

Some recent summaries of Maya archaeology emphasise that there was no collapse – at least not in the apocalyptic sense that the word often now signifies, and that the megadrought school envisions. The Maya did not disappear, their civilisation and culture were not lost. This is not a new or revisionist view or simply a reaction against recent environmental narratives of collapse. In 1973, E. Wyllis Andrews stated: 'Much has been published in recent years about the collapse of Maya civilization and its causes. It might be wise to preface this chapter with a simple statement that in my belief no such thing happened'. In James Aimers review entitled 'What Maya collapse?' he too supports Andrews' view, but adopts 'collapse' as a shorthand for what is also now called the Terminal Classic period, the period from around AD 750 to 1050.[45]

The Classic Maya world was made up of numerous urban centres generally conceived of as the centres of kingdoms or states; some were bigger and more influential, ruled by strong dynasties, while others were smaller and sometimes fell under the influence of the more powerful states. Arlen and Diane Chase, with Michael Smith, have proposed that there were fourteen primary capitals.[46] These states were neither culturally identical nor unified, although they were related in a complex political, social, and economic web, with interaction fuelling the creation of similarities and differences by actors within the whole system of the Maya culture zone. Demarest writes of a polythetic set of Classic Maya traits, such as an 'emphasis on combined ideological, ritual, political, and military power of the central figure, the *k'uhul ajaw* ('holy lord')', as defining the Classic Maya.[47]

So every Maya centre was unique, though they shared many commonalities that allow us to view them as a whole. Northern and southern centres differed somewhat in architectural styles and the use of epigraphy. And at centres like Caracol, rather than a powerful ruling dynasty as was present earlier, a system with a more egalitarian feel may have been in place in the Late Classic; we have to be open to the normal dynamism of politics and social life in Classic Maya states.[48]

Neither did all Maya states occupy the same kinds of environment: 'the land … was vast and environmentally diverse, covering nearly half a million square kilometres and ranging from high volcanic mountain ranges with narrow cool valleys to dense rainforest interspersed with swamps and rivers to the dry forest plains of the north', Linda Schele and David Freidel explain.[49] In such a varied local environments, can megadroughts really be thought to account for the whole collapse? It seems doubtful.

Rather than thinking of a single and 'instantaneous' Classic Maya collapse that affected the whole region, the Terminal Classic period can best be conceptualised as a long period that was experienced in a variety of ways by people of different status at different places.[50] Aimers notes that Maya scholars also refer to 'collapse' as decline, transition, transformation, or crumble, and the range of terms expresses the idea of variety well.[51] Individual kingdoms and sites certainly did experience collapse and subsequent depopulation – states that had existed ended, but this did not happen all at once nor for a single reason. Demarest now places the beginnings of the earliest collapses at AD 695 in the south central Pasion region, and these continued to AD 800.[52] He notes that 'all of these radical changes occurred a full century before most proposed global, silver-bullet solutions to the collapse issues, including drought'. But that was not the end – collapses within the Classic Maya zone continued to happen over the next two centuries.

The Maya landscape as a whole looked different at the end of the Terminal Classic when compared to the earlier Classic period, and the Classic era political system based on divine kingship did not survive.[53] But this should not surprise us – which society has remained the same for five centuries? But while most states did collapse, and some areas apparently became widely depopulated, others did not, for example, Lamanai in Belize.[54] Some states even experienced increased population and continued building, as well as active trade.[55] As a whole, we are entitled to retain the concept of collapse as applied to specific states and regional networks, but on a larger geographic and chronological scale the Maya world transformed; but it certainly did not end.

POLITICAL COLLAPSES AND CULTURAL TRANSFORMATIONS

Rather than concentrating on knockout disasters that caused 'the Maya collapse' at a given point in time, many scholars focus on the fates of the individual Maya kingdoms.[56] After all, there was no Maya empire, rather there was a connected world that had developed together, that shared a degree of culture and similar languages, that were interconnected by trade, and had economies (political and wealth) that were connected to some extent but with plenty of individual variation.[57] Even though Maya states may not have been entirely 'territorial', it may be helpful to image the Maya world as something like medieval Europe, a world with a shared heritage, with Latin as a common written and spoken language and Christianity as a common religion. The Classic Maya spoke many languages but tended to write in a prestige language – classic Ch'olt'ian.[58] Europe was a world of connected cultures and economies, but full of opportunistic rulers, dynasties, and barons (and others) ready to take on one or another of their neighbours. In the years after the Western Roman Empire, its successor states came and went – the Vandal states in Iberia and North Africa and others, and this went on for hundreds of years until the modern contemporary nations came to occupy the space of Europe.[59] Why should we imagine the Maya lands and rulers as so very different?

Arthur Demarest sees collapse as progressing in stages, the first stage taking place in the Petexbatun region at the end of the seventh to ninth centuries, with an increase in intersite warfare and outmigration[60] or nucleation of population into defensible centres such as Aguateca.[61] The story hinges on politics and rivalry, as the fate of states often has done. The site of Dos Pilas, for example, appears to have been founded (late, by AD 650) by a member of the Tikal royal family, perhaps a disenfranchised claimant to the throne, taking over the area from two former kingdoms. The new Dos Pilas dynasty and state was sponsored by Calakmul, Tikal's great rival to the north. Gaining a regional hegemony with Calakmul's help, it seems that this support was withdrawn, or, at any rate, reduced in the reign of K'awill Chan K'inich (*c.* AD 741–761); over the eighth century Calakmul declined in power and regional influence.[62] Dos Pilas was not able to continue its domination of the other sites in the area, and its power also waned. Inhabitants took apart temples and palaces in order to build defensive walls – evidently the threat of conflict was clear and present (Figure 10.3).[63] The city was abandoned around AD 761, and this did not happen peacefully; there was probably a battle there as spearpoints and decapitated skulls have been found.[64] Everyone did not disappear, though many may have fled, unable to make a living in an increasingly dangerous and unstable militarised land.

Aguateca, a much more defensible site than Dos Pilas, received an influx of population at the beginning of the eighth century, including elites and rulers from Dos Pilas (Figure 10.4).[65] Kings continued to rule from there for the next fifty years, the last known being Lachan K'awiil Ajaw B'ot (AD 802–807). Around AD 800 to 830, Aguateca too was attacked and burned, with destruction focussed on the elite areas of the site. Takeshi Inomata, who has investigated the site, concludes that since 'the enemies did not leave their own material remains … their identity is only a subject of speculation', but 'the thorough destruction of the epicenter and the lack of enemy occupations in this center imply that the intention of the enemies was not to conquer or subjugate this center but to terminate it as a political and economic power'.[66] Some kingdoms collapsed because

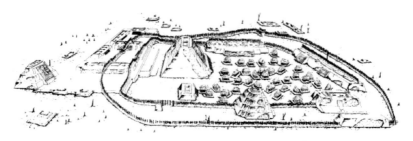

FIGURE 10.3. The transformation of Dos Pilas into a defended centre.
Source: Courtesy of Arthur Demarest (artist: Luis Fernando Luin).

of direct military action aimed at their annihilation. Depopulation would have been caused by these specific events, but this should be seen as a process taking place over time (decades at least).

The destabilisation and fall of Dos Pilas and later Aguateca allowed the further development of nearby kingdoms, such as Cancuen, further south.[67] Cancuen began life in AD 656 as another strategic move by Calakmul; it was founded in a well-watered riverine area to control a strategic political and economic crossroads running north/south and east/west.[68] Cancuen went on to thrive in its own right during the eighth century, between AD 740 and 790. A massive palace was constructed, as were other elite dwellings, at the heart of the site on a peninsula, with a port, plazas, and ballcourts, but habitation stretched out over a much larger area. Cancuen was adapting itself to the changing realities of the time in terms of a degree of 'power sharing' between the elite, control over long distance interactions, trade and exchange, and alliances. Demarest has identified this as a shift 'from Terminal Classic to Postclassic economic patterns'.[69] But

FIGURE 10.4. Aguateca, a naturally defensible location with cliffs and a gorge. *Source*: Courtesy of Arthur Demarest (artist: Luis Fernando Luin).

although 'they seem to have been doing the right things to survive the transition from the Classic to the Postclassic ... they didn't survive'.[70] Like Dos Pilas and Aguateca, Cancuen was violently destroyed around AD 800 – the royal family were ritually executed along with more than thirty nobles, including children; they were placed in a cistern in their royal regalia and the site was abandoned.[71]

In this river fed 'wet zone' the relatively rapid series of collapses did not happen because of climate change, it happened because of a descent into increasingly violent conflict caused by the ambitions of rulers and elites; the desire to rule bigger and better states (with more and grander monuments) created 'status rivalry' between states and pressures on long distance exchange systems that provided the lords with exotica needed to display (and claim) their high statuses within their states.[72] In addition, states became less stable as the elite class grew and alternative lineages claimed more power and a higher status, claiming higher titles and building rival palaces. Conflict would have encouraged farmers to leave the area, and as dynasties and states collapsed, so depopulation increased; the collapse was 'marked by the demise of the *k'uhul ajaw* system of governance *followed* by the abandonment of many Maya settlements in the South'.[73]

Elsewhere in the Maya region, at Copan, William Fash suspects that 'competition between noble lines, or between noble lines and the Copan dynasty, probably contributed significantly to the breakdown of the kingdom'.[74] The last carved monument is dated to AD 822, but during the reign of the king, Yax Pasaj Chan Yoaat (AD 763 to *c.* 810), the kingdom may already have begun to fragment. The evidence for this is the appearance on many of his monuments of a number of 'companions' who also took part in king-like activities: 'seating' and 'scattering' rituals.[75] In addition, nobles were building palaces and having carved hieroglyphic benches made. This was happening by AD 780. Soon after, the ruler of a local centre called Los Higos seems to have proclaimed his independence by erecting a stela of his own in AD 781. Although Yax Pasaj did commemorate his time in power in AD 802 at Copan, no monument commemorates the special calendrical year AD 810, the end of a significant k'atun date, which was recorded at Quiriga. Copan, which probably had a peak population of 15,000–20,000 during AD 750–800, seems to have remained at least partly inhabited, though on a much reduced level, until around AD 1200, and there was continued construction and elite activity at the site after AD 800.[76]

Fash suggests that revolts of nobles, rather than peasant's revolts, may have happened at many other sites too. Indeed, at other major sites too we see similar patterns of the breakdown of control by ruling dynasties, and this is not particularly surprising. Although we tend to think in terms of states being fairly stable once they are established – as we imagine our own to be (how could they possibly end, except by disaster?) – ancient rulers who attempted to manage 'states', and dynasties that attempted to keep and transfer power to the next generation faced significant challenges – not least the desire of others to dispute or share power, or resist the claims of authority of rulers in some way.

Such revolts, conflicts between rival lineages, are recorded in later Postclassic Maya times, as at Mayapan, as de Landa wrote:

And this they did, killing at the same time all his sons, except one who was absent. They sacked his house and took away the lands which he had in cacao and in other fruits, saying that they paid themselves for what he had taken from them. The quarrels between the Cocoms, who said that they had been unjustly expelled, and the Xius, lasted so long, that after they had lived in that city for more than five hundred years, they abandoned it and left it in solitude, each party returning to his own country.[77]

It is not possible here to survey the collapses of the entire Maya culture zone. But we can emphasise that Classic collapses happened over a long span of time, with the last taking place at Chichen Itza in the much drier northern Yucatan in the mid-eleventh century.[78] Many of the collapses seem to have been violent and the destruction of communities must have been traumatic – more for some than others, no doubt.

I cannot do better than sum up the Classic Maya collapse in the words of Maya specialists Don and Prudence Rice and Arthur Demarest:

What actually collapsed, declined, gradually disappeared, or was transformed at the end of the Classic period was a specific type of political system and its archaeological manifestations: a system of theater-states, identified by Emblem Glyphs, dominated by the k'ul ajawob (holy kings) and their inscribed stone monuments, royal funerary cults, and tomb-temples, the political hegemonies of these divine lords, and their patronage networks of redistribution of fineware polychrome ceramics, high status exotics, and

ornaments. Its ending is often accompanied within a century by the depopulation of major cities, drastic reduction in public architecture, and other
changes. Notably, however, in other areas, such as Belize, the Mopan Valley,
and the northern lowlands, the close of the Classic period saw more gradual
change or even florescence. There clearly was no 'uniform' collapse phenomenon, but rather a sequence of highly variable changes. Yet in all cases
there was a pronounced change in the Classic Maya socio-political order
by the end of the Terminal Classic (varying from AD 950–1100), with the
'termination' of the divine k'ul ajaw institution and most of its distinctive,
archaeologically manifest features of elite culture.[79]

WHAT HAPPENED NEXT?

The feature most Maya specialists mean when they talk of the Classic
collapse is not site abandonment or depopulation, but the end of a
particular kind of socio-political organisation and order, and the
material cultural expression of it that had grown up over the previous
centuries. Demarest summarises what it was that 'collapsed, declined,
or was transformed by the end of the Classic period' thus:

> It was a specific type of political system and its material culture: a system of
> competitive states with most forms of power (religious, military, and politi-
> cal) focused on their 'Holy Lords,' the *k'uhul ajaw*.[80]

Chase and Chase see a new Postclassic focus on symbolic egalitarianism – the age of super-kings, the *k'uhul ajaws*, with their
self-aggrandising agendas was ended in the collapse, their rule and
ideology consciously rejected by subsequent generations.[81] But the past
was remembered and selectively recycled in some places – despite significant changes, abandonments and destructions, and shifts in population, the Postclassic was no dark age – complex society was still present.

As Anthony Andrews points out, the Postclassic Maya 'built pyramids, palaces, temples, shrines, and a wide range of residential
structures'; the buildings they constructed were covered in colour-
fully painted stucco.[82] The incoming Spanish saw Maya communities with several thousand houses. Even in the south, where Late
and Terminal Classic abandonment and depopulation was most
pronounced, the populations 'may have been much larger than
the archaeological and historical evidence suggests' because of the
perishable nature of domestic architecture.[83] Society in some places

was highly stratified, urban, and still literate, although Stephen Houston observes that the later writing of the Maya is 'notoriously difficult to study'.[84]

Two northern sites and one eastern site bridge the Terminal to Postclassic divide – Chichen Itza, Mayapan, and Lamanai. Chichen Itza became a major regional player in northern Yucatan from the early ninth century.[85] There are long count dates, the last possibly being from AD 897 (there may be one from AD 998, but this is not certain). Even so, Andrews and colleagues see Chichen Itza as continuing to be a power for some time after AD 900. The changing material culture, the end of long count records 'may reflect a shift to a public narrative iconographic program, directed to an increasingly cosmopolitan and multi-ethnic population'.[86] Murals from the Temple of the Jaguars, for example, show a pitched battle with a multitude of combatants; Webster points out that 'they differ markedly from Classic war depictions, which usually focus on individual kings, elite warriors, or prisoners'.[87] Such novel representations could indicate a shift away from a ruler focus towards the 'symbolic egalitarianism' that the Chases identify.

The Chichen Itza collapse, now dated to the early eleventh century,[88] was remembered by later generations, and de Landa was informed thus:

There once reigned three lords who were brothers, and who came to that land from the west. And they brought together in these cities a great number of towns and people, and ruled over them for some years with justice and peace ... soon they split into factions, so wanton and licentious in their ways, that the people came so greatly to loath them that they killed them, laid the town waste and themselves dispersed, abandoning the buildings and this beautiful site ...[89]

We should note here that Maya people voted with their feet, killing bad rulers and destroying and abandoning towns that had no infrastructure or agricultural problems – there is no reason to suspect they did not do this in earlier times too.

Masson and colleagues discussed the formation of the Postclassic state of Mayapan, the successor of Chichen Itza in the north. They have demonstrated that aspects of the Classic and Terminal Classic past were actively adopted or deliberately rejected by the people there.[90] For example, major monuments based on those at Chichen Itza were constructed, including a quadripartite serpent temple, a colonnaded hall, and a round temple, but other building models and behaviours were rejected – there were no long count dates recorded in stone, no ballcourts, and no large scale offerings were deposited in cenotes (sinkholes).

The city of Mayapan was the capital of a large regional state; population estimates for the city range from 8,400 to 21,000.[91] It was governed not by a 'holy lord' but by a council (*multepal*) of major landowners, dominant lineage groups who banded together in a 'voluntary confederacy'; they owned the surrounding towns and villages but resided with their followers in the city.[92] The Mayapan confederacy collapsed as lineage groups (the Cocoms and Xius, mentioned earlier) competed with each other – the state fragmented in the AD 1440s. However, members of the prominent families continued to live in the area a century later.

Aimers, in a paper called 'Anti-apocalypse', points to the long duration of the transition from Classic to Postclassic, and to the new Postclassic sites, most of which were founded in Late or Terminal Classic times.[93] Many of these were in the north, in Yucatan, rather than in the river-fed southern lowlands, although there were important sites in the Peten Lakes area too. In the eastern area, at the important centre of Lamanai, on the New River in Belize, there was no collapse; the city flourished during the Terminal and Postclassic period, and into the colonial period, even surviving into the period of the British occupation of Belize (Figure 10.5).[94] At Lamanai, as at Chichen Itza and Mayapan, stone buildings continued to be used, renovated, and built, and there was no break in Maya culture.

There are several possible reasons why Lamanai was more resilient than other Maya states and statelets – its people may not have engaged in excessive elite competition within the region or in militaristic competition with other sites, for example. Lamanai may also have played a role in the shifting of regional trade from inland to coastal routes, which seems to have taken place from the Classic to Postclassic times.[95] Aimers' work demonstrates that Lamanai pottery shows clear links with the major northwestern site of Mayapan, and may have been as important a site, but it was also connected with many other coastal sites such as Cozumel and Tulum to the north. Research at Lamanai may yet have much to tell us.

FIGURE 10.5. Impression of Lamanai.
Source: Courtesy of Stan Loten.

BARBARIAN INVASION: CONTINUITY AND CULTURAL DESTRUCTION

The Maya, like many peoples encountered by roving European adventurers, on the hunt for wealth, profit, and advantage in the second millennium AD, came off worse for the encounter, both by accident of Old World diseases and by design of conquest and Christianisation. Cortes met Maya people on landing in Yucatan in 1519, and these Maya lived in dispersed settlements, villages and towns with stone buildings and perhaps small pyramid temples, like at Cozumel. The city of Mayapan had only recently been abandoned by the Maya in the early 1460s, but the Maya had settled into the Postclassic culture, adapted to their world, over centuries. Further west the indigenous people lived in cities that impressed the Spanish enough for them to make comparisons with Cairo and Seville, but the search for gold left Yucatan and the Maya out of the picture until some years later.

When Cortes arrived, the Maya were divided into several groups or provinces (*kuchcabaloob*), perhaps between sixteen and twenty-four.[96] Archaeologists argue about the classification of these groupings – as states, city-states, chiefdoms, etc., and it seems best to conclude that arrangements were varied and constantly shifting – so permanent boundaries are not really clear. At Mayapan and possibly also at Chichen Itza, there had been *multepal*, councils of prominent people. The Postclassic Maya world they found was still thriving, with strong regional trade tying areas together.

Although Maya literacy practices were affected by the Classic collapse, the Postclassic was still a literate world, but one of painted books rather than carved monumental texts, which extolled kings' doings. Diego de Landa, one of the architects of Maya cultural destruction – a book burner extraordinaire – described Maya books thus in 1566:

> They wrote their books on a long sheet doubled in folds, which was then enclosed between two boards finely ornamented; the writing was on one side and the other according to the folds. The paper they made from the roots of a tree, and it gave a white finish excellent for writing upon. Some of the principal lords were learned in these sciences, from interest, and for the greater esteem they enjoyed thereby; yet they did not make use of them in public.[97]

Literacy practices had changed – with the removal of the holy lords, the elite driven literacy of the Classic period would not remain a fossilised relic.[98] But the reaction of the Europeans to indigenous religion and culture was one characterised by zealous Christianity. This had a terrible impact on traditional culture, and of the hundreds of books that once existed, only three now remain. Frans Blom quotes one Father Cogulludo, another destroyer of ancient Maya culture, who in his *History of Yucatan* stated:

> With a desire to stamp out this idolatry, I assembled all the books and ancient characters which the Indians had, and in order to deprive them of every occasion and memory of their ancient rites, then, where ever we could find books, we burned them publicly, in the day of the Auto de Fe, and together with their rituals, we also burned the history of their ancient times.[99]

Another technique in deliberate cultural destruction was the re-education of children; de Landa describes this too:

> The method taken for indoctrinating the Indians was by collecting the small children of the lords and leading men, and establishing them around the monasteries in houses which each town built for the purpose … Then among these children they gathered them in for catechism, from which

frequent visiting many asked for baptism, with much devotion. The children then, after being taught, informed the friars of idolatries and orgies; they broke up the idols, even those belonging to their own fathers ... Even when they were threatened by their people they were not deterred ...[100]

Despite indoctrination and the inevitable changes wrought by disease and colonialism, Maya identities were preserved, though changed.

Some Maya states continued to exist alongside the Spanish invaders, for a time. The Itza of Nojpeten, on Lake Peten Itza, held out until they were conquered by the Spanish in a major campaign – their city was stormed on 13th March AD 1697.[101] Nojpeten was an island city with temples, palaces, and thatched houses, possibly founded by Itza who had migrated from northern Yucatan, possibly from Chichen Itza.[102] Many of the city's inhabitants fled or were killed and the Spanish soon set about destroying what they found.[103] Subsequently the process of Christianising the Itza began; the king Ajaw Kan Ek' was baptised, renamed Joseph Pablo Kan 'Ek and eventually was moved to Santiago de Guatemala, where he and his son were given a degree of freedom.[104]

New towns and missions were founded to subjugate and convert the Itza and their neighbouring peoples.[105] They had been ravaged by smallpox, which killed many. But after only a few years, in AD 1704, there was an uprising – unsuccessful – of local Maya. That was not the end of the story. A number of later Maya uprisings followed – including the so-called Caste War, which lasted from 1847 to 1901.[106] Many Maya people continued to fight for their rights even into the twentieth century – in Guatemala, where Maya form the majority of the population, tens of thousands were killed and the government accused of committing genocide against the Maya in a thirty-six-year civil war that began in 1960.[107] Maya history did not end with the Classic Maya collapse.

FINAL THOUGHTS

Patricia McAnany and Tomas Negron ask 'why is Western society so intrigued by the ancestors of contemporary Maya people, and so willing to label one of their societal transformations a 'failure?'"[108] If the collapse was a breakdown or a rejection of a kind of ideological, economic, and political arrangement, where divine kings claimed a central place in competitive states, then was collapse a bad thing for most Maya people? If we see the Maya people as deliberate actors with their own motivations, we have to conclude that some (many?) chose 'collapse'. There was no instant annihilation of population – people just behaved differently, ebbing away from some places over a hundred or more years and adopting less visible lifestyles. To those who see monument-building states with royal leaders as more worthy than less impactful lives, the Maya collapse may well be tragic – but as David Pendergast says, 'it is only if we persist in seeing the Classic as the embodiment of perfection in all aspects of life that we can view the succeeding centuries as all dross and dreariness'.[109]

To stick to the myth of an apocalyptic Classic Maya collapse where everyone died of hunger and thirst is to dismiss, or even fail to see, a thousand years of Postclassic Maya history, and the countless lives and stories therein. It also helps to excuse or brush aside some of the messier and less pleasant parts of a much less mysterious and more recent colonial history that still needs to be confronted.

The modern Maya population of Central America is higher than the population of Scotland, almost as high as that of Switzerland, although there is nothing that could exactly be described as a Maya state. In the various states where they do live, created through European colonialism, Maya people are still suffering the consequences of violent colonialism and centuries of continued exploitation, and prejudice, although increasingly their presence is recognised and voices heard more widely. Archaeology and archaeologists can and often do try to play a positive role here, and one responsibility that they and other scientists have is surely to encourage a richer and more balanced appreciation of the Maya story.

The relationship of modern Maya to a 'Maya' identity, and to their Classic Maya ancestors and ancestral culture, is not straightforward, though, as Robey Callahan noted when interviewing modern Maya in Coba about the film *Apocalypto*. Many of the interviewees spoke a Maya language, and did not speak Spanish, the prestige language, well, but some felt inferior because their Mayan, with its loan words from Spanish, is different to the classicised Yucatec Maya language of the film, and to the deliberately 'purified' Mayan spoken by some of the local political activists. There was also a clear cultural distance too – the film, they thought, was about 'the Maya' – not them. In modern parlance, people used 'Maya' to describe very traditional people or the very poor, and the 'Maya' and their monuments are associated with the wild jungle and not the domestic village.

Recognising that the myth of an apocalyptic Maya collapse fails to tell the whole story does not mean that the Classic Maya collapse goes out the window entirely – in my view, it actually makes it much more interesting and relevant. Instead of a knockout blow that simply killed huge numbers of people, we need to appreciate a much more complex picture, one of competition, rivalry, vast differences in wealth and status, and social exclusion, which was at the time bad for some and good for others.

If the collapse of past societies is going to be used to develop models for present day sustainable communities, it is important to see that myths of collapse can get in the way. James Aimers comment that 'few scholars see the collapse as a result of purely environmental factors', and his use of 'collapse' is 'as shorthand ... to refer to the interval between the height of the Classic period and the subsequent Postclassic period, the dates and characteristics of which varied across the lowlands between approximately AD 750 and AD 1050'.[110] As he says:

we need to consider cultural responses to crises like drought. People are not plants or animals, they react and try to adapt by changing ideas, organizational structures, and practices, but not always successfully.[111]

Bartolome de las Casas is not a name that many westerners grow up knowing, unlike the names of Columbus and Cortes, but he deserves to be much better known.[112] Born in AD 1484, he and his father migrated to Hispaniola in 1502, and, after witnessing the horrors of conquest and colonialism, he dedicated the rest of his life to recording and fighting its worst excesses – beginning even before Cortes got to Yucatan. In 1542 he wrote *A Short Account of the Destruction of the Indies*, dedicated to Philip II of Spain, in which he catalogued the atrocities he saw and heard about. Although he agreed with the Pope that the Spanish had legal sovereignty – and that this gave the Christian Spanish a reason for being in the pagan Americas – this he argued was no carte blanche for ignoring indigenous people's claim to their land and property, nor to enslave or mistreat them. He argued that indigenous royalty and nobility had the same status as others in the Spanish 'commonwealth'.

De las Casas is less fun to read than many books about the mysteries of collapse and the romance of lost cities; in fact, the accounts in *Destruction* are so horrible that no one would wish them to be true. But such views are perhaps more important in the long run, and we can consider whether it is best to substitute a modern myth of apocalyptic collapse, caused by external forces, for a real recorded history of the most appalling behaviour, cruelty, selfishness and greed. It is sobering to dwell on the words of William George Lovell who suggests that 'viewed in historical perspective, it is disconcerting to think how much the twentieth century resembles the sixteenth, for the parallels between cycles of conquest hundreds of years apart are striking'.[113]

THE BLACK LEGEND AND POPULATION IN MESOAMERICA

'The Black Legend' – the term was first used by Julian Juderias in 1914 – 'depicted the Spaniards as brutal and bloody colonists who systematically victimized their native subjects' leading to massive loss of life and culture among the indigenous peoples of the Americas.[114] As a myth, it became popular amongst the early modern English; by the late eighteenth century it was widely known, especially in Protestant parts of Europe. The Black Legend takes as its primary sources writings such as Bartolome de las Casas' book *A Short Account of the Destruction of the Indies* and Garcilaso de la Vega's history of Peru (de la Vega was half Spanish half Inka), both of which catalogue the atrocities of conquistadors. Although the Black Legend reflected 'the hideous truth of a Black Reality ... its overall portrayal is crude and simplistic', according to W. George Lovell.[115]

Although there is a persistent myth that the Americas were 'a sparsely populated wilderness', historians and others have increasingly come to recognise that the Americas were very well populated before the Colonial era, and that the landscapes of the two continents had been humanly modified. William Denevan makes this point in a key 1992 article 'The pristine myth: The landscape of the Americas in 1492'. What caused drastic depopulation, as is well-recognised now, was the devastating effects of Old World diseases on native populations; thus not only was the cruelty of colonial behaviour to blame for population collapse. Because of depopulation, Denevan suggests that quite possibly 'the human presence' in the Americas 'was less visible in 1750 than it was in 1492'.[116]

Despite the behaviours described in the Black Legend and the effects of new diseases on New World peoples, what is astonishing about the massive and very real demographic collapse that hit the Americas is that it did not utterly destroy all native cultures, many of which survive in some form to this day, not only in the Maya lands, but also in the Andes and elsewhere. However, it seems that in some places, for example, the Amazon, which is now recognised to have housed complex, even urban, agricultural-based societies, the ravages of disease did bring about cultural, political, population, and social collapse in the wake of the new arrivals.[117]

11

Collapse in the Andes

The ruins of Tiahuanaco have been regarded by all students of American antiquities as in many respects the most interesting and important, and at the same time most enigmatical ...

E. George Squier[1]

INTRODUCTION

Most people have heard of the Inka of Peru, and would recognise a picture of the famous Inka city of Machu Picchu, perched on a mountain top overlooking the Urabamba Valley, near their capital city of Cuzco. At its height, their vast empire stretched 3,000 miles along the mountains and coast of western South America. The empire was destroyed by the Spaniards in the sixteenth century – its fall brought about by a barbarian invasion, it could be said, as well as the spread of Old World disease. But the Inka were not the only complex society to develop in the region, rather they were the latest in a line of indigenous societies and empires to grow up before the colonial period (Table 11.1). In this chapter, we shall look at the collapse of three of these, the Moche of the north Andean coast and the highland altiplano states of Tiwanaku and Wari (Figure 11.1).

There are several reasons for looking at three collapses in a single chapter. One is that the cultures of the Andean region were interconnected and overlapped culturally, geographically, politically, and temporally, and they form something of a continuum. In some ways, this is

TABLE 11.1 *Some periods and cultures of the Andean region*

Periods	Cultures	Approximate dates
Early Intermediate Period		100 BC-AD 650
	Moche	200 BC-AD 750
	Tiwanaku	AD 300–1000
Middle Horizon		AD 650–1000
	Wari	AD 600–1000
Late Intermediate Period		AD 1000–1475
Late Horizon		AD 1200–1475
	Inka	AD 1200–1533

Source: Page 642, Moseley, M. E. and Heckenberger, M. J. (2009). 'From village to empire in South America.' In Scarre, C. (ed.). *The Human Past: World Prehistory & The Development of Human Societies*. Second edition. London: Thames and Hudson, pp. 640–677.

reminiscent of the city-states of Mesopotamia, which were periodically independent, then sometimes drawn into empires, and which belonged to a shared culture zone. Another reason is that scholars have identified different patterns of response to the same circumstances, in terms of collapse. Also, for some of these collapses we really have so little to go on that we can deal reasonably with several collapses in one place.

THE MOCHE

The Moche culture, named for the valley where it was first identified and where many of its largest monuments are located, developed in the valleys of the north coast of Peru in a dry desert environment where they used irrigation-based agriculture (Figure 11.2).[2] Archaeologists have divided the Moche culture into a five-stage chronology based on pottery: I to V, early to late.[3] This is set into the wider Andean chronological scheme, where the Moche culture spans the Early Intermediate Period to the Middle Horizon, roughly from AD 200 to 750 (though the initial period started gradually and has different dates in different areas). The transition between periods IV and V marks the Moche collapse.[4]

Moche is usually considered, archaeologically speaking, as a culture – an artistic style best seen on pottery. So when we speak of 'the Moche', we are really referring to the people who used Moche material culture over a long period – to what degree this reflects ethnicity is

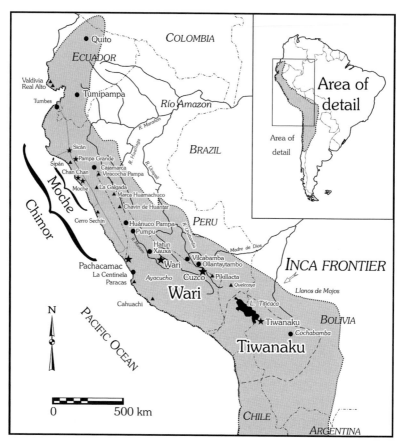

FIGURE 11.1. Map of the ancient Andes.
Source: From D'Altroy, T. N. (2014). 'The Late Intermediate Period and Late Horizon.' In Renfrew, C. and Bahn, P. (eds.). *Cambridge World Prehistory*. *Volume III*. Cambridge: Cambridge University Press, 1143 (map 2.26.1).

arguable.[5] As for the political organisation of the Moche area, Jeffrey Quilter explains that there are several competing models, and this has a bearing on the collapse and its aftermath.[6] The first model is that of a single conquest state that expanded its influence regionally; it was ruled from Moche and sponsored the common artistic style and replicated an architectural pattern in various centres. A second model sees two politically independent Moche regions, a northern region including the Jequetepeque Valley, with a three-phase ceramic sequence, and a southern one with the standard five-period ceramic,

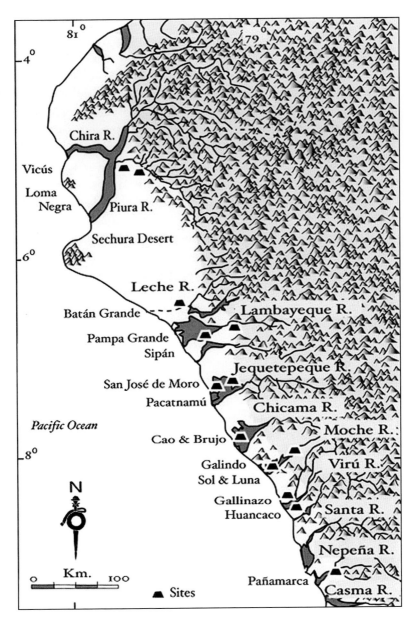

FIGURE 11.2. The Moche area in northern Peru.
Source: Reproduced with permission of Springer New York.

based at Moche. In the third model, the Moche area is dotted with independent and competing kingdoms sharing a common culture. John Verano suggests that Moche ceramics show scenes of combat, similar to those of the Maya, which depict conflict between cities and royal leaders.[7] Another idea is that the Moche may have occasionally formed a federation, with Moche as the primary site. Others argue that there were chiefdoms rather than states. It is possible, as Quilter points out, that all or some of these reflect reality at some point in time. Some authors detect a certain 'militarism' in the archaeological evidence, and this may have played a role in the Moche expansion.[8]

At any rate, Michael Moseley and Charles Stanish both identify a Moche state which had developed by the fourth century AD.[9] The new artistic culture was a state-sponsored style adopted as the state expanded. The capital was at Moche (Cerro Blanco), where the great mud-brick pyramids of the Huaca del Sol and the Huaca de la Luna dominated an urban landscape with compounds, squares, streets, canals, and craft production areas. The Huaca del Sol was the biggest monument of its kind in South America, while the city may have been the first in South America, and was quite possibly a royal residence as well as a ceremonial space. The Huaca de la Luna was decorated with murals. Another key site is Sipan, famous for the 'Lord of Sipan' burial, discovered by Walter Alva and Christopher Donnan; the lord, dressed for war, was buried with more than four hundred precious objects, a large solid gold headdress, with retainers on either side of his body (Figure 11.3).[10] The Moche also engaged in human sacrifice at temples and accompanying the burials of high status individuals like the Lord of Sipan, and images of the sacrifice of prisoners of war are shown on pottery.[11]

Collapse

The Moche collapse is dated to around AD 600, the transition from period IV to V. Garth Bawden lists the features of collapse as including the abandonment of the capital city and the founding of new settlements (Galindo and Pampa Grande), which were located in valley necks, the abandonment of agricultural land, and significant changes in elite iconography.

Both Bawden and Quilter identify three major themes in the explanation of the Moche collapse. These are external causes - the impact

FIGURE 11.3. Royal tomb (Tomb 1) at Sipan.
Source: Courtesy of Getty Images.

of Wari imperialism/influence; environmental reasons, including El Nino events, floods, and droughts; and internal causes such as revolt or revolution.[12] Let us look at each in turn.

The Impact of Wari Imperialism

One explanation of collapse focusses on the rise of the Wari state. This was an expansive state or empire, that was located to the southeast of the Moche region, based in the high Andean altiplano. It was expanding its influence to the north at around the same time as the Moche collapse, leading some to link the two.[13] However, Shimada and colleagues have pointed out that Wari expansion does not explain the location of Wari V sites in valley neck areas, where the priority seems to have been to control water flow. They also observe that Wari ceramics and features only appear in or after Wari V, which they take to suggest a much later influence; Wari may have been an influence on the post-collapse Moche V. Stanish too suggests that Wari 'seems to have had some political access to former Moche territory'; this might be taken to imply a connection between Wari expansion and Moche collapse or it may just mean that Wari culture filled a post-collapse vacuum.[14] In the latter two scenarios, we also should remember that the Moche may not have been passive victims but perhaps made active choices about their cultural and political values. So, while there may be some connection here, it is far from certain or clearcut.

Environmental Causes

A number of scholars have proposed environmental causes for the Moche collapse. Some of these were reviewed by Shimada and colleagues.[15] They included periods of aridification or reduced rainfall and cold periods that sparked agricultural crises and also caused the changes in settlement patterns mentioned earlier. Whilst they agree with the general tenor of these arguments, Shimada and team found the evidence and argumentation a little weak. They based their own argument – that the sixth century was punctuated by drought events, for example, a seventeen year one at AD 524, and that there was an especially abrupt and severe thirty year megadrought from AD 562 to 594 – on analysis of cores taken from the Quelcayya ice cap. The later drought was followed by a wetter phase. They argue that the cores give a precise record of precipitation in the northern coastal area and so are an improvement over previous work.

In addition to droughts, some scholars have blamed El Nino events for causing serious rains and flooding that would have washed away the dusty soil from farmlands, damaged canals, and swept away and/or damaged buildings, including even the Huaca del Sol.[16] Sediments washed out to shore and then back to the beaches would have been blown back again, further ruining agricultural land. Drinking water would have been tainted and disease and pestilence spread. This is the narrative offered by Michael Moseley in the 1990s and followed by Brian Fagan and others.[17] In a 2008 chapter, Moseley and colleagues Christopher Donnan and David Keefer again found evidence to suggest such a pattern of events at Dos Cabezas in the Jequetepeque Valley, north of the Moche Valley.[18]

Shimada, critical of the El Nino theory, has identified eight El Nino events in the sixth and seventh centuries, but explains that it is difficult to date them precisely and to correlate them with the

IV-V transition.[19] Moseley and colleagues note that the particularly severe El Nino happened between AD 450 and 750.[20] The El Nino theory, Shimada argues, does not explain why the Moche moved their capital further north to Pampa Grande, as El Nino events would have been more severe to the north. He also notes that the occurrence of an El Nino event would not explain changes in the southern Moche area or the moving of settlements to valley necks. It is also worth considering why the Moche survived some events but not others.

El Nino events can still be deadly in modern times. In 1997–1998 a severe El Nino event 'swept away roads and bridges, homes and farms, lives and livelihoods. It created a vast lake in a north Peruvian desert, and ruined the fisheries of Chile'.[21] The desert in question was the Sechura desert, in the north of the Moche region, north of Pampa Grande; it became a lake several thousand square kilometres in size. In the wake of the floodwaters, disease and diarrhoea, malaria and dengue fever became rife. In Peru, 350,000 people were made homeless. It seems unlikely that the Moche would not have been similarly affected by the natural environment.

Quilter states that the Moche 'were powerless in the face of grand catastrophes such as earthquakes and disastrous rains and floods brought by El Nino events' but also reminds us that 'in the aftermath of such upheavals, however, they rebuilt their infrastructure and started anew, at least until the waning days of their existence as a distinct culture'.[22] The Moche did indeed respond to the crises that affected them, and few, if any, scholars believe that environmental issues were the whole story of Moche collapse.

Response to Crisis

The Moche carried on in the face of whatever crises they were facing, proving their resilience as a society. The collapse at the IV-V boundary is perhaps better termed a 'transformation' than a collapse.[23] As Moseley makes clear, in period V the Moche reorganised themselves in 'revolutionary changes' – 'some, but by no means all,' he explains, 'were responses to environmental stresses'.[24] Moche was rebuilt before being abandoned, and the appearance of a front-facing staff-holding deity on a court of the Huaca de la Luna might point to an initial change in religious outlook – the figure is similar to the Tiwanaku staff-god.[25]

As mentioned earlier, Moche itself was eventually abandoned and the capital probably moved north to Pampa Grande in the Lambayeque Valley, around fifty kilometres from the coast. Pampa Grande probably had a population of ten or fifteen thousand and at its centre was the four-tiered Huaca Fortaleza, surrounded by elite residence compounds. Unlike the Huaca del Sol and the Huaca de la Luna, which were solid brick structures, the Huaca Fortaleza was built more economically with earth fill and a brick exterior. A lot of attention was paid to storage of food and precious items.

In the Moche Valley the site of Galindo was founded; both Galindo and Pampa Grande were further from the coast in valley necks, suggesting their locations were connected with the control of water; the southern part of the valley was abandoned. The southern region, the Viru Valley and those further south, seems to have been abandoned, and these probably became independent polities.[26] In the northern valleys, Moche settlements were located in the middle of the valleys, perhaps to protect them from the effects of El Nino events.

What kind of changes were taking place? Moseley points to increased instability and conflict, indicated by the construction of forts and fortifications on the coast and inland.[27] Galindo was one such walled settlement, and archaeologists have found piles of sling stones there. Also at the site were many rooms with food storage vessels; there was an increased emphasis on organised defence and provisioning/storage. Should we see this as fragmentation of a formerly unified state, or an increase in conflict between smaller local states? Over time, the settlement of Galindo expanded outside the walls, which may suggest the return of a degree of stability.

In some places, funerary customs also changed. In earlier times, there had been cemeteries, but none are found at Galindo or Pampa Grande. At Galindo some burials are within houses or chambers in the town. Bodies were now buried in a sideways position. Bawden states that 'the magnitude of these innovations in a social domain imbued with supernatural significance clearly marks profound religious change'.[28] Other areas display continuity, however, such as the Jequetepeque Valley.

Religious and/or ideological change can be detected through significant changes in iconography as well. In Moche V there is a turn towards marine themes in pottery decoration, whereas many of the former gods and themes were no longer depicted or were used in new ways. Donna McClelland calculated that more than half of Moche V bottles had marine themes.[29] One possible explanation of this is that the marine environment had sustained the Moche through the difficult times at the end of Moche IV. Important figures were a character called 'wrinkle face' and an anthropomorphised iguana, shown with sea shells, who travelled on a reed boat.[30] Bawden suggests that the period V iconography reveals a myth cycle that 'reflects ideological adjustment in response to terminal Moche IV disruption'. He also notes the disappearance of portrait vessels, 'symbols of the triumph of individualizing ideology', and interprets this as a sign of rejection of the earlier Moche ideological system.

The Moche IV-V transition seems to have been a successful response to a possible environmental crisis, and to a century of harsh conditions. The polity, based in the north, continued to exist on a large scale for another century and a half. Survival through the sixth century shows the strength and resilience of the Moche IV system, and the Moche V system was a successful adaptation. It is quite possible that the transition represents a new strategy by the ruling elite or some kind of revolution, perhaps led by another leading family or elite groups.

Revolution?

The regenerated Moche V system was not to last, and it is the end of this phase, around AD 750, that is better termed as collapse. At this time both Pampa Grande and Galindo were abandoned. Jonathan Haas notes of Pampa Grande that the pyramids, Huaca Fortaleza, and elite adobe residences were burned, whereas other parts of the city were not.[31] He also suggests that a mural on the Huaca de la Luna, which shows ceramics and other objects rebelling against their users, indicates a concept of revolution and rebellion and the subversion of accepted order. The Moche V collapse seems to be a case of the rejection of a wider ideological system that had lasted for centuries.

Moche society had been rigidly stratified: there was a wealthy ruling elite (like the Lord of Sipan), who would have been a small minority of the total population, presumably also an intermediate elite of some kind, and common people, farmers and the like. Social divisions were made manifest not only in grave goods and rituals but also architecturally. Haas points to the architecture of Moche, where elite compounds were in the ceremonial centre of the city, with lower status housing scattered around outside the central area. A sharp divide is also evident at Pampa Grande and Galindo where there were walled compounds with well-made adobe residences, formally laid out, but outside these compounds there were irregular structures with cobble walls filled with rubble. Could social and political conditions have led to a revolution – and should we imagine an elite or popular revolution?

Urbanism was abandoned and populations resettled the valleys in a rural settlement pattern – there was no apocalyptic loss of life. In the north, there was cultural continuity, with Moche styles fading out and new (related) styles being developed.[32] In the south, as we noted, Wari influence became more apparent.[33]

Leaving the Moche of northern Peru we shall now head south and east to the highland Andean altiplano, the home of the Tiwanaku and Wari empires.

TIWANAKU

As a prehistoric and illiterate society, Tiwanaku's history has been reconstructed from archaeology, and views of it have changed over time, although much still remains uncertain, perhaps unknowable. Colonial Spanish visited the site at least as early as 1549, when it was described by Pedro Cieza de Leon, who was drawn by its importance to the Inka. In the nineteenth century, Ephraim George Squier produced a plan of the site and illustrations of the ruins, describing it as the 'American Stonehenge'. Squier, followed later by Wendell Bennett, who undertook the first modern archaeological studies in the 1930s and 40s, imagined that Tiwanaku could be at most a ritual centre with only a small permanent population – because of its location in the cold and windy altiplano almost 4,000 m above sea level.

Subsequent work has changed our views of Tiwanaku. As Charles Stanish points out, 'the culture of Tiwanaku represents one of the great civilizations of the ancient world. It is easily on a par in size, complexity, and sophistication with the more well-known civilizations of the Near East, Mediterranean, and Asia'.[34] The city itself was some four to six square kilometers in size, and may have had a population of some 30,000 to 60,000 – the Titicaca Basin may have had a population as high as 100,000.[35] Tiwanaku culture spread far and wide, as indicated, for example, by the distribution of a new ceramic assemblage, including the *kero*, a tall drinking cup for beer, and the city governed an empire with colonies such as those in the Moquega Valley area, Peru.[36] This empire may not have comprised a continuous geographic territory, rather, the Tiwanaku elite may have sought to control strategic areas of military and economic importance; as such, the empire may have been multi-ethnic and multi-lingual and diverse in its make-up.

Central Tiwanaku city is dominated by impressive monumental construction, while the outskirts of the city were densely populated.[37] The city centre has two main complexes, one in the northeast, where the Akapana and Kalasasaya are located, and another, the Pumapunku, to the southwest.

The Akapana is a seven-terraced stone-faced mound some 16.5 m high and 197 × 257 m wide. It has two main staircases on the west leading up from a landing decorated with chacapuma, grinning human-felines, grasping severed human heads, and faced an eastern plaza. The top of the mound contained a number of residential buildings, which were possibly occupied by rulers. There was also a sunken court area on top. The Akapana was not just a static monument but was the site of feasting and ceremonies; as a living site it was periodically repaired and improved over a long time. Each refurbishment might be linked to a new ruler or ruling family. Human remains have also been found in and around the Akapana. Analysis has shown these to be the remains of non-local people who suffered a variety of trauma such as violent cutting or bludgeoning. The site is linked to fertility and abundance and, because of the nature of the human remains found there, was probably also symbolic of Tiwanaku's power over other peoples.

FIGURE 11.4. The Sun Portal at Tiwanaku.
Source: Ephraim Squier (1877). *Peru: Incidents of Travel and Exploration in the Land of the Incas*. Holt.

Other monuments of the northeast group included the Kalasasaya, which is an elevated area north of the Akapana. It has an east-west axis and was oriented to the cardinal points. The monument was built over an early high status residence, and so might have served to link a later powerful group with ancestors or Tiwanaku founders. At the west side was a sunken court, and just outside the Kalasasaya was the Sunken Temple. Part of the Kalasasaya was used as an observatory, and to this area the iconic Sun Portal may be linked (Figure 11.4).

Like the Akapana, the Pumapunku ritual complex was an ongoing project through the generations. It similarly consisted of a plaza and a raised area with a sunken court. Built with elaborate drains and with a sacred spring to the southwest, the complex was linked with water.

Tiwanaku subsisted in what is often described as a marginal agricultural landscape in the altiplano by modifying the landscape through a system of raised field farming. As Clark Erickson explains, this type of agriculture relies on the construction of platforms for crops surrounded by canals or ditches.[38] These prevent flooding and waterlogging of crops, increase the soil fertility, and retain moisture, while also improving the micro-climate. Another system of sunken gardens, *cochas*, was used too – these sunken gardens relied on the water table for moisture. These styles of agriculture allowed the city of Tiwanaku and the Titicaca Basin to flourish and for the population to grow.

The Megadrought Hypothesis

Undoubtedly, a megadrought hypothesis is the most popular explanation of the Tiwanaku collapse, and has been for some time; as Clark Erickson has pointed out, environmental explanations of the collapse have regularly recurred through the twentieth century.[39] In recent times, Tiwanaku scholar Alan Kolata has made the case for this in his 1993 book *The Tiwanaku*, as well as with colleagues in various papers.[40]

Kolata and his research group investigated the ancient climate of the Tiwanaku area by studying sediment cores drilled from Lake Titicaca. The sediment cores were radiocarbon dated to provide dates and the pollen analysed for clues about the ancient climate and the level of Titicaca. Of these he states:

Analysis of these data indicate a radical climate change in the south-central Andes during the post-AD 1000 era that took the form of a significant decrease in annual precipitation ... The south central Andes suffered from a catastrophic and persistent drought that began around AD 1000 and persisted virtually unabated for many decades.[41]

Supporting evidence for aridification comes from ice cores drilled in the Quelccaya glacier, about 200 km northwest of Titicaca. The ice cores preserve a record of precipitation indicated by the thickness of snow layer deposits. These seem to indicate wetter periods from AD 610 to 650 and 760 to 1040, and drier periods from AD 650 to 730; a severe drought, he argues, is indicated in post-Tiwanaku times.

What was the result of this drought? In a 1997 paper, Michael Binford and colleagues, including Kolata, argue that the level of Lake Titicaca dropped by a massive 12 to 17 m around AD 1100, coinciding with the Tiwanaku collapse.[42] The lake would have receded far from Tiwanaku and the neighbouring city of Lukurmata. The drought would also have reduced precipitation levels and lowered the water table. These changes would have affected the agricultural basis of Tiwanaku, reducing the carrying capacity of the landscape, meaning that fewer people could be supported. Settlement patterns shifted, with the cities of Tiwanaku and Lukurmata, on the shores of Titicaca, being eventually largely abandoned.

In this scenario, collapse did not happen all at once, though. The Tiwanaku Empire stretched over different environmental areas and it is hypothesised that colonies, such as the one in the Moquega Valley, collapsed first, with the Tiwanaku homeland itself and its raised field systems affected later on. However, as with climate change hypotheses in other collapses, the megadrought explanation has not gone unchallenged.

Critics of Climate Change

There are three main critics of the megadrought hypothesis: Michael Calaway, Clark Erickson, and Patrick Ryan Williams.

Calaway, in a 2005 article published in *Antiquity*, reanalysed and critiqued the data taken to indicate megadrought – the lake sediment cores and ice cores from Quelccaya.[43] Of the sediment cores, he notes a problem with dating climate events and assessing their duration. The method of dating visible changes, by radiocarbon dating gastropod shells, he suggests is prone to error, since the gastropods could have moved within the sediment. Given that periods of 500 to 1,000 years can be represented by three or four centimetres of sediment, slight movements could cause a high degree of error. In addition, he cautions that the sediment record do not indicate the duration of a drought event, only that the lake had been at a low level: 'the low water levels could have been present for just part of a year or over a period of 50 years in duration'.[44]

Another chronological problem Calaway mentions is caused by trying to reconcile palaeoclimatic and archaeological data: 'Palaeoclimatologists are comfortable discussing climate change on a scale of millennia, while archaeologists strive for a narrow margin of dates in order to hypothesise events such as civilisation collapse on a scale of centuries'.[45]

Ice cores are often taken as a good proxy for palaeoclimatic data in a chronological context – allowing us to trace climate changes over time. However, this is not necessarily the case. As Calaway explains, ice core records do not always match up with recorded annual levels of rain or snow in historical times.[46] This can be due to the peculiarity of local conditions – local wind patterns, especially in mountainous areas, can affect snow deposition and ablation; areas close together can produce quite different results. He points out too that there were two ice core samples taken from Quelccaya, the second of which, with its thicker deposits, should indicate a wetter period in the AD 1100s, around the time of the collapse.[47]

All in all, Calaway concludes that no megadrought can be inferred from the data presented, going so far as to say that 'a false empirical reality' has been presented 'to the archaeological community':

Palaeoclimatic abstractions are introduced into the archaeological realm as scientific fact. Archaeologists then use this 'fact' as a foundation for cultural theoretical models. Arguments for civilisation collapse tend to move increasingly further away from any solid foundation in the palaeoclimatic data. This is clearly evident in the Tiwanaku case study and may be should prompt further investigations into other, non-environmental, interpretations of civilisation collapse.[48]

Erickson too critiques the notion of an agricultural collapse caused by a megadrought. In his view Tiwanaku collapsed before the supposed drought took place. He also notes that raised field agriculture continued around Lake Titicaca at Huatta and Koani Pampa for three centuries after collapse. But what is especially interesting is his discussion of community responses to historically recorded droughts in the Titicaca region. Rather than causing an agricultural collapse, a drop in lake level would open up more land for farming – people would track the shoreline. The soil in these newly exposed areas is rich and is valued by farmers, who can grow crops in abundance. Aerial photographs taken during low lake levels during the 1970s exposed just such raised field systems and canals that are more usually hidden underwater.

Also in the historical record are many years of drought and flooding – flooding usually followed drought. In the seventeenth century, Erickson points out, there were thirty-six continuous years of drought, twenty-nine in the eighteenth century, and fifteen years in the twentieth century.[49] None of these droughts caused a collapse, permanent migration out of the region, or the abandonment of agriculture. Local Huattenos who Erickson interviewed 'eloquently spoke both of the horrors of long-term drought and the joy of farming' the newly exposed lands; 'they described piles of threshed quinoa and potatoes as large as houses'. Even if there was a megadrought, it need not have spelled the end for Tiwanaku.

Williams focuses on the Moquega Valley region, where both Tiwanaku and the Wari Empires had colonies within sight of each other – Wari up high at Cerro Baul and Tiwanaku further down river at Omo – where there was a significant religious and political centre, with a ceremonial area built based on the Akapana in Tiwanaku itself, and also at Chen Chen.[50] In a study of the water resources used by inhabitants, he observed changes over time that reduced Chen Chen's agricultural output in the later Tiwanaku period. Chen Chen was also destroyed and abandoned, Williams suspects, in a revolt by local inhabitants, who may have been obliged to produce maize for elites at Tiwanaku itself.

Maize was an important crop, which was used to make *chicha*, a fermented maize beer used in feasting and ceremonies, where it was often drunk from a ceramic *kero*. However, it was not grown on the altiplano but was grown at lower elevations such as the middle Moquega Valley and exported to Tiwanaku. Karen Anderson explains that 'with the advent of the state, the distribution of maize increased substantially, especially at Tiwanaku, where it was found in surprisingly high quantities, considering the difficulty of growing it in the high elevation environment'.[51] Paul Goldstein even suggests that Tiwanaku's political economy was driven by *chicha*, and that this was one reason for colonising areas like the Moquega Valley and Cochabamba.[52] The collapse of the Moquega colonies may, Williams suggests, have destabilised 'the authority structure of the state in the heartland itself'.[53] The capital, and the ruling elite, would have been deprived of a major source of maize for making *chicha*.

A Long and Complex Collapse

Despite charges of environmental determinism from other scholars, Alan Kolata, in identifying megadrought as 'the ultimate threat and proximate cause' of the Tiwanaku state's collapse, also stated that the process must have taken some generations to work out, and 'was accompanied by historically specific instances of social competition, conflict and realignments that are unrecorded in the archaeological record'.[54] In other words, climate change can only have been one factor in the events that played out; human agency was at work too. Nor was the collapse an apocalyptic demographic decline – Kolata states, 'the people of Tiwanaku themselves did not perish *en masse*'.[55] Therefore we should expect a degree of continuity from Tiwanaku into later times.

More recently, archaeologist and Tiwanaku specialist John Wayne Janusek has woven together various strands to create his own view of the Tiwanaku collapse.[56] Like Kolata, he views the collapse as a long process rather than a sudden event, 'collapse … was a volatile and at times violent process of socio-political fragmentation and cultural innovation characterized by a long sequence of events spanning several generations'.[57] Some of the signs of violent fragmentation of the state and its social fabric and ideology include the deliberate destruction of buildings and the defacing of monuments, again perhaps indicative of revolution:

Defacing and decapitating images of Tiwanaku deities and elite ancestors was ritualized hostility wrought to efface the power of Tiwanaku elites and destroy the ideological foundation of their identities. Burning and destroying their places of residence effectively erased their place and power in society, if not their lives.[58]

One monument, known as the Putuni Monolith, which perhaps represented an ancestor of an elite family, was decapitated and buried. Despite the deliberate anti-elite actions, Janusek does not believe in a commoners' revolution, rather he suggests that it was elite factions that were 'turning away' from the status quo that had prevailed in earlier times.

Apart from the defacement of monuments that represented a particular Tiwanaku ideology, Janusek notes that the urban collapse took place over some time.[59] Population began to move out of Tiwanaku in a process that spanned a century or more, leaving the city drastically reduced to perhaps 3 per cent of its earlier size. At the same time low quality 'shanty houses' were built over areas that had previously been used in elite-sponsored feasting and ritual. Elite residences, such as the Putuni compound, were also destroyed, as were the East and West palaces. But people spread out, they did not disappear; the number of small settlements grew, and thus decentralisation may have been part of the development of late Tiwanaku. We can imagine more and smaller communities, which were perhaps more autonomous, and which may have drained the central power of Tiwanaku itself.

After Tiwanaku

What happened after Tiwanaku's age of empire? One archaeological indicator of collapse is the abandonment of 'the state ceramic style – including Tiwanaku iconography, technology, and various vessel forms'.[60] This suggests a failure and rejection of the long-lived Tiwanaku cultural package, with its emphasis on *chicha*-drinking.

Kenny Sims has studied the Tumilaca culture of the Moquega Valley.[61] He observes that decorative themes on Tumilaca pottery derive from Tiwanaku styles, with an important difference – elite 'imperial' religious-political symbolism, such as the Front Face Deity and the Puma Head, is missing – deliberately left out in a rejection of a former identity. In addition, there seems to be systematic destruction of Tiwanaku cemeteries, households, and temples, which symbolise a break from a former status quo. In Sims' words:

collapse appears as the transformation of local Tiwanaku groups into an assertive and independent set of Tumilaca communities whose ethnic identity – although derived from Tiwanaku – was founded in a new and independent political organization.[62]

Elsewhere, too, there was a rejection of Tiwanaku symbols. At Cochabamba, new geometric style pottery replaced the Tiwanaku style.[63]

Scholars now see the generation of the Inka state as beginning in the aftermath of the collapse of Tiwanaku and Wari, and their legacy was used in different ways. As the Inka homeland was near the former centre of Wari, they naturally made use of Wari precedents in their settlements, buildings, and organisation. But in Inka lore, the memory of Wari fared less well; as John Wayne Janusek observes, 'it is as if their imperial strategies were best appropriated and their cultural legacy forgotten'.[64] It was the Tiwanaku culture to which the Inka turned for constructing their mythical past.

According to Inka royalty, the city of Tiwanaku, at the southern end of Lake Titicaca, was the place where the creator god Viracocha first made people and 'designed' the different nations of people, each with their language and distinctive cultures. It was embedded in their worldview. As a former imperial capital, Tiwanaku, three weeks journey from Cuzco, was also an inspiration for Inka monumental building and sculpture. It even served as a royal residence – Manco Capac, son of the last ruling Inka, Wayna Capac, was born there – as well as being a site of ceremonial feasting.

Inka narratives also record a period of Auca Runa, warlike people, in which people were savage, often waged war, and built refuge sites in the mountains. This 'warring states' period bears some resemblance to the post-collapse period of Tiwanaku, in that pukaras, high altitude settlements, first appeared at this time.

So the culture and empire of Tiwanaku, as well as the post-collapse era, bequeathed a legacy to the later Inka, who chose to adopt particular aspects of their Andean heritage.

THE WARI COLLAPSE

What of Tiwanaku's northern neighbour – the Wari Empire? Wari developed somewhat later than Tiwanaku, and has different characteristics, though each affected the other's processes of development and expression.[65] Opinions on what Wari was vary between a religious ideology that was widely adopted, a militaristic state and empire that grew through conquest, and a zone of automous centres all sharing a culture.[66] There seems to be some consensus that Wari can be considered an imperial state, but questions about what Wari was must affect how we consider its collapse. One potential indicator of Wari imperialism is the 'colonies' it founded, which 'emphasized great visibility in and surveillance over local regions', and which were significantly different from local sites.[67]

The city of Wari grew up piecemeal, but in the eighth century, significant changes were made to Wari's urban structure, with the construction of a more gridlike series of patio groups and this style spread in the eighth and ninth centuries through the Wari zone.[68] This 'closed' and 'restrictive' pattern contrasts with Tiwanaku's more 'open' urban style – and perhaps this was a deliberate strategy of difference. This 'controlled' scheme may have been influenced by some of the regional centres that were constructed, such as Pikillacta. It is perhaps indicative of an ideological and/or political shift that affected the Wari area.

Even less is known about the Wari collapse than about Tiwanaku's; as John Wayne Janusek recently stated, 'the reasons for and trajectory of Wari state collapse are unknown'.[69] It seems likely that the Wari state was functioning up to AD 950–1000, and that it collapsed at around the same time as Tiwanaku. Prior to this, changes were made to the city of Wari – parts of the city were levelled, with new compounds constructed over the top; these were irregular in shape, unlike previous Wari architecture, with thick, curved walls. Slightly later it becomes clear that habitation was decreasing in some parts of the city and, although there was some new construction, some areas that had been cleared were never built on. Some areas merely contained outhouses, converted from the earlier buildings, and there were also trash dumps. It seems to Janusek that the city was abandoned whilst under construction.

These visible changes to Wari in its late period are perhaps indicative of another change in ideology and social structure, with a rejection of the former symbolic language of Wari culture; it could mean that a new group came to power, even though it may not have been able to consolidate its power for very long. Thus we could imagine that at Wari in its late period different elite factions were competing for power more openly or divisively, threatening the unity of the state. It is possible that revolutionary ideas spread between Wari and Tiwanaku in the tenth century AD; as we know from the Arab Spring revolutions that took place from 2010, dissent can spread rapidly, especially when one regime is successfully toppled. In Wari's colonies there is also evidence for deliberate abandonment. In some areas villages were abandoned, with the population moving to fortified sites higher up. At Pikillacta and elsewhere, building complexes that had probably been connected with regional administration were sealed, as if the occupants would return later, but they never did.

FINAL THOUGHTS

In the case of the Moche, Tiwanaku, and Wari collapses we are very limited in the evidence we have – there are no texts that reveal personalities, events, or opinions, nothing that might guide us or give us insights into the political life of these cultures, states, or empires. It is clear, though, that during their long spans, each society grew, adapted, and changed. The Moche survived probable environmental catastrophes which may have led to changes in their ideological system; eventually humans seem to have caused the demise of Moche V. At Tiwanaku too it seems that an elite ideology was generally rejected, and this may have been the case at Wari too.

We cannot regard any of these societies as a failure: the Moche adapted to changing times and Moche culture continued as an influence later on; Tiwanaku, the city, state, and eventually empire, endured for some five or six centuries, from around AD 500 to 1000/1100, twice the span of the later Inka Empire; the Wari Empire too spanned almost this length of time. These Andean cultures were remarkably resilient systems populated by resilient people and communities.

Collapse, though, whatever the causes were, and these are bound to be many and various, was not only an end but also a beginning. There was no post-imperial dark age for the Moche, Tiwanaku, or Wari as they disintegrated into smaller units with more localised cultures. And in the aftermath of collapse, in each case, we see the selective reuse of cultural features, which were eventually incorporated, in different ways, into the expansive Inka Empire.

TIWANAKU AS A NATIONAL SYMBOL

For many people outside Bolivia and the southern Andes, the ancient city of Tiwanaku first came to attention when it was used in 2006 by Evo Morales as the venue for a special ceremony preceding his inauguration on 23 January as Bolivia's first indigenous president (he was also the first indigenous president in the whole of South America).[70] Barefoot and dressed in traditional Andean costume, Morales was ritually purified by *yatiri*, Aymara 'spiritual specialists', processed around the site, over the Akapana, and addressed the crowd from the Kalasasaya.

As David Kojan has pointed out, Tiwanaku, and its use in this modern ritual, is symbolic in a number of ways, according to the different narratives that it is part of.[71] For archaeologists, Morales' event points up the success of archaeological work at the site, which is now important not only in Bolivia but also in world archaeology and heritage. It also symbolises Bolivian national identity, and embodies indigenous identities and cultural heritage, which have survived years of colonialism to once again become central. In addition, the site and Morales' ceremony also represents a protest by the poor and under-represented indigenous people against the forces of colonialism, corporate culture and globalisation.

Although the southern Andean site and culture of Tiwanaku is perhaps less internationally well known than other pre-historic South American cultures such as the Moche, with their famous art, or the 'line-producing' Nazca, or Inka sites like Machu Picchu, it was, and clearly is a site of significance. Certainly the Tiwanaku are less famous than the Inka, whose empire embraced the same regions as Tiwanaku some five centuries later. But the Inka later regarded the site as sacred and may have re-erected some of its monuments, also incorporating the site into their own myths. Bernabe Cobo's account from the seventeenth century records that the emperor Inka Pachacuti was so impressed by the building techniques in the fifteenth century that he ordered his masons to use them in Cuzco.

12

Angkor and the Khmer

... we must not be led by its undeniable brilliance to bestow unqualified praise on Khmer civilization. It contained within itself the seeds of its own destruction.

B.-P. Groslier[1]

ANGKOR COMES TO LIFE

The image of the grand temple of Angkor Wat in Cambodia, surrounded by jungle, is famous throughout the world (Figure 12.1). It conjures up images of a lost sophisticated society, enriched by art and dancing girls. For a Western audience, Angkor was first brought to life by Henri Mouhot, a French explorer, who was born in 1826.[2] Mouhot, primarily a naturalist and explorer, and not an archaeologist, visited Cambodia between 1858 and 1860, and later published illustrated accounts of his travels in English and French. He was led to Angkor by a missionary – he was not looking for an ancient city, but what he found has fascinated subsequent generations. Naturally, as Angkor was fitted into the grand historical narratives from the perspective of Western scholarship, researchers have sought to explain the collapse of Angkor, the fall of the kingdom, and the abandonment of the city.

This chapter will begin by outlining the background to the formation of the Angkor (or Khmer) state before examining the city itself. Then the discussion will turn to what kind of collapse is envisioned and the reasons given to explain it.

FIGURE 12.1. Façade of Angkor Wat, drawn by Henri Mouhot.

THE ANGKOR STATE

The Angkor state survived and thrived for several centuries – leading Michael Coe to label the period from AD 802 to 1327 the Classic period of Angkor history (Figure 12.2).[3] This Classic period was also an imperial period in which Angkor expanded to control an area that stretched through Cambodia east to Laos and north into Thailand. This expansion and consolidation was due primarily to one man, king Jayavarman II, also known as Parmeshvara, who was crowned as *chakravartin*, or 'universal monarch', in AD 802, in a ritual that took place at the holy mountain of Mahendraparvata (Phnom Kulen). The ritual is recorded in a bilingual Khmer and Sanskrit inscription from a stela from Sdok Kak Thom in Thailand. This inscription is important because it also records the names of Angkor's kings over a period of 250 years. These and later kings engaged in successive and often impressive building programmes, but often had to fight to secure their own positions, deal with vassal states seeking independence, and confront rival states.

Jayavarman's capital was not Angkor but Hariharalaya, which was further expanded by his son Jayavarman III and in particular

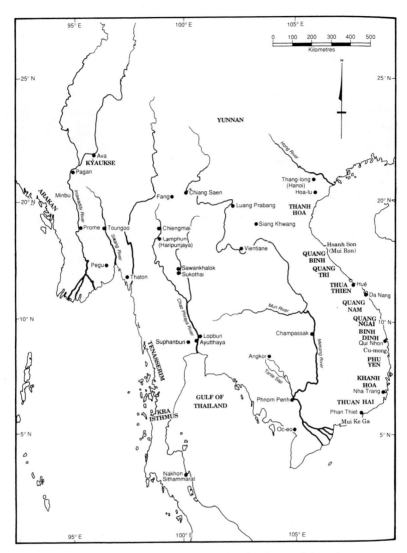

FIGURE 12.2. Map of southeast Asia, showing Angkor and Ayutthaya.
Source: From Tarling, N. (ed.). (1992). *The Cambridge History of Southeast Asia. Volume One*. Cambridge: Cambridge University Press, 138 (map 3.1).

by Indravarman I (AD 877–889).[4] Indravarman's building pro-gramme at Hariharalaya set the precedent for Khmer building in stone and for later building at Angkor itself. He was also responsible for constructing the first Angkorian *baray*. This was a rectangular 'reservoir' more than two miles long and about half a mile wide, filled by river water, and capable of holding more than 7.5 million cubic metres of water. It was named the Indratataka, or the 'Sea of Indra'. After Indravarman's death, there was a period of conflict after which Yashovarman I (AD 889/890–900) became king; it was he who moved the capital to Angkor (Yashodharapura – 'Glory-hearing city').[5]

Three decades later Jayavarman IV (*c.* AD 928–941) chose to move the capital to Koh Ker, around fifty miles northeast of Angkor.[6] He had already built an impressive pyramid temple, Prasat Thom, there before he became king and he perhaps had some special attachment to the area; he also built the Rahal Baray and a grand moated palace. In any case, a few years after Jayavarman's death Rajendravarman II (AD 944–968) returned political power to Angkor in AD 944.

The most notable Khmer kings must include Suryavarman II (*c.* AD 1113–1150), who fought his way to the throne against his great-uncle.[7] He was responsible for the construction of Angkor Wat, a temple complex of 21 ha situated in an artificial lake. The temple is laid out around a central shrine that was initially dedicated to Vishnu (though it later became Buddhist) – the five central towers representing the peaks of the sacred Mount Meru; this was surrounded by concentric rectangular enclosures, terraces, and courtyards.[8] Though only one of the many impressive stone-built complexes of the Khmer, Angkor Wat is undoubtedly the best known.

Jayavarman VII (AD 1181–1215), Coe notes, was 'arguably not only the greatest of all the Khmer kings but also the greatest personage in Cambodian history'.[9] Not only did he defeat the neighbouring Chams in a battle recorded on the walls of his massive Bayon temple complex, he also constructed his capital of Angkor Thom within Angkor (Figure 12.3). Angkor Thom is famous for the massive sculpted faces that look out from over its gates. Like earlier kings, Jayavarman built a new great baray, the 'Sea of Victory', with an island temple at its centre. Caring for his people, he also built more than a hundred hospitals around the Khmer Empire.[10] In his reign the Khmer Empire reached its most expansive point, possibly having some twenty-three provinces, indicated by Jayavarman's distribution of Buddhist statues to various regions.[11]

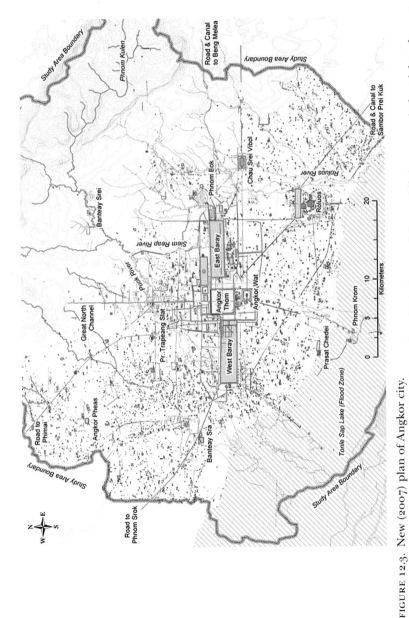

FIGURE 12.3. New (2007) plan of Angkor city.
Source: Evans, D. et al. (2007). 'A comprehensive archaeological map of the world's largest preindustrial settlement complex at Angkor, Cambodia.' *PNAS* 104(36): 14277–14282.

The kings were the supreme power in the Khmer state. Of the nineteenth-century Cambodian kings, Coe quotes Aymonier, who wrote:

The State is the King, whose power is limitless, and who is the absolute leader of the country, of its armies, of all its political and administrative affairs. The sovereign appoints and dismisses all dignitaries, great mandarins and provincial governors; he establishes and shares out taxes in fixed shares, and disposes to his liking the kingdom's revenues, of which he is the great usufructor. Supreme judge, he has the power of life and death, of mercy, of revision of judgments ... Unique legislator, his ordinances have the force of law; he makes and revises codes, he promulgates them in solemn audience.[12]

But they needed help to run the kingdom. Without any hereditary elite class, the Khmer state was governed by kings through a cadre of administrators at different levels – a mandarin class, whose members received the title *khlon*.[13] However powerful a king was supposed to be, the existence of channels for the exercise of power, and the multiple loyalties of individuals, created divisions and tensions within the state. Coups and faction must always have been threats, especially with a large royal family.

Since a high point must be followed inevitably by decline, in the common narrative of collapse, that is usually how subsequent centuries are characterised. But as we shall see, this may be more myth than history.

THE COLLAPSE

What kind of collapse do researchers imagine for Angkor? Since it was 'discovered' by westerners, surrounded by and being absorbed by tropical jungle, Angkor has been seen as an abandoned ruin. Thus, depopulation and urban abandonment are seen as facets of an Angkorian collapse. Monumental building also ceased after the death of Jayavarman VII.[14] As for the Khmer Empire, this is also seen as coming to an end, or at least to retract severely. Coe sees the Classical period of Angkor as ending with the death of Shrindrajayavarman in AD 1327 and with the last Sanskrit inscription made to mark the accession of Jayavarmadiparameshvara – the subsequent period is sometimes labelled a dark age, owing to the lack of inscriptions.[15] A social collapse is also envisioned by some; a 2010 study states that

'Angkor declined from a level of high complexity and regional hege-mony' after the fourteenth and early fifteenth centuries.[16] The col-lapse is sometimes pinned down to a precise point in time: AD 1431, when the city was sacked by the Thai king Borommaracha II and thereafter largely abandoned.

The Angkor collapse thus seems to tick many of the boxes for fea-tures of collapse outlined in Chapter 1; it seems to have been rapid, political and social, and to have affected factors such as monumental building, the use of inscriptions, and changes in population levels and settlement patterns.

A 'HYDRAULIC CITY'?

The Angkor state's wealth was ultimately derived from rice agricul-ture, and for some this, in combination with water management and population, holds the key to understanding Angkor's end. Angkor itself was strategically located on the edge of the flood zone of the Tonle Sap, the great lake of central Cambodia, which would flood each year, quadrupling in size (Figure 12.3). In the same way the annual Nile flood in Egypt fertilised the riverbanks for agriculture, making Egypt exceptionally rich, the Tonle Sap would enrich its flood zone for growing rice. The lake was also a rich source of fish and was big enough for naval battles to take place. Water and water management were key to the Khmer state.

Crucial to this theory of collapse is the 'hydraulic city' model of the Angkor agricultural economy, developed by Bernard-Philippe Groslier and since adopted by others such as Jacques Dumarcay.[17] They argue that Angkor had a very high population, which grew because of the baray system. In their view the barays were used to irri-gate rice fields, making them highly productive and capable of bear-ing three or four crops per year. In Groslier's opinion, on the basis of irrigation agriculture, Angkor could have supported a massive popu-lation of 1.9 million people, making it the largest city in the world at the time, and bigger even than Rome at the height of empire.[18] As barays silted up, rulers were forced to construct new ones, and to raise the dikes surrounding them.

The hydraulic city model has not gone unchallenged.[19] Some point to the lack of references in inscriptions to the use of barays for agriculture. Others rely on the information provided by the eyewit-ness account of Angkor in AD 1296–1297, written by the Chinese dip-lomat Zhou Daguan. He spent some eleven months at Angkor, and so had plenty of time to see what farming techniques were used in the area. Zhou described the barays and the temples on them, but did not link these with irrigation or agriculture.[20] He did describe agri-culture specifically but not irrigation. Rather, he described the flood-retreat farming, where rice would be grown on the land that had been covered by the flooded Tonle Sap lake. Zhou explains that three to four rice crops could be grown, but as Charles Higham points out, he does not say the harvests came from a single place.[21]

Coe notes three other criticisms of the hydraulic city model.[22] First, some say that the barays would impede water flow to the rice fields and that new barays would cause down-slope barays to dry up. The baray system would therefore not have been an effective water management strategy. Second, that baray waters would not have been good for fertilising the soil because of their acidity and lack of organic material. And third, Groslier's figures have been challenged, with Robert Acker calculating that hydraulic agriculture could only have supported 7.8 per cent of Angkor's citizens.

MONSOONS AND MEGADROUGHTS

As with many other societies that we have seen, climate change has been adduced as the cause (or at least as one cause) of Angkorian collapse – the end of both the city and kingdom. Most recently, Brendan Buckley and colleagues have proposed this.[23] In their view a megadrought, a decades-long drought, in combination with severe monsoons (and unidentified 'other factors'), was responsible for the demise of Angkor. In their reconstruction, they argue that droughts punctuated by heavy rains caused the silting up of canals and barays, which the city relied on. The damage to Angkor's hydraulic infra-structure rendered the city unsustainable – it could not support its own massive population and the Angkor state collapsed under the strain. This story has been given a popular airing in the *National Geographic,* and further research in the West Baray at Angkor, con-ducted by Mary Beth Day and colleagues, seems to have confirmed the picture.[24]

Buckley and colleagues' evidence for this reconstruction of the fourteenth and fifteenth century climate in Cambodia consists of tree-ring data, speleothem, and also historical evidence. The tree ring data comes from three locations: Mae Hong Son in northern Thailand, Mu Cang Cai in northern Vietnam, and the Bidoup Nui Ba National Park, in southern Vietnam. The speleothem records come from the Dandak Cave in India and the Wanxiang Cave in China. The historical data comes from Sri Lanka and Phitsanulok in Thailand. What we should straightaway consider is that two strands of the evidence come from a considerable distance away from Angkor – the Vietnamese tree that was investigated, for example, is located seven hundred kilometres from the city; how accurate a reflection of Angkor's climate and environmental situation do they provide? We may be on surer ground with Day's research, which pertains directly to Angkor's hydraulics, and in combination they seem to support each other.

But a significant problem with the megadrought collapse model appears when we look at the wider southeast Asian context. For example, we find that the Thais, under U Thong, founded the capital of their new kingdom at Ayutthaya in AD 1351, a city which endured for some four centuries until it was destroyed by the Burmese in AD 1767.[25] Ayutthaya, like Angkor, falls within the area of the evidence drawn upon by Buckley, so, surely, we should expect a similar crisis there. But we find no such crisis – or if there was one, the Thais weathered it. Coe quotes the words of a seventeenth century Dutch traveller, who described a flourishing Ayutthaya thus:

The streets of the walled town are many of them large, straight and regular, with channels running through them, although for the most part of small narrow lanes, ditches, and creeks most confusedly placed; the citizens have an incredible number of small boats ... which come to their very doors, especially at floods and high water.[26]

What may be more important than environmental changes is that the Thais were growing in power at the expense of Angkor, even while they emulated the city in many ways.

Buckley and colleagues cite evidence of silting from a canal that carries the Siem Reap River, east of Angkor Thom – but, while it may have silted up, the canal is still carrying that river. But what needs explaining here is why the canal was not cleared – given the level of hydraulic engineering and know-how developed by the Khmer, flooding and siltation events alone explain little about collapse.

But could climate change have had different effects in different places? Since the hydraulic model seems to be generally accepted now, some argue that Angkor's infrastructure was too rigid to be able to respond to change; other kingdoms with different local environments and subsistence strategies could have responded differently. In any case, the Khmer relocated their capital to the south – possibly in part for environmental reasons in addition to the pressure put on them by the waxing Thai state. Coe remarks that this move may have been carried out in a 'piecemeal process' rather than all at once.[27]

KINGSHIP AND STABILITY

Bernard-Philippe Groslier, whose words preface this chapter, believed that the Khmer civilisation contained the seeds of its own destruction. In his view the state was ultra-focussed on the kings and was wholly geared towards supporting them and their massive and self-aggrandising building programmes; he wrote of a 'cult of the king-god'.[28] The country was, he said, 'milked dry' and 'exhausted', all in the king's name. But although the Angkor state did not wear itself out, it was beset by problems at its heart.

One issue was that of the succession and transfer and relocation of royal power, all of which have beset many monarchical societies. Renee Hagesteijn sums up the problems experienced by Angkor thus, 'Angkor ... had more than six different capitals, four usurpations, and eleven other non-lineal successions (out of 27)'.[29] But how was power transferred normally? We often think of power in monarchies as being smoothly passed from father to son in 'ideal' circumstances, but this may not have been the case with the Khmer. Michael Vickery proposes that kingship rotated between different branches of the extended royal family.[30] He suggests, therefore, that one 'usurper *par excellence*', Jayavarman IV (*c.* AD 928–941), could, as a grandson of an earlier king, actually have been the rightful successor of Yashovarman I (AD 889–900), rather than Yashovarman's sons Harshavarman I and Ishnavarman II.[31] Jayavarman started construction of his own rival capital at Lingapura in AD 921 and he probably was quite justified in doing so.[32] But this demonstrates a potentially serious problem for the state. Vickery suggests that problems most often occurred when kings tried to pass on power to their sons; he notes several instances of this where the sons' reigns were 'brief' and 'ephemeral'. And the longer things went on, the more royal relatives, and 'rightful' heirs, there would be.

Hagesteijn also points out that, although there was a formal institution of kingship, individual kings still had to win support and renown for themselves, 'the authority of the early Southeast Asian rulers for a considerable part depended on achievement, distribution of material means and patron-client relations'.[33] Kings could thus be more and less successful, and stronger or weaker.

The reigns of 'weak' kings were marked by fragmentation and internal conflict, as well as potential invasion or military defeat. After the death of Jayavarman IV, in AD 941, a number of vassal kings broke away from the Khmer state during the reign of Harshavarman II; at this time no major monuments were built. Rajendravarman undertook the reconquest of these regions.[34] Around AD 1000 a little known king, Udayadityavarman I, died and the state was again split in two – divided between two princes, Jayaviravarman and Suryavarman.[35] Suryavarman, after nine years of probably 'very bloody struggle', triumphed in around AD 1011 and consolidated his empire.[36] The Sdok Kak Thom inscription records 'the devastation caused by civil war'.[37]

The reign of Harshavarman III (AD 1066–1080) saw fourteen years of internal disruption and defeat by Chams.[38] The next ruler, and founder of a new dynasty, was Jayavarman VI, whose father was probably a local ruler in Thailand to begin with.[39] It seems likely that he came to power in a revolt against Harshavarman.[40] A few years after the death of Suryavarman II, the builder of Angkor Wat, a new king Yashovarman II came to power. Some think he was an usurper, but he was assassinated in 1165 by a 'rebel bureaucrat' who in turn became king.[41] Tribhuvanadityavarman was subsequently killed by the Chams in AD 1177.

The fourteenth and early fifteenth centuries are less well known because of the lack of inscriptions, which makes a reconstruction of Angkor's history difficult. It would be easy to characterise this as a period of crisis, a prelude to inevitable collapse, but this is premature and a circular argument. It can be said, though, that the Angkor state was resilient enough to survive potential collapse caused by infighting at the top, even if internal conflict and the problems it caused were a periodic occurrence that could have led to collapse at many points.

THE KHMER AND THEIR NEIGHBOURS

The Khmer state did not exist in isolation in southeast Asia. One persistent thorn in the side of Angkor's kings were the Cham of Vietnam.[42] In the reign of the Angkor king Harshavarman III (AD 1066–1080) they may have taken advantage of internal discord to attack and defeat the Khmer.[43] The same was to happen a century later in AD 1177, after the death of Suryavarman II (AD 1113–1150), which was followed by some decades of chaos.[44] The forces of the Cham king Jaya Indravarman sailed up the Tonle Sap into the lake and sacked the city, burning its wooden buildings and looting treasures; the king was killed. The Chams were later defeated on the lake by Angkor's new king Jayavarman II (AD 1181–1215), who had been living with the Cham in their capital of Vijaya.[45] Apparently the Chams seriously damaged Angkor's hydraulic infrastructure, which was then overhauled by Jayavarman. Jayavarman turned the kingdom round and brought the Khmer Empire to its territorial peak, and built roads, bridges, and even hospitals in addition to temples and the mysterious 'Houses of Fire', which may have been highway 'rest houses' or temples.[46]

As mentioned earlier, in AD 1351 a new Thai state was founded at Ayutthaya by a man named U Thong.[47] U Thong came from a Chinese family but had married into two ruling families – those of Lopburi and Suphanburi, which he united into a new kingdom. Lopburi had been a vassal of Angkor, but seceded by the mid-thirteenth century, perhaps demonstrating a period of weakness at Angkor that locals could take advantage of.[48] This new kingdom was expansionist from the outset; U Thong went to war with Angkor and may even have taken the city. As Keith Taylor explains, 'this reveals that, at its inception, Ayutthaya was fighting to appropriate the claim to regional overlordship that had been held for many generations by Angkor'.[49] His policy was followed by his son Ramesuan

(AD 1388–1395) and grandson Ramaracha (1395–1409), the former of which may again have sacked Angkor. Borommaracha II sacked the city for a third time in AD 1431, after which the Khmer moved their capital south.

The great game between the states and peoples of southeast Asia puts in context the history of the Khmer and their supposed collapse. A state and empire, the Khmer's fortunes rose and fell alongside the fates of their neighbours. Expansion by one state would cause resentment and an aggressive response in another, as happened when other states attacked Angkor. Neighbours and vassals would very often take advantage of recurrent bouts of instability in the Angkor state.

FROM HINDUISM TO BUDDHISM

The Khmer kingdom had grown up under Indian cultural influence; India and southeast Asia had been in trading contact since 350 BC or even earlier.[50] Hindu religious philosophies were adopted, as were gods, especially Shiva and Vishnu, as was India's classical language Sanskrit. Early accounts stressed that this influence was probably key in the formation of the Angkor state. But as Higham states, 'local rulers chose to adopt Indic gods and language to their own advantage' – there was no simple imposition of culture. As time passed and Buddhism developed in India, it too spread to southeast Asia. Just as Christianity colonised the Roman Empire, changing aesthetic and social values and outlooks, so Buddhism, over time, colonised the Angkor state.

Zephir argues that the adoption of Buddhism was 'one of the most profound and enduring changes' Angkor experienced.[51] He comments that while it accompanied the political weakening of the state, it was not a cause of this. But the adoption of Buddhism was not welcomed by all, nor did it immediately take root. The great Jayavarman VII was both a Buddhist and a great warrior – he was responsible for building Angkor Thom and the Bayon, a mixed temple that was for Buddhist worship but that included Hindu gods in its scheme (Figure 12.4).[52]

However, on Jayavarman's death, there was a profound reaction against Buddhism and a period of iconoclasm. Coe states that 'every single Buddha image in Angkor was systematically broken up

FIGURE 12.4. Face towers, the Bayon, Angkor Thom.
Source: Courtesy of Yoshie Nakata.

or defaced ... This meant ... chipping out ... an estimated 45,000 images ...'.[53] Some statues were recarved into Hindu style and some texts completely erased. A Japanese team of excavators found pits containing 272 Buddha statues that had been smashed and deliberately buried. The iconoclasm was so vast that Coe believes 'it must have been a king, for the extent of the vandalism staggers the imagination'. What happened and who was responsible is something of a mystery, but, if the policy was designed to eradicate Buddhism, it failed – when Zhou Daguan visited Angkor, later in the thirteenth century, he observed that most of the population were Buddhists and that the city was full of monks.[54]

The shift to Buddhism, though not a cause of any collapse, did affect the material culture of Angkor, and this connects it to our ideas of collapse and decline. Sanskrit, associated with Hinduism, fell out of use and stone temples gave way to wooden ones, which had in any case always been constructed alongside them; this changed the archaeological visibility of Khmer society to modern eyes, helping to construct an image of decline and collapse. In addition, Pali inscriptions came to replace Sanskrit ones, the first from the early fourteenth century, with more from the sixteenth to eighteenth centuries.[55]

THE KHMER AFTER ANGKOR

While the Angkor collapse is often put at AD 1431, this was in no way the end of the Khmer state. While Angkor itself was given up as the capital, the kings moved out to a new capital at Srei Santhor, further south, under king Ponhea Yat; many people will have moved with the court, depopulating the city.[56] Ponhea Yat soon abandoned that site, possibly because of floods, in favour of Phnom Penh; though, according to Zephir, it was periodically reused until the end of the seventeenth century and remained the royal residence. Justin Corfield explains this move as politically, militarily, and economically motivated – the Khmer were seeking closer ties with China and distancing themselves from the Thais in the northwest.[57] He also suggests that Ponhea Yat may have had more supporters in the south, and thus he and his successors could be more secure in their rule if based there. Other sites too, including Lovek and Udong, became capitals in the following years. Helen Ibbitson Jessup characterises this as 'not so much defeat as adaptation'.[58]

Angkor itself was neither completely abandoned nor forgotten – pilgrims continued to visit Angkor Wat. It even regained its status as capital under Ang Chan I (AD 1516–1566) or his son Paramaraja I (AD 1566–1576). At this time new stone monuments were created, including colossal Buddha statues and some of the earlier reliefs were completed.[59]

Neither did Khmer culture disappear. One of the major differences between the Classical and Postclassic Khmer was that wood became the usual medium for sculpture and building, and Jessup explains that 'it is customary to interpret the disappearance of stone architecture as a sign of declining power and wealth in Cambodia'.[60] However, she argues that this was a change not a decline – many elite structures had been built of wood in earlier times, and wood architecture could be very impressive, even if they did not last as long (she rightly notes the amazing Japanese wood-construction tradition, which can still be seen in temples like Todai-ji, in Nara; Japanese temples are usually reconstructed every few decades). Also, there were practical and spiritual reasons for the change: wood was more easily obtainable in the south than stone, and the ephemerality of wood could have appealed to the now Buddhist Khmer. These changes seem similar in kind to the changes in architectural style and spiritual outlook in the later Roman Empire, when bits of old buildings (spolia) were reused in less impressive (to many, compared with the Classical monuments) new constructions, and the new Christian outlook placed more importance on the spiritual than the worldly.

The Postclassic Khmer state, with its southern base, was more international in outlook when compared to the relative insularity of the Classic period. Coe describes the post-Angkor capitals as 'thoroughly international, with foreign quarters for Malay, Japanese and Chinese traders' – Europeans visited too; he notes a population of at least 3,000 Chinese at Lovek in the 1540s.[61] International trade was to become increasingly important in subsequent centuries. But the Khmer were still under threat from the Thais, who captured Lovek in 1594. Also in the sixteenth century the Khmer state began to be drawn into relations with expanding European adventurers and missionaries, with mixed results; in 1863 Cambodia became a French protectorate.[62]

All in all, it can be said that the Khmer state that was founded by king Jayavarman II in AD 802 was a remarkably long-lived and adaptable entity. Undoubtedly, it experienced ups and downs in its fortunes, with its regional influence and extent waxing and waning, but that is hardly surprising. If there were environmental difficulties, then these could have prompted some of the changes that rulers made, including shifting the capital, but we must also see these in the context of conflict and the strategy of rulers. The state underwent significant changes over time, but it seems incorrect to identify a fifteenth century collapse when there was political and cultural continuity; certainly there was no social collapse or reduction in the level of complexity in the region, as has sometimes been claimed.

ANKGOR AND THE MAYA – TWO PEAS IN A POD?

Some compare the Angkorian collapse to that of the Classic Maya – both being tropical civilisations with theatre-state architecture for kings to affirm and show off their power. But is this comparison a good one? A major difference is that while the Angkor state grew into an empire, the Classic Maya world was one of many independent states in a culture-zone; although some states did acquire influence over others, no states acquired very large empires. The Classic Maya collapse was the ending of many states over two or three centuries, with abandonment of many major sites and a rejection of an ideological system involving holy kings. But it is questionable whether what happened to the Khmer kingdom is best seen as a collapse at all. Although the city of Angkor was *largely* abandoned, it was not completely abandoned or indeed lost, and it served as the capital again for a while some time after AD 1431. The state did not come to an end either – the modern Cambodian state is a linear successor of the Angkor state. Also, there seems to have been no reduction in social complexity. The Khmer kings moved their capital, as the Hittites and Romans had done, for strategic and economic reasons, and they continued to exist and to adapt.

FINAL THOUGHTS

The well-known story of the end of Angkor conflates two things – the city of Angkor and the Angkor or Khmer state. While the city was largely abandoned, the state did not end, nor did social complexity in southeast Asia reduce. Climate change did not bring about the end of the Khmer state, even if it did contribute, as it may have done, to the decision to move the capital from Angkor to the south.

Hagesteijn has characterised the Angkor state's 500-year history as two centuries of formation followed by a heyday and three centuries of disintegration, 'a slow process – before the actual fall takes place'.[63] But is a three-century decline a useful way of looking at the Angkor state's trajectory? Does a rise-and-fall narrative do justice to Khmer history? The Chinese visitor Zhou Daguan's description of Angkor in AD 1296–1297 does not seem to be one of decline or pre-collapse jitters – rather he pictures a bustling city and a thriving society.[64]

As Keith Taylor puts it:

the end of Angkorian history came not with a dramatic collapse but rather as a reorientation of the Khmer polity: from dependence on rice fields to a greater reliance upon wealth generated by trade and commerce; from continental empire to maritime entrepot; from a religious culture that was priestly to one that was monastic.[65]

ANGKOR AS A SYMBOL

Cambodia became a French colony in 1863, though not without difficulty – there was a Khmer rebellion, unsuccessful, in 1884.[66] The French colonial ideology of a civilising mission overlay economic exploitation. The country was then occupied by the Japanese from 1941 to 1945 and soon after ejected the French. Turbulent times lay ahead; in 1975 the Khmer Rouge came to power, killing an estimated 1.5 million, perhaps 15 per cent of the population, and causing many more to emigrate.[67] They were defeated by the Vietnamese in 1978.

Now, Angkor Wat and the Classic Khmer culture have become important modern and internationally known symbols of modern, post-occupation, and post–Khmer Rouge Cambodia. Angkor was added to the UNESCO list of world heritage sites in 1992, ensuring its appeal as a global tourist destination and its position as special cultural heritage. The towers of Angkor Wat appear on the Cambodian flag. Tim Winter points out that, in this regard, Angkor plays 'a pivotal role as a unifying marker of modern cultural, national, and ethnic identity'.[68] But while welcome, this also poses problems – the focus on Angkor plays up the past of Cambodia's rulers but pushes aside the social histories of the vast majority.

Another issue connects with authenticity and the preservation, or manipulation, of the area around Angkor. This has long been home to local communities; some 50,000 people live within the Angkor park area. But these people are now legally restricted in what they can do, for fear of altering the landscape and area from how tourists may expect to see and experience it. This ties us back into the Angkor collapse narrative – 'throughout its history Angkor has become framed by the international tourist industry as a desolate, abandoned landscape', even though the site was never fully abandoned and the Khmer state has a still-continuing history.[69] There is still a Cambodian king on the throne, descended from an ancient family of kings and queens.

13

The Incredible Survival of Rapa Nui

It is a sad fact that in these islands, as in North America, wherever the white man establishes himself the aborigines perish.

H. V. Barclay[1]

RAPA NUI: HOME OF THE MYSTERIOUS *MOAI*

Rapa Nui, Easter Island, has been the setting of popular mystery stories – often presented as history – for the past half century (Figure 13.1). For many, it was made famous by the mid-1950s expeditions of the Norwegian adventurer Thor Heyerdahl, through his books, including *Aku-Aku*, and films, or by Erich von Daniken, who suggested that aliens had been stranded there, had become bored, and taught the islanders to make statues. Even in the nineteenth century, when J. Linton Palmer reported his visit to the island in 1868 with the HMS Topaze, Rapa Nui was already well-known for its statues – *moai* – giant carved figures, some weighing up to 270 tons, that were transported and erected around the island over hundreds of years.[2] Perhaps more than a thousand *moai* were carved. Some were placed on *ahu*, ritual platforms next to the coast, others lie in the quarry at Rano Raraku, and yet others were left, perhaps deliberately, somewhere in between, possibly serving as clan boundary markers.[3]

When Europeans first reached Rapa Nui, beginning with the Dutchman Jacob Roggeveen in 1722, they found it hard to believe

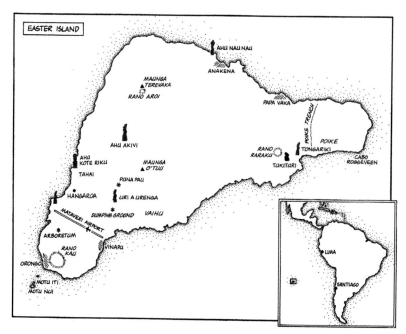

FIGURE 13.1. Map of Rapa Nui/Easter Island.
Source: Boersema, J. J. (2015). *The Survival of Easter Island: Dwindling Resources and Cultural Resilience*. Cambridge: Cambridge University Press, p. xi, Map 1.

that the Polynesian inhabitants with their leaky canoes could have any relation to the obviously sophisticated and complex culture that had set up the *moai*. Rogeveen stated:

> At first, these stone figures caused us to be filled with wonder, for we could not understand how it was possible that people who are destitute of heavy or thick timber, and also of stout cordage, out of which to construct gear, had been able to erect them; nevertheless some of these statues were a good 30 feet in height and broad in proportion.[4]

So it seemed to others too. In 1868, Christian missionaries, who had been living on Easter Island for four years, engaged in converting the Rapa Nui from their traditional religion and culture, did not think the locals had anything to do with the stone statues, which, they believed, must therefore have been made by an earlier race. Palmer, too, thought a lack of chisels ruled out the present 'race', whom he nevertheless had a high opinion of, calling them 'good people'.

When Palmer's visit was reported to the Royal Geographical Society in 1870, a debate ensued about the origins of the islanders, and whether they could have been responsible for making the statues – the president said 'they seemed to point to former times and to powerful people'.[5] Some agreed that the islanders themselves could not have been responsible for the statues and thought a Peruvian origin for the statue-builders seemed likely. They saw parallels with the Tiwanaku culture of the Andes. Others, though, including some who had visited Rapa Nui and the Pacific in the 1820s, thought a Polynesian origin suited the statues and the islanders. A Mr Franks commented:

with regard to the origin of the stone images ... the small wooden figures, which are still made and sold to visitors, bear a certain similarity to the stone images, which would scarcely exist if the present inhabitants were not intimately connected with the race that formed the earlier statues.[6]

He also noted that other Pacific islanders raised statues of chiefs, and that on Rapa Nui this may have been done in stone due to a lack of wood.

In the twentieth century, Heyerdahl's adventures may have been popular, but his theorising about the origins of the statue builders attracted a great deal of criticism and has been generally rejected by more recent scholars. He had adopted a version of the Peruvian origin story for the Rapa Nui peoples, already rejected for good reasons in the Royal Geographical Society decades earlier, but in his view these Peruvians were really a 'white' race who had originated in the Middle East, and who had spread their 'superior' culture and abilities amongst the various 'inferior' peoples they encountered. Graham Holton has described well how Heyerdahl's historical program was shot through with racial and diffusionist thinking that was widespread in Europe at the end of the nineteenth century and into the twentieth, but that denies indigenous peoples their rightful history.[7]

But for many people today it is still the carving, transportation, raising of the *moai*, their subsequent toppling, and end of this monumental megalithic tradition and the culture that supported it that remain at the heart of the 'mystery' of Rapa Nui. The *moai*, like the fine monuments we often admire in other cultures, represent Rapa

Nui's civilisation – its supposed cultural peak from which it collapsed, leaving the present-day islanders living 'amid the ruins of their ancestors' remarkable accomplishments'.[8] The image of the *moai* and the traditions they represent are thus bound up in the story of the collapse of the island's culture and population.

THE ROAD TO DISASTER – THE ECOCIDE NARRATIVE

The story of Rapa Nui has become a by-line for environmental short sightedness and recklessness and the overuse of finite resources – ecocide – Benny Peiser calls it 'the poster child of a new environmental historiography'.[9] 'In just a few centuries,' states Jared Diamond, 'the people of Easter Island wiped out their forest, drove their plants and animals to extinction, and saw their complex society spiral into chaos and cannibalism,' and he asked: 'Are we about to follow their lead?'[10]

Diamond was not the first to turn Rapa Nui into a microcosm of the Earth, nor to imagine a terrible collapse that happened before Europeans 'discovered' the island. A recent historian of Easter Island, Steven Fischer, notes that the Comte de la Pérouse, who visited the island for a single day in April 1786, during his royal-sponsored Pacific expedition, speculated on the 'imprudence' of the islanders for apparently deforesting their island and the idea of a collapse that changed the island's society:

Nothing is more certain than this people's present form of governance has made all classes and stations so similar to one another that one no longer encounters a chief among the same whose influence would be of such importance that a large number of people should take pains to immortalize his memory through the erection of a statue. Instead of those colossi, in the present day, one accordingly erects small pyramid-shaped stone mounds whose tips are painted with a type of limewater.[11]

William Mulloy may first have made the modern connection between deforestation, *moai*, and collapse, now the mainstays of the Easter Island story, in 1970.[12] He thought that civil war resulted from overpopulation and competition over land and fishing rights. In the 1980s, Patrick Kirch, an archaeologist specialising in the Pacific, connected the *moai* tradition with ecological and social collapse – 'a downward spiral of cultural regression ... under pressures of over-population and environmental degradation'.[13]

Clive Ponting began his popular green history of the world, which focuses on human-caused environmental problems, population growth, and collapse, by suggesting that Easter Island provided a 'lesson' for global society today.[14] Ponting emphasises Rapa Nui society as 'primitive' with 'squalid' huts, 'almost perpetual warfare', and cannibalism – 'what amazed and intrigued the first European visitors was the evidence, amongst all this squalor and barbarism, of a once flourishing and advanced society'.[15] Biogeographer John Flenley takes a similar line, stating that Europeans found islanders 'scratching a living among what appeared to be the ruins of a collapsed civilization'.[16]

Archaeologist Paul Bahn with John Flenley, in their 1992 book *Easter Island, Earth Island*, had also wondered about the environmental and moral significance of the island's fate:

The person who felled the last tree could see that it was the last tree. But he (or she) still felled it. This is what is so worrying. Humankind's covetousness is boundless. Its selfishness appears to be genetically inborn. Selfishness leads to survival. Altruism leads to death. The selfish gene wins. But in a limited ecosystem, selfishness leads to increasing population imbalance, population crash, and ultimately extinction.[17]

Not that the Rapa Nui had become extinct. But the idea of a pre-contact collapse from civilisation, the reasons, and the blame for it seemed clear enough, as Diamond reasserted, 'it was the islanders themselves who had destroyed their own ancestor's work'.[18]

This narrative of collapse suggests that a small initial population, perhaps no more than thirty people, arrived from the west onto the forested island, 'a pristine paradise', sometime around AD 800–900 or sometime before, even as early as AD 300.[19] The new arrivals, with their imported plants and animals, had a limited impact for a few hundred years, during which time the population grew only slowly. But then, after AD 1000, they began in earnest to cut down the island's *Jubaea* palm forests, clearing and burning areas for agricultural use and using the timber for canoe building, construction, fires, moving *moai*, rope, and all manner of things, creating a visible decline in tree pollen, as seen in core samples taken by modern researchers at Rano Kau.[20] The dating of these events, though, has recently been challenged and some, including Easter Island archaeologists Terry Hunt and Carl Lipo, think the settlers arrived sometime later, perhaps around AD 1200, and had an immediate effect on the environment.[21]

The initial population started to construct *ahu* platforms and *moai*, with construction and population rising rapidly around AD 1300. By AD 1400, forests in some areas might have been completely gone, though Bahn and Flenley estimate the last wood was cut for fire in around AD 1640.[22] Islanders then had to burn grasses and other materials instead of wood. The population, which had grown as the trees were cut to make and move more *moai* and to provide more land, which became eroded as more trees were cleared, reached its peak in AD 1680. But the islanders grew increasingly hungry as there was less and less food to go around – they could not access sea foods without good wooden canoes and they had eaten many of the island's birds to extinction. At this time they began to rely more heavily on their chickens, kept in chicken huts. The island could no longer support its vast population and slipped into collapse, famine, and civil war.

The island's violent conflict is signaled in the archaeological record by *mata'a*, which Captain Cook's companion Forster noted in 1774, writing that some islanders 'had lances or spears made of thin ill-shaped sticks, and pointed with a sharp triangular piece of black glassy lava'.[23] *Mata'a* blades become common in the seventeenth and eighteenth centuries, and based on interpretations of the islanders' oral traditions, are taken to represent the rise of a warrior class. Some islanders took to living in caves for safety as people began to eat each other and topple statues, competing for the scarce resources that were available.

In this context, it is sometimes proposed that a new religion and social order spread. The new Bird Man cult involved selected islanders, called *hopu*, who would compete on behalf of their patron to retrieve the first tern's egg from the offshore island of Motu Nui. The winning patron would become *tangatu manu* for a year and receive benefits such as food and the exclusive right for his clan to collect eggs and young birds – making the dangerous competition a way of distributing resources amongst the island's clans.[24]

POPULATION, DEPOPULATION, AND COLLAPSE

The ecocide collapse narrative strongly depends on the idea of a high, and in the long run unsustainable, island population, but reconstructing past populations from times before census records existed is no easy matter. Generally archaeologists and palaeodemographers use a variety of techniques to estimate possible ranges of population, often drawing on surveys that reveal the numbers of habitation sites or cemeteries at particular periods (which may not all be used at the same time), making best guesses at what a 'typical' household size might be, and working out figures from there. Unsurprisingly, estimates, even based on essentially the same data, can often range quite widely, and in part what numbers are deemed plausible depends on the assumptions or argument of the observer.

Diamond estimates that Rapa Nui had a population of around 2,000 at contact, based on the early reports about the island, but thinking of the *moai* he suggests that 'their sheer number and size suggest a population much larger'. In his 1995 article, he notes that archaeologists often use a population of around 7,000, but also sees other estimates of up to 20,000 as not 'implausible for an island of Easter's area and fertility'.[25] In his 2005 book he opts for 15,000 plus, noting higher estimates of 30,000.[26]

However, the claim that the island's population ever rose to unsustainably high levels is just that, a claim, although it is a vital one for the ecocide/overshoot collapse model to work. Archaeologist Terry Hunt reminds us that these high figures are just speculation and they conclude that population probably grew at a rate of about 3 per cent from initial settlement, rising to a stable maximum of around 3,000 to 4,000 by AD 1350–1370, a figure that would have fluctuated with local circumstances but that is more in line with estimates of contact level populations.[27] That the island had a low sustainable population through time, rather than a massively high one, seems likely enough.

What happened to the population after contact, the real disaster for the island, is better known, though less frequently dealt with than the islands 'mysterious' prehistoric past. In 1862 and 1863, the island was plundered for its human resources and many islanders were transported to Peru, effectively as slave labour – slavery had been outlawed in Peru, creating a labour shortage for which a solution was being sought.[28] The scheme to use Pacific islanders as cheap 'legal' labour in Peru – the contracts that bound people to years of labour rather than people themselves were bid for – was the brainchild of Joseph Charles Byrne, who died before the plan could be carried out. Islanders would jump at the chance to join the civilised world, he argued.

One of the first chapters in the disaster story happened in 1862, when Easter Islanders, identifying themselves as from Anakena, arrived on Tahiti, where the disapproving French authorities freed them. In December that year, the young heir, *atariki*, Manu Rangi and others were also captured by the ship *Cora*, but the islanders seized the boat and sailed to Tahiti, returning to Easter Island in 1864. Some captains, like Sasuategi, operated in a fair system, with contracts ('signed' with an 'x'), translators (though no one really spoke the local Rapa Nui language), and 'decent' conditions, and for some 238 islanders who signed up, their conditions and contracts were upheld, but this was the exception. Less scrupulous captains tempted islanders to the beaches by gifts laid on the sand, then captured them, tied them up, and shipped them out – those who fled were caught or shot. Though the Peruvian authorities tried to halt the practice, they may just have driven it underground – international pressure, partly from the Catholic Church, concerned over the fate of their converts, eventually led to some repatriation.

Perhaps up to 1,500 islanders were taken over the year, forced to work as agricultural labourers, domestic servants, and alongside other Polynesians in the fatal guano mines of the Chincha Islands – guano was a valued commodity and source of income at the time, being used as agricultural fertiliser and in explosives; in 1864–1866 a war was fought between newly independent Peru and the former colonial power Spain over control of the guano-rich islands. Many, including the island's '*ariki mau*' died far from home as a result of the conditions, as well as disease and overwork. Twelve islanders returned, but smallpox returned with them, and the reduced population of around 1,500 was perhaps halved again as the disease spread – as happened in the Marquesas and elsewhere. At this point, many aspects of the island's traditional culture vanished – they could not be reproduced or sustained with the evils of conversion, disease, and depopulation.

The deaths brought disputes over land and resources, and caused real conflict on the island.

This episode, 'the Rape of Rapa Nui', has left an enduring legacy of bitterness towards Peru, yet even after the population collapse caused by slaving and disease, Palmer noted that these people living on half a rat per day were yet the 'most happy in the world', even though 'they are rapidly dying out'.[29] The real population and cultural collapse happened because of contact with Europeans and South Americans, and not because of ecocidal behaviour on the part of the Rapa Nui themselves.[30]

DEFORESTATION

Aside from the population size, the other key pillar in the prehistoric collapse scenario is, of course, what caused the deforestation of the island and its transformation into a grassland. The ecocide idea focuses on the use of *Jubaea* palms for the *moai* tradition, the visibility of declining resources, and the islander's irrational response in continuing to use them – their focus on the short term. Such short-term thinking is certainly common enough in modern societies, but it is not clear whether it applies in the case of Rapa Nui. Did the islanders go *moai* mad and use up all their wood?

Hunter-Anderson thought that, given the number of *moai* and the fact that they could have been made and moved over nine centuries, only around one statue per year was being moved.[31] Even if statue building started several hundred years later – and as mentioned, scholars are now beginning to think that the island was colonised several centuries after AD 800–900 – and finished earlier, halving the time, that figure increases to only around two to three '*moai* events' per year. Considering that statue size and the distance they were moved varied, from 4 feet to 33 feet tall, not all would have required the same effort. Almost 400 were found still in the quarry (plus 200 unfinished statues); 324 made it to coastal *ahu*, and 92 lie inland, often thought to be abandoned but possibly deliberately used as boundary markers.[32]

She also considered that *Jubaea* logs, which can last for many years in a usable condition, would have been reused, but she thinks that they in any case were probably not used to move statues, as cutting and moving heavy logs would increase the effort required to do the job; this goes against ethnographic data on how people work. In Oceania, she notes, the normal way to move large and heavy objects is to drag them over a slickened path prepared from some organic material such as grass or palm fronds, not to use log rollers. Dragging may use larger numbers of people, but participation in these events may have been a positive feature of communal social life; we should avoid thinking about it simply in terms of our modern time and labour saving ideas of efficiency. It remains uncertain then whether the *moai* tradition was a cause of deforestation on the island. Interestingly, Hunter-Anderson has also speculated that the trend to deforestation began before the island was settled.

Others have suggested that deforestation may have been caused by climate change. However, evidence from the Rano Raraku lake suggests that palm trees were present on the island for some 35,000 years, and that no climate changes in that vast stretch of time hindered their survival.[33] Climate change is therefore unlikely, at least on its own, to have brought about any deforestation on the island.

A more recent focus has been on the role of rats in hindering forest regeneration. Flenley and Bahn suspected this, and noted that most palm nuts recovered, except a few fragments from Anakena, showed evidence of being gnawed by rats, though they emphasise that it was still humans that cut the trees down in the first place.[34] Hunt and Lipo suggest that rats, brought by settlers, would have grown rapidly in numbers, consuming the *Jubaea* palm nuts as their primary food, but also feeding on other seeds, seedlings, and bark, contributing in a major way to preventing sustainable forestry; they would also have eaten birds eggs and hatchlings, reducing another food resource.[35] Rats, though, were not simply pests, as we might think, they also formed a part of the islanders low-meat diet, and may have been brought along deliberately with the early colonists. Katherine Routledge, who undertook one of the earliest full studies of the island in 1913, describes how at feast times, rats were caught in the hen houses – regular feasting on them may have kept down numbers and prevented rats from eating eggs and chicks.[36] This strategy may have been used in earlier times too, perhaps with unintended consequences.

Andreas Mieth and Hans-Rudolf Bork point out that these samples of gnawed palm nuts came from caves, where rats would be likely to eat all of them; only 10 per cent of samples they counted from the Poike Peninsula had signs of gnawing, and they doubt the idea of a rat invasion.[37] Looking at *Jubaea* forests in La Campana National Park in Chile, they note that despite the evidence for rats eating seeds, the forest is nevertheless regenerating naturally, with flourishing seedlings in evidence. On Rapa Nui, they also found evidence of prehistoric palm forest regeneration after tree cutting in the crater at Rano Raraku. Hunter-Anderson noted evidence also from Chile that rats actually helped *Jubaea chilensis* to reproduce – gnawing by rats stimulated seed germination. But she thinks that the subtropical *Juania australis* is a better candidate than the tropical *Jubaea chilensis* for the Easter Island palm tree.[38]

The very idea that Easter Island was once a forested island – with perhaps 70 per cent tree cover, based on pollen evidence from sediment cores from the islands three volcanic craters, has also been questioned by recent investigations. Valenti Rull, the head of the Botanical Institute of Barcelona's palynology and paleoecology lab, suggests that there is not yet enough evidence to be certain of this, and that other reconstructions are possible, 'the magnitude of ecological and cultural inferences about Easter Island's history contrasts with the limited number of cores studied, their fragmentary nature and the low resolution of the analyses, the few proxies used (mostly pollen)'.[39] The exact reasons for the apparent deforestation of the island remain uncertain, but even a lack of trees did not end the island's remarkable culture.

AGRICULTURE AND FISHING

Did Easter Island have a complex state society that Diamond imagines – with chiefs, bureaucrats, and carvers 'whose jobs depended on deforestation'?[40] Is it necessary or plausible to imagine Rapa Nui as an island state, with such clear divisions of labour that are found in other archaic states? Again, Lipo, Hunt, and Hundtoft argue instead, on the basis of the transmission of local traditions, for a relatively small and autonomous local kin-based organisation, not an island wide chiefdom or mini-state, and they believe that this 'groupness' might help explain competition and the development of cultural forms such as *moai* making on the island – as parts of costly signalling of status or position.[41]

Rapa Nui's deforestation, whatever its causes, took place over several centuries, and the islanders of each generation would be hard pushed to survive if they were unable to adapt their lifestyles. Islanders developed a system of gardening using *manavai*, walled gardens which protected crops from the wind and increased moisture, almost 1,500 of which are now known.[42] Usually around 45 m² in size, though some were bigger, *manavai* are found clustered together in groups of up to fifty. These were often located near the windy shoreline. Agriculture was also practiced in upland areas, as in the Vaita region, below Rano Aroe, at the fourteenth century circular house site at Maunga Tari, which was excavated by Christopher Stevenson, Thegn Ladefoged, and Sonia Haoa.[43] The house, in an area full of agricultural remains, was surrounded by planting pits, into which household waste, including fish scales, had been put to improve the soil, and there was also a rock garden nearby. Planting pits demonstrated that the islanders used lithic mulching, where pebbles and stones are used to reduce soil erosion from wind and water and which increase soil temperature and moisture.[44]

When Rogeveen was met by the Rapa Nui, 'they brought a large quantity of sugar cane, fowls, yams, and bananas' – striped linen cloth, 'with which they appeared to be well pleased', was exchanged for sixty chickens and thirty bunches of bananas.[45] Nowadays, islanders still use banana trunks for banana sled skiing; even without forests, the islanders could produce high yields of various foods at the time of contact. Contrary to later reports, Rogeveen thought that 'the island was full of trees, which were in full fruit' – and he may have seen and meant banana plants, which resemble trees. Palmer reported plenty of fresh water, though no flowing rivers, consumption of large fish, crabs, shellfish, and rats, and noted that the soil of the hills and valleys 'being nothing but decomposed lava, is very fertile ... [and] as a rule, seems moist enough not to require particular irrigation'.[46]

We should not imagine that there were no trees at all on the island going into historical times. The paper mulberry, whose bark was used for *tapa* cloth in parts of Polynesia, also survived; it prefers moist volcanic soils and can grow up to 12 m in height, though it is usually harvested when around 3–4 m.[47] When cultivated, it regenerates rapidly, and it is grown alongside other crops such as sweet potato and breadfruit. In Hawaii, young plants were protected from wind with dry banana leaves, and stone walls were used to protect plantations in the Marquesas. Apart from *tapa* cloth, the bark could also be used to make rope and cord, and as kindling. Although Europeans generally thought that islanders had little idea about agriculture, it is rather the case that the outsiders had very little understanding of how the islanders understood and successfully modified their landscape to suit their needs.

Much is made of the fact that the islanders, without forests and wood for canoes, had a much reduced access to sea food, and were also unable to leave the island to make a home elsewhere. The questionable quality of Rapa Nui canoes is also emphasised in early sources and repeated by modern ones – they were patchwork, leaky, and needed constant bailing out. But their canoes clearly did function, and for the contact period, after the supposed ecological disaster and cultural and population collapse, the sources allow us to identify a long-lived canoe building tradition, which presumably originated in pre-contact times.[48]

The 'very many' canoes seen by Rogeveen in 1722 were up to 3 m long, not hollowed from trees but made of pieces of wood glued together with organic material; in 1770 Gonzales reported seeing two canoes.[49] Cook in 1774 reported three or four canoes of 3–4 m in length, built in the same tradition as those seen half a century earlier, of which George Forster wrote:

Their canoe was another curiosity, being patched up of many pieces, each of which was not more than four or five inches wide, and two or three feet long. Its length might be about ten or twelve feet, its head and stern were raised considerably, but its middle was very low. It had an outrigger, or balancer, made of three slender poles, and each of the men had a paddle, of which the blade was likewise composed of several pieces.

The canoes were reported as carrying two to four people. La Perouse thought the canoes were most similar to those of the Society Islands, where hollowed and sewn plank canoes were used, and, as single canoes with outriggers or as double canoes (two single canoes joined together), even narrow canoes may have been used away from the shore and even for inter-island travel.[50] In 1825, two visitors to Easter Island reported seeing three canoes each, either sailing or beached, and in 1870 a Dr Philippi reported stitched plank canoes of eighteen to twenty feet, with carved figures at bow and stern.

That declining palm forests affected boatbuilding seems unlikely, since Polynesians did not use palm trees to build canoes – palm wood is not suitable, and breadfruit, mahogany, apple, and other woods are preferred.[51] Throughout Polynesia a great variety of canoe types and traditions could be found, with larger and smaller, more and less sturdy examples to be found, depending on what resources were available – the first Easter Islanders may have landed on an island already without the resources to build new ocean-going canoes (Figure 13.2). Hunter-Anderson suggests that the patchwork canoes could have been made from *toromiro* wood, which was also used for carving anthropomorphic and animal statues of a foot or more in length; the *toromiro* tree survived on the island and carving was a still-living tradition when Palmer was on the island.[52]

Regardless of whether or not the islanders had become isolated from the Polynesian world, there are reports of canoes travelling 5 km offshore, which would give access to deep water and sea food, and with the tradition of canoes we have discussed, there is no need to doubt the islanders' access to the sea. These canoes may not have been big, but Polynesian people elsewhere were also using small canoes. Regardless of whether or not such canoes were fit for long voyages, the islanders ingeniously used the available resources to build serviceable boats in what was a long-lived tradition.

What of the islanders' descent into cannibalism and civil war? Captain Cook reported seeing cannibalism practiced by the Maori, but on Rapa Nui there are no witness statements or archaeological evidence to prove it took place, although it is a frequent subject in the island's myths. One story, told to the crew of the HMS Topaze in 1868, related how the islanders killed, cooked, and ate two or three Peruvians, in response to Peruvian slaving on the island – one British officer responded, 'with such provocation it is not surprising', but was the story literally true or something told as a warning to outsiders?[53] The evidence for cannibalism remains 'narrative not archaeological'.[54] The *mata'a* blades, cited as evidence of increased warfare,

FIGURE 13.2. Tongan canoes, with sails and cabins, and two Tongan men paddling a smaller canoe in the foreground. *Source*: Derived from 'Boats of the Friendly Isles' a record of Cook's visit to Tonga, 1773–4, during his second circumnavigation of the world. Hodges, William, 1744–1797. drawn from nature by W. Hodges. Engraved by W. Watts. No. XLII. Published February 1st, 1777, by Wm. Strahan, in New Street Shoe Lane, and Thos. Cadell in the Strand, London. Alexander Turnbull Library: Reference No.B-054-047.

have also been reinterpreted as more general multipurpose tools –
though some islanders, like Sergio Rapu, a local archaeologist, disagree, 'don't tell me those obsidian tools were just for agriculture …
I'd love to hear that my people never ate each other. But I'm afraid
they did'.[55]

MOAI, TOPPLING, AND STONEWORKING CULTURE

Back to the *moai*, which are usually taken as the visible indicators
of civilisation and collapse on Rapa Nui. *Moai* production is seen as
ceasing rapidly, hence the unfinished and abandoned *moai* in the
quarries and elsewhere. But regarding *moai* production as a kind
of 9-to-5 job in a production line industry that could cease in this
way seems highly suspect. Recent work by archaeologists dwells on
how *moai* served to mark out cultural and peopled landscapes on the
island, symbolic landscapes replete with layers of meaning and experience, and how acts of making and moving were not simply 'work'
in the sense we understand it, but were social acts done in physical
spaces that created and recreated the island's culture and heritage.[56]

Investigation of the quarry at Rano Raraku suggests that the
quarry itself was encultured by the presence of *moai* – not abandoned
or unfinished but deliberately positioned on its flanks. The act of
quarrying too shows little standardisation – each carving bay, as
Routledge pointed out, had been 'worked differently, and each has
a character of its own'; perhaps each was used by a different community. *Moai* on the roads leading to and from Rano Raraku, long
thought to have been abandoned, also seem likely to have been deliberately placed, perhaps marking off the space of the road from the
off-road area, delineating spaces that had a spiritual significance.

But as Sue Hamilton and colleagues make clear, stone was a part
of the islanders' lives that went far beyond *moai* – the island is covered
in stones that were given meanings through use and which allowed
social acts to take place, and stone working never stopped. Far from
an industry in our sense, working with stone may have been a key
pastime of islanders, no doubt surrounded by layers of social and
symbolic meaning and taboo. While it may have become impossible
to transport *moai* because of lack of trees, depending on the methods
of movement thought plausible (the most recent theory, which works

in practice, being that they were rocked along on their bases), *moai* were still a part of island culture when Europeans arrived. Indeed, it may be wrong to regard monuments in stone as 'finished works' rather than modifiable ongoing cultural artefacts – *ahu* were certainly reformed and recycled periodically.[57]

The *moai* were not simply abandoned because of early deforestation. Statues were upright in 1722, and some were still upright in 1838; some were toppled by 1774 and only twenty were left standing by 1804 – eight in 1830, but it was only by 1868 that none remained upright.[58] The statues therefore remained part of the islanders' lives until well into the contact period – even if new *moai* were not being raised. Toppling and breaking a statue may have removed its power, but the act demonstrates that *moai* remained meaningful focuses of attention – it may have always been the case that they were toppled periodically in conflicts or for other reasons.[59] Terry Hunt and Carl Lipo suggest that many statues may have fallen simply due to lack of maintenance. They also suggest that it was contact with Europeans, and the opportunity to obtain their exotic goods – including prestigious hats, which islanders famously took every opportunity to acquire – which led to *moai* becoming a redundant part of Rapa Nui life.[60]

European presence, occasional as it may have been, may well have thrown a spanner into the works of the *moai*-based culture. Evidence suggests that 'cargo cults' sprang up on Easter Island, through which islanders hoped to attract back visitors bearing exotica. The building of ship shaped houses, in which Rapa Nui folk acted out rituals of 'being' European sailors, were a part of this. Carvings and paintings of European-style and hybrid ships were made on buildings and even on *moai* (Figure 13.3).[61] It is possible that *rongorongo* writing, discussed more below, may have been an imitation of the European habit of writing – without its symbols having any literal meaning.

COLLAPSE DENIED

The well-known model of a spectacular demographic and cultural collapse on Easter Island before contact with Europeans is coming under increased scrutiny – and increased criticism. In a 2002

FIGURE 13.3. *Moai* 263 at Rano Raraku with a carving of a European ship. *Source*: Courtesy of J. Pollard, A. Paterson, and K. Welham.

article, Paul Rainbird charted how contact with Europeans destabilised the status quo of the island and its culture.[62] He argued that new diseases such as syphilis were far more damaging than intra-island conflict, which did not really seem to be indicated by the skeletal remains of the islanders. It was contact that drove ecodisaster – the introduction of animals that hindered new tree growth. As he concludes:

it was the collision with the modern world system from the eighteenth century onwards that was directly responsible for the destruction of a fertile environment, and a rich and in part unique culture, to one depopulated and suited only to sheep grazing as received in the present day.[63]

Benny Peiser too has been critical of the focus on a supposed pre-contact collapse, to be blamed on the ignorance of islanders, at the expense of what we actually know to have happened to the islanders after contact.[64]

More recently, the work of Mara Mulrooney and colleagues has made it very clear that any real evidence for a pre-contact collapse is lacking.[65] She has explored the use of the date of AD 1680 as a symbolic marker of the island's supposed collapse. Through study of land use and obsidian hydration dating, that is dating and tallying the number of obsidian tools commonly used on the island and taking these as an index of land use, she has found it to be a meaningless date. What she has shown in her research on the Hanga Ho'onu area is that there was a steady decline in land use from around AD 1700, which became more precipitous between AD 1750 and 1799. The area was eventually abandoned around AD 1850 and after. This shows clearly that it was in the contact-era that depopulation and shifts in habitation were taking place.

The most recent work on the island's fate also casts doubt on a demographic collapse model. Christopher Stevenson and colleagues undertook an island-wide survey using obsidian hydration dating and found that patterns of land use varied across the island in the eighteenth century.[66] They argue that in some areas land use declined in pre-contact times, while at others it did not; the reasons for these changes they identify as the interrelation of local climate, rainfall, and environmental conditions. They conclude that land use declined in two out of three study areas, probably due to periodic drought in combination with the local soil conditions. Although suggesting that the abandonment of some areas could have caused pressure on resources still produced elsewhere, they imply that the widely accepted concept of a collapse is misleading.

FINAL THOUGHTS: A TROUBLED PAST AND FUTURE?

What can we conclude about the prehistoric Easter Island collapse? First of all, the Rapa Nui neither exterminated themselves or their culture, nor did they ruin their environment through carelessness or ignorance – with or without *moai*, they were well adapted to life in a precarious and marginal environment that they successfully transformed over time. By using techniques such as lithic mulching, banana growing, and chicken rearing, as well as accessing seafood by canoe, and even by (possibly 'farming' and) consuming rats, the islanders were able to make a living from the island into post-contact times. Though Europeans, through 'enlightened' European eyes, looked at the islanders and saw squalor and barbarism, poverty and wilderness, some of them also saw fine, good, happy people living in a fertile environment that supported them well enough– there is no need to see the Rapa Nui as merely 'scratching a living'.

The islanders did change the environment of the island, as Polynesian settlers did wherever they landed, but even if the island was deforested, perhaps by people and rats in combination, contact era Easter Island was doing ok. It was contact and after, the actions and influences of missionaries and slavers, as well as the role of newly introduced animals and diseases, that really harmed the island's indigenous people and culture, as H. V. Barclay, commander of the HMS Topaze, said in 1868. It was outsiders who turned the island into a vast sheep farm.[67] The idea that there was a prehistoric population collapse, with an attendant cultural collapse, seems an invention of modern scholarship, building on certain early impressions of the island and its culture. What is certain is that a population and cultural collapse did happen in the nineteenth century, to the shame of the so-called 'developed' world, but in keeping with its colonialist outlook.

Despite the odds, the Rapa Nui folk survived, but now, with a population of about 5,000, half being ancestral islanders, they face new threats from the outside world – tourism and modern culture. Twelve flights per week embed Rapa Nui into the global community, bringing some 50,000 tourists per year, and bringing food and fuel daily from Chile. In a recent article for *National Geographic*, Mahina Lucero Teao explained the island's new dependency on tourism, 'without it everyone would be starving on the island', and the mayor, Luz Zasso Paoa, stated that the island's 'patrimony is the base of our economy. You're not here for us, but for that patrimony'.[68]

Modernity and a place in the global community – 'development' – seems a mixed blessing for Rapa Nui. Many locals do not want to work in tourism, so many jobs are done by immigrant Chileans, whilst Easter Islanders travel to Chile for higher education; Spanish is spoken and islanders often marry mainlanders. The latest incarnation of the island may be as a heritage site rather than the site of a living dynamic culture. Change is normal enough, but the price of modernity is visible in the identity of the islanders themselves and in the pressures on the island's water supply and infrastructure – the islanders have even started asking tourists to take their rubbish away with them. The island and its people and culture were perhaps far more sustainable before contact with the outside, not less.

RONGORONGO WRITING

'Of all the mysteries about Easter Island, none is as unresolved or as controversial as *rongorongo*...' writes Shawn McLaughlin.[69] The script was first seen by Europeans in 1864, when the missionary Eugene Eyraud reported seeing 'wooden tablets or staffs covered with sorts of hieroglyphic characters' in many of the island's dwellings. The symbols, which include animals, plants, geometric, and celestial objects, were carved onto wood using shark's teeth or obsidian flakes. Islanders reported to Katherine Routledge that they used to write on banana leaves before switching to more durable wood, and that learners still used banana leaves to practice on. A hundred and fifty years later, much about *rongorongo* remains unknown – there has been no universally agreed complete decipherment. Given that no other Polynesian culture developed writing, many have wondered how the script originated. Although there are competing theories, it is perhaps most likely that the script was invented after islanders saw the writing of European sailors – thus it was an indigenous but externally inspired creation.

The full name, *kohau motu mo rongorongo,* means 'lines of inscriptions for recitation', and this may give a clue to its possible use – the symbols may have been a kind of *aide memoire* or a mnemonic device rather than being strictly 'read' as we read pages of text. Various researchers from the 1860s onwards tried to get islanders to recite from the script, in order to find out what they said and to translate the script, but these were generally unsuccessful. In 1886 William Thomson of the American ship *Mohican* recorded a story of an old man called Daniel Ure Va'e Iko, supposedly the last man who could read *rongorongo.* Daniel would not touch the real tablets because, he said, of the warnings of the priests, and using photographs he did chant, but apparently his recitals were very similar even with different tablets.

The islanders claimed that the ancestral founder Hotu Matu'a brought with him sixty-seven tablets when he first came to Rapa Nui, but there is no evidence for *rongorongo* prior to the mid-nineteenth century. The script had a very short life of perhaps less than a century; undoubtedly the conversion to Christianity, slave raids, and decimation of the island's population contributed to its demise, and the lack of knowledge about it. In the 1870s, Alphonse Pinart reported seeing tablets used for wrapping fishing nets around. It is likely that *rongorongo* lost its relevance as Christianity took hold, and Thomson reported that the islanders said they destroyed the tablets under pressure from the missionaries. The ingenuity and creativity of the islanders, however, is evident in the fact that they went on to invent two more scripts, *ta'u* in the 1880s and *mama* or *va'eva'e* in the early twentieth century. Now there are only twenty-five *rongorongo* carved objects remaining, with some 14,000 incised glyphs; none of these artefacts remain in their place of origin, Easter Island.

14

Conclusions

Prudent men should judge of future events by what has taken place in the past and what is taking place in the present ...

Miguel de Cervantes[1]

COLLAPSE: PAST AND FUTURE

We have now finished our tour through some, but by no means all, of the past collapses identified by archaeologists and historians. At the beginning of the book, I set out to explain the place of collapse in our cultural heritage and how certain ways of thinking about historical endings are embedded in our popular modern culture. I also described and evaluated some of the ways scholars define and think of collapse. I hope to have shown through the case studies that not all the things identified as 'collapse' are the same, and that, while some involved very significant events and changes, some rapid and some playing out over decades or even centuries, not all were apocalyptic or catastrophic, as they are often made out to be. In some cases, collapse may not be the most appropriate characterisation of what happened. We have seen how human populations are in fact remarkably resilient, and that cultures, too, often continue in some form even when states or empires disappear, with successor populations making deliberate choices about the heritage and identities they choose to carry on or to reject. I hope that I have stressed enough how collapses were primarily human stories.

Throughout the book I have tried to emphasise the complexity of collapse and the problem with trying to explain collapse through single or simple explanations – especially environmental ones. It is true that in our contemporary world climate change, human-caused environmental damage, and population growth are very serious concerns, but we should be careful both about projecting our problems onto past societies and about appropriating the past to make lessons for the present. Most archaeologists who think about collapse understand that it is a complex process, with many variables and multiple causes, and very few, if any, would nowadays put forward 'silver bullet' explanations; some would even question whether particular collapses should really be called 'collapses' at all, as opposed to being longer transformations. It is important that this be recognised in the popular media and in other fields of research besides archaeology, especially those where scholars seek to identify and explain collapses by climatic or environmental theories. We must also recall, when trying to explain collapse, that, in some cases, we have little evidence to go on and do not yet even agree on what some societies were.

Despite these caveats, there are important conclusions that we can draw from the study of collapse for the present, if we want to. For me, the main point is the fact that human agency, human choice, is central to each story of change. People react to circumstances, make decisions, and have the power to drive change. Usually, they are not simply victims of circumstances beyond their control. That said, human agency is not unlimited – societies are complex and made up of individuals and groups with differing aspirations, motivations, and different degrees of power to act and shape society – the ability to respond exists in this context. As I write, we can see this with Islamic State, who are attempting to form a state across international borders through appeal, violence, and coercion, and who are attempting to create a break with the past through the erasure of rival cultures, heritage, and ideologies; clearly not all the people they are affecting have the power to resist change, even if they have the desire to do so.[2]

So, not everything is controllable either at a society-wide or at an individual level. A functioning society faced with problems, say several bad agricultural years, a war or invasion, faction amongst the elite, plague, or disaffection amongst sectors of the population, may be able to do little about them directly, and each of these factors could promote a situation where collapse would become more likely. Collapse would not necessarily be inevitable though, because people could react to some extent to mitigate such problems. Particular constellations of factors occurring together would make collapse much more likely, and this is where chance too can play a role in collapse and in historical change.

To me, the message to take from many collapses is clear – collapse cautions us to build fair and inclusive societies that minimise room for disaffection and for potentially harmful divisions to arise. To create more sustainable societies we need not only to understand the natural environment, its impact on us and our impacts on it, and to live within our means, but also to realise true political and social sustainability, and consensus, in societies that ensures the well-being of all now and in the future. Although looking at past collapses can teach us these lessons, we need only look around us today to see the truth of them.

COMPARING COLLAPSES

This book, while making use of various examples of past collapses, has not attempted to make a formal comparative study in order to find one-size-fits-all explanations. But we can see some broad patterns emerging. For example, we looked at five clear instances of imperial collapses – the Akkadian, Hittite, Roman, and Tiwanaku, and briefly the Wari, empires. In each case we could claim that, even though they endured for centuries, the empires were inherently unstable, prone to fragmentation, and likely to collapse. From the Hittite and Roman empires, we can see the problems of provincial revolt or secession, of royal succession and the transmission of power through the generations, and the power of factions, all of which could cause serious divisions to arise and increase the weakness of central authority and unity. Both also had problems with 'barbarians' on the fringes of empire, who contested imperial control and power. We see similar features with the Classic Maya states and with the Angkor kingdom (or empire – depending on how we define it). But in each case we also see that aspects of the civilisations, the cultures, social and political, continued and were reused by successors. What we know of the

Hittite and Roman cases, and the Maya and Angkor cases, could help fill in the gaps with the Akkadian, Tiwanaku and Wari collapses.

Empires and states have in common that they are built up of smaller units that cohere to varying degrees. In Old Kingdom Egypt, what has been called collapse, and seen as an apocalyptic, famine-ridden, and chaotic First Intermediate Period, seems rather to have been a lively time of social fluidity and the localisation of culture. An unintended outcome of delegating power to regional governors created the context for them to become more important than, and independent from, central power. The centre became less important, less relevant, and while the texts are ambivalent, this shows in the archaeology.

We might also see parallels between the Mycenaean and Maya collapses. In both cases we are dealing not with empires but with culture zones made up of competing rival states with dominant lineages. Each state too was made up of competing members of the elite – aristocrats and prominent families, as well as individuals, who would seek to maximise benefit to themselves. Each collapse involved ideological changes – the loss of a particular kind of kingship and socio-political ideology, as well as economic changes, and an end of literacy and large scale elite-sponsored building projects. The Maya collapse involved warfare, as well as the eventual abandonment of many sites and a decline in population in many areas, and it is very likely that the Mycenaean collapse also involved conflict – inter and/or intra-state; it too saw a probable reduction in population, especially in particular areas. Although population decline is a factor in both, this is something that happened over time and was quite possibly part of the aftermath of collapse – we need not imagine sudden mass deaths.

An important difference between these examples is that the culture zones existed on quite different scales – there were many more Maya polities than Mycenaean kingdoms. Also, the Mycenaean collapse was fairly rapid, taking place probably over a few decades, whereas the Maya collapse took place over as much as three centuries, which has led to some wondering why it is termed a collapse at all. In each case, we see individual states collapsing, leading to an overall change in culture. Even so, in both civilisations there were continuities and sites that were not destroyed or abandoned.

Of the Indus Valley and Minoan civilisations, so many questions remain to be answered. In both cases, and especially in the case of the Angkor state as well, it may not be helpful to think of collapse at all. In the Indus Valley case we do know that there was an eastward shift in habitation over time, quite possibly as a reaction to irregular and changing river flows in the western region. Changes in the patterns of international trade (possibly the collapse of the Akkadian Empire) may have caused problems for the economies of Harappan cities, but most people would have been small-scale farmers in any case. What should be noted is the successful adaptation of the Harappan people to changing circumstances. And again there are observable continuities.

As for Crete, the aspects of Minoan civilisation continued, though it is unclear what happened to the Minoan states, whether there was conflict between rival states that caused eventual mutual collapse, a culture change driven from within, possibly after a natural disaster, and/or aspects of Mycenaean culture adopted by Minoans or imposed by mainland Mycenaeans. Did Minoan states, such as Knossos, seek to create some kind of hegemony, like the larger Maya states or the Akkadian dynasty, which might have led to unsettled conditions and resentment?

The fates in Mesoamerica of Rio Viejo and Teotihuacan are also difficult to understand and interpret and of the Moche, Tiwanaku, and Wari. The changes in the archaeological record clearly reflect social and political changes over time, but it is difficult, perhaps ultimately impossible, to fill out this story with characters or events, other than the mute record of when particular buildings were constructed, modified, destroyed, or abandoned (as for the Minoans and Mycenaeans too). It might be possible to trace something of a history of a strong royal line at Teotihuacan (we know that there were rulers from Maya records) through this evidence, but the evidence can only take us so far. The changes apparent in the archaeological record suggest that there may have been several such dynasties over time. Teo remained inhabited and important on a local level until much later times, when the Spanish came. In both cases we might be seeing the material remains of revolutions – indeed, the destruction or abandonment of 'ruling elite culture', and sometimes iconoclasm, is a factor in many collapses.

The stories of the Postclassic Maya and Easter Island, we have seen, are tragic ones for the indigenous peoples, involving deliberate cultural annihilation. Much of the debate on the prehistory of Easter Island hinges on the idea of an overlarge population that collapsed when it outstripped the carrying capacity of the island, plunging it into civil war, cultural collapse, and cannibalism. It is not at all clear that this is really what happened, since the islanders seemed to be doing fine upon contact. What is clear though is that contact with outsiders, Europeans and South Americans, slavers, priests, and agricultural businesses, did drive population and cultural change and collapse, and also changed the natural environment of the island to make it suitable for use as a sheep farm. The most remarkable thing is that there are still some islanders left. Returning to the idea of lessons for the present, the lesson here is surely concerned with exploitation, human and environmental, with the value of multiple cultures, with the fate of peoples and their heritages, rather than human-caused environmental damage or climate change.

DOOM, DECLINE, AND COLLAPSE

Today's news media, science magazines, and even academic journals are full of doom and gloom, and seem often to paint a picture of inexorable decline and destruction. Marilyn Matthews, writing in the journal *Psychological Perspectives*, gives a rundown of some of the threats that seem to many people to be increasingly challenging modern ways of life, and even humanity itself:

In the few short years of the 21st century alone, we have witnessed countless global events that have powerful and immediate effects: typhoons, hurricanes, and tsunamis; earthquakes, floods, and volcanoes; and wars that devastate cultures, people, and resources. The increasing threat of annihilation from the natural disasters and the wars augmented by our own runaway technology seems to have penetrated – and activated – the human psyche at a very deep level. Are these the labor pains of an immense and unprecedented evolution of humanity, the death and rebirth of humans into a new world that only we can create?[3]

Her discussion is written from an explicitly American perspective, and she begins with a claim that Americans have suffered a loss of illusion – that the myth of American invulnerability and greatness has been shattered, partly by the 11 September bombings, partly by corruption and scandal – before moving on to the 'poverty, deceit, and corruption' in Western culture, and to global events and humanity in general. It is a depressing picture that does not dwell on the myriad positive features of modern life and a globalised society that could be listed – not least the development and spread of human rights thinking, an increase in the availability of clean water, education, and birth control, and improvements in medical technology and our understanding of disease and development of sanitation. The discourse of doom exists alongside all of these positive developments.

But Matthews is not alone in her perception of threats and of global apocalypse; apocalyptic thinking is fairly widespread. A recent poll of 16,262 adults in twenty-one countries actually asked people around the world whether they thought the world was about to end.[4] The research, conducted by Ipsos Global Affairs for Reuters news agency, found that around one in seven, 14 per cent of people, think the world will end in their lifetime. The figures were highest amongst people in the United States and Turkey (22 per cent), and lowest in France (6 per cent). Although this means that 86 per cent of people do not think the world will end in their lifetime, it still makes for exciting news, and the results were widely reported.

The poll also connects more directly to our theme of past collapse and the uses of 'history', because Ipsos also asked people about 'the 2012 prophecy' – the idea, based on some people's interpretations of the ancient Maya calendar, that the world will end in December 2012 (it did not …). Interestingly, 10 per cent (though who knows if they were being serious) agreed that 'the Mayan calendar, said to 'end' in 2012, marks the end of the world'. Results again varied by location, with 20 per cent in China agreeing, compared with only 4 per cent in Germany and Indonesia. The results of the poll also varied according to other factors; participants under thirty-five years, and those with a lower educational level and income, were more likely to believe that they would experience an apocalypse. A recent academic study also suggested that religious people are more likely to think apocalyptically, and to believe they will witness the end.[5] Part of this apocalyptic turn may be due to the prominence of apocalyptic collapse in the media, films, literature, documentaries, and popular science magazines (as well as in religious texts) – but ideas of an imminent apocalypse, millenarian thinking, have long been a part of the human social experience.

Jared Diamond's best-selling book *Collapse* was later turned into a *National Geographic* documentary, spreading his views on collapse to a whole new and even wider audience. It focussed much more explicitly on 'now', but retained some of the historical background of the Anasazi collapse that featured in his book. It also featured Joseph Tainter, who, while critiquing overshoot and ecocidal models of collapse of the kind proposed by Diamond, nevertheless thinks a present day collapse would be not only possible but could happen in six months; it would be the most damaging in human history because of the complexity of our society, our global interdependency, and the massive global population. The documentary follows archaeologists of the future, picking over the bones of our present left in the deserts like the statue of Ozymandias, asking questions of why we behaved the way we did rather than recognising our impacts and changing our ways.

Aspects of the documentary dwell on our supposed 'mastery' of the planet and our 'greatness' – 'the greatest civilisation in history' – cherished delusions, which underscore our preferred attitudes, wishful thinking, and inability (or unwillingness) to recognise and act upon our deleterious impacts on the planet. Divorced from production and insulated by the complex webs of modernity, as most of us are, we are shown our unsustainable water-hungry agricultural monocultures and technologies of power generation that change the atmosphere. Watching the documentary is as salutary as any environmental focus on human degradation of the landscape, but the overall impression the film gave was not that a global collapse is imminent, but that southern California and Los Angeles are unsustainable human projects and are in danger of environmental collapse.

In fact, this is something that Lester Milbraith pointed out to his surprised University of California students in the 1990s.[6] He argued that southern California was the most unsustainable part of two of the most unsustainable societies on earth:

The southern Californians have erected a huge metropolitan area with nearly 20 million inhabitants on a terrain of mountains and valleys that is essentially a desert and highly susceptible to earthquakes. The city must import all its water, energy, and food from elsewhere. Its transportation system depends overwhelmingly on heavy, fast, automobiles that travel on multi-lane freeways that criss-cross the area. If southern Californians had set out to design an unsustainable society, they could hardly have exceeded the reality of today's LA area.

The kind of collapse envisioned is apocalyptic – but different in kind to the collapses we have examined in this book.

But although present day systems, such as mass urbanisation and agricultural monoculture, are very widely recognised as environmentally harmful and potentially unsustainable, and we can certainly recognise the impacts of past societies on landscapes, the contemporary situation is far far worse than any that past peoples could have created. If we think of history as an ethical pursuit, it is questionable to project our own problems onto past peoples; in some sense, by doing this, we are robbing 'them' of a history that is independent of 'our' present.

COLLAPSE, POPULATION, AND THE ENVIRONMENT

I have attempted to go somewhat against the current grain of explaining collapses by reference to environmental causes and natural disasters in a simple cause and effect fashion. All societies have existed embedded in their environments, and environmental change of any sort can drive all manner of other shifts – but there is often no simple connection of climate change or anthropogenic environmental damage to collapse. As archaeologist Patrick Ryan Williams has said, 'collapse and survival are social processes, affected by but not driven by their environments'.[7] Even Jared Diamond has stated that 'I don't know of any case in which a society's collapse can be attributed solely to environmental damage'.[8] That said, more research and increasing amounts of evidence will allow us to say more securely whether and when climatic changes did coincide with collapses, and the development of increasingly accurate chronologies should help us assess whether there could be causative links between them. We must always beware of seeing coincidences automatically as causes though and we must still focus on the human stories of how collapse played out – these are the stories we should want to learn about, rather than simply posit climate change = collapse.

It is beyond doubt that extreme weather events, droughts, and high rainfall, will have affected agrarian societies, sometimes very severely – they continue to affect us today. But since human societies have existed around the globe for thousands of years, and many are little known and not included in the roster of collapses (though presumably many could be), it is basically unrealistic to expect climate change to have been the main driver of change; certainly its effects will have been mediated by the individual society and the unique circumstances at the time. There is a tendency in current affairs to claim apparent changes in weather as evidence of climate change, but, as environmental archaeologist Dina Dincauze explains, 'Because climate is so variable and dependent upon contingencies at many scales, thinking in terms of climatic averages or norms is likely to be misleading … It is better to emphasize dynamism and variability …'.[9] Climate, conditions measured over long spans of time, is always changing; weather is always open to potential variation – what we see in our lifetime encourages a very short-term perspective. For climate to play a key role in all collapses, and to be valid as a general explanation of collapse, it has to apply in all cases, not only those few where evidence suggests a temporal coincidence, and not only in the well-known cases of collapse.

I think it more likely that weather events (sometimes protracted) may have played a greater role historically than climate change – the distinction being that a run of bad years, which may go unnoticed in records of climate changes on a more geological scale, could be disastrous for any agricultural society, and could undermine its social, political, and economic infrastructure. Such events could precipitate a lack of confidence in any system, or its failure, especially when an urban centre is involved, and could drive social, political, and ideological change. This is especially the case when elites were ideologically connected to water supply, production, and stability, but also in cases where shortage could simply drive severe discontent (think Roman grain riots – though lack of supply, as in many cases of famine, was dictated by human choices such as the hoarding of foodstuffs by those with more power). The same goes for geological hazards such as earthquakes and volcanoes, which have been ever-present dangers in certain locations, but which could, depending on the circumstances and event itself, drive change of various kinds. Even so, many societies lived alongside these hazards (think of highly seismic Japan, for example).

But more than that, I suggest that it is the human stories and choices that underpin collapses. The environment may well be part of the cause of some collapses, but it cannot be seen apart from the human factors. For example, Rebecca Stone points out that, whereas the Moche may have been profoundly affected by El Nino events, the later Chimu, who occupied the same space as their Moche forebears, adapted their culture when such events struck – she argues that they changed their adaptive strategy from one based on canals to one based on the conquest of fertile, well-watered valleys.[10] Particular environments are often created and maintained by human organisation, and when that breaks down, it may look like environmental collapse. Warfare, a constant in human history, has the potential to wreck agriculture and the maintenance of agricultural, economic, and social infrastructure, and cumulatively to cause destabilisation and collapse. People, though, will then adapt to the new circumstances with a mix of traditional knowledge and innovation.

It is not hard to see how a kind of 'ratchet effect' operates in human societies, with each generation brought up and existing in unique circumstances, where the reality they are born into, the political and social circumstances, and the choices they make take them further away from a situation that existed earlier on – from the realities of their parents' or grandparents' generations. Human social change, often regarded teleologically (and in a self-satisfied manner) as progress – for example, industrialisation – can be explained in such a way, but so can collapse and its aftermath, which is usually seen as the opposite of progress.[11] Again it comes out clearly with the story of the Western Roman Empire that incremental change on many levels, in line with events that unfolded, brought about a set of circumstances and realities very different in the fifth century AD to that of the second or third. But much of the change was simply change and adaptation to circumstances – not necessarily a 'bad thing', to generalise grossly. Political collapse happened alongside these changes, and ultimately drove more.

None of this is to say that, in the present day, climate change and anthropogenic damage to the environment do not pose most serious threats to modern global society – they do. Evidence suggests that the circumstances that humans have created since industrialisation, including the massive increase in human population and resource use, as well as global economic integration, do indeed put our societies and way of life, as well as our planet and its species and ecosystems, at profound risk – apocalyptic collapse is more of a possibility for us than for any generation in the past. In 2011 a report detailing the catastrophic human impact on the oceans was published by IPSO – the International Programme on the State of the Ocean.[12] The report makes for uncomfortable reading as it catalogues the increasingly rapid degradation of the ocean and marine ecosystems – which ultimately support all life on earth – due to human action. The increased warming, acidification, and hypoxia that can be seen now are all features associated with earlier mass extinction events that have taken place on earth, and in the words of IPSO's Dr Alex Rogers – 'if the oceans go down, it's game over'.

An earlier and equally frightening report on conservation and biodiversity was published in *Science,* based on the International Union for Conservation Red List.[13] Noting the vital role that vertebrates play in ecosystems, the authors of the paper reported that a fifth of vertebrates are currently classified as 'threatened', and that fifty-two species of vertebrates a year move a category closer to extinction. Key causes of biodiversity loss include agricultural expansion, logging, overexploitation, and the presence of invasive species – all caused by humans and their choices. Although the report highlighted some successes due to conservation efforts, it concluded that global biodiversity remains under serious threat. A paper by Anthony Barnosky and colleagues in *Nature* asks whether we might now be experiencing the Earth's sixth 'mass extinction event'.[14]

Reading such reports, it is easy to feel that human behaviour over the last 10,000 years or so, since more people started practicing more intensive agriculture around the world and populations started growing and increasing their impacts on the planet, has really just added up to a catalogue of cumulative environmental abuse that seems to go hand in hand with the development of complex societies.

Indeed, as we have seen, many environmental historians, including Jared Diamond and Clive Ponting, have written in this vein. Lester Milbraith has called this 'the tragic success of the human species ...' and explains that 'by being singlemindedly successful at doing what society expects of us, we have created a civilization that is headed for breakdown'.[15] Such thinking tends to be 'progressivist' and teleological – it suggests a worsening over time, linking together many disparate instances of human history into an overarching narrative. It also tends to see human–environment interaction as automatically destructive both for the environment and for the human societies based on it rather than a more complex ecological relationship that can be a success for both. However, when it comes to applying this to past societies, or to using this model to explain their collapse, I agree with Eric Zencey:

the ecology movement would have done better – and would do better in the future – if its partisans drew their image of time not from the romantic notion of history with its apocalyptic redemption, but from nature, where there is no apocalypse – just continual, and sometimes dramatic, adaptation and change.[16]

Arguments about past collapses based on overshoot arguments, where high populations are estimated, always rely on guesses about populations – however educated those guesses are – derived from archaeological evidence; it is circular argumentation to assume that where there was a collapse, a high population must have existed to create the circumstances of destabilisation or collapse. In many cases of collapse, such as Easter Island or the Classic Maya, population figures remain unknown, with high and low estimates given by different experts. Overshoot arguments seem, on balance, much more likely to be relevant to the contemporary world, given the massive and unprecedented increase in population in a historically very short period of time – the last three centuries or so. The issue of population and global carrying capacity is of prime concern for governments and international organisations and was the subject of a recent United Nations report (Figure 14.1).[17]

I would like to end the book with two more, slightly different, contemporary examples that should provide notes of caution for us when we think about collapse, and which reassert the primacy of people in

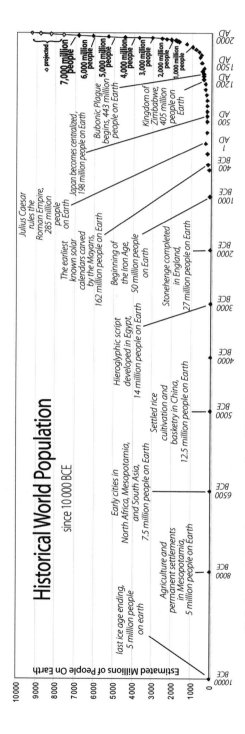

FIGURE 14.1. Global population change over time (UNEP).

Source: UNEP Global Environment Alert Service (2012). *One Planet, How Many People? A Review of Earth's Carrying Capacity.* Available at: http://na.unep.net/geas/archive/pdfs/GEAS_Jun_12_Carrying_Capacity.pdf

historical change of the kind reflected in material culture – the kind detectable by archaeology.

FROM STATELY HOMES TO GOLF CLUBS

Visible changes to material culture and patterns of habitation do not always indicate the kind of political change or revolution that we would think of as collapse. Change and transformation are normal, and reflect changes in social values and practice as well as economic shifts including changes in subsistence, agriculture, and trade.

A good example of the kind of change that future archaeologists, looking back at the last three centuries in the British Isles, might mistake for collapse is the transformation of elite habitations – castles, stately homes, and the like.[18] The stately homes of the UK developed out of the earlier prestige centres of local aristocrats. As conflict became less common, defence became less important, and architectural styles and site locations changed, with a changing desire for both display and privacy.[19]

In the eighteenth and nineteenth centuries, newly wealthy industrialists built their own stately homes in imitation of aristocratic ideals and the symbolic architectural language of power, sometimes also marrying into the aristocracy to further increase their social status. By the twentieth century, it was becoming increasingly difficult for the landed elite, whether aristocratic or new money, to maintain their stately homes. The First and Second World Wars denuded many homes of the staff required to maintain them, and with the addition of inheritance taxes, the effect was to bankrupt this elite class. While many homes were destroyed, others were bought and taken, stone by stone, to new locations overseas, such as the USA. Many surviving examples are now managed by heritage organisations or have been transformed into golf clubs, hotels, or subdivided into prestigious apartments. These changes could be said to represent (and to be recognisable to a future archaeologist as) a 'rapid' elite collapse, one taking place over, say, a century – but given our knowledge of what actually happened, we know that there really was no collapse, let alone apocalyptic change. But there was a great deal of transformation, with historically specific events taking place and reflecting and driving change.

In archaeology, the subdivision of ancient high status buildings is often said to represent decline and 'squatter' occupation after a period of elite use. Could we say the same about Britain's stately homes? We might rather see such changes as representing growing social equality, and we might see increased access to them as an increasing democratisation of culture. No doubt some might see that, from a classed perspective, as 'barbarisation'. We might also recall Ipuwer's characterisation of the Egyptian First Intermediate Period as one of the reversal of the 'proper' social order. In heritage terms it is interesting that the homes of the former elite are now a focus for the construction of a shared past – even though it is one that excludes the lives of the vast majority – the ordinary folk. Our modern architecture, mass public housing, a reduced focus on sturdy elite buildings, and a greater focus on the utilitarian or functional in public buildings, would also reflect to future archaeologists ongoing social and economic changes. But would we want them to paint this as decline or failure?

In archaeology we must remain open to the possibility – the probability rather – that a lot may be going on that we simply cannot see – the future archaeology of Britain would tell us that changes were happening but, without texts, might reveal little about the actors and processes involved. There are some things we only know about because texts of one sort or another tell us about them – and even these are not always straightforward in interpretation – but in prehistoric cases, where there is no (or no deciphered) writing, or where texts are very limited in scope, it is the archaeological evidence that we rely on. Archaeological evidence too has to be interpreted in order to make a satisfying narrative, and this is often not a straightforward task either. But while admitting that our picture is inevitably partial, there are clear instances in both the modern and ancient worlds where distinctive changes in material culture accompany revolutions (such as the destruction of palaces or political centres and iconoclasm). Seen in hindsight, long social change, revolutions, and regime changes may all appear to archaeologists as collapse.

ROME AND DETROIT: COLLAPSE IN THE MAKING?

Although the ancient and modern worlds differ in so many ways, not least in the scale and complexity of many modern day organisations and technologies, the effects of changing balances of political, economic, and military power, nodes of production and trade networks are clearly present in both. Recognising these clear parallels allows us to shed light on processes which are common to both, and helps us to evaluate our responses to the change that we identify in the past and the present.

Modern industrialisation has had a range of effects on human societies; one of the clearest is in the distributions of populations towards urban areas, a process which is visible in industrialising regions such as China, where the number of cities increased from just under 200 to more than 600 between 1978 and 2000 (though cities in the ancient world also had a draw).[20] But for countries which underwent a transition to industrial urban economies earlier, such as the UK, the global situation has changed things, and in many cases what had become traditional industries have disappeared from some areas. Nowadays, governments and local authorities running them are challenged by urban decay, visible in the abandonment and dereliction of buildings and even whole areas, and of movements out of areas by some groups.[21]

In many of the ancient societies we have looked at, urbanisation, increasing complexity, and population growth was followed by 'decay' – breakdown of urban infrastructure, simpler buildings, abandonment, and the movement of population. Centres attract people, whether economically or because of their ideology, or for other reasons, grow for a while, and when circumstances change their population levels and regional importance reduce. Looked at in isolation, it seems like a clear 'rise and fall' pattern, but we have to take into account that some sites may be on the up when others are on the way down – events are running side by side, with interactions 'across'; in addition, shifts in religion or ideology, economic changes, or shifts in trade patterns may be taking place too, reducing the importance or function of some sites, and increasing that of others.

A well-known example of urban decay is the American city of Detroit, which was once the fourth largest city in the USA, with a maximum population of almost two million people. Detroit grew because of a booming automobile industry, which drew people in to share in the economic success. In the 1950s, citizens of the Detroit area enjoyed relatively high incomes and levels of home ownership, but between 2000 and 2010, the population fell by 25 per cent.[22] In recent years, Detroit has come to be seen as a dying city with 'a desolate post-industrial cityscape', with some districts and even public buildings left derelict, and public services restricted to only 'viable' parts.[23] The population, which has declined steadily since its 1950s peak, is now around 700,000, its lowest level since 1910. In the future, this might look like collapse.

But Detroit remains a functioning city, and it is unlikely that it will become a ghost town, or a completely abandoned 'lost city'. One of the interesting possibilities that may transform the landscape and economies of Detroit, and other cities, is an increase in urban farming, which would transform derelict land into useful and productive land, with a range of economic and social benefits.[24] A drive towards increasing locally sourced food reduces dependency on the global supply chain that, whilst creating a cheap food economy, is itself dependent on a continuing cheap oil economy and is perhaps unsustainable.

This urban transformation is reminiscent of some of the patterns of rise and fall, and also some of the features of collapse, that we see in the archaeological record, and clearly suggests how some past transformations must equally have been normal adaptations to changing circumstances that involved changing networks of resources, and motivated individuals acting on their own agency. The rise of urban farming – the changing use of a once urbanised landscape – reminds me of the 'dark earth' of Late and post-Roman towns, where urban spaces may also have changed their functions. We can see in the case of Detroit that the population decline is quite rapid, but still takes place over decades. But as with other well-known redistributions of people, like the Highland clearances in eighteenth and nineteenth century Scotland and the Celtic migrations to the New World and Antipodes, there is no need to suggest that anything apocalyptic happened, even if parts of these stories are traumatic for those involved, and however abandoned buildings or landscapes can make things look.

Of course, if we pick on particular areas in isolation, population might seem to disappear. But, while population can decline for many reasons, we also see that it can mean people choosing to go somewhere else – many Romans from Rome went to Constantinople when it was reconstituted as the eastern capital, and especially during the troubles of the fifth century (and a thousand years later many Constantinopolitans fled west when the Ottomans arrived). It can also mean that the traces the population leaves behind are less visible, which can happen through changing building habits or distributions of people in the landscape, for example. Populations may nucleate at certain points, where they are archaeologically more visible, or be spread thinly over the landscape, leaving few traces for archaeologists to find. There may be false comparisons with overestimates of earlier population, based on site counts which assume habitation of all sites during a particular period.

Even before the end of the Western Roman Empire, the city of Rome experienced depopulation, and as Richard Krautheimer says, 'After the Gothic Wars, Rome had become a rural town dependent on agricultural produce close at hand, within the Aurelian walls, or just outside' (Table 14.1).[25] But, of course, at Rome and other places there was continuity too. Indeed, there was a twice-weekly cattle market held in the Theatre of Marcellus into the twentieth century – a startlingly long tradition, though not the original use of the building; a continuity from the aftermath of empire. Formerly urban areas throughout the empire contain layers of what archaeologists refer to as 'dark earth', between Roman and medieval, which may be indicative of new agricultural practices in these places (some urban agriculture/market gardening took place normally, as at Pompeii).[26] Future archaeologists might detect this in Detroit and other cities increasing urban farming.

So-called urban decay was mitigated by developing new aesthetic tastes and by practical and legal measures. In AD 459, a law was passed allowing spoliation – the robbing and use of material from buildings deemed 'beyond repair' – what we might think of as brownfield sites, 'the physical collapse of the city from the fourth century on built Christian Rome'.[27] The law obviously reflects what had become normal practice, and in fact represents a very sensible saving of energy in reusing already quarried and cut stone and also the changing value

TABLE 14.1 *Population estimates for the city of Rome through time*

Year	Population estimate
c. 100 BC	250,000
31 BC	500,000/750,000
AD 0–200	1,000,000 (emperors not resident after AD 284)
AD 400	500,000–800,000 (Constantinople dedicated in AD 330, Ravenna becomes western capital in AD 402)
AD 452	500,000
AD 500	100,000
AD mid-6th	30,000 (Procopius claimed a population of 500 men were left)
AD *c.* 570	90,000 (temporary increase including refugees, especially monks, taking refuge from invading Langobards)
AD 9/10th – 12/13th	35,000
AD 1527	55,000

Note: The city did not exist in isolation. Krautheimer notes a proportion of one to ten of city to district population after AD 1400, a dynamic proportion dependent on various changing factors
Source: Figures from the *Oxford Classical Dictionary*; page 42, Christie N. (2011). *The Fall of the Western Roman Empire: An Archaeological and Historical Perspective*. London: Bloomsbury; pages 65, 231–232, Krautheimer, R. (2000). *Rome: Profile of a City, 312–1308*. Princeton UP, Princeton; page 8 & refs, Robinson, O. F. (1994). *Ancient Rome: City Planning and Administration*. London: Routledge.

of older buildings within the community. The medieval cathedral and tower at Pisa used Roman stone, with many inscriptions clearly visible, and this reflects not only simple reuse, but a claim of *romanitas* for Pisa – a visible, if slightly odd to modern eyes, connection with the Roman past.[28] It is a wonder, in fact, that so much remains from the ancient world – in medieval times much more must still have been visible, even if the buildings were often seen as convenient quarries.

In the case of Detroit, the abandonment of buildings and districts, the redistribution of population, and the transformation of land use need not represent a wholly negative picture, the way collapse or decline is often imagined. The changes taking place could make the new Detroit more sustainable and less vulnerable to fluctuations and networks over which organisations and local people have little control. In other words, Detroit is adapting, and while it may look very different to fifty years ago, it would be strange to think of the process simply as a decline or a failure.

Rome and Detroit are very different cases, but in some ways both clearly experienced the effects of changes in the networks that drew people in and helped fuel their expansion. Such systems are highly complex, and this kind of hyperconnectivity marks out the period of globalisation which the world is now experiencing, though hyperconnectivity could also happen in the smaller systems of the ancient world. Indeed, since the nineteenth century, it has become increasingly recognised that participation in global systems can have profound repercussions at local levels, and that these can drive social change in local areas.

GLOBAL RISKS AND APOCALYPTIC THREATS

Throughout this book, I have taken an anti-apocalyptic view of collapse, seeing it as part of normal transformations of history, often constructed in hindsight affected by the nature of our traditions combined with archaeological evidence and the modern 'discovery' (or 'invention') of the past. However, there is a growing interest in global catastrophic threats that would be potentially apocalyptic. This interest is not new, but grows with scientific research and enquiry – a century ago H. G. Wells, the father of futurology, stated:

It is impossible to show why certain things should not utterly destroy and end the human race and story; why night should not presently come down and make all our dreams and efforts vain ... something from space, or pestilence, or some great disease of the atmosphere, some trailing cometary poison, some great emanation of vapour from the interior of the earth, or new animals to prey on us, or some drug or wrecking madness in the mind of man.[29]

A recent academic book musing on potential threats, entitled *Global Catastrophic Risks*, included categories such as risks from nature, risks from unintended consequences, and risks from hostile acts (Table 14.2).[30] These range from massive volcanic episodes and planet-killing asteroids, through climate change and plagues, to global totalitarian takeover. Whilst totalitarianism need not bring population or societal collapse, many of the threats could result in the kind of apocalyptic scenarios beloved of the science fiction culture that we use to reflect on such possibilities.

TABLE 14.2 *Global catastrophic risks*

Risks from nature
Super-volcanism/eruptions
Comets and asteroids
Supernovae, gamma ray bursts, etc.
Risks from unintended consequences
Climate change
Plagues and pandemics
Artificial intelligence
Catastrophe, social collapse, and human extinction
Risks from hostile acts
Nuclear war
Nuclear terrorism
Biotechnology
Nanotechnology
Totalitarianism

Source: Bostrom, N. and Cirkovic, M. M. (2008). *Global Catastrophic Risks*. Oxford: Oxford University Press.

Sociologists like Manuel Castells and others are now fond of seeing societies as networks, and modern societies, indeed global society, comprise complex systems of networks.[31] One of the key threats to the global status quo comes from the hyperconnectivity, mentioned earlier, and the increasing complexity of interlinked global economies and cultures. The more dependent a society is on a system it cannot control, the more vulnerable it becomes to disturbances in any part of that system. Collapse of global systems, or parts of them, have knock on effects throughout the system, as has been seen in the financial crisis that 'began' in 2007–2008 and ushered in a period of global recession. At the time of writing, the crisis is affecting normal Cypriots, whose savings the government planned to appropriate in a one-off tax to raise money necessary to win an EU bailout package, and whose access to their own money is being limited by capital controls.[32] Even more recently, Greece has been suffering badly from its debt burden, which has been caused by and affects its links to other European countries and its membership of the Euro. What Greece chooses to do will have ramifications, economic and political, across Europe, potentially affecting the existence of the European Union itself. In 2016, the UK held a referendum on membership of the EU, voting to leave, but it will remain tied in both to the EU and the wider world; it has perhaps given away more power and control through this decision than it will get back.

This connectivity and the global risks to stability are amply demonstrated in the World Economic Forum's annual global risk report. Risks are subdivided into five categories: economic, environmental, geopolitical, societal, and technological. The ninth edition, *Global Risks 2014*, summarises the top five risks predicted since 2007 in terms of likelihood and impact (Table 14.3).[33] Many of the threats identified by experts who responded to the risk survey the WEF carries out are economic and financial, and this is a sure indication of the deep reach of global economic interdependence; but the most likely risks predicted in 2011 were meteorological catastrophes, hydrological catastrophes, corruption, biodiversity loss, and climatological catastrophes. In 2014, extreme weather events, climate change, and water crises ranked alongside issues such as unemployment and underemployment, cyber-attacks, and financial crises.

The Universite Catholique de Louvain's Centre for Research on the Epidemiology of Disasters also publishes a regular bulletin called CRED Crunch, in which they provide data about natural disasters around the world. A recent issue reported on the increased incidence of natural disasters between 1950 and 2011 (Figure 14.2). It seems clear that the number of reported disasters has been on the increase, especially in Asia.

Figures like those collated by CRED may well make it seem like the world is becoming a more dangerous place, but we have to take into account in particular the rising global population; this puts more people into the path of natural and normal risks and hazards, resulting in more death and damage. We also need to consider the recording and communication of hazards and disasters, which is now much more precise and far-reaching than ever. To some extent the danger we perceive and experience is a result of increasing population and increasing attention, not a change in the environment itself – in this sense it is not 'turning against us' or punishing us for our 'ecosins', though we put increasing pressure on it, which will feed back into our societies.

TABLE 14.3 *The World Economic Forum's top five global risks by likelihood and impact*

	2008	2009	2010	2011	2012	2013	2014
Likelihood	Asset price collapse	Asset price collapse	Asset price collapse	Meteorological catastrophes	Severe income disparity	Severe income disparity	Income disparity
Impact	Asset price collapse	Asset price collapse	Asset price collapse	Fiscal crises	Major systemic financial failure	Major systemic financial failure	Fiscal crises

Source: Page 17, The World Economic Forum. (2014). *Global Risks 2014, Ninth Edition.* Geneva: World Economic Forum.

362

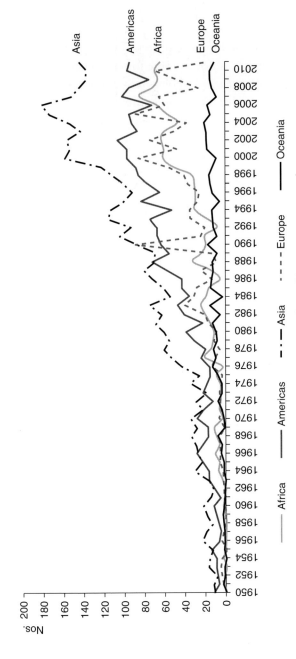

FIGURE 14.2. Reported natural disasters 1950–2011 (CRED Crunch).
Source: CRED Crunch Issue 30, January 2013. Available at: http://cred.be/sites/default/files/CredCrunch30.pdf

FINAL THOUGHTS

This book has been selective both in the examples of collapse chosen and the stories told about them, which reflect my own research and personal interests, views, and experiences, though I have sought not to exclude theories deliberately or to be overly partisan. In a book of this size and scope, it is not possible to be comprehensive about collapse or all the collapses that scholars have discussed. I have attempted to give a general view of how people think about collapse in different ways, and to show how a number of proposed collapses have been approached by archaeologists and others in order to introduce some of the theories, issues, and problems of the subject. I have emphasised that I think many things called 'collapse' are misunderstood, because we tell particular stories about past societies and because the category of 'collapse' is much broader than we usually think – thus, many collapses found discussed together may in reality represent very different things; though some comparisons may be useful, we need to account for what collapse was in each case. Also, the case-studies I chose could have been narrated very differently, taking different base theories as starting points, for example, and more or different examples could have been selected, such as the dynasties of China,[34] the kingdoms of Africa apart from Egypt,[35] and many less well-known examples of what might be called 'collapse' that deserve fuller treatment in their own right.

I am as prone as others to weave a narrative that seems to me to make sense. Others will read the evidence and sources differently, arrive at different conclusions, and tell other stories. They are entitled to do so, and indeed should do so. By approaching collapse from various angles of evidence, interpretation, and interest, we may progress towards better knowledge of what we understand by collapse and what could and might have happened in the different collapses and transformations that we identify. This can help us to understand how states 'fail' in the contemporary world, and also how to create and maintain societies which are not only environmentally but also socially and politically sustainable – key to this must be the recognition of change as a constant, as well as adaptability, both practical and cultural. New evidence will appear, old evidence will be reinterpreted, and theories will come and go. Thus, I have avoided proposing any general theory of collapse and any effort at having the final word on collapse – I do not think a general theory of any kind of utility can be devised, and there will undoubtedly be many more studies of collapse in the future.

Nevertheless, in this book I have sought to emphasise that collapse is rarely, if ever, apocalyptic, and that people, communities, and cultures tend to continue through collapse, even while some parts of material and non-material culture may be abandoned – especially those phenomena connected with rulers and elites. This reflects the choices taken by people at particular times and in particular circumstances – all unique and by and large unrecoverable. Examining the collapse of the Roman West demonstrated that even when we can attempt to piece together some motivations and stories from primary sources, we do not arrive at a simple or unified narrative – just like our modern societies today, there was always a lot going on, and a lot of people with divergent interests and views. In part, the ambiguity that surrounds many instances of collapse is what allows us to use them to tell stories that have contemporary resonance, however fantastic these are.

This view of collapse may seem much less dramatic or exciting than those that appear in headlines, documentaries, or feature films, but this is not really surprising. And it is not surprising either that there are no straightforward answers to collapse, certainly not when we recognise the complexity of the context and questions we are asking. As Arthur Demarest recently stated:

As information becomes more complete, the silver bullets seldom work. The case of the well-documented decline and fall of Rome shows that answers to questions of the "collapse" of civilizations become increasingly complex with the emergence of additional information. The "mysteries" and the questions also become less dramatic – and, in a sense, less interesting. But then that is what answers do![36]

I would like to end this book by suggesting that the less evidence there is – historical or narrative evidence certainly – and the more distant a society is from 'us' in time, space, or culture, the more prone we are to see its collapse as something that must be explained in some unusual and possibly overly simple way – we create modern myths for ancient history. If our aim is to learn from the past, for example, to create more sustainable communities, then this is dangerous, since it can often mean ignoring the complexity of societies and the very real human factors in collapse. As Cervantes wrote, quoted in the opening epigraph of this chapter, we can and should learn from the present as much as the past. Just looking around us now we can readily see problems, environmental, political, and social, that require addressing, and we can predict the problems and scenarios that we may face if we hesitate to do so; there is no need to appropriate ancient history to find examples or lessons to be learned.[37]

Yet, in studying the past, we are affected by our inherited views as well as our present day concerns, and tend to telescope past events and processes so that they may seem more sudden and terrible than they were – though, doubtless, many terrible things happened to people, as they have in recent history too. We construct out of the past a range of 'others' that offer us mirrors with which to view ourselves, through study and research, through information and entertainment. But we do this at our peril, as much as our illumination. So let us end with what seems an apposite quote from an essay by George Orwell:

Contrary to popular belief, the past was not more eventful than the present. If it seems so, it is because when you look backward things that happened years apart are telescoped together, and because very few of your memories come to you genuinely virgin.[38]

Yet, if the past was not more eventful than the present, we can be equally sure that, in human terms, it was not any less eventful either.

Notes

Preface

1 Grabbe, L. L. (2007). 'What historians would like to know ...' *Near Eastern Archaeology* 70(1): 13.

2 Diamond, J. (2005). *Collapse: How Societies Choose to Fail or Succeed.* London: Penguin; Tainter, J. A. (1988). *The Collapse of Complex Societies.* Cambridge: Cambridge University Press.

3 Davies, N. (2011). *Vanished Kingdoms: The History of Half-Forgotten Europe.* London: Allen Lane.

4 On the alleged Chaco Canyon ecocidal collapse, see now Wills, W. H., Drake, B. L., and Dorshow, W. B. (2014). 'Prehistoric deforestation at Chaco Canyon?' *Proceedings of the National Academy of Sciences* 111(32): 11584–11591; generally see Kantner, J. (2004). *Ancient Puebloan Southwest.* Cambridge: Cambridge University Press; on Cahokia see Pauketat, T. R. (2004). *Ancient Cahokia and the Mississipians.* Cambridge: Cambridge University Press.

5 Marshall, M. (2012). 'Climate change: The great civilization destroyer.' *New Scientist* 215(2876): 32–36; Weiss, H. and Bradley, R. S. (2001). 'What drives societal collapse?' *Science* 291: 609–610.

1. Introducing Collapse

1 Page 126, Wheeler, M. (1968). *The Indus Civilization.* Cambridge: Cambridge University Press.

2 24 February 2012, BBC Radio 4 news.

3 Medina-Elizalde, M. and Rohling, E. J. (2012). 'Collapse of Classic Maya civilization related to modest reduction in precipitation.' *Science* 335: 956–959.

4 Page 133, Orwell, G. (2000/1940). 'My country left or right?' In *Essays*. London: Penguin, pp. 133–138.

5 *The Times of India*. (2012). 'Climate killed Harappan civilization.' (29 May). Available at: http://articles.timesofindia.indiatimes.com/2012-05-29/science/31886985_1_harappan-river-monsoon; Giosan, L., Clift, P. D., Macklin, M. G., Fuller, D. Q., Constantinescu, S., Durcan, J. A., Stevens, T., Duller, G. A., Tabrez, A. R., Gangal, K., Adhikari, R., Alizai, A., Filip, F., Van Laningham, S., and Syvitski, J. P. (2012). 'Fluvial land-scapes of Harappan civilization.' *Proceedings of the National Academy of Sciences* 109(26): E1688–E1694.

6 Marshall, M. (2012). 'Climate change: The great civilization destroyer.' *New Scientist* 215(2876): 32–36.

7 Drake, B. L. (2012). 'The influence of climatic change on the Late Bronze Age collapse and the Greek Dark Ages.' *Journal of Archaeological Science* 39(6): 1862–1870.

8 Hutton, R. (2013). 'A pagan riddle we will never solve.' *BBC History Magazine* (Christmas): 24–28.

9 Page 1541, Hornblower, S. and Spawforth, A. (eds.). (2003). *Oxford Classical Dictionary*. Revised third edition. Oxford: Oxford University Press.

10 Sommer, R. (2008). 'Drama and narrative.' In Herman, D., Jahn, M., and Ryan, M.-L. (eds.). *Routledge Encyclopedia of Narrative Theory*. London: Routledge, pp. 119–124.

11 Page 48, Scodel, R. (2010). *An Introduction to Greek Tragedy*. Cambridge: Cambridge University Press.

12 Aristotle *Poetics* 1.6.

13 Part 5, Nietzsche, F. 'What I owe the ancients.' *Twilight of the Idols*. London: Penguin, pp. 116–121.

14 Portmann, J. (2000). *When Bad Things Happen to Other People*. London: Routledge.

15 See Dundes, A. (ed.). (1988). *The Flood Myth*. Berkeley and Los Angeles: University of California Press.

16 Ryan, W. B. F. and Pitman, W. C. (1999). *Noah's Flood: The New Scientific Discoveries about the Event That Changed History*. New York: Simon and Schuster; see also Giosan, L., Filip, F., and Constatinescu, S. (2009). 'Was the Black Sea catastrophically flooded in the early Holocene?' *Quaternary Science Reviews* 28: 1–6.

17 Vidal-Naquet, P. (2007). *The Atlantis Story: A Short History of Plato's Myth*. Exeter: Exeter University Press.

18 Page 81, Cameron, A. (1983). 'Crantor and Posidonius on Atlantis.' *Classical Quarterly* 33: 81–91.

19 Page 38, Plato. (1977). *Timaeus and Critias*. Translated by D. Lee. London: Penguin.

20 Compare, for example, Morgan, K. A. (1998). 'Designer history: Plato's Atlantis story and fourth-century ideology.' *Journal of Hellenic Studies* 118: 101–118; and Zangger, E. (1993). 'Plato's Atlantis account – a dis-torted recollection of the Trojan War.' *Oxford Journal of Archaeology* 12(1): 77–87.

21 Page 124, n. 5, Cameron, A. (2004). *Greek Mythography in the Roman World.* Oxford: Oxford University Press.

22 Page 343, Koelsch, W. A. (2006). 'W. E. Gladstone and the reconstruction of Bronze Age geography.' *International Journal of the Classical Tradition* 12(3): 329–345.

23 Page 189, Frost, K. T. (1913). 'The *Critias* and Minoan Crete.' *Journal of Hellenic Studies* 33: 189–206.

24 Frost (1913), 190.

25 Daly, N. (2011). 'The volcanic disaster narrative: From pleasure garden to canvas, page, and stage.' *Victorian Studies* 53(2): 255–285.

26 *New York Times*, 9 June 1889.

27 Pages 9, 10, 55, Brown, L. (2011). *World on the Edge: How to Prevent Environmental and Economic Collapse.* New York: Norton.

28 Page 5, Moser, S. (2006). *Wondrous Curiosities: Ancient Egypt in the British Museum.* Chicago: University of Chicago Press.

29 O'Brien, S. (2013). 'Parables of decline: Popular fears and the use of crises in Aegean archaeological interpretation.' In van der Wilt, E. M. and Jimenez, J. M. (eds.). *Tough Times: The Archaeology of Crisis and Recovery.* Oxford: Archaeopress, pp. 13–22.

30 Page 60, Tainter, J. A. (2006). 'Archaeology of overshoot and collapse.' *Annual Review of Anthropology* 35: 59–74.

31 Page 105, Demarest, A. A. (2001). 'Climatic change and the Maya collapse: The return of catastrophism.' *Latin American Antiquity* 12(1): 105–107.

32 Pages 4–5, Tainter, J. A. (1988). *The Collapse of Complex Societies.* Cambridge: Cambridge University Press.

33 Tainter, J. A. (2000). 'Problem solving: Complexity, history, sustainability.' *Population and Environment: A Journal of Interdisciplinary Studies* 22: 3–41.

34 Page 256, Cowgill, G. L. (1988). 'Onward and upward with collapse.' In Yoffee, N. and Cowgill, G. L. (eds.). *The Collapse of Ancient States and Civilizations.* Tucson: Arizona University Press, pp. 244–276.

35 Page 45, Yoffee, N. (1988). 'The collapse of ancient Mesopotamian states and civilization.' In Yoffee, N. and Cowgill, G. L. (eds.). *The Collapse of Ancient States and Civilizations.* Tucson: Arizona University Press, pp. 44–68.

36 Rempel, J. and Yoffee, N. (1999). 'The end of the cycle? Assessing the impact of Hellenization on Mesopotamian civilization.' In Bock, B., Cancik-Kirschbaum, E., and Richter, T. (eds.). *Munuscula Mesopotamica: Festschrift fur Johannes Renger.* Munster: Ugarit-Verlag, pp. 385–398.

37 Geller, M. J. (1997). 'The last wedge.' *Zeitschrift fur Assyriologie* 87: 43–95.

38 Berglund, J. (1986). 'The decline of the Norse settlements in Greenland.' *Arctic Anthropology* 23: 109–135; Berglund, J. (2010). 'Did the medieval Norse society in Greenland really fail?' In McAnany, P. A. and Yoffee, N. (eds.). *Questioning Collapse: Human Resilience, Ecological Vulnerability, and the Aftermath of Empire.* Cambridge: Cambridge University Press,

pp. 45–70; Buckland, P. et al. (2008). 'Land management at the bishop's seat, Gardar, medieval Greenland.' *Antiquity* 82(315). Available at: www .antiquity.ac.uk/projgall/buckland315/

39 Stahle, D. W. et al. (1998). 'The lost colony and Jamestown droughts.' *Science* 280: 564–567; pages 162–189, Wellard, J. (1980). *The Search for Lost Cities.* London: Constable.

40 Diamond, J. (2005). *Collapse: How Societies Choose to Fail or Succeed.* London: Penguin.

41 Diamond (2005), 271–273.

42 Schwartz, G. M. (2006). 'From collapse to regeneration.' In Schwartz, G. M. and Nichols, J. J. (eds.). *After Collapse: The Regeneration of Complex Societies.* Tucson: Arizona University Press, pp. 3–17.

43 Page 3628, Butzer, K. W. and Endfield, G. H. (2012). 'Critical perspectives on historical collapse.' *Proceedings of the National Academy of Science* 109(10): 3628–3631.

44 Page 450, Young, M. N. and Leemans, R. (2007). 'Group report: Future scenarios of human-environment systems.' In Costanza, R., Graumlich, L. J., and Steffen, W. (eds.). *Sustainability or Collapse? An Integrated History and Future of People on Earth.* Cambridge: Dahlem University Press and Massachusetts Institute of Technology, pp. 447–470.

45 Costanza, R., Graumlich, L. J., and Steffen, W. (eds.). (2007). *Sustainability or Collapse? An Integrated History and Future of People on Earth.* Cambridge: Dahlem University Press and Massachusetts Institute of Technology.

46 Cojanu, V. and Popescu, A. I. (2007). 'Analysis of some failed states: Some problems of definition and measurement.' *The Romanian Economic Journal* 10(25): 113–132; Thurer, D. (1999). ''The failed state' and international law.' *ICRC.* Available at: www.icrc.org/eng/resources/documents/misc/ 57jq6u.htm

47 Pages 53, 60–61, Gardiner, P. L. (1952). *The Nature of Historical Explanation.* London: Oxford University Press.

48 Fisher, N. (2006). 'Citizens, foreigners, and slaves in Greek society.' In Kinzl, K. H. (ed.). *A Companion to the Classical Greek World.* Oxford: Blackwell, pp. 327–349. For another interpretation of Messenian identity, see Luraghi, N. (2002). 'Becoming Messenian.' *The Journal of Hellenic Studies* 122: 45–69.

49 Balter, M. (2010). 'The tangled roots of agriculture.' *Science* 237: 404–406.

50 Rowley, T. and Wood, J. (2000). *Deserted Villages.* Third revised edition. Oxford: Shire Archaeology.

51 Campbell, R. B. (2009). 'Toward a networks and boundaries approach to early complex polities.' *Current Anthropology* 50(6): 821–848.

52 Guy, R. K. (2010). 'Ideology and organization in the Qing empire.' *Journal of Early Modern History* 14: 355–377.

53 Shelach, G. and Pines, Y. (2006). 'Secondary state formation and the development of local identity: Change and continuity in the state of Qin

(770–221 BC).' In Stark, M. T. (ed.). *Archaeology of Asia*. Oxford: Blackwell, pp. 202–230.

54 Renfrew, C. and Cherry, J. F. (1986). *Peer Polity Interaction and Socio-Political Change*. Cambridge: Cambridge University Press.

55 Page 1, Renfrew, C. (1986). 'Introduction: peer polity interaction and sociopolitical change.' In Renfrew, C. and Cherry, J. F. (1986). *Peer Polity Interaction and Socio-Political Change*. Cambridge: Cambridge University Press, pp. 1–18.

56 Tainter (1988), 17–18; Turnbull, C. M. (1972). *The Mountain People*. New York: Simon and Schuster.

57 Battersby, C. (1978). 'Morality and the Ik.' *Philosophy* 53(204): 201–214; Calhoun, J. B. (1972). 'Plight of the Ik and Kaiadilt is seen as a chilling possible end for man.' *Smithsonian Magazine* November: 27–32.

58 Heine, B. (1985). 'The Mountain People: Some notes on the Ik of north-eastern Uganda.' *Africa* 55(1): 3–16.

59 Renfrew and Cherry (1986).

60 Anderson, E. N. and Chase-Dunn, C. (2005). 'The rise and fall of great powers.' In Chase-Dunn, C. and Anderson, E. N. (eds.). *The Historical Evolution of World-Systems*. New York: Palgrave Macmillan, pp. 1–19; Hall, T. D., Kardulias, N. P., and Chase-Dunn, C. (2011). 'World-systems and archaeology: Continuing the dialogue.' *Journal of Archaeological Research* 19: 233–279.

61 Parkinson, W. A. and Galaty, M. L. (eds.). (2009). *Archaic State Interaction: The Eastern Mediterranean in the Bronze Age*. Santa Fe: School for Advanced Research Press.

62 Van Engelsdorp, D. et al. (2009). 'Colony collapse disorder: A descriptive study.' *Public Library of Science One* 4: e6481.

63 Gray, S. (2011). 'Vanishing city: The story behind Detroit's shocking population decline.' *Time*. Available at: http://newsfeed.time.com/2011/03/24/vanishing-city-the-story-behind-detroit%E2%80%99s-shocking-population-decline/

64 Kirch, P. V. and Rallu, J. L. (eds.). (2007). *The Growth and Collapse of Pacific Island Societies: Archaeological and Demographic Perspectives*. Honolulu: University of Hawaii Press.

65 Noble, D. C. (2002). 'Sickness, starvation, and death in early Hispaniola.' *Journal of Interdisciplinary History* 32(3): 349–386; Poole, R. M. (2011). 'What became of the Taino?' *Smithsonian Magazine* October.

66 Tainter (1988).

67 Page 101, Boyes, W. and Melvin, M. (2009). *Fundamentals of Economics*. Fourth edition. Boston: Houghton Mifflin.

68 Costanza, Graumlich, and Steffen (2007).

69 Huntington, E. (1917). 'Climate change and agricultural exhaustion as elements in the fall of Rome.' *The Quarterly Journal of Economics* 20: 173–208.

70 Weiss and Bradley (2001).

71 Marshall (2012).

72 Middleton, G. D. (2012). 'Nothing lasts forever: Environmental discourses on the collapse of past societies.' *Journal of Archaeological Research* 20(3): 257–307.

73 Butzer, K. (2012). 'Collapse, environment, and society.' *Proceedings of the National Academy of Sciences* 109(10): 3632–3639; Butzer and Endfield (2012); Middleton (2012); Tainter, J. A. (2008). 'Collapse, sustainability, and the environment: How authors choose to fail or succeed.' *Reviews in Anthropology* 37: 342–371.

74 Ponting, C. (1991). *A Green History of the World*. London: Sinclair-Stevenson. Republished (1994). *A Green History of the World: The Environment and the Collapse of Great Civilizations*. New edition. London: Penguin, and again (2007). *A New Green History of the World: The Environment and the Collapse of Great Civilizations*. Revised edition. London: Penguin.

75 Diamond, J. (1994). 'Ecological collapse of past civilizations.' *Proceedings of the American Philosophical Society* 138(3): 363–370.

76 Page 282, Diamond, J. (1992). *The Third Chimpanzee*. New York: HarperCollins.

77 Chew, S. C. (2001). *World Ecological Degradation: Accumulation, Urbanization, and Deforestation, 3000 BC – AD 2000*. Walnut Creek: AltaMira; Chew, S. C. (2002). 'Globalisation, ecological crisis, and dark ages.' *Global Society* 16: 333–356; Chew, S. C. (2005). 'From Harappa to Mesopotamia and Egypt to Mycenae: Dark Ages, political-economic declines, and environmental/climatic changes.' In Chase-Dunn, C. and Anderson, E. N. (eds.). *The Historical Evolution of World-Systems*. New York: Palgrave Macmillan, pp. 52–74.

78 Redman, C. L. (1999). *Human Impact on Ancient Environments*. Tucson: University of Arizona Press.

79 Page 83, Lowenthal, D. (2005). 'Natural and cultural heritage.' *International Journal of Heritage Studies* 11(1): 81–92.

80 Simkhovitch, V. G. (1916). 'Rome's fall reconsidered.' *Political Science Quarterly* 31(2): 201–243.

81 Buntgen, U. et al. (2011). '2500 Years of European climate variability and human susceptibility.' *Science* 331: 578–582; Ponting (2007); Tainter, J. and Crumley, C. L. (2007). 'Climate, complexity, and problem solving in the Roman Empire.' In Costanza, R., Graumlich, L. J., and Steffen, W. (eds.). *Sustainability or Collapse? An Integrated History and Future of People on Earth*. Cambridge: Dahlem University Press and Massachusetts Institute of Technology, pp. 61–75.

82 Diamond (2005), 11, 15.

83 Diamond (2005), 487.

84 Tainter (2006).

85 Lawler, A. (2010). 'Collapse? What collapse? Societal change revisited.' *Science* 330: 907–909; McAnany, P. A. and Yoffee, N. (eds.) (2010). *Questioning Collapse: Human Resilience, Ecological Vulnerability, and the Aftermath of Empire*. Cambridge: Cambridge University Press; Middleton (2012).

86 Diamond, J. (2010). 'Two views of collapse.' *Nature* 463: 880–881; McAnany, P. A. and Yoffee, N. (2010). 'Questioning how different societies respond to crises.' *Nature* 464: 977.

87 Will, W. H., Drake, B. L., and Dorshow, W. B. (2014). 'Prehistoric deforestation at Chaco Canyon?' *Proceedings of the National Academy of Sciences. Early edition.* Available at: www.pnas.org/cgi/doi/10.1073/pnas.1409646111

88 Page 170, Cline, E. H. (2014). *1177 BC: The Year Civilization Collapsed.* Princeton: Princeton University Press.

89 Arthur Demarest, personal communication.

90 Page 234, Kaufman, H. (1988). 'The collapse of ancient states and civilizations as an organizational problem.' In Yoffee, N. and Cowgill, G. L. (eds.). *Collapse of Ancient States and Civilizations.* Tucson: University of Arizona Press, pp. 219–235.

91 Marcus, J. (1998). 'The peaks and valleys of ancient states: An extension of the dynamic model.' In Feinman, G. M. and Marcus, J. (eds.). *Archaic States.* Santa Fe: School of American Research Press, pp. 59–94.

92 Marcus (1998), 85.

93 Nelson, S. M. (2006). 'Archaeology in the two Koreas.' In Stark, M. (ed.). *Archaeology in Asia.* Oxford: Blackwell, 37–54.

94 Potter, D. S. (2004). *The Roman Empire at Bay, AD 180–395.* London: Routledge.

95 Stoneman, R. (1994). *Palmyra and its Empire: Zenobia's Revolt against Rome.* Ann Arbor: University of Michigan Press.

96 Arthur Demarest, personal communication.

97 Ibn Khaldun (1967). *The Muqaddimah: An Introduction to History.* Abridged edition. Princeton: Princeton University Press.

98 Anderson, E. N. and Chase-Dunn, C. (2005). 'The rise and fall of great powers.' In Anderson, E. N. and Chase-Dunn, C. (eds.). *The Historical Evolution of World-Systems.* New York: Palgrave Macmillan, pp. 1–19; Turchin, P. (2003). *Historical Dynamics: Why States Rise and Fall.* Princeton: Princeton University Press; Turchin, P. (2006). *War and Peace and War: The Rise and Fall of Empires.* New York: Plume; Turchin, P. and Nefedov, S. A. (2009). *Secular Cycles.* Princeton: Princeton University Press.

99 Herodotus *Histories* book 1.

100 Anderson and Chase-Dunn (2005), 5.

101 Taagepera, R. (1979). 'Size and duration of empires: Growth-decline curves, 600 BC to 600 AD.' *Social Science History* 3(3 & 4): 115–138.

102 Turchin (2006), 208.

103 Turchin and Nefedov (2009), 312.

104 Turchin and Nefedov (2009), 121.

105 Kaufman (1988), 234.

106 Tainter, J. A. (2004). 'Review of *Historical Dynamics: Why States Rise and Fall* by Peter Turchin.' *Nature* 427: 488–489.

107 Page 237, Seitz, J. L. and Hite, K. A. (2012). *Global Issues: An Introduction.* Fourth edition. Chichester: Wiley-Blackwell.

108 McAnany and Yoffee (2010).

109 Holling, C. S. (1973). 'Resilience and stability of ecological systems.' *Annual Review of Ecological Systems* 4: 1–23.

110 Walker, B. et al. (2004). 'Resilience, adaptability and transformability in social-ecological systems.' *Ecology and Society* 9(2): 5. Available at: www .ecologyandsociety.org/vol9/iss2/art5/

111 McAnany and Yoffee (2010), 10.

112 Page 75, Walker, B. and Salt, D. (2006). *Resilience Thinking: Sustaining Ecosystems and People in a Changing World.* Washington DC: Island Press.

113 Page 242, Eisenstadt, S. N. (1988). 'Beyond collapse.' In Yoffee, N. and Cowgill, G. L. (eds.). *Collapse of Ancient States and Civilizations.* Tucson: University of Arizona Press, pp. 236–243.

114 Redman, C. L. (2005). 'Resilience theory in archaeology.' *American Anthropologist* 107(1): 70–77.

115 McAnany and Yoffee (2010), 10.

116 Tainter, J. A. (1999). 'Post-collapse societies.' In Barker, G. (ed.). *Companion Encyclopedia of Archaeology.* London: Routledge, pp. 988–1039.

117 Tainter (1999), 1025.

118 Lawler (2010), 907.

119 Schwartz and Nichols (2006).

120 Bronson, B. (2006). 'Patterns of political regenerations in Southeast and East Asia.' In Schwartz, G. M. and Nichols, J. J. (eds.). *After Collapse: The Regeneration of Complex Societies.* Tucson: University of Arizona Press, pp. 137–143.

121 Bronson (2006), 140.

122 Kintigh, K. W. et al. (2014). 'Grand challenges for archaeology.' *Proceedings of the National Academy of Sciences* 111(3): 879–880.

123 EC. (2003). *Water for Life.* Luxembourg: European Commission, Office for Official Publications of the European Communities.

124 Ponting (1991/1994/2007).

125 Page 2, De Waal, A. (1991). *Evil Days: Thirty Years of War and Famine in Ethiopia.* New York: Human Rights Watch.

2.   Egypt: The Old Kingdom Falls

1 Quoted on page 1, Bell, B. (1971). 'The Dark Ages in ancient history: 1. The first Dark Age in Egypt.' *American Journal of Archaeology* 75: 1–26.

2 Following the dates in Shaw, I. (ed.). (2000). *The Oxford History of Ancient Egypt.* Oxford: Oxford University Press. Compare Clayton, P. A. (2006). *Chronicle of the Pharaohs.* London: Thames and Hudson.

3 Page 72, Wilkinson, T. (2010). *The Rise and Fall of Ancient Egypt.* London: Bloomsbury.

4 Wilkinson (2010), 76–80.

5 Wilkinson (2010), 90.

6 Clayton (2006), 59; Wilkinson (2010), 91–92.

7 Page 8, Baines, J. and Lacovara, P. (2002). 'Burial and the dead in ancient Egyptian society: Respect, formalism, neglect.' *Journal of Social Archaeology* 2(1): 5–36.

8 Page 10, Baines and Lacovara (2002), 5–36.

9 Seidlmayer, S. (2000). 'The First Intermediate Period (c. 2160–2055 BC).' In Shaw, I. (ed.). *The Oxford History of Ancient Egypt*. Oxford: Oxford University Press, pp. 108–136.

10 Moeller, N. (2005). 'The First Intermediate Period: A time of famine and climate change?' *Ägypten und Levante* 15: 153–167.

11 Seidlmayer (2000), 112.

12 Seidlmayer (2000), 113–114, 116.

13 Bell (1971).

14 Pages 166–199, Parkinson, R. B. (1997). *The Tale of Sinuhe and Other Ancient Egyptian Poems 1940–1640 BC*. Oxford: Oxford University Press.

15 Faulkner, R. O. (1965). 'The Admonitions of an Egyptian Sage.' *The Journal of Egyptian Archaeology* 51: 53–62. See also Hassan, F. A. (2007). 'Droughts, famine, and the collapse of the Old Kingdom: Re-reading Ipuwer.' In Hawass, Z. and Richards, J. (eds.). *The Art and Archaeology of Ancient Egypt: Essays in Honour of David B. O'Connor. Vol. 1*. Cairo: Conseil Supreme des Antiquites de'l Egypte, pp. 357–377.

16 Wilkinson (2010), 124–125.

17 Quoted in Bell (1971).

18 Bell (1971), 18.

19 Hassan (2007).

20 Parkinson (1997), 166; page 94, Van De Mieroop, M. (2011). *A History of Ancient Egypt*. Oxford: Blackwell.

21 Page 110, Gardiner, A. (1961). *Egypt of the Pharaoahs*. Oxford: Oxford University Press.

22 Page 135, Fagan, B. (2004). *The Long Summer: How Climate Changed Civilization*. New York: Basic Books.

23 Pages 253–254, Burroughs, W. J. (2005). *Climate Change in Prehistory: The End of the Reign of Chaos*. Cambridge: Cambridge University Press.

24 Seidlmayer (2000), 135.

25 Krom, M. D. et al. (2002). 'Nile River sediment fluctuations over the past 7000 yr and their key role in sapropel development.' *Geology* 30(1): 71–74.

26 Bernhardt, C. E., Horton, B. P., and Stanley, J-D. (2012). 'Nile Delta vegetation response to Holocene climate variability.' *Geology* 40(7): 615–618.

27 Seidlmayer (2000), 119.

28 Van De Mieroop (2011), 96.

29 Butzer, K. W. (2012). 'Collapse, environment, and society.' *Proceedings of the National Academy of Science* 109(10): 3632–3639.

30 Moeller (2005), 167, and personal communication.

31 Seidlmayer (2000), 119.

32 Wilkinson (2010), 105.

33 Clayton (2006), 64; Wilkinson (2010), 106.

34 Wilkinson (2010), 107.

35 Wilkinson (2010), 107–109.

36 Janssen, J. C. (1978). 'The early state in ancient Egypt.' In Claessen, H. J. and Skalnik, P. (eds.). *The Early State*. The Hague: Mouton, pp. 213–234; Seidlmayer (2000).

37 Wilkinson (2010), 112.

38 Seidlmayer (2000), 110.

39 Seidlmayer (2000), 123.

40 Page 66, Morris, E. (2006). "'Lo, nobles lament, the poor rejoice': State formation in the wake of social flux.' In Schwartz, G. M. and Nichols, J. J. (eds.). *After Collapse: The Regeneration of Complex Socities*. Tucson: The University of Arizona Press, pp. 58–71, also citing page 76, Brunton, G. (1927). *Qau and Badari I*. London: British School of Archaeology in Egypt.

41 Seidlmayer (2000), 113.

42 Morris (2006), 67.

43 Van De Mieroop (2011), 81.

44 Morris (2006), 70.

45 Morris (2006), 71.

46 Van De Mieroop (2011), 126–150.

47 Page 183, Bourriau, J. (2000). 'The Second Intermediate Period (ca. 1650–1550 BC).' In Shaw, I. (ed.). *The Oxford History of Ancient Egypt*. Oxford: Oxford University Press, pp. 172–206.

48 Van De Mieroop (2011), 261.

3. Akkad: The End of the World's First Empire

1 Pages 204–215, Pritchard, J. B. (ed.). (1975). *The Ancient Near East, Volume II: An Anthology of Texts and Pictures*. Princeton: Princeton University Press. Also: Cooper, J. S. (1983). *The Curse of Agade*. Baltimore: Johns Hopkins University Press. The text can also be found in translation at: http://etcsl .orinst.ox.ac.uk/section2/tr215.htm

2 Page 34, Westenholz, A. (1999). 'The Old Akkadian Period: History and culture.' In Sallaberger, W. and Westenholz, A. *Mesopotamien. Akkade-Zeit und Ur III-Zeit*. Orbis biblicus et Orientalis 160/3. Freiburg: Universitatsverlag Freiburg Schweiz, pp. 17–117.

3 Mears, D. (2002). 'The first great conqueror.' *Military History* 19(4): 47–52; Page 64, Van De Mieroop, M. (2007). *A History of the Ancient Near East, ca. 3000–323 BC*. Oxford: Blackwell.

4 Van De Mieroop (2007), 68.

5 Weiss, H. et al. (1993). 'The genesis and collapse of third millennium north Mesopotamian civilization.' *Science* 261: 995–1004; Weiss, H. (2013). 'The northern Levant during the Intermediate Bronze Age.' In Killebrew, A. E. and Steiner, M. L. (eds.). *The Oxford Handbook of the Archaeology of the Levant*. Oxford: Oxford University Press, pp. 367–387.

6 Page 33, Weiss, H. (1996). 'Desert Storm.' *The Sciences* (May/June): 30–36. Publications about Tell Leilan can be accessed via the Tell Leilan Project website: http://leilan.yale.edu/index.html

7 Weiss (1996), 33; Oates, J. et al. (2007). 'Early Mesopotamian urbanism: A new view from the north.' *Antiquity* 81: 585–600.

8 Weiss et al. (1993).

9 Van De Mieroop (2007), 64.

10 Weiss et al. (1993), 999.

11 Weiss et al. (1993), 1000–1002.

12 Cullen, H. M. et al. (2000). 'Climate change and the collapse of the Akkadian empire: Evidence from the deep sea.' *Geology* 28: 379–382.

13 Page 448, Matthews, R. (2009). 'Peoples and complex societies of ancient southwest Asia.' In Scarre, C. (ed.). *The Human Past: World Prehistory & The Development of Human Societies*. Second edition. London: Thames and Hudson, pp. 432–471.

14 Pages 178–187, Dincauze, D. F. (2000). *Environmental Archaeology: Principles and Practice*. Cambridge: Cambridge University Press.

15 Page 1/6, Butzer, K. W. (2012). 'Supporting information.' Available at www.pnas.org/cgi/content/short/1114845109

16 Courty, M.-A. (2001). 'Evidence at Tell Brak for the Late ED III/Early Akkadian Air Blast Event (4 kyr BP).' In Oates, D., Oates, J., and McDonald, H. (eds.). *Excavations at Tell Brak Volume 2: Nagar in the Third Millennium BC*. Cambridge: McDonald Institute for Archaeological Research, pp. 367–372.

17 Weiss (1996), 36.

18 Wilkinson, T. (1998). 'Akkadian empire: Where to look?' *Science* 279: 1283–1284.

19 Page 148, Wossink, A. (2009). *Challenging Climate Change: Competition and Cooperation Among Pastoralists and Agriculturalists in Northern Mesopotamia (c. 3000–1600 BC)*. Leiden: Sidestone Press.

20 Page 131, Barjamovic, G. (2013). 'Mesopotamian empires.' In Bang, P. F. and Scheidel, W. (eds.). *The Oxford Handbook of the State in the Ancient Near East and Mediterranean*. Oxford: Oxford University Press, pp. 120–160.

21 Page 1500, Oates, J. (2014). 'Mesopotamia: The historical periods.' In Renfrew, C. and Bahn, P. (eds.). *The Cambridge World Prehistory*. Cambridge: Cambridge University Press, pp. 1498–1507.

22 Pages 19–20, Zettler, R. L. (2003). 'Reconstructing the world of ancient Mesopotamia.' *Journal of the Economic and Social History of the Orient* 46(1): 3–45; Van De Mieroop (2007), 4.

23 Page 170, Paulette, T. (2012). 'Domination and resilience in Bronze Age Mesopotamia.' In Cooper, J. and Sheets, P. (eds.). *Surviving Sudden Environmental Change: Answers from Archaeology*. Boulder: University of Colorado Press, pp. 167–195.

24 Paulette (2012), 169–170.

25 Cooper (1983).

26 Quoted in Weiss (1996), 31.

27 Marshall, M. (2012). 'Climate change: The great civilization destroyer.' *New Scientist* 215(2876): 32–36; Weiss (1996).

28 Pages 62–66, Kramer, S. N. (1963). *The Sumerians*. Chicago: Chicago University Press; pages 103–108, Leick, G. (2001). *Mesopotamia: The Invention of the City*. London: Penguin.

29 Leick (2001), 106.

30 Kramer (1963), 62–66; Marshall (2012); Zettler (2003), 18.

31 Leick (2001), 103.

32 Leick (2001), 107.

33 Pages 82–85, Chavalas, M. W. (ed.). (2006). *The Ancient Near East: Sources in Translation*. Oxford: Blackwell.

34 Pages 407–408, Ur, J. (2010). 'Cycles of civilization in Northern Mesopotamia, 4400–2000 BC.' *Journal of Archaeological Research* 18: 387–431.

35 Ur (2010), 407–408.

36 Van De Mieroop (2007), 69.

37 Westenholz (1999), 41.

38 Page 859, McMahon, A. (2008). 'Mesopotamia, Sumer, and Akkad.' In Pearsall, D. (ed). *Encyclopedia of Archaeology*. New York: Academic Press, pp. 854–865.

39 Van De Mieroop (2007), 69.

40 Van De Mieroop (2007), 67, 73.

41 Pages 34–35, Michalowski, P. (2008). 'The mortal kings of Ur: A short century of divine rule in ancient Mesopotamia.' In Brisch, N. (ed.). *Religion and Power: Divine Kingship in the Ancient World and Beyond*. Chicago: The Oriental Institute, University of Chicago, pp. 33–46; Tinney, S. (1995). 'A new look at Naram-Sin and the 'Great Rebellion'.' *Journal of Cuneiform Studies* 47: 1–14; Van De Mieroop (2007), 68.

42 Westenholz (1999), 47.

43 Bernbeck, R. (2008). 'Royal deification: An ambiguation mechanism for the creation of courtier subjectivities.' In Brisch, N. (ed.). *Religion and Power: Divine Kingship in the Ancient World and Beyond*. Chicago: The Oriental Institute, University of Chicago, pp. 157–170.

44 Van De Mieroop (2007), 72.

45 Page 100, Speiser, E. A. (1952). 'Some factors in the collapse of Akkad.' *Journal of the American Oriental Society* 72(3): 97–101.

46 Van De Mieroop (2007), 71

47 Glassner, J.-J. (1986). *La Chute d'Akkade. Le Evenement et sa memoire*. Berliner Beitrage zum vorderen Orient, 5. Berlin: Dietrich Reimer Verlag and (1994). 'La Chute de l'empire d'Akkade, les volcans d'Anatolie et la desertification de la vallee du Habur.' *Le Nouvelles de l'archeologie* 56: 49–51.

48 Pages 377–380, Liverani, M. (2001). 'The fall of the Assyrian empire: Ancient and modern interpretations.' In Alcock, S. E., D'Altroy, T. N., Morrison, K. D., and Sinopoli, C. M. (eds.). *Empires*. Cambridge: Cambridge University Press, pp. 374–391; Zettler (2003), 24.

49 Kuzucuoglu, C. and Marro, C. (eds.). (2007). *Human Societies and Climate Change at the End of the Third Millennium: Did a Crisis Take Place in Upper Mesopotamia? (Societes humaines et changement climatique a la fin du troisieme millenaire: Une crise a-t-elle eu lieu en haute Mesopotamie?).* Istanbul: Institut Francais d'Etudes Anatoliennes Georges-Dumezil; Wossink (2010).

50 Ur (2010), 413.

51 Van De Mieroop (2007), 71; Westenholz (1999), 57.

52 Barjamovic (2013), 131–133.

53 Page 45, Chavalas, M. W. (2005). 'The age of empires, 3100–900 BCE.' In Snell, D. (ed.). *A Companion to the Ancient Near East.* Oxford: Blackwell, pp. 34–47.

54 Jacobsen, T. and Adams, R. M. (1958). 'Salt and silt in ancient Mesopotamian agriculture.' *Science* 128: 1251–1258.

55 Paulette (2012), 174.

56 Cohen, A. C. (2007). 'Barley as a key symbol in early Mesopotamia.' In Cheng, J. and Feldman, M. H. (eds.). *Ancient Near Eastern Art in Context. Studies in Honor of Irene J. Winter by Her Students.* Leiden: Brill, pp. 411–422.

57 Powell, M. (1985). 'Salt, seed, and yields in Sumerian agriculture: A critique of the theory of progressive salinization.' *Zeitschrift fur Assyriologie* 75: 7–38.

58 Artzy, M. and Hillel, D. (1988). 'A defence of the theory of progressive soil salinization in ancient southern Mesopotamia.' *Geoarchaeology: An International Journal* 3(3): 235–238; Page 27, Hughes, J. D. (2015). 'The ancient world, c. 500 BCE to 500 CE.' In McNeil, J. R. and Mauldin, E. S. (eds.). *A Companion to Global Environmental History.* Chichester: Wiley-Blackwell, pp. 18–38.

59 Altaweel, M. and Watanabe, C. E. (2012). 'Assessing the resilience of irrigation agriculture: Applying a social-ecological model for understanding the mitigation of salinization.' *Journal of Archaeological Science* 39: 1160–1171.

60 Page 183, Yoffee, N. (2010). 'Collapse in ancient Mesopotamia: What happened, what didn't.' In McAnany, P. A. and Yoffee, N. (eds.). *Questioning Collapse: Human Resilience, Ecological Vulnerability, and the Aftermath of Empire.* Cambridge: Cambridge University Press, pp. 176–203.

61 Leick (2001), 136–140.

62 Chavalas (2006), 45.

63 Barjamovic (2013), 133.

64 Van De Mieroop (2007), 83.

65 Liverani (2001), 379.

66 Phys.org. (2012). 'Scientists discover genetic factor that makes barley plants resistant to salt.' *Phys.org.* Available at http://phys.org/news/2012-10-scientists-genetic-factor-barley-resistant.html

67 Van De Mieroop, M. (2012). 'Gutians.' *Encyclopaedia Iranica.* Available at www.iranicaonline.org/articles/gutians

4. The Indus Valley: A Truly Lost Civilisation?

1 Wheeler, R. E. M. (1947). 'Harappa 1946: The defences and cemetery R37.' In Lahiri, N. (ed.). (2000). *The Decline and Fall of the Indus Civilization*. Delhi: Permanent Black, pp. 50–57.
2 Page 185, Possehl, G. L. (2002). *The Indus Civilization*. Walnut Creek: AltaMira.
3 Strabo *Geography* 15.19.
4 Possehl (2002), chapter 1; Pages 71–74, Wellard, J. (1980). *The Search for Lost Cities*. London: Constable.
5 Quoted in Possehl (2002), 15.
6 Page 532, Coningham, R. (2009). 'South Asia: From early villages to Buddhism.' In Scarre, C. (ed.). *The Human Past*. London: Thames and Hudson, pp. 518–551; Kenoyer (2015), 41; Kenoyer (2008a). 'Indus civilization.' In Pearsall, D. (ed.). *Encyclopedia of Archaeology*. New York: Academic Press, pp. 715–733.
7 Pages 183–192, Coningham, R. and Young, R. (2015). *The Archaeology of South Asia: From the Indus to Asoka, c. 6500 BCE – 200 CE*. Cambridge: Cambridge University Press.
8 Kenoyer (2015), 28–29.
9 Meadows, R. H. and Kenoyer, J. M. (2000). 'The Indus Valley mystery.' *Discovering Archaeology*. March/April: 38–43.
10 Kenoyer (2015), 59.
11 Page 150, Manuel, M. (2010). 'Chronology and culture-history in the Indus Valley.' In Gunawardhana, P., Adikari, G., and Coningham, R. A. E. (eds.). *Sirinimal Lakdusinghe Felicitation Volume*. Battaramulla: Neptune, pp. 145–152.
12 Kenoyer, J. M. (1998). *Ancient Cities of the Indus Valley Civilization*. Oxford: Oxford University Press.
13 Pages 277–279, Possehl, G. L. (1998), 'Sociocultural complexity without the state: The Indus civilization.' In Feinman, G. M. and Marcus, J. (eds.). *The Archaic State*. Sante Fe: School of Advanced Research Press, pp. 261–291.
14 Coningham, R. and Manuel, M. (2009). 'Priest-kings or Puritans? Childe and willing subordination in the Indus.' *European Journal of Archaeology* 12(1–3): 167–180.
15 Kenoyer (2015), 46.
16 Kenoyer, J. M. (2008b). 'Indus urbanism: New perspectives on its origin and character.' In Marcus, J. and Sabloff, J. A. (eds.). *The Ancient City: New Perspectives on Urbanism in the Old and New World*. Santa Fe: School for Advanced Research, pp. 183–208.
17 Page 95, Kennell, N. M. (2010). *Spartans: A New History*. Chichester: Wiley-Blackwell.
18 Wheeler, M. (1968). *The Indus Civilization*. Third edition. Cambridge: Cambridge University Press.
19 Coningham and Young (2015), 234–240.

20 Possehl (1998); Thompson, T. J. (2005). 'Ancient stateless civilization: Bronze Age India and the state in history.' *The Independent Review* 10(3): 365–384.

21 Kenoyer (2015), 43.

22 Kenoyer, J. M. (2006). 'Cultures and societies of the Indus Tradition.' In Thapar, R. (ed.). *Historical Roots in the Making of 'the Aryan'.* New Delhi: National Book Trust, pp. 21–49.

23 Kenoyer (2015), 49.

24 Kenoyer (2015), 51.

25 Parpola, A. and Brunswig, R. H. (1977). 'The Meluhha village: Evidence of acculturation of Harappan traders in late third millennium Mesopotamia.' *Journal of the Economic and Social History of the Orient* 20(2): 129–165; Possehl (2002), 215; Possehl, G. L. (2007). 'The Middle Asian Interaction Sphere: Trade and contact in the 3rd millennium BC.' *Expedition* 49(1): 40–42.

26 Kenoyer (1998), 73–76, 83–89; Kenoyer (2015), 48.

27 Kenoyer (2008a), 729–730; Whitehouse, D. (1999). 'Earliest writing found.' Available at: http://news.bbc.co.uk/2/hi/science/nature/334517.stm

28 Kenoyer (1998), 69.

29 Kenoyer (2008a), 722–725.

30 Coningham and Manuel (2009).

31 Cork, E. (2005). 'Peaceful Harappans? Reviewing the evidence for the absence of warfare in the Indus civilization of north-west India and Pakistan (c. 2500–1900 BC).' *Antiquity* 79: 411–423.

32 Kenoyer (2015), 38, 44.

33 Cork (2005).

34 Lovell, N. (2014). 'Additional data on trauma at Harappa.' *International Journal of Paleopathology* 6: 1–4; Robbins Schug G. et al. (2012). 'A peaceful realm? Trauma and social differentiation at Harappa.' *International Journal of Paleopathology* 2: 136–147.

35 Keir Strickland, personal communication.

36 Coningham and Young (2015), 192–202.

37 Possehl (2002), 237–238.

38 Wheeler (1968), 131–133.

39 Howell, C. (2002). 'Aryan conquest of India (c. 1500 BC).' In Sandler, S. (ed.). *Ground Warfare: An International Encyclopedia, Volume 1 A-G.* Santa Barbara: ABC-Clio, p. 66.

40 Wellard (1980), 83–84.

41 Wheeler (1968), 131.

42 Coningham and Young (2015), 265–266.

43 Coningham and Young (2015), 266.

44 Possehl (2002), 238.

45 Kenoyer (1998), 174.

46 Kenoyer (1998), 174.

47 Page 73, Wheeler, M. (1966). *The Civilizations of the Indus and Beyond.* London: Thames and Hudson.

48 Lal, B. B. (2005). 'Aryan invasion of India: Perpetuation of a myth.' In Bryant, E. F. and Patton, L. L. (eds.). *The Indo-Aryan Controversy: Evidence and Inference in Indian History.* London: Routledge, pp. 50–74.

49 Possehl (2002), 15.

50 The Times of India. (2012). 'Climate killed Harappan civilization.' *The Times of India* (May 29). Available at: http://articles.timesofindia.indiatimes .com/2012-05-29/science/31886985_1_harappan-river-monsoon

51 Giosan, L. et al. (2012). 'Fluvial landscapes of Harappan civilization.' *Proceedings of the National Academy of Sciences* 109(26): E1688–E1694.

52 Dixit, Y., Hodell, D. A., and Petrie, C. A. (2014). 'Abrupt weakening of the summer monsoon in northwest India ≈4100 yr ago.' *Geology* 42(4): 339–342.

53 Lawler, A. (2008). 'Indus collapse: The end or beginning of an Asian culture?' *Science* 320: 1281–1283.

54 Kenoyer (2015), 51.

55 Bell, B. (1971). 'The Dark Ages in ancient history: 1. The first Dark Age in Egypt.' *American Journal of Archaeology* 75: 1–26. See also Dalfes, H. N., Kukla, G., and Weiss, H. (eds.). (1997). *Third Millennium BC Climate Change and Old World Collapse.* Berlin: Springer; Weiss (1996); Redman, C. L. et al. (2007). 'Group report: Millenial perspectives on the dynamic interaction of climate, people, and resources.' In Costanza, R., Graumlich, L. J., and Steffen, W. (eds.). *Sustainability or Collapse? An Integrated History and Future of People on Earth.* Cambridge: Dahlem University Press and Massachusetts Institute of Technology, pp. 115–148; Weiss, H. and Bradley, R. S. (2001). 'What drives societal collapse?' *Science* 291: 609–610.

56 Staubwasser, M. et al. (2003). 'Climate change at the 4.2 ka BP termination of the Indus valley civilization and Holocene south Asian monsoon variability.' *Geophysical Research Letters* 30(8): 1425.

57 Page 133, Redman, C. L. et al. (2007). 'Group report: Millenial perspective on the dynamic interaction of climate, people, and resources.' In Costanza, R., Graumlich, L. J., and Steffen, W. (eds.). *Sustainability or Collapse? An Integrated History and Future of People on Earth.* Cambridge: Dahlem University Press and Massachusetts Institute of Technology, pp. 115–148.

58 Madella, M. and Fuller, D. Q. (2006). 'Palaeoecology and the Harappan civilization of South Asia: A reconsideration.' *Quaternary Science Reviews* 25: 1283–1301.

59 Lawler (2008), 1282.

60 Possehl (2002), 243.

61 Kenoyer (1998), 174.

62 Kenoyer (2015), 60–61; Kenoyer (1998), 183; Lawler (2008), 1282.

63 Coningham and Young (2015), 268; Kenoyer (1998), 173; Possehl (2002), 238.

64 Pages 483, 485, Lambrick, H. T. (1967). 'The Indus flood-plain and the 'Indus' civilization.' *The Geographical Journal* 133(4): 483–495.

65 Page 290, Raikes, R. L. (1964). 'The end of the ancient cities of the Indus.' *American Anthropologist* 66(2): 284–292, 294–299.

66 Raikes (1964), 296.

67 Lambrick (1967), 493.

68 Possehl (2002), 238.

69 Giosan et al. (2012).

70 Dales, G. F. (1965). 'Civilization and floods in the Indus Valley.' *Expedition* 7: 10–19; Dales, G. F. and Raikes, R. L. (1968). 'The Mohenjo-Daro floods: A rejoinder!' *American Anthropologist* 70(5): 957–961; Possehl, G. L. (1967). 'The Mohenjo-Daro floods: A reply.' *American Anthropologist* 69(1): 32–40; Raikes, R. L. (1967). 'The Mohenjo-Daro floods: Further notes.' *Antiquity* 41: 64–66; Mughal, M. R. (1990). 'The decline of the Indus Civilization and the Late Harappan period in the Indus Valley.' *Lahore Museum Bulletin* 3(2): 1–22.

71 Page 398, McIntosh, J. (2002). *A Peaceful Realm: The Rise and Fall of the Indus Civilization.* Boulder: Westview Press

72 Kenoyer (1998), 173; Kenoyer (2008a), 719.

73 Cameron Petrie, personal communication; Singh, R. N. and Petrie, C. A. (2009). 'Lost rivers and life on the plains.' In Chaudhri, A. R. (ed.). *Saraswati River – A Perspective.* Haryana: Saraswati Nadi Shodh Sansthan, pp. 102–111.

74 McIntosh (2002), 396.

75 Robbins Schug G. et al. (2013). 'Infection, disease, and biosocial processes at the end of the Indus civilization.' *Public Library of Science, ONE* 8(12): e84814. doi:10.1371/journal.pone.0084814

76 Coningham and Young (2015), 272.

77 Robbins Schug et al. (2012).

78 McIntosh (2002), 399; Possehl (2002), 237.

79 Kenoyer (2015), 59.

80 Coningham and Young (2015), 273–274.

81 Coningham and Young (2015), 270–271.

82 Wheeler (1968), 127.

83 Coningham and Young (2015), 270.

84 Possehl (2002), 238.

85 Manuel (2010), 147.

86 Possehl (2002), 47–50.

87 Wheeler (1966), 76–77.

88 Kenoyer (2015), 59; Manuel, (2010), 152; Pages 461–462, Possehl, G. L. (1997). 'The transformation of the Indus civilization.' *Journal of World Prehistory* 11: 425–472; Possehl (1998), 290.

89 Lawler (2008), 1283.

90 Possehl (2002), 250.

91 Kenoyer (1998), 180.

92 Page 350, Allchin, B. and Allchin, R. (1982). *The Rise of Civilization in India and Pakistan.* Cambridge: Cambridge University Press.

93 Possehl (1997), 462

94 Parpola, A. (2010). 'A Dravidian solution to the Indus script problem.' *Kalaignar M. Karunanidhi Classical Tamil Research Endowment Lecture World Classical Tamil Conference 25th June 2010*; Parpola, A. (2005). 'Study of the Indus script.' *Paper read at the 50th ICES Tokyo Session, 19 May 2005.* Available at: www.harappa.com/script/indusscript.html

95 Reddy, K. (2007). *Indian History.* New Delhi: Tata McGraw Hill, pp. A93–A94

96 Kenoyer, J. M. (2005). 'Culture change during the Late Harappan period at Harappa: New insights on Vedic Aryan issues.' In Bryant, E. F. and Patton, L. L. (eds.). *The Indo-Aryan Controversy: Evidence and Inference in Indian History.* London: Routledge, pp. 21–49.

97 I thank Nadine Moeller for drawing my attention to this, and Felix Hoflmayer for discussion and references. See Regev, J., Miroschedji, P., and Boaretto, E. (2012). 'Early Bronze Age chronology: Radiocarbon dates and chronological models from Tel Yarmuth (Israel).' *Radiocarbon* 54(3–4): 505–524; Regev, J. et al. (2012). 'Chronology of the Early Bronze Age in the southern Levant: New analysis for a high chronology.' *Radiocarbon* 54(3–4): 525–566.

98 Forsen, J. (1992). *The Twilight of the Helladics: A Study of the Disturbances in East-Central and Southern Greece towards the End of the Early Bronze Age.* Jonsered: SIMA; Forsen (2010). 'Mainland Greece.' In Cline, E. H. (ed.). *The Oxford Handbook of the Aegean Bronze Age.* Oxford: Oxford University Press, pp. 53–65.

99 Wheeler (1966), 73.

100 Coningham and Young (2015), 275.

101 Possehl (2002), 127–139.

102 Coningham (2009), 532.

5. The End of Minoan Crete

1 Pages 216–217, Wardle, K. A. (1994). 'The palace civilizations of Crete and Greece.' In Cunliffe, B. (ed.). *The Oxford Illustrated Prehistory of Europe.* Oxford: Oxford University Press, pp. 202–243.

2 Soles, J. S. (1995). 'The functions of a cosmological center: Knossos in palatial Crete.' In Laffineur, R. and Niemeier, W.-D. (eds.). *Politeia: Society and State in the Aegean Bronze Age. Aegaeum 12.* Liege: University of Liege, pp. 405–414.

3 Wardle (1994), 204.

4 Page 12, Gere, C. (2009). *Knossos: Priests of Modernism.* Chicago: Chicago University Press. On Evans and his influence, see also MacGillivray, J. A. (2001). *Minotaur: Sir Arthur Evans and the Archaeology of the Minoan Myth.* London: Pimlico; Papadopoulos, J. K. (2005). 'Inventing the Minoans: Archaeology, modernity, and the quest for European identity.' *Journal of Mediterranean Archaeology* 18(1): 87–149.

5 Manning, S. W. (1986). 'The military function in Late Minoan I Crete: A note.' *World Archaeology* 18(2): 284–288; Molloy, B. (2012). 'Martial Minoans? War as social process, practice and event in Bronze Age Crete.' *The Annual of the British School at Athens* 107: 87–142.

6 Bietak, M. (2000). 'Minoan paintings in Avaris, Egypt.' In Sherratt, S. (ed.). *The Wall Paintings of Thera: Proceedings of the First International Symposium. Volume I.* Piraeus: The Thera Foundation, pp. 33–42.

7 Knappett, C. and Nikolakopoulou, I. (2008). 'Colonialism without colonies? A Bronze Age case study from Akrotiri, Thera.' *Hesperia* 77: 1–42.

8 Page 141, Younger, J. G. and Rehak, P. (2008). 'The material culture of Neopalatial Crete.' In Shelmerdine, C. W. (ed.). *The Cambridge Companion to the Aegean Bronze Age.* Cambridge: Cambridge University Press, pp. 140–185.

9 Wardle (1994), 208.

10 Page 151, Hallager, E. (2010). 'Crete.' In Cline, E. H. (ed.). *The Oxford Handbook of the Aegean Bronze Age.* Oxford: Oxford University Press, pp. 149–159.

11 Younger and Rehak (2008), 140.

12 Pages 311–312, Preston, L. (2008). 'Late Minoan II to IIIB Crete.' In Shelmerdine, C. W. (ed.). *Cambridge Companion to the Aegean Bronze Age.* Cambridge: Cambridge University Press, pp. 310–326.

13 Jan Driessen, personal communication.

14 Younger and Rehak (2008), 140.

15 Preston (2008), 311.

16 Page 425, Marinatos, S. (1939). 'The volcanic destruction of Minoan Crete.' *Antiquity* 13: 425–439; Preston (2008), 311; Younger and Rehak (2008), 141.

17 Marinatos (1939), 429.

18 Marinatos (1939), 425.

19 Quoted in Papadopoulos (2005), 106.

20 Papadopoulos (2005), 133.

21 Monaco, C. and Tortorici, L. (2004). 'Faulting and effects of earthquakes on Minoan archaeological sites in Crete (Greece).' *Tectonophysics* 382: 103–116.

22 Marinatos (1939).

23 Marinatos (1939), 429.

24 Marinatos (1939), 430.

25 Doumas, C. (2010). 'Akrotiri.' In Cline, E. H. (ed.). *The Oxford Handbook of the Aegean Bronze Age.* Oxford: Oxford University Press, pp. 752–761.

26 Page 537, Anon. (1880). 'M. Fouque's Santorin and its Eruptions.' *The Popular Science Monthly* 17: 534–538.

27 Pages 157–183, De Boer, J. Z. and Sanders, D. T. (2002). *Volcanoes in Human History: The Far-Reaching Effects of Major Eruptions.* Princeton: Princeton University Press.

28 Ammianus Marcellinus *Res Gestae* 26.10

29 Marinatos (1939), 436.

30 McCoy, F. and Heiken, G. (2000). 'Tsunami generated by the Late Bronze Age eruption of Thera (Santorini), Greece.' *Pure and Applied Geophysics* 157: 1227–1256; McCoy, F. and Heiken, G. (2000). 'The Late Bronze Age explosive eruption of Thera (Santorini), Greece: Regional and local effects.' In McCoy, F. and Heiken, G. (eds.). *Volcanic Hazards and Disasters in Human Antiquity.* Boulder: The Geological Society of America, pp. 43–70.

31 Page 85, Driessen, J. and MacDonald, C. F. (2000). 'The eruption of the Santorini volcano and its effects on Minoan Crete.' In McGuire, W. G., Griffiths, D. R., Hancock, P. L., and Stewart, I. S. (eds.). *The Archaeology of Geological Catastrophes* (Special Publications 171). London: Geological Society, pp. 81–93.

32 Marinatos (1939), 437.

33 De Boer and Sanders (2002), 171.

34 De Boer and Sanders (2002), 171–172.

35 Pichler, H. and Schiering, W. (1977). 'The Thera eruption and Late Minoan-IB destructions on Crete.' *Nature* 267: 819–822.

36 Manning, S. W. (2010). 'Eruption of Thera/Santorini.' In Cline, E. H. (ed.). *The Oxford Handbook of the Aegean Bronze Age.* Oxford: Oxford University Press, pp. 457–474.

37 McCoy and Heiken (2000), 1223.

38 Driessen and MacDonald (2000), 83.

39 Driessen and MacDonald (2000), 83.

40 Driessen, J. (2013). 'The troubled island ... 15 years later.' Presentation at Heidelberg 26/1/13. Available at: www.academia.edu/2971816/The_ Troubled_Island._15_years_later

41 Trevelyan, L. (2012). 'Haiti's tent cities signal long road to quake recovery.' Available at: www.bbc.co.uk/news/world-latin-america-16508545

42 Higgins, C. M. (2009). *Popular and imperial responses to earthquakes in the Roman empire.* Unpublished MA Thesis, College of Arts and Sciences of Ohio University.

43 Pages 252–253, Lupack, S. (2010). 'Minoan religion.' In Cline, E. H. (ed.). *The Oxford Handbook of the Aegean Bronze Age.* Oxford: Oxford University Press, pp. 251–262.

44 Driessen, J. (2002). 'Towards and archaeology of crisis: Defining the long-term impact of the Bronze Age Santorini eruption.' In Torrance, R. and Grattan, J. (eds.). *Natural Disasters and Cultural Change.* London: Routledge, pp. 250–263.

45 Rehak and Younger (1998), 100–101.

46 Preston (2008), 313.

47 Preston (2008).

48 Wallace, S. (2010). *Ancient Crete: From Successful Collapse to Democracy's Alternatives, Twelfth to Fifth Centuries BC.* Cambridge: Cambridge University Press.

49 Dickinson, O. (2014). 'How warlike were the Mycenaeans, in reality?' In Galanakis, Y., Wilkinson, T., and Bennet, J. (eds.). *ΑΘΥΡΜΑΤΑ: Critical*

Essays on the Archaeology of the Eastern Mediterranean in Honour of E. Susan Sherratt. Oxford: Archaeopress, pp. 67–72.

50 Driessen, J. and Langohr, C. (2007). 'Rallying 'round a Minoan past: The legitimation of power at Knossos during the Late Bronze Age.' In Galaty, M. L. and Parkinson, W. A. (eds.). *Rethinking Mycenaean Palaces II.* Los Angeles: The Cotsen Institute of Archaeology, University of California, pp. 178–189.

51 Page 540, McDonald, C. (2010). 'Knossos.' In Cline, E. H. (ed.). *The Oxford Handbook of the Aegean Bronze Age.* Oxford: Oxford University Press, pp. 529–542.

52 Rehak and Younger (1998). 99.

53 Killen, J. T. (1995). 'Some further thoughts on 'collectors'.' In Laffineur, R. and Niemeier, W.-D. (eds.). *Politeia: Society and State in the Aegean Bronze Age. Aegaeum 12.* Liege: University of Liege, pp. 213–226.

54 Preston (2008), 315.

55 Preston (2008), 315.

56 Preston (2008), 314.

57 Pages 270–273, Cline, E. H. (1995). 'Tinker, tailor, soldier, sailor: Minoans and Mycenaeans abroad.' In Laffineur, R. and Niemeier, W.-D. (eds.). *Politeia: Society and State in the Aegean Bronze Age. Aegaeum 12.* Liege: University of Liege, pp. 265–287.

58 Driessen and Langohr (2007).

59 McDonald (2010), 540.

60 Parkinson, W. A. and Galaty, M. L. (2007). 'Secondary states in perspective: An integrated approach to secondary state formation in the prehistoric Aegean.' *American Anthropologist* 109(1): 113–129.

61 Driessen and Langohr (2007).

62 Page 197, Hitchcock, L. A. (2010). 'Minoan architecture.' In Cline, E. H. (ed.). *The Oxford Handbook of the Aegean Bronze Age.* Oxford: Oxford University Press, pp. 189–199; Preston (2008), 317.

63 Preston (2008), 316.

64 McDonald (2010), 540–541.

65 Jan Driessen, personal communication.

66 Driessen (2013).

67 Hitchcock, L. A. and Maeir, A. M. (2014). 'Yo-ho, yo-ho, a seren's life for me!' *World Archaeology* 46(4): 624–640.

68 Wallace (2010), 51, 66.

6. The Kingdoms of Mycenaean Greece

1 Page 3, Drews, R. (1993). *The End of the Bronze Age: Changes in Warfare and the Catastrophe ca. 1200BC.* Princeton: Princeton University Press.

2 Kilian, K. (1988). 'The emergence of wanax ideology in the Mycenaean palaces.' *Oxford Journal of Archaeology* 7: 291–302; Wright, J. (2006) 'The formation of the Mycenaean palace.' In Deger-Jalkotzy, S. and Lemos,

I. S. (eds.). *Ancient Greece from the Mycenaean Palaces to the Age of Homer.* Edinburgh: Edinburgh University Press, pp. 7–52.

3 Stocker, S. R. and Davis, J. L. (2004). 'Animal sacrifice, archives, and feasting at the Palace of Nestor.' *Hesperia* 73(2): 179–195.

4 Parkinson, W. A. and Galaty, M. L. (2007). 'Secondary states in perspective: An integrated approach to state formation in the prehistoric Aegean.' *American Anthropologist* 109(1): 113–129.

5 Bennet, J. (1995). 'Space through time: Diachronic perspectives on the spatial organization of the Pylian state.' In Laffineur, R. and Niemeier, W-D. (eds.). *Politeia. Society and state in the Aegean Bronze Age. Aegaeum 12.* Liège: University of Liège, pp. 587–602; Bennet, J. (1999). 'Pylos: The expansion of a Mycenaean center.' In Galaty, M. L. and Parkinson, W. A. (eds.). *Rethinking Mycenaean Palaces: New Interpretations of an Old Idea.* Los Angeles: The Cotsen Institute of Archaeology, pp. 9–18.

6 Bennet, J. (2006). 'The Aegean Bronze Age.' In Morris, I., Saller, R., and Scheidel, W. (eds.). *The Cambridge Economic History of the Greco-Roman World.* Cambridge: Cambridge University Press, pp. 175–210; Deger-Jalkotzy, S. (2008). 'Decline, destruction, aftermath.' In Shelmerdine, C. W. (ed.). *The Cambridge Companion to the Aegean Bronze Age.* Cambridge: Cambridge University Press, pp. 387–415; Dickinson, O. (2010). 'The collapse at the end of the Bronze Age.' In Cline, E. H. (ed.). *The Oxford Handbook of the Aegean Bronze Age.* Oxford: Oxford University Press, pp. 483–490; Dickinson, O. (2006). *The Aegean from Bronze Age to Iron Age: Continuity and Change Between the Twelfth and Eighth Centuries.* London: Routledge; Middleton, G. D. (2010). *The Collapse of Palatial Society in Late Bronze Age Greece and the Postpalatial Period.* Oxford: Archaeopress.

7 Popham, M. (1994). 'The collapse of Aegean civilization at the end of the Late Bronze Age.' In Cunliffe, B. (ed.). *The Oxford Illustrated Prehistory of Europe.* Oxford: Oxford University Press, pp. 277–303.

8 Rutter, J. B. (1992). 'Cultural novelties in the post-palatial Aegean world: Indices of vitality or decline?' In Ward, W. A. and Joukowsky, M. S. (eds.). *The Crisis Years: The 12th Century BC: From Beyond the Danube to the Tigris.* Dubuque: Kendall/Hunt Publishing Company, pp. 61–78.

9 Hall, J. M. (1997). *Ethnic Identity in Greek Antiquity.* Cambridge: Cambridge University Press; Hall, J. M. (2002). *Hellenicity: Between Ethnicity and Culture.* Chicago: The University of Chicago Press.

10 Dickinson (2010), 486.

11 Carpenter, R. (1966). *Discontinuity in Greek Civilization.* Cambridge: Cambridge University Press.

12 Bryson, R. A, Lamb, H. H., and Donley, D. R. (1974). 'Drought and the decline of Mycenae.' *Antiquity* 48: 46–50.

13 Page 72, Desborough, V. (1972). *The Greek Dark Ages.* London: Ernest Benn Ltd; Dickinson, O. (1974). "Drought and the decline of Mycenae': Some comments.' *Antiquity* 48: 228–230.

14 Middleton (2010), 36.

15 Marshall, M. (2012). 'Climate change: The great civilization destroyer.' *New Scientist* 215(2876): 32–36.

16 Drake, B. L. (2012). 'The influence of climatic change on the Late Bronze Age collapse and the Greek dark ages.' *Journal of Archaeological Science* 39: 1862–1870.

17 Drake (2012), 1866.

18 Middleton, G. D. (2015). 'Telling stories: The Mycenaean origins of the Philistines.' *Oxford Journal of Archaeology* 34(1): 45–65.

19 Kaniewski D. et al. (2013) 'Environmental roots of the Late Bronze Age crisis.' *Public Library of Science ONE* 8(8): e71004.

20 Langgut, D., Finkelstein, I., and Litt, T. (2013). 'Climate and the Late Bronze Age collapse: New evidence from the southern Levant.' *Tel Aviv* 40: 149–175.

21 Neumann, J. (1993). 'Climatic changes in Europe and the Near East in the second millennium.' *Climatic Change* 23(3): 231–245.

22 Kaniewski, D., Guiot, J., and Van Campo, E. (2015). 'Drought and societal collapse 3200 years ago in the eastern Mediterranean: A review.' *WIREs Climate Change*, doi: 10.1002/wcc.345.

23 Middleton (2015).

24 Middleton (2010), 31, 41–45.

25 Popham (1994), 286.

26 Page 147, Cline, E. H. (2014). *1177 BC: The Year Civilization Collapsed.* Princeton: Princeton University Press.

27 Reicherter, K. (2011). 'Frontiers of earthquake archaeology: The Olympia and Samicum cases (Peloponnese, Greece).' 2nd INQUA-IGCP-567 International Workshop on Active Tectonics, Earthquake Geology, Archaeology and Engineering, Corinth, Greece, pp. 194–197.

28 Page 21, Nur, A. and Burgess, D. (2008). *Apocalypse: Earthquakes, Archaeology, and the Wrath of God.* Princeton: Princeton University Press.

29 Kilian, K. (1996). 'Earthquakes and archaeological context.' In Stiros, S. and Jones, R. E. (eds.). *Archaeoseismology.* Athens: The British School at Athens and Institute of Geology and Mineral Exploration, pp. 63–68.

30 Page 182, French, E. B. and Stockhammer, P. (2009). 'Mycenae and Tiryns: The pottery of the second half of the thirteenth century BC – contexts and definitions.' *Annual of the British School at Athens* 104: 175–232.

31 Nur, A. and Cline, E. H. (2000). 'Poseidon's horses: Plate tectonics and earthquake storms in the Late Bronze Age Aegean and eastern Mediterranean.' *Journal of Archaeological Science* 27: 43–63.

32 Tacitus *Annals* 2.47

33 Ambraseys, N. N. (2006). 'Earthquakes and archaeology.' *Journal of Archaeological Science* 33: 1008–1016.

34 Ambraseys (2006), 1015.

35 Maran, J. (2009). 'The crisis years? Reflections on signs of instability in the last decades of the Mycenaean palaces.' *Scienze dell'antichita. Storia Archeologia Antropologia* 15: 241–262.

36 2017. 'Reading the thirteenth century BC in Greece: Crisis, decline, or business as usual?' In Cunningham, T. and Driessen, J. (eds.). *Crisis to Collapse: The Archaeology of Social Breakdown. Aegis 11.* Louvain: Louvain University Press, pp. 87–97.

37 Maran (2009), 255.

38 Maran (2009), 255.

39 Parkinson, W. A. and Galaty, M. L. (eds.). (2009). *Archaic State Interaction: The Eastern Mediterranean in the Bronze Age.* Santa Fe: School for Advanced Research Press.

40 Sherratt, E. S. (2003). 'The Mediterranean economy: 'Globalization' at the end of the second millennium BCE.' In Dever, W. G. and Gitin, S. (eds.). *Symbiosis, Symbolism, and the Power of the Past: Canaan, Ancient Israel, and Their Neighbors from the Late Bronze Age through Roman Palaestina.* Winona Lake: Eisenbrauns, pp. 37–62.

41 Schon, R. (2009). 'Think locally, act globally: Mycenaean elites and the Late Bronze Age world-system.' In Parkinson, W. A. and Galaty, M. L. (eds.). *Archaic State Interaction: The Eastern Mediterranean in the Bronze Age.* Santa Fe: School for Advanced Research Press, pp. 213–236.

42 Schon (2009), 233.

43 Donlan, W. (1993). 'Duelling with gifts in the *Iliad*: As the audience saw it.' *Colby Quarterly* 29(3): 155–172.

44 Page 50, Galaty, M. L. et al. (2009). 'Interaction amidst diversity: An introduction to the eastern Mediterranean Bronze Age.' In Parkinson, W. A. and Galaty, M. L. (eds.). *Archaic State Interaction: The Eastern Mediterranean in the Bronze Age.* Santa Fe, NM: School for Advanced Research Press, pp. 29–51

45 Pages 271–274, Vermeule, E. T. (1972). *Greece in the Bronze Age.* Chicago, University of Chicago Press; Vermeule, E. T. (1960). 'The fall of the Mycenaean Empire.' *Archaeology* 13: 66–75.

46 Sandars, N. K. (1978). *The Sea Peoples: Warriors of the Ancient Mediterranean 1250–1150 BC.* London: Thames and Hudson.

47 Popham (1994), 287.

48 Sherratt, E. S. (2001). 'Potemkin palaces and route-based economies.' In Voutsaki, S. and Killen, J. (eds.). *Economy and Politics in the Mycenaean Palace States.* Cambridge: The Cambridge Philological Society, pp. 214–238; Sherratt (2003).

49 Sherratt (2001), 234.

50 Sherratt, E. S. (1998). ''Sea Peoples' and the economic structure of the late second millennium in the eastern Mediterranean.' In Gitin, S., Mazar, A., and Stern, E. (eds.). *Mediterranean Peoples in Transition: Thirteenth to early Tenth Centuries BCE.* Jerusalem: Israel Exploration Society, pp. 292–313; Sherratt (2003).

51 Middleton (2010), 32–36.

52 Kopanias, K. (2008). 'The Late Bronze Age Near Eastern cylinder seals from Thebes (Greece) and their historical implications.' *Mitteilungen des Deutschen Archaologischen Instituts, Athenische Abteilung* 123: 39–96.

53 Page 702, Dakouri-Hild, A. (2010). 'Thebes.' In Cline, E. H. (ed.). *The Oxford Handbook of the Aegean Bronze Age.* Oxford: Oxford University Press, pp. 690–711.

54 Page 107, Burns, B. E. (2010). *Mycenaean Greece, Mediterranean Commerce, and the Formation of Identity.* Cambridge: Cambridge University Press.

55 Middleton (2010), 48–50.

56 Walløe, L. (1999). 'Was the disruption of the Mycenaean world caused by repeated epidemics of bubonic plague?' *Opuscula Atheniensia* 24: 121–126; Williams, E. W. (1962). 'The end of an epoch.' *Greece and Rome* 9(2):109–125. See also Naphy, W. and Spicer, A. (2004). *Plague: Black Death and Pestilence in Europe.* Stroud: Tempus.

57 Drews (1993).

58 Drews (1993), 104.

59 Drews (1993), 221–222.

60 Middleton (2010), 47–48.

61 Rystedt, E. (1997). 'Approaching the question of Bronze-to-Iron-Age continuity in Ancient Greece.' *Current Swedish Archaeology* 5: 147–154.

62 Rutter (1992).

63 Page 729, Maran, J. (2010). 'Tiryns.' In Cline, E. H. (ed.). *The Oxford Handbook of the Aegean Bronze Age.* Oxford: Oxford University Press, pp. 722–734.

64 Pages 677–678, French, E. (2010). 'Mycenae.' In Cline, E. H. (ed.). *The Oxford Handbook of the Aegean Bronze Age.* Oxford: Oxford University Press, pp. 671–679.

65 I thank Jerry Rutter for telling me about this site and for sending me the latest publication. Gauss, W. et al. (2013). 'Aigeira 2012. Bericht zu Aufarbeitung und Graben.' In *Jahreshefte des Osterreichischen Archaologischen Institutes in Wien. Band 82* Wien: Osterreichisches Archaologisches Institute, pp. 69–91.

66 Mountjoy, P. A. (2011). 'A Bronze Age Ship from Ashkelon with particular reference to the Bronze Age ship from Bademgedigi Tepe.' *American Journal of Archaeology* 115(3): 483–488; Papadopoulos, A. (2009). 'Warriors, hunters and ships in the Late Helladic IIIC Aegean: Changes in the iconography of warfare.' In Bachhuber, C. and Roberts, R. G. (eds.). *Forces of Transformation: The End of the Bronze Age in the Mediterranean.* Oxford: Oxbow Books, pp. 69–77.

67 Page 531, Vlachopoulos, A. G. (2008). 'A Late Mycenaean journey from Thera to Naxos: The Cyclades in the twelfth century BC.' In Brodie, N., Doole, J., Gavalas, G., and Renfrew, C. (eds.). *Horizon. A Colloquium on the Prehistory of the Cyclades.* Cambridge: McDonald Institute for Archaeological Research, pp. 519–531.

68 Page 687, Davis, J. L. (2010). 'Pylos.' In Cline, E. H. (ed.). *The Oxford Handbook of the Aegean Bronze Age.* Oxford: Oxford University Press, pp. 680–689.

69 For example: Iacovou, M. (1999). 'The Greek exodus to Cyprus: The antiquity of Hellenism.' *Mediterranean Historical Review* 14(2): 1–28;

Yasur-Landau, A. (2010). *The Philistines and Aegean Migration at the End of the Late Bronze Age.* Cambridge: Cambridge University Press.

70 Middleton (2015).

71 Voskos, I. and Knapp, A. B. (2008). 'Cyprus at the end of the Late Bronze Age: Crisis and colonization or continuity and hybridity?' *American Journal of Archaeology* 112: 659–684. I thank Bernard Knapp for drawing my attention to this article.

72 Sherratt, S. (2003). 'Visible writing: Questions of scripts and identity in Early Iron Age Greece and Cyprus.' *Oxford Journal of Archaeology* 22(3): 225–242.

73 Iacovou (1999).

74 Hall (1997; 2002).

75 Bernard Knox's introduction to Finley, M. I. (1982). *The World of Odysseus.* New York: New York Review of Books, pp. vii–xviii.

76 Latacz, J. (2004). *Troy and Homer: Towards a Solution of an Old Mystery.* Oxford: Oxford University Press.

77 Cline, E. H. (2013). *The Trojan War: A Very Short Introduction.* Oxford: Oxford University Press.

7.   The Hittites and the Eastern Mediterranean

1 Page 101, Edens, C. (1997). 'Bogazkoy.' In Bahn, P. (ed.). *Lost Cities.* London: Weidenfeld and Nicolson.

2 Bryce, T. (2006a). 'The Eternal Treaty from the Hittite perspective.' *British Museum Studies in Ancient Egypt and Sudan* 6: 1–11.

3 Beckman, G. M., Bryce, T. R., and Cline, E. H. (2011). *The Ahhiyawa Texts.* Atlanta: Society of Biblical Literature.

4 Killebrew, A. E. and Lehmann, G. (eds.). (2013). *The Philistines and Other 'Sea Peoples' in Text and Archaeology.* Atlanta: Society of Biblical Literature.

5 Page 195, Van De Mieroop, M. (2007). *A History of the Ancient Near East, ca. 3000–323 BC.* Oxford: Blackwell.

6 Yasur-Landau, A. (2010). *The Philistines and Aegean Migration at the End of the Late Bronze Age.* Cambridge: Cambridge University Press.

7 Pages 52–53, Drews, R. (1993). *The End of the Bronze Age: Changes in Warfare and the Catastrophe ca. 1200 BC.* Princeton: Princeton University Press.

8 Sandars, N. K. (1978). *The Sea Peoples" Warriors of the Ancient Mediterranean.* London: Thames and Hudson.

9 Pages 112–114, Cline, E. H. (2014). *1177 BC: The Year Civilization Collapsed.* Princeton: Princeton University Press.

10 Kaniewski, D. et al. (2011). 'The Sea Peoples, from cuneiform tablets to carbon dating.' *Public Library of Science, One* 6(6): e20232: 1–7; Kaniewski, D. et al. (2013). 'Environmental roots of the Late Bronze Age crisis.' *Public Library of Science, One* 8(8): e71004: 1–10.

11 Dothan, T. and Dothan, M. (1992). *The Peoples of the Sea.* New York: Macmillan; Stager, L. E. (1995). 'The impact of the Sea Peoples in Canaan (1185–1050 BCE).' In Levy, T. E. (ed.). *The Archaeology of Society in the Holy Land.* Leicester: Leicester University Press, pp. 332–348; Yasur-Landau (2010).

12 Hitchcock, L. A. and Maeir, A. M. (2014). 'Yo-ho, yo-ho, a seren's life for me!' *World Archaeology* 46(4): 624–640.

13 Page 126, Knapp, A. B. (1992). 'Bronze Age Mediterranean island cultures and the ancient Near East.' *The Biblical Archaeologist* 55(3): 112–128.

14 Page 335, Bryce, T. (2005a). *The Kingdom of the Hittites*. New edition. Oxford: Oxford University Press.

15 De Souza, P. (1999). *Piracy in the Graeco-Roman World*. Cambridge: Cambridge University Press.

16 Van De Mieroop (2003), 194.

17 Page 386, Kuhrt, A. (1995). *The Ancient Near East*. London: Routledge.

18 Wilson, J. A. (1956). 'The royal myth in ancient Egypt.' *Proceedings of the American Philosophical Society* 100: 439–442.

19 Page 56, Wilkinson, T. (2010). *The Rise and Fall of Ancient Egypt*. London: Bloomsbury.

20 Page 245, Van De Mieroop, M. (2010). *The Eastern Mediterranean in the Age of Ramesses II*. Chichester: Wiley-Blackwell.

21 Page 55, Bryce, T. (2012). *The World of the Neo-Hittite Kingdoms: A Political and Military History*. Oxford: Oxford University Press; page 299, Sagona, A. and Zimansky, P. (2009). *Ancient Turkey*. Abingdon: Routledge; Van De Mieroop (2007), 193–195.

22 Bryce (2012), 83–98.

23 Genz, H. (2013). 'No land could stand before their arms, from Hatti… on…'? New light on the end of the Hittite Empire and the Early Iron Age in central Anatolia.' In Killebrew, A. E. and Lehmann, G. (eds.). *The Philistines and Other 'Sea Peoples' in Text and Archaeology*. Society of Biblical Literature, pp. 469–477.

24 Middleton, G. D. (2015). 'Telling stories: The Mycenaean origin of the Philistines.' *Oxford Journal of Archaeology* 34(1): 45–65.

25 Bryce (2005a), 322, 331–332.

26 Bryce (2005a), 331.

27 Bryce (2006a), 8.

28 Kaniewski, D., Guiot, J., and Van Campo, E. (2015). 'Drought and societal collapse 3200 years ago in the eastern Mediterranean: A review.' *WIREs Climate Change*, doi: 10.1002/wcc.345.

29 Gorny, R. L. (1989). 'Environment, archaeology, and history in Hittite Anatolia.' *Biblical Archaeologist* 52: 78–96.

30 Gorny (1989), 91.

31 Kaniewski, Guiot, and Van Campo (2015).

32 Page 35–37, Bryce, T. (2005b). 'The last days of Hattusa: The mysterious collapse of the Hittite empire.' *Odyssey* January/February: 32–41, 51

33 Bryce (2012), 20.

34 Bryce (2005a), 332.

35 Bryce (2005a), 300.

36 Bryce (2005a), 300.

37 Bryce (2012), 26–30.

38 Trevor Bryce, personal communication; Bryce (2005a), 268–271.

39 Bryce (2005b).

40 Bryce (2005a), 329.

41 Bryce (2005a), 327–328.

42 Bryce (2005a), 328.

43 Bryce (2005b).

44 Glatz, C. and Matthews, R. (2005). 'Anthropology of a frontier zone: Hittite-Kaska relations in Late Bronze Age north-central Anatolia.' *Bulletin of the American School of Oriental Research* 339: 47–65.

45 Bryce (2005a), 217–218.

46 Matthews, R. (2004). 'Landscapes of terror and control: Imperials impacts in Paphlagonia.' *Near Eastern Archaeology* 67(4): 200–211.

47 Glatz and Matthews (2005), 56

48 Bryce (2005a), 230–231.

49 Bryce (2005a), 230.

50 Page 81, Collins, B. J. (2007). *The Hittites and Their World.* Atlanta: Society of Biblical Literature.

51 Bryce (2005a), 205–206, 232–233.

52 Quoted on page 206, Bryce (2005a).

53 Bryce (2005a), 220.

54 Bryce (2005a), 232–233.

55 Glatz and Matthews (2005), 50.

56 Roller, L. E. (2011). 'Phrygia and the Phrygians.' In Steadman, S. R. and McMahon, G. (eds.). *The Oxford Handbook of Ancient Anatolia.* Oxford: Oxford University Press, pp. 560–578; Voigt, M. M. (2011). 'Gordion: The changing political and economic roles of a first millennium BCE city.' In Steadman, S. R. and McMahon, G. (eds.). *The Oxford Handbook of Ancient Anatolia.* Oxford: Oxford University Press, pp. 1069–1094.

57 Neumann, J. (1993). 'Climatic changes in Europe and the Near East in the second millennium.' *Climatic Change* 23(3): 231–245.

58 Herodotus, *Histories* 7.73.

59 Roller (2011), 560–561.

60 Sagona and Zimansky (2009), 352–353.

61 Roller (2011), 561.

62 Voigt (2011), 1077.

63 Kealhofer, L. et al. (2009). 'Post-collapse: The re-emergence of polity in Iron Age Bogazkoy, central Anatolia.' *Oxford Journal of Archaeology* 28(3): 275–300.

64 Kealhofer et al. (2009), 277.

65 Voigt (2011), 1077.

66 Sagona and Zimansky (2009), 352.

67 Cited in Kealhofer et al. (2009), 277.

68 Bryce (2005b).

69 Bryce (2012), 28–29, 86.

70 Bryce (2012); Collins (2007), 197–218.

71 Bryce (2012), 83–88.

72 Harrison, T. P. (2009). 'Neo-Hittites in the 'Land of Palistin': Renewed investigations at Tell Ta'yinat on the Plain of Antioch.' *Near Eastern Archaeology* 72(4): 174–189.

73 Bryce (2005a), 312–313, 350; Hawkins, J. D. (1988). 'Kuzi-Tesub and the 'Great Kings' of Karkamis.' *Anatolian Studies* 38: 99–108.

74 Bryce (2005a), 350.

75 Bryce (2012), 195–196.

76 Harrison (2009).

77 Bryce (2012), 130–131.

78 Bryce (2012), 110–114.

79 Bryce (2012), 125–128.

80 Bryce (2012), 124.

81 Hawkins (1988), 106.

82 Page 213, Dodd, L. S. (2007). 'Strategies for future success: Remembering the Hittites during the Iron Age.' *Anatolian Studies* 57: 203–216.

83 Hawkins, J. D. (2009). 'The Arzawa letters in recent perspective.' *British Museum Studies in Ancient Egypt and Sudan* 14: 73–83.

84 Pages 363–366, Bryce, T. (2011). 'The Late Bronze Age in the west and the Aegean.' In Steadman, S. R. and McMahon, G. (eds.). *The Oxford Handbook of Ancient Anatolia*. Oxford: Oxford University Press, pp. 363–375.

85 Bryce (2011), 366.

86 Bryce (2011), 367.

87 Bryce (2011), 366–367.

88 Bryce (2011), 366–368.

89 Bryce (2011), 372.

90 Page 82, Bryce, T. (2006b). *The Trojans and Their Neighbours*. Abingdon: Routledge.

91 Bryce (2006b), 145; Trevor Bryce, personal communication.

92 Bryce (2006b), 147.

93 Page 451, Knapp, A. B. (2013). *The Archaeology of Cyprus: From Earliest Prehistory through the Bronze Age*. Cambridge: Cambridge University Press; page 188, Steel, L. (2004). *Cyprus Before History: From the Earliest Settlers to the End of the Bronze Age*. London: Duckworth.

94 Hitchcock and Maeir (2014).

95 Steel (2004), 187–188.

96 Steel (2004), 208.

97 Bauer, A. A. (1998). 'Cities of the sea: Maritime trade and the origin of the Philistine settlement in the Early Iron Age southern Levant.' *Oxford Journal of Archaeology* 17(2): 149–168; Sherratt, E. S. (1998). "Sea Peoples' and the Economic Structure of the Late Second Millennium in the Eastern Mediterranean.' In Gitin, S., Mazar, A., and Stern, E. (eds.) *Mediterranean Peoples in Transition: Thirteenth to Early Tenth Centuries BCE*. Jerusalem. pp. 292–313.

98 Van De Mieroop (2010), 247–249.

99 Dale, A. (2011). 'Alcaeus on the career of Myrsilos: Greeks, Lydians and Luwians at the east Aegean west Anatolian interface.' *Journal of Hellenic Studies* 131: 15–24.

100 Page 415, Wallace, R. W. (2013). 'Charismatic leaders.' In Raaflaub, K. A. and Van Wees, H. (eds.). *A Companion to Archaic Greece*. Oxford: Wiley-Blackwell, pp. 411–426.

8.   The Fall of the Western Roman Empire

1   Page xvii, Traina, G. (2011). *428 AD: An Ordinary Year at the End of the Roman Empire.* Princeton: Princeton University Press.

2   See: www.utexas.edu/courses/rome/21oreasons.html

3   BBC (2004). 'The Roman Empire's collapse in the fifth century.' *In Our Time.* BBC Radio 4. Available at: www.bbc.co.uk/podcasts/series/ioth/all

4   Page 509, Gibbon, E. (1994 [1781]). *The History of the Decline and Fall of the Roman Empire. Volume 2.* London: Penguin.

5   Pages 53–73, Galinsky, K. (1992). *Classical and Modern Interactions.* Austin: University of Texas Press; Kagan, D. (1992). *The End of the Roman Empire.* Lexington: D. C. Heath.

6   Pages 110–113 and generally, Ferris, I. (2000). *Enemies of Rome.* Stroud: Sutton.

7   Page 416, Ammianus Marcellinus. (1986). *The Later Roman Empire (AD 354–378).* London: Penguin.

8   Page 173, 176, Halsall, G. (2007). *Barbarian Migrations and the Roman West, 357–568.* Cambridge: Cambridge University Press.

9   Halsall (2007), 138–162.

10 Ammianus Marcellinus (1986), 417.

11 Halsall (2007), 177–179.

12 Halsall (2007), 179–180.

13 Halsall (2007), 184.

14 Halsall (2007), 211.

15 Halsall (2007), 195–200, 209.

16 Bury, J. B. (1967). *The Invasion of Europe by the Barbarians.* New York: W. W. Norton; Halsall (2007), 284–319.

17 Moorhead, S. and Stuttard, D. (2010). *AD 410: The Year that Shook Rome.* London: British Museum Press; Halsall (2007), 255.

18 Halsall (2007), 254.

19 Rogers, A. and Hingley, R. (2010). 'Edward Gibbon and Frances Haverfield: The traditions of imperial decline.' In Bradley, M. (ed). *Classics and Imperialism in the British Empire.* Oxford: Oxford University Press, pp. 189–209.

20 Page 237, Mommsen, T. E. (1942). 'Petrarch's conception of the 'Dark Ages'.' *Speculum* 17(2): 226–242.

21 See for example: Herman, A. (1997). *The Idea of Decline in Western History.* Free Press: New York.

22 For the period, see Peachin, M. (2006). 'Rome the superpower.' In Potter, D. (ed.). *Companion to the Roman Empire.* Oxford: Blackwell, pp. 126–152.

23 For Aristides' speech, see: http://coursesa.matrix.msu.edu/~fisher/hst205/readings/RomanOration.html

24 Page 198, Bronson, B. (1988). 'The role of barbarians in the fall of states.' In Yoffee, N. and Cowgill, G. L. (eds.). *The Collapse of Ancient States and Civilizations.* Tucson: University of Arizona Press, pp. 196–218.

25 Page 146 n. 3, Runciman, W. G. (2009). *The Theory of Cultural and Social Selection*. Cambridge: Cambridge University Press.

26 Rogers and Hingley (2010), 203–204.

27 Rogers and Hingley (2010), 203.

28 Page 505, Parker, P. (2009). *The Empire Stops Here*. London: Pimlico.

29 Pages 414–415, Goldsworthy, A. (2009). *How Rome Fell*. New Haven: Yale University Press.

30 Quoted in Kagan (1992), 12.

31 Brown, P. (1997). '*So debate* the world of Late Antiquity revisited.' *Symbolae Osloenses* 72: 1, 5–30.

32 Haywood, R. M. (1960). *The Myth of Rome's Fall*. London: Alvin Redman.

33 White, L. (ed.). (1966). *The Transformation of the Roman World*. Oakland: University of California Press.

34 Procopius. *History of the Wars* III. 2.13.

35 Pages 432–433, Heather, P. (2005). *The Fall of the Roman Empire*. London: Pan.

36 Page 481, Liebschuetz, W. (2007). 'Warlords and landlords.' In Erdkamp, P. (ed.). *A Companion to the Roman Army*. Oxford: Blackwell, pp. 479–494.

37 Page xv, Totman, C. D. (1980). *The Collapse of the Tokugawa Bakufu, 1862–1868*. Honolulu: The University of Hawaii Press.

38 Pages 172–173, Bury, J. B. (1958). *History of the Later Roman Empire, 395–565. Volume. I*. New York: Dover. See also Hughes, I. (2010). *Stilicho: The Vandal Who Saved Rome*. Barnsley: Pen and Sword.

39 Page 91, Mitchell, S. (2007). *A History of the Later Roman Empire, AD 284–641*. Oxford: Blackwell.

40 Willey, D. (2010). '24 August 410: The date it all went wrong for Rome?' Available at: www.bbc.co.uk/news/world-europe-11066461; King, R. (2010). 'Hadrian's Wall lights up to mark 1600th anniversary of the end of Roman rule.' Available at: www.dailymail.co.uk/news/article-1257842/Hadrians-Wall-lights-mark-1600th-anniversary-end-Roman-rule.html; For the 'Romans go home' celebrations (the phrase comes from the Monty Python film *The Life of Brian*, set in Roman occupied Judaea), see 'Cardiff University's Roman anniversary role.' Available at: www.bbc.co.uk/news/uk-wales-south-east-wales-10665360

41 For the sack, see Moorhead, S. and Stuttard, D. (2010). *AD 410: The Year that Shook Rome*. London: British Museum Press.

42 Pages 194, 232, Li, F. (2006). *Landscape and Power in Early China: The Crisis and Fall of the Western Zhou*. Cambridge: Cambridge University Press.

43 P. 351, Shaughnessy, E. L. (1999). 'Western Zhou history.' In Loewe, M., and Shaughnessy, E. L. (eds.). *The Cambridge Ancient History of China*. Cambridge: Cambridge University Press, pp. 292–351.

44 Ando, C. (2008). 'Decline, fall, and transformation.' *Journal of Late Antiquity* 1(1): 31–60; Marcone, A. (2008). 'A long Late Antiquity: Considerations on a controversial periodization.' *Journal of Late Antiquity* 1(1): 4–19.

45 Page 304, Potter, D. (2009). *Rome in the Ancient World: From Romulus to Justinian*. London: Thames and Hudson.

46 Traina (2011).

47 Potter (2009), 304, 320. See Haldon, J. F. (1990). *Byzantium in the Seventh Century.* Cambridge: Cambridge University Press, pp. 41–70; and Kaegi, W. E. (2003). *Heraclius: Emperor of Byzantium.* Cambridge: Cambridge University Press.

48 O'Donnell, J. J. (2008). *The Ruin of the Roman Empire: A New History.* New York: Ecco.

49 Page 463, Pohl, W. (2005). 'Justinian and the barbarian kingdoms.' In Maas, M. (ed.). *The Cambridge Companion to the Age of Justinian.* Cambridge: Cambridge University Press, pp. 448–476.

50 Pohl (2005), 464.

51 Page 389, Brown, P. (2012). *Through the Eye of a Needle: Wealth, the Fall of Rome, and the Making of Christianity in the West, 350–550 AD.* Princeton: Princeton University Press.

52 On the fragmentation of the western army, see Liebeschuetz (2007); Whitby (2007). On *limatanei* reinstated by Justinian after reconquest from the Vandals, see Whitby (2007), 523. On soldiers without an empire: Eugippius *Life of Severinus* 20 – George Robinson's translation can be found here: www.tertullian.org/fathers/severinus_02_text.htm

53 On Romulus Augustulus, see Mathisen, R. W. and Nathan, G. (1997). *De Imperatoribus Romanus.* Available at: www.roman-emperors.org/auggiero .htm; Murphy, C. (2006). 'The road from Ravenna.' *The Atlantic Monthly* (September): 127–132.

54 Murdoch, A. (2006). *The Last Roman: Romulus Augustulus and the Decline of the West.* Stroud: Sutton.

55 After Potter (2009), 308.

56 Croke, B. (1983). 'AD 476: The manufacture of a turning point.' *Chiron* 13: 81–119.

57 Haywood (1960), 168.

58 Zosimus. *The New History of Count Zosimus* 2.34.1-2, quoted in Elton, H. (2012). 'Warfare and the military.' In Lenski, (ed.). *Cambridge Companion to the Age of Constantine.* Cambridge: Cambridge University Press, pp. 325–346.

59 Zosimus. *The New History of Count Zosimus* 1.57.1; Page 413, Goffart, W. (1971). 'Zosimus, the first historian of Rome's fall.' *The American Historical Review* 76(2): 412–441.

60 Jordanes. *The Origin and Deeds of the Goths* 48. Translated by Charles Mierow, Dodo Press.

61 Page 51, Rebenich, S. (2009). 'Christian asceticism and barbarian incursion: The making of a Christian catastrophe.' *Journal of Late Antiquity* 2(1): 49–59.

62 Adapted from Moorhead and Stuttard (2010), 124 and Schaff, P. *Nicene and Post-Nicene Fathers. Series II, Volume VI.* Available at: http://en.wikisource.org/wiki/Nicene_and_Post-Nicene_Fathers:_Series_II/Volume_VI/The_Letters_of_St._Jerome/Letter_127

63 Bury (1958), 311.

64 Bowersock, G. W. (1996). 'The vanishing paradigm of the fall of Rome.' *Bulletin of the American Academy of Arts and Sciences* 49: 29–43.

65 Bowersock (1996), 42.

66 Heather (2005), 459.

67 Halsall (2007), 19.

68 Halsall (2007), 19.

69 Halsall (2007), 34.

70 Ammianus Marcellinus. (1986), 127–128.

71 Page 13, Ward-Perkins, B. (2005). *The Fall of Rome and the End of Civilization.* Oxford: Oxford University Press.

72 Ward-Perkins (2005), 87.

73 Ward-Perkins (2005), 87–120.

74 Chapter 3, Whittaker, C. R. (2004). *Rome and its Frontiers: The Dynamics of Empire.* London: Routledge.

75 Jones, A. H. M. (1964). *The Later Roman Empire: 284–602.* Oxford: Blackwell.

76 Buntgen, U. et al. (2011). '2500 Years of European climate variability and human susceptibility.' *Science* 331: 578–582.

77 Huntington, E. (1917). 'Climate change and agricultural exhaustion as elements in the fall of Rome.' *The Quarterly Journal of Economics.* XX: 173–208.

78 Simkhovitch, V. G. (1916). 'Rome's fall reconsidered.' *Political Science Quarterly* 31(2): 201–243.

79 Brown (2013), 386.

80 Potter, D. S. (2004). *The Roman Empire at Bay, AD 180–395.* New edition. London: Routledge; Williams, S. (2000). *Diocletian and the Roman Recovery.* London: Routledge.

81 Scarre, C. (1995). *Chronicle of the Roman Emperors.* London: Thames and Hudson.

82 Brown (2013), 393.

83 Williams (2000).

84 See Lenski, N. (ed.). (2012). *The Cambridge Companion to the Age of Constantine.* Cambridge: Cambridge University Press.

85 Page 91, Mitchell, S. (2007). *A History of the Later Roman Empire, AD 284–641.* Oxford: Blackwell.

86 Procopius. *History of the Wars* III.2.25–26.

87 Page 35, Laiou, A. E. and Morrison, C. (2007). *The Byzantine Economy.* Cambridge: Cambridge University Press; Page 386, Ward-Perkins, B. (2000). 'Specialized production and exchange.' In Cameron, A., Ward-Perkins, B., and Whitby, M. (eds.). *The Cambridge Ancient History, Volume XIV, Late Antiquity: Empire and Successors.* Cambridge: Cambridge University Press, pp. 346–391.

88 Page 163, Lancon, B. (2000). *Rome in Late Antiquity: Everyday Life and Urban Change.* Edinburgh: Edinburgh University Press.

89 Loseby, S. T. (2000). 'Power and towns in late Roman Britain and early Anglo-Saxon England.' In Ripoll, G. and Gurt, J. M. (eds.). *Sedes Regiae (ann. 400–800).* Barcelona: Reial Academia de Bones Lletres, pp. 319–370; Ward-Perkins (2000), 375.

90 Lancon (2000), 14–15, 36–44, 119.

91 Lancon (2000), 14, 119–120.
92 Page 69, Croke, B. (2005). 'Justinian's Constantinople.' In Maas, M. (ed.). *The Cambridge Companion to the Age of Justinian*. Cambridge: Cambridge University Press, pp. 60–86.
93 Lancon (2000), 16; Ward-Perkins (2000), 379–380.
94 'Goths' in Lemprière, J. (1792) *A Classical Dictionary*. Second edition. London: T. Cadell.
95 Page 84, Gibbon, E. (2005 [1776]). *The History of the Decline and Fall of the Roman Empire. Volume 1*. London: Penguin.
96 Goffart, W. (2008). 'Rome's final conquest: The Barbarians.' *History Compass* 6(3), 855–883.
97 Pages 1018, 1023, Mathisen, R. W. (2006). *Peregrini, barbari,* and *cives Romani*: Concepts of citizenship and the legal identity of barbarians in the Later Roman Empire.' *American Historical Review* 111(4): 1011–1040.
98 Page 164ff., Ebrey, P. B. (2010). *The Cambridge Illustrated History of China*. Cambridge: Cambridge University Press.
99 Pirenne, H. (2001). *Mohammed and Charlemagne*. New York: Dover.
100 Pages 223–224, Wickham, C. (2009). *The Inheritance of Rome: A History of Europe from 400 to 1000*. London: Penguin.
101 Hodges, R. and Whitehouse, D. (1983). *Mohammed, Charlemagne & the Origins of Europe*. London: Duckworth.

9. Collapse and Revolution in Mesoamerica

1 Polybius *The Histories* 6.2,
2 Pages 246–250, Machiavelli, N. (2008). *Discourses on Livy*. Oxford: Oxford University Press.
3 See Goody, J. (2006). *The Theft of History*. Cambridge: Cambridge University Press.
4 Fargher, L. F. et al. (2011). 'Tlaxcallan: The archaeology of an ancient republic in the New World.' *Antiquity* 85: 172–186.
5 Page 16, Idzerda, S. J. (1954). 'Iconoclasm during the French Revolution.' *The American Historical Review* 60(1): 13–26.
6 Losebrink, H.-J. and Reichardt, R. (eds.). (1997). *The Bastille: A History of a Symbol of Despotism and Freedom*. Durham: Duke University Press.
7 See for example Reichardt, R. and Kohl, H. (2008). *Visualizing the Revolution: Politics and the Pictorial Arts in Late Eighteenth Century France*. London: Reaktion Books.
8 Betros, G. (2010). 'The French Revolution and the Catholic church.' *History Today*. Available at: www.historytoday.com/gemma-betros/ french-revolution-and-catholic-church
9 Joyce, A. A. et al. (2014). 'Political transformations and the every-day in Postclassic Oaxaca.' *Ancient Mesoamerica* 25(2): 389–410; Joyce, A., Arnaud Bustamente, L., and Levine, M. (2001). 'Commoner power: A case study from the Classic Period collapse on the Oaxaca coast.' *Journal of Archaeological Method and Theory* 8(4): 343–385.

10 Joyce, A. A. and Weller, E. T. (2007). 'Commoner rituals, resistance, and the Classic-to-Postclassic transition in ancient Mesoamerica.' In Gonlin, N. and Lohse, J. C. (eds.). *Commoner Ritual and Ideology in Ancient Mesoamerica*. Boulder: University Press of Colorado, pp. 143–184.

11 Joyce and Weller (2007), 144.

12 Joyce and Weller (2007), 145.

13 Joyce et al. (2001), 354.

14 Joyce and Weller (2007), 165.

15 Joyce. et al. (2014), 393; Joyce et al. (2001), 355–361.

16 Joyce et al. (2001), 356.

17 Joyce et al. (2001), 346.

18 Joyce et al. (2001), 373.

19 Cowgill, G. L. (2015). *Ancient Teotihuacan: Early Urbanism in Central Mexico*. Cambridge: Cambridge University Press; Nichols, D. L. (2015). 'Teotihuacan.' *Journal of Archaeological Research*. DOI 10.10007/s10814-015-9085-0; Cowgill, G. L. (2012a). 'Concepts of collapse and regeneration in human history.' In Nichols, D. L. and Pool, C. A. (eds.). *The Oxford Handbook of Mesoamerican Archaeology*. Oxford: Oxford University Press, pp. 301–308.

20 Millon, R. (1988). 'The last years of Teotihuacan dominance.' In Yoffee, N. and Cowgill, G. L. (eds.). *The Collapse of Ancient States and Civilizations* Tucson: Arizona University Press, pp. 102–164.

21 Cowgill (2015), 1, 143–144.

22 Pages 281–287, 297–299, Evans, S. T. (2004). *Ancient Mexico & Central America*. London: Thames and Hudson; Cowgill (2015), 195–203; Nichols (2015).

23 Pages 271–274, Sanders, W. T. and Evans, S. T. (2006). 'Rulership and palaces in Teotihuacan.' In Christie, J. J. and Sarro, P. J. (eds.). *Palaces and Power in the Americas: From Peru to the Northwest Coast*. Austin: University of Texas Press, pp. 256–284.

24 Pages 10–11, Cowgill, G. L. (2012b). 'Migrants and the fall of Ancient Teotihuacan in Central Mexico.' Paper for ASU workshop 'Late lessons from early history', May 4–5 2012; Beekman, C. S., Cowgill, G. L., Dakin, K., Hopkins, N. A., Rosenswig, R. M., Sampeck, K. E., Swanton, M., de Ávila, A., van Doesburg, B., and Wichmann, S. (2011). 'Comments on Kaufman and Justeson: 'The history of the word for cacao in Ancient Mesoamerica'.' *Ancient Mesoamerica* 21(2): 415–441.

25 Nichols (2015).

26 Price, T. D., Manzanilla, L., and Middleton, W. D. (2000). 'Immigration and the ancient city of Teotihuacan in Mexico: A study using strontium isotope ratios in human bone and teeth.' *Journal of Archaeological Science* 27: 903–913.

27 Cited by Cowgill, G. L. (2008a). 'An update on Teotihuacan.' *Antiquity* 82: 962–975; Robertson, I. G. (1999). 'Spatial and multivariate analysis, random sampling error, and analytical noise: empirical Bayesian methods at Teotihuacan, Mexico.' *American Antiquity* 64: 137–52.

28 Millar, F. (1998). *The Crowd in Rome in the Late Republic*. Ann Arbor: University of Michigan Press; North, J. (1994). 'Democracy in Rome.' *History Today* (March): 38–43.

29 Sanders and Evans (2006).

30 Evans (2004), 253–260; pages 614–615, Webster, D. and Evans, S. T. (2009). 'Mesoamerican civilization.' In Scarre, C. (ed.). *The Human Past: World Prehistory & the Development of Human Societies*. London: Thames and Hudson, pp. 594–639.

31 Pages 177–178, Chase, A. F., Chase, D. Z., and Smith, M. E. (2009). 'States and empires in ancient Mesoamerica.' *Ancient Mesoamerica* 20: 175–182.

32 Cowgill (2015), 75.

33 Cowgill (2015), 116; Sanders and Evans (2006), 259–261.

34 Quoted in Sanders and Evans (2006), 261.

35 Evans (2004), 266; Cowgill (1997), 155.

36 Nichols (2015).

37 Cowgill (2015), 116.

38 Cowgill (2015), 93–94.

39 Quoted in Sanders and Evans (2006), 261.

40 Sanders and Evans (2006), 262.

41 Pages 144–145, Cowgill, G. L. (2008b). 'State and society at Teotihuacan, Mexico.' *Annual Review of Anthropology* 26: 129–161; Cowgill (2015), 97.

42 Sanders and Evans (2006), 262.

43 Cowgill (2015), 93.

44 Evans (2004), 266.

45 Cowgill (2015), 109; Sanders and Evans (2006), 263–264.

46 Sanders and Evans (2006), 263.

47 Cowgill (2015), 109.

48 Evans (2004), 267.

49 Cowgill (1997), 155.

50 Sanders and Evans (2006), 266.

51 Cowgill (2015), 193.

52 Cowgill (2015), 115.

53 Cowgill (2015), 191–193.

54 Cowgill (2015), 192–193.

55 Beramendi-Orosco, L. E. et al. (2009). 'High resolution chronology for the Mesoamerican urban center of Teotihuacan derived from Bayesian statistics of radiocarbon and archaeological data.' *Quaternary Research* 71: 99–107; Manzanilla, L. Lopez, C., and Freter, A. (1996). 'Dating results from excavations in the quarry tunnels behind the Pyramid of the Sun at Teotihuacan.' *Ancient Mesoamerica* 7: 245–266; Manzanilla, L. R. (2015). 'Cooperation and tensions in multi-ethnic corporate societies using Teotihuacan, Central Mexico, as a case study.' *Proceedings of the National Academy of Sciences* 112(30): 9210–9215.

56 Cowgill (2015), 233.

57 Page 226, Sugiyama, S. (2012). 'Ideology, polity, and social history of the Teotihuacan state.' In Nichols, D. A. and Pool, C. A. (eds.). *The Oxford*

Handbook of Mesoamerican Archaeology. Oxford: Oxford University Press, pp. 215–229.

58 Cowgill (2015), 233; Nichols (2015).

59 Cowgill (2012); page 3, Storey, R. (1991). 'Residential compound organization and the evolution of the Teotihuacan state.' *Ancient Mesoamerica* 2(1): 107–118.

60 Cowgill (2015), 233.

61 Lachniet, M. et al. (2012). 'A 2400 yr Mesoamerican rainfall reconstruction links climate and cultural change.' *Geology* 40(3): 259–262.

62 McClung de Tapia, E. (2012). 'Silent hazards, invisible risks: Prehispanic erosion in the Teotihuacan Valley, central Mexico.' In Cooper, J. and Sheets, P. (eds.). *Surviving Sudden Environmental Change: Understanding Hazards, Mitigating Impacts, Avoiding Disasters.* Boulder: University Press of Colorado, pp. 143–165.

63 Cited in Cowgill (2015), 235.

64 Stahle, D. W. et al. (2011). Major Mesoamerican droughts of the past millennium. *Geophysical Research Letters* 38, L05703, DOI:10.1029/2010GL046472.

65 Cited on page 94, Manzanilla, L. (2003). 'The abandonment of Teotihuacan.' In Inomata, T. and Webb, R. W. (eds.). *The Archaeology of Settlement Abandonment in Middle America.* Salt Lake City: The University of Utah Press, pp. 91–101.

66 Manzanilla (2003), 100.

67 McClung de Tapia (2012), 149.

68 Page 197, Sanders, W. T. (2003). 'Collapse and abandonment in Middle America.' In Inomata, T. and Webb, R. W. (eds.). *The Archaeology of Settlement Abandonment in Middle America.* Salt Lake City: The University of Utah Press, pp. 193–202.

69 McClung de Tapia (2012), 151.

70 Cowgill (2015), 237; Hirth, K. G. (1995). 'Urbanism, militarism, and architectural design: An analysis of Epiclassic socio-political structure at Xochichalco.' *Ancient Mesoamerica* 6: 237–250.

71 Gonzalez Crespo, N. et al. (1991). 'Archaeological investigations at Xochichalco, Morelos, 1984 and 1986.' *Ancient Mesoamerica* 6: 223–236.

72 Cowgill (2015), 237.

73 Page 120, Beekman, C. S. and Christensen, A. F. (2003). 'Controlling for doubt and uncertainty through multiple lines of evidence: A new look at the Mesoamerican Nahua migrations.' *Journal of Archaeological Method and Theory* 10(2): 111–164; Cowgill (2015), 237–239.

74 Cowgill (2012b). Crider, D. et al. (2007). 'In the aftermath of Teotihuacan: Epiclassic pottery production and distribution in the Valley of Mexico.' *Latin American Antiquity* 18(2): 123–143.

75 Cowgill (2015), 238; Nichols (2015).

76 Pages 311–312, Parsons, J. R. and Sugiura, Y. (2012). 'Teotihuacan and the Epiclassic in Central Mexico.' In Nichols, D. L. and Pool, C. A. (eds.). *The Oxford Handbook of Mesoamerican Archaeology.* Oxford: Oxford

University Press, pp. 308–323; Rattray, E. C. (1996). 'A regional perspective on the Epiclassic period in Central Mexico.' In Mastache, A. G., Parsons, J. R., Santley, R. S., and Puche, M. C. (eds.). *Arqueologia Mesoamericana: Homenaje a William T. Sanders.* Mexico City: Instituto Nacional de Antropologia e Historia, pp. 213–231.

77 Manzanilla, Lopez, and Freter (1996); Manzanilla, L. (2005). 'Migrantes epiclasicos en Teotihuacan. Propuesta metodologica para analisis de migraciones del Clasico al Posclasico.' In Manzanilla, L. (ed.). *Reacomodos demograficos del Clasico al Posclasico en el centro de Mexico.* Mexico City: Universidad Nacional Autonoma de Mexico Instituto de Investigaciones Antropologicas, pp. 261–274.

78 Cowgill, G. L. (2012). 'Migrants and the Fall of Ancient Teotihuacan in Central Mexico.' Paper for ASU "Late Lessons from Early History" Workshop Ancient and Modern Migrations, Saguaro Lake Ranch, Arizona; Cowgill, G. L. (2013). 'Possible migrations and shifting identities in the central Mexican Epiclassic.' *Ancient Mesoamerica* 24(1): 131–149.

79 Sugiyama (2012), 226.

80 Hirth (1995), 237.

81 Cowgill, personal communication; Millon (1988), 146–147.

82 Sugiyama (2012), 226.

83 Nichols (2015): Sanders, W. T. (2006). 'Late Xolalpan-Metepec/ Oxtotipac-Coyatlatelco; Ethnic succession or changing patterns of political economy: A reevaluation.' In Solar, L. (ed.). *El Fenomeno Coyatlatelco en el Centro de Mexico: Tiempo, Espacio, y Significado.* Mexico City: Instituto Nacional de Antropologia e Historia, pp. 183–200.

84 Cowgill (2012b), 12.

85 Millon (1988), 150.

86 Millon (1988), 154.

87 Manzanilla (2003).

88 Millon (1988), 156–157.

89 Manzanilla (2015), 9210.

90 Manzanilla (2015), 9214.

91 Cowgill (2015), 235.

92 Millon (1988), 156–157.

93 Millon (1988), 148.

94 Pages 71–72, Beekman, C. S. (2010). 'Recent research in western Mexican archaeology.' *Journal of Archaeological Research* 18: 41–109.

95 Hahn, J. (2008). 'The conversion of the cult statues: The destruction of the Serapeum 392 AD and the transformation of Alexandria into the 'Christ-loving' city.' In Hahn, J., Emmel, S., and Gotter, U. (eds.). *From Temple to Church: Destruction and Renewal of Local Cultic Topography in Late Antiquity.* Leiden: Brill, pp. 335–365.

96 Rattray, E. C. (2006). 'El Epiclasico de Teotihuacan y Azcapatzalco.' In Solar, L. (ed.). *El Fenomeno Coyotlatelco en el Centro de Mexico: Tiempo, Espacio y Significado.* Mexico City: Instituto Nacional de Antropologia e Historia, pp. 187–200.

97 Parsons and Sugiura (2012), 311–312.

98 Cowgill (2015), 239.

99 Nichols (2015).

100 Evans (2004), 373; Sanders (2003), 197. Cowgill (2012), 4, citing McClung de Tapia, E. (2009). 'Los ecosistemas del Valle de Teotihuacan a lo largo de su historia.' In *Teotihuacan: Ciudad de los Dioses*. Mexico City: Instituto Nacional de Antropología e Historia, pp. 36–45; McClung de Tapia (2012).

101 Cowgill (2008a), 971.

102 Nichols (2015).

103 Cowgill (2015), 14.

104 Crider et al. (2007), 126. Garraty, C. P. (2006). 'Aztec Teotihuacan: Political processes at a Postclassic and Early Colonial city-state in the Basin of Mexico.' *Latin American Antiquity* 18(4): 363–387.

105 Pages 132–133, Goldstone, J. A. (2014). *Revolutions: A Very Short Introduction*. Oxford: Oxford University Press.

106 Nichols (2015); Sanders and Evans (2006), 270–274.

10.   The Classic Maya Collapse

1 Page 299, Gill, R. B. et al. (2007). 'Drought and the Maya collapse.' *Ancient Mesoamerica* 18: 283–302.

2 Aimers, J. J. (2007). 'What Maya collapse? Terminal Classic variation in the Maya Lowlands.' *Journal of Archaeological Research* 15: 329–377.

3 Webster D. (2006). 'The mystique of the ancient Maya.' In Fagan, G. G. (ed.). *Archaeological Fantasies: How Pseudoarchaeology Misrepresents the Past and Misleads the Public*. London: Routledge, pp. 129–153.

4 Page 26, Webster, D. (2007) 'The uses and abuses of the ancient Maya.' The Emergence of the Modern World Conference, Otzenhausen, Germany.

5 Galindo, J. (1831). 'Ruins of Palenque.' *London Literary Gazette* 769: 665–667 [also reprinted in Galindo 1833]; Galindo, J. (1833). 'Description of the Usumacinta, in Guatemala.' *Journal of the Royal Geographic Society of London* 3: 59–64; Galindo, J. (1836). 'On Central America.' *Journal of the Royal Geographic Society of London* 6: 119–135.

6 Stephens, J. L. (1969 [1841]). *Incidents of Travel in Central America, Chiapas, and Yucatan. Volume I*. New York: Harper and Brothers.

7 Galindo (1831), 666–667.

8 Stephens (1969), 104–105.

9 Page iv, de Landa, D. (1978[1566]). *Yucatan Before and After the Conquest*. New York: Dover.

10 Page 183, Fash, W. L. (1994). 'Changing perspectives on Maya civilization.' *Annual Review of Anthropology* 23: 181–208.

11 Webster, D. (2000). 'The not so peaceful civilization: A review of Maya war.' *Journal of World Prehistory* 14(1): 65–119; Martin, S. and Grube, N. (2008). *Chronicles of the Maya Kings*. Second edition. London: Thames and Hudson.

12 Page 80, Gunn, J. D., Matheny, R. T., and Folan, W. J. (2002). 'Climate change studies in the Maya area: A diachronic analysis.' *Ancient Mesoamerica* 13: 79–84.

13 Cecil, J. (2011). 'The fall of the Mayan civilization.' Available at: www .bbc.co.uk/history/ancient/cultures/maya_01.shtml

14 Logan, W. (2010). 'Shelley's wrinkled lip, Smith's gigantic leg.' *Parnassus: Poetry in Review* 32(1/2); Rodenbeck, J. (2004). 'Travelers from an antique land: Shelley's inspiration for 'Ozymandias.'' *Alif: Journal of Comparative Poetics* 24: 121–148.

15 Pages 183–184, Webster, D. (2002). *The Fall of the Ancient Maya: Solving the Mystery of the Maya Collapse.* London: Thames and Hudson.

16 Quoted in Webster (2002), 185–186.

17 Quoted in Webster (2002), 212.

18 Webster (2002), 186.

19 Pages 272–275, Neiman, F. D. (1997). 'Conspicuous consumption as wasteful advertising: A Darwinian perspective on spatial patterns in Classic Maya terminal monument dates.' *Archeological Papers of the American Anthropological Association* 7(1): 267–290.

20 Webster (2002), 192, 194.

21 Webster (2002), 194.

22 Quoted in Webster (2002), 187.

23 Huntington, E. (1917). 'Maya civilization and climate change.' *Proceedings of the 19th Congress of Americanists.* Washington, D.C.: The Congress, pp. 150–164.

24 Gunn, Matheny, and Folan (2002).

25 Gunn, Matheny, and Folan (2002), 80.

26 Gill et al. (2007); Gill, R. B. (2000). *The Great Maya Droughts: Water, Life, and Death.* Albuquerque: University of New Mexico Press.

27 Cecil, J. (2011). 'The fall of the Mayan civilization.' Available at: www .bbc.co.uk/history/ancient/cultures/maya_01.shtml

28 Gill (2000); Gill et al. (2007); Pringle, H. (2009). 'A new look at the Mayas' end.' *Science* 324: 454–456.

29 Haug, G. H. et al. (2003). 'Climate and the collapse of Maya civilization.' *Science* 299: 1731–1735; Hodell, D. A., Curtis, J. H., and Brenner, M. (1995). 'Possible role of climate in the collapse of Classic Maya civilization.' *Nature* 375(1): 391–394; Hodell, D. A., Brenner, M., and Curtis, J. H. (2005). 'Terminal Classic drought in the northern Maya lowlands inferred from multiple sediment cores in Lake Chichancanab (Mexico).' *Quaternary Science Reviews* 24: 1413–1427; Hodell, D. A., Brenner, M., and Curtis, J. H. (2007). 'Climate and cultural history of the Northeastern Yucatan peninsula, Quintana Roo, Mexico.' *Climatic Change* 83: 215–240.

30 Kennett, D. J. et al. (2012). 'Development and disintegration of Maya political systems in response to climate change.' *Science* 338: 788–791.

31 Page 50, Curtis, J. H., Brenner, M., and Hodell, D. A. (2001). 'Climate change in the circum-Caribbean (Later Pleistocene to present) and implications for regional biogeography.' In Woods, C. A. and Sergile,

F. E. (eds.). *Biogeography of the West Indies: Patterns and Perspectives.* Second edition. Boca Raton: CRC Press, pp. 35–54.

32 Hodell et al. (2005).

33 Gill et al. (2007), 288; Peterson, L. and Haug, G. (2005). 'Climate and the collapse of the Maya.' *American Scientist* 93: 322–327.

34 Culbert, T. P. (1988). 'The collapse of Classic Maya civilization.' In Yoffee, N. and Cowgill, G. L. (eds.). *The Collapse of Ancient States and Civilizations.* Tucson: Arizona University Press, pp. 69–101.

35 Aimers (2007), 348; Hodell et al. (2007); Leyden, B. W., Brenner, M., and Dahlin, B. H. (1998). 'Cultural and climatic history of Coba, a lowland Maya city in Quintana Roo, Mexico.' *Quaternary Research* 49: 111–122. Most recently, also Iannone, G. (ed.). (2014). *The Great Maya Droughts in Cultural Context: Case Studies in Resilience and Vulnerability.* Boulder: University Press of Colorado.

36 Page 105, Demarest, A. A. (2001). 'Climate change and the Classic Maya collapse: The return of catastrophism.' *Latin American Antiquity* 12: 105–107.

37 Page 450, Suhler, C. et al. (2004). 'The rise and fall of terminal classic Yaxuna, Yucatan, Mexico.' In Demarest, A. A., Rice, P. M., and Rice, D. S. (eds.). *Terminal Classic in the Maya Lowlands: Collapse, Transition and Transformation.* Boulder: University Press of Colorado, pp. 450–484.

38 Page 155, McAnany, P. A., and Negron, T. G. (2010). 'Bellicose rulers and climatological peril? Retrofitting twenty-first century woes on eighth century Maya society.' In McAnany, P. A. and Yoffee, N. (eds.). *Questioning Collapse: Human Resilience, Ecological Vulnerability, and the Aftermath of Empire.* Cambridge: Cambridge University Press, pp. 142–175; Webster (2002), 245–246.

39 Peterson and Haug (2005).

40 Page 271, Demarest, A. A. (2004). *Ancient Maya: The Rise and Fall of a Rainforest Civilization.* Cambridge: Cambridge University Press.

41 Demarest (2004), 257–260.

42 Pages 295–302, Houston, S. D. and Inomata, T. (2009). *The Classic Maya.* Cambridge: Cambridge University Press; Demarest, A. A. (2006). *The Petexbatun Regional Archaeological Project: A Multidisciplinary Study of the Maya Collapse.* Nashville: Vanderbilt University Press; Dunning, N. P., Beach, T., and Rue, D. (1997). 'The palaeoecology and ancient settlement of the Petexbatun region, Guatemala.' *Ancient Mesoamerica* 8: 255–266; Wright, L. E. and White, C. D. (1996). 'Human biology in the classic Maya collapse: Evidence from paleopathology and paleodiet.' *Journal of World Prehistory* 10: 147–198.

43 Wahl, D. (2008). 'Late Holocene climate variability in the southern Maya Lowlands.' Presentation to Joint Meeting of The Geological Society of America, Soil Science Society of America, American Society of Agronomy, Crop Science Society of America, Gulf Coast Association of Geological Societies with the Gulf Coast Section of SEPM. Available at: https://gsa.confex.com/gsa/2008AM/finalprogram/abstract_151679.htm

44 Iannone (2014).

45 Aimers (2007), 329–331.

46 Page 178, Chase, A. F., Chase, D. Z., and Smith, M. E. (2009). 'States and empires in Ancient Mesoamerica.' *Ancient Mesoamerica* 20: 175–182.

47 Pages 23–24, Demarest, A. A. (2013). 'The collapse of the Classic Maya kingdoms of the southwestern Peten: Implications for the end of Classic Maya civilization.' In Arnauld, M.-C. and Breton, A. (eds.). *Millenary Maya Societies: Past Crises and Resilience*, pp. 22–48. Electronic document, published online at Mesoweb: www.mesoweb.com/publications/MMS/2_Demarest.pdf

48 Chase, Chase, and Smith (2009), 176.

49 Page, 39–41, Schele, L. and Freidel, D. (1990). *A Forest of Kings: The Untold Story of the Ancient Maya.* New York: Harper Perennial.

50 Aimers (2007); Demarest, A. A., Rice, P. M., and Rice, D. S. (eds.). (2004). *Terminal Classic in the Maya Lowlands: Collapse, Transition and Transformation.* Boulder: University Press of Colorado; Iannone, G. (2005). 'The rise and fall of a Maya petty royal court.' *Latin American Antiquity* 16: 26–44.

51 Aimers (2007), 331.

52 Page 202, Demarest, A. A. (2014). 'The Classic Maya collapse, water, and economic change in Mesoamerica: Critique and alternatives from the 'wet zone'.' In Iannone, G. (ed.). *The Great Maya Droughts in Cultural Context: Case Studies in Resilience and Vulnerability.* Boulder: University Press of Colorado, pp. 177–206; Demarest (2013), 30–31.

53 Freidel, D. (2008). 'Maya divine kingship.' In Brisch, N. (ed.). *Religion and Power: Divine Kingship in the Ancient World and Beyond.* Chicago: Oriental Institute, University of Chicago, pp. 191–206.

54 Page 18, Pendergast, D. M. (1993). 'The center and the edge: Archaeology in Belize, 1809–1992.' *Journal of World Prehistory* 7: 1–33.

55 Masson, M. A. and Mock, S. B. (2004). 'Ceramics and settlement patterns at Terminal Classic-period lagoon sites in northeastern Belize.' In Demarest, A. A., Rice, P. M., and Rice, D. S. (eds.). *The Terminal Classic in the Maya Lowlands: Collapse, Transition, and Transformation.* Boulder: University Press of Colorado, pp. 367–401.

56 See Demarest, Rice, and Rice (2004).

57 Sabloff, J. A. (1986). 'Interaction among Maya polities: A preliminary examination.' In Renfrew, C. and Cherry, J. F. (eds.). *Peer Polity Interaction and Socio-Political Change.* Cambridge: Cambridge University Press, pp. 109–116.

58 Page 457, Houston, S., Baines, J., and Cooper, J. (2003). 'Last writing: Script obsolescence in Egypt, Mesopotamia, and Mesoamerica.' *Comparative Studies in Society and History* 45(3), 430–479.

59 Davies, N. (2011). *Vanished Kingdoms: The History of Half-Forgotten Europe.* London: Allen Lane.

60 On outmigration, see McAnany, P. A., Sabloff, J. A., Lamoureux St. Hilaire, M., and Iannone, G. (2015). 'Leaving Classic Maya cities: Agent-based

modeling and the dynamics of diaspora.' In Emberling, G. (ed.). *Counternarratives and Macrohistories: New Agendas in Archaeology and Ancient History*. New York: Cambridge University Press, pp. 259–288.

61 Demarest (2014); Demarest (2013).

62 Martin and Grube (2008), 114–115.

63 Demarest (2013), 31.

64 Demarest, A. A. et al. (1997). 'Classic Maya defensive systems and warfare in the Petexbatun region: Archaeological evidence and interpretations.' *Ancient Mesoamerica* 8: 229–253.

65 Inomata, T. (1997). 'The last day of a fortified Maya center.' *Ancient Mesoamerica* 8: 337–351.

66 Inomata (1997), 348.

67 Martin and Grube (2008), 65.

68 Demarest (2014), 190.

69 Demarest (2013), 34.

70 Demarest (2014), 202–203.

71 Demarest (2014), 203.

72 Demarest (2013), 36–37; Demarest (2014), 190.

73 Page 209, Scherer, A. K. and Golden, C. (2014). 'Water in the west: Chronology and the collapse of the Classic Maya river kingdoms.' In Iannone, G. (ed.). *The Great Maya Droughts in Cultural Context: Case Studies in Resilience and Vulnerability*. Boulder: University Press of Colorado, pp. 207–229.

74 Page 175, Fash, W. L. (1991). *Scribes, Warriors, and Kings: The City of Copan and the Ancient Maya*. London: Thames and Hudson.

75 Martin and Grube (2008), 210–211.

76 Webster, D. and Freter, A. (1990). 'Settlement history and the Classic collapse at Copan: A redefined chronological perspective.' *Latin American Antiquity* 1(1): 66–85.

77 Quoted in Fash (1991), 175.

78 Andrews, A. P., Andrews, E. W., and Robles Castellanos, F. (2003). 'The northern Maya collapse and its aftermath.' *Ancient Mesoamerica* 14: 151–156.

79 Page 9, Rice, P. M., Demarest, A. A., and Rice, D. S. (2004) 'The Terminal Classic and the 'Classic Maya Collapse' in perspective.' In Demarest, A. A., Rice, P. M., and Rice, D. S. (eds.). *Terminal Classic in the Maya Lowlands: Collapse, Transition and Transformation*. Boulder: University Press of Colorado, pp 1–11.

80 Demarest (2013), 23.

81 Chase, D. Z. and Chase, A. F. (2006). 'Framing the Maya collapse: Continuity, discontinuity, method, and practice in the Classic to Postclassic southern Maya lowlands.' In Schwartz, G. M. and Nichols, J. J. (eds.). *After Collapse: The Regeneration of Complex Societies*. Tucson: University of Arizona Press, pp. 168–187.

82 Page 50, Andrews, A. P. (1993). 'Late Postclassic Lowland Maya archaeology.' *Journal of World Prehistory* 7: 35–69.

83 Andrews (1993), 49.

84 Houston, Baines, and Cooper (2003), 461–462.
85 Andrews, Andrews. and Robles Castellano (2003), 152.
86 Andrews, Andrews, and Robles Castellano (2003), 152.
87 Webster (2002), 204.
88 Andrews, Andrews, and Robles Castellano (2003), 152.
89 Quoted in Webster (2002), 205.
90 Masson, M. A., Hare, T. S., and Peraza Lope, C. (2006). 'Postclassic Maya society regenerated at Mayapan.' In Schwartz, G. M. and Nichols, J. J. (eds.). *After Collapse: The Regeneration of Complex Societies.* Tucson: University of Arizona Press, pp. 188–207. See also Demarest (2004), 277–293; Masson, M. A. (1997). 'Cultural transformation at the Maya Postclassic community of Laguna de On, Belize.' *Latin American Antiquity* 8: 293–316; Milbraith, S. and Peraza Lope, C. (2003). 'Revisiting Mayapan: Mexico's last Maya capital.' *Ancient Mesoamerica* 14: 1–46.
91 Andrews (1993), 48.
92 Kepecs, S. and Masson, M. (2003). 'Political organization in Yucatan and Belize.' In Smith, M. E. and Berdan, F. F. (eds.). *The Postclassic Mesoamerican World.* Salt Lake City: The University of Utah Press, pp. 40–44.
93 Aimers, J. (2006–2007). 'Anti-Apocalypse: The Postclassic period at Lamanai, Belize.' *Archaeology International* 10: 45–48.
94 Graham, E. (2000/2001). 'Collapse, conquest, and Maya survival at Lamanai, Belize.' *Archaeology International* 4: 52–56; Pendergast, D. M. 'Stability through change: Lamanai, Belize, from the ninth to the seventeenth century.' In Sabloff, J. A. and Andrews, E. W. (eds.). *Late Lowland Maya Civilization: Classic to Postclassic.* Alberquerque: School of American Research, University of New Mexico Press, pp. 223–249.
95 Golitko, M. et al. (2012). 'Complexities of collapse: The evidence of Maya obsidian as revealed by social networks graphics analysis.' *Antiquity* 86: 507–523.
96 Andrews (1993), 45.
97 de Landa (1978), 13.
98 Houston, Baines, and Cooper (2003).
99 Page 410, Blom, F. (1933). 'Maya books and sciences.' *The Library Quarterly* 3(4): 408–420.
100 de Landa (1978), 29.
101 Jones, G. D. (1998). *The Conquest of the Last Maya Kingdom.* Stanford: Stanford University Press.
102 Jones (1998), xix.
103 Jones (1998), 300–302.
104 Jones (1998), 374–377.
105 Jones (1998), 387.
106 Reed, N. A. (2001). *The Caste War of Yucatan.* Revised edition. Stanford: Stanford University Press.

107 Lovell, W. G. (1988). 'Surviving conquest: The Maya of Guatemala in historical perspective.' *Latin American Research Review* 23(2): 25–57.
108 McAnany and Negron (2010), 165.
109 Pendergast (1986), 249.
110 Aimers (2007), 331–332.
111 James Aimers, personal communication.
112 de las Casas, B. (2004). *A Short Account of the Destruction of the Indies.* London: Penguin.
113 Lovell (1988), 47.
114 Page 117, Johnson, L. 'The Black Legend.' In Herrera-Sobek, M. (ed.). *Celebrating Latino Folklore: An Encyclopedia of Cultural Traditions.* Santa Barbara: ABC Clio, pp. 117–119; page 119, Restall, M. (2003). *Seven Myths of the Spanish Conquest.* Oxford: Oxford University Press.
115 Page 427, Lovell, W. G. (1992). "Heavy shadows and black night': Disease and depopulation in Colonial Spanish America.' *Annals of the Association of American Geographers* 82(3): 426–443.
116 Page 369, Denevan, W. M. (1992). 'The pristine myth: The landscape of the Americas in 1492.' *Annals of the Association of American Geographers* 82(3): 369–385.
117 Heckenberger, M. and Neves, E. G. (2009). 'Amazonian archaeology.' *Annual Review of Anthropology* 38: 251–266.

11.   Collapse in the Andes

1 Page 274, Squier, E. G. (1877). *Peru: Incidents of Travel and Exploration in the Land of the Incas.* New York: Harper and Brothers.
2 Bawden G. (1999). *The Moche.* Oxford: Blackwell; Benson, E. P. (2012). *The Worlds of the Moche on the North Coast of Peru.* Austin: University of Texas Press; Bourget, S. and Jones, K. L. (eds.). (2008). *The Art and Archaeology of the Moche.* Austin: University of Texas Press; Stanish, C. (2001). 'The origin of state societies in South America.' *Annual Review of Anthropology* 30: 41–64.
3 Pages 153–154, Quilter, J. (2002). 'Moche politics, religion, and warfare.' *Journal of World Prehistory* 16(2): 145–195.
4 Page 264, Bawden, G. (1995). 'The structural paradox: Moche culture as political ideology.' *Latin American Antiquity* 6(3): 255–273; Benson (2012), 131–140.
5 Quilter, J. (2010). 'Moche: Archaeology, ethnicity, identity.' *Bulletin de l'Institut d'Etudes Andines* 39(2): 225-241.
6 Quilter (2002), 155, 158–161.
7 Cited in Quilter (2002), 161.
8 Stanish (2001), 58.
9 Page 166, Moseley, M. E. (1992). *The Incas and Their Ancestors.* London: Thames and Hudson; Stanish (2001), 53.
10 Pages 103–107, Stone, R. R. (2012). *Art of the Andes: From Chavin to Inca.* Third edition. London: Thames and Hudson.

11 Sutter, R. C. and Cortez, R. J. (2005). 'The nature of Moche human sacrifice: A bio- archaeological perspective.' *Current Anthropology* 46 (4): 521–549.
12 Bawden (1995), 264; Quilter (2002), 155.
13 Page 255, Shimada, I. et al. (1991). 'Cultural impacts of severe droughts in the prehistoric Andes: Application of a 1,500-year ice core precipitation record.' *World Archaeology* 22(3): 247–270.
14 Stanish (2001), 60.
15 Shimada et al. (1991), 255–256.
16 Wright, K. R. and Dracup, J. (1997). 'Flooding and the demise of the Moche Empire.' In Gruntfest, E. (ed.). *What We Have Learned Since the Big Thompson Flood*. Boulder: Natural Hazards Research and Applications Information Center, University of Colorado, pp. 161–167.
17 Pages 143–168, Fagan, B. (2009). *Floods, Famines, and Emperors: El Nino and the Fate of Civilizations*. New York: Basic Books; Moseley (1992), 211.
18 Moseley, M. E., Donnan, C. B., and Keefer, D. K. (2008). 'Convergent catastrophe and the demise of Dos Cabezas: Environmental change and regime change in ancient Peru.' In Bourget, S. and Jones, K. L. (eds.). *The Art and Archaeology of the Moche: An Ancient Andean Society of the Peruvian North Coast*. Austin: University of Texas Press, pp. 81–92.
19 Page 130, Shimada, I. (1994). *Pampa Grande and the Mochica Culture*. Austin: University of Texas Press.
20 Moseley, Donnan, and Keefer (2008), 89.
21 Anon. (1998). 'The season of El Nino.' *The Economist* (May 7th). Available at: www.economist.com/node/127009
22 Quilter (2002), 158.
23 Quilter (2002), 146.
24 Moseley (1992), 212.
25 Moseley (1992), 211.
26 Bawden (1996), 265; Moseley (1992), 212.
27 Moseley (1992), 212.
28 Bawden (1996), 265.
29 Cited in Benson (2012), 137.
30 Moseley (1992), 215.
31 Page 93, Haas, J. (1981). 'Class conflict and the state in the New World.' In Jones, G. D. and Kautz, R. R. (eds.). *Transition to Statehood in the New World*. Cambridge: Cambridge University Press, pp. 80–102.
32 Luis Jaime Castillo, cited in Quilter (2002), 153.
33 Benson (2012), 136.
34 Page 151, Stanish, C. (2013). 'What was Tiwanaku?' In Vranich, A. and Stanish, C. (eds.). *Visions of Tiwanaku*. Los Angeles: Cotsen Institute of Archaeology Press, pp. 151–166.
35 Stanish (2001), 53–54.
36 Page 167, Anderson, K. (2008). 'Tiwanaku influence on local drinking patterns.' In Jennings, J. and Bowser, B. J. (eds.). *Drink, Power, and Society in the Andes*. Gainesville: University of Florida Press, pp. 167–199.

37 Pages 113–118, Janusek, J. W. (2008). *Ancient Tiwanaku.* Cambridge: Cambridge University Press.

38 Erickson, C. L. (1992). 'Prehistoric landscape management in the Andean highlands: Raised field agriculture and its environmental impact.' *Population and Environment* 13(4): 285–300.

39 Erickson, C. L. (1999). 'Neo-environmental determinism and agrarian 'collapse' in Andean prehistory.' *Antiquity* 73: 634–642.

40 Kolata, A. L. (1993). *The Tiwanaku: Portrait of an Andean Civilization.* London: Wiley-Blackwell.

41 Kolata (1993), 285, 289.

42 Binford, M. et al. (1997). 'Climate variation and the rise and fall of an Andean civilization.' *Quaternary Research* 47: 235–248.

43 Calaway, M. J. (2005). 'Ice-cores, sediments and civilisation collapse: A cautionary tale from Lake Titicaca.' *Antiquity* 79: 778–790.

44 Calaway (2005), 786.

45 Calaway (2005), 787.

46 Francou, B. et al. (2003). 'Tropical climate change recorded by a glacier in the central Andes during the last decades of the twentieth century: Chacaltaya, Bolivia, 16° S.' *Journal of Geophysical Research D: Atmospheres* 108: 4154; Vuille, M. et al. (2003). '20th century climate change in the tropical Andes: Observations and model results.' *Climate Change* 59: 75–99.

47 Calaway (2005), 783.

48 Calaway (2005), 779, 788.

49 Erickson (1999), 637.

50 Williams, R. P. (2002). 'Rethinking disaster-induced collapse in the demise of the Andean highland states: Wari and Tiwanaku.' *World Archaeology* 33: 361–374.

51 Anderson (2008), 167.

52 Goldstein, P. S. (2003). 'From stew-eaters to maize-drinkers: The chicha economy and the Tiwanaku expansion.' In Bray, T. L. (ed.). *The Archaeology and Politics of Food and Feasting in Early States and Empires.* New York: Kluwer Academic/Plenum, pp. 143–172.

53 Williams (2002), 372.

54 Kolata (1993), 290–291.

55 Kolata (1993), 299.

56 Janusek, J. W. (2005). 'Collapse as cultural revolution: Power and identity in the Tiwanaku to Pacajes transition.' In Vaughn, K. J., Ogburn, D. E., and Conlee, C. A. (eds.). *The Foundations of Power in the Prehispanic Andes.* Washington, D.C.: American Anthropological Association, pp. 175–209.

57 Janusek (2005), 188.

58 Janusek (2005), 194.

59 Janusek (2008), 294.

60 Anderson (2008), 188–189.

61 Sims, K. (2006). 'After state collapse: How Tumilaca communities developed in the Upper Moquega Valley, Peru.' In Schwartz, G. M. and Nichols,

J. J. (eds.). *After Collapse: The Regeneration of Complex Societies.* Tucson: The University of Arizona Press, pp. 114–136.

62 Sims (2006), 131.

63 Anderson (2008), 189.

64 Janusek (2008), 305.

65 Janusek (2008), 250.

66 Janusek (2008), 252.

67 Janusek (2008), 262.

68 Janusek (2008), 256.

69 Janusek (2008), 291.

70 BBC. (2010). 'Evo Morales sworn in as Bolivia's 'spiritual leader'.' Available at: http://news.bbc.co.uk/2/hi/americas/8473899.stm

71 Kojan, D. (2008). 'Paths of power and politics: Historical narratives at the Bolivian site of Tiwanaku.' In Habu, J., Fawcett, C., and Matsunaga, J. M. (eds.). *Evaluating Multiple Narratives: Beyond Nationalist, Colonialist, Imperialist Archaeologies.* New York: Springer, pp. 69–85.

12. Angkor and the Khmer

 1 Groslier, B.-P. quoted on page 115, Zephir, T. (1998). *Khmer: Lost Empire of Cambodia.* London: Thames and Hudson.

 2 Dagens, B. (1995). *Angkor: Heart of an Asian Empire.* London: Thames and Hudson.

 3 Page 97, Coe, M. D. (2003). *Angkor and the Khmer Civilization.* London: Thames and Hudson.

 4 Coe (2003), 101.

 5 Coe (2003), 102–103, 106.

 6 Coe (2003), 108; Zephir (1998), 58.

 7 Coe (2003), 116.

 8 Coe (2003), 117–121.

 9 Coe (2003), 122.

10 Coe (2003), 125.

11 Coe (2003), 141.

12 Quoted in Coe (2003), 135.

13 Coe (2003), 133–144.

14 Coe (2003), 130; Zephir (1998), 91.

15 Coe (2003), 130.

16 Page 6750, Buckley, B. M. et al. (2010). 'Climate as a contributing factor in the demise of Angkor, Cambodia.' *Proceedings of the National Academy of Sciences* 107(15): 6748–6752.

17 Dumarcay, J. and Royere, P. (2001). *Cambodian Architecture, Eighth to Thirteenth Centuries.* Leiden: Brill; Groslier, B.-P. (1979). 'La cite hydraulique angkorienne: Exploitation ou surexploitation du sol?' *Bulletin de l'Ecole Francaise d'Extreme-Orient* 66: 161–202.

18 Coe (2003), 146–147.

19 Coe (2003), 147; pages 156–160, Higham, C. (2001). *The Civilization of Angkor.* London: Phoenix.

20 Higham (2001), 134.

21 Higham (2001), 160.

22 Coe (2003), 147.

23 Buckley et al. (2010).

24 Day, M. B. et al. (2012). 'Paleoenvironmental history of the West Baray, Angkor (Cambodia).' *Proceedings of the National Academy of Sciences* 109(4): 1046–1051; Stone, R. (2009). 'Divining Angkor.' *National Geographic* 216(1): 26–55.

25 Coe (2003), 191; page 170, Taylor, K. W. (1999). 'The early kingdoms.' In Tarling, N. (ed.). *The Cambridge History of Southeast Asia. Volume One Part One. From Early Times to c. 1500.* Cambridge: Cambridge University Press, pp. 137–182.

26 Coe (2003), 192.

27 Coe (2003), 208.

28 Zephir (1998), 115.

29 Page 113, Hagesteijn, R. (1987). 'The Angkor state: Rise, fall and in between.' In Claeseen, H. J. M. and Van De Velde, P. (eds.). *Early State Dynamics (Studies in Human Society. Vol. 2).* Leiden: Brill, pp. 154–169.

30 Page 244, Vickery, M. (1985). 'The reign of Suryavarman I and royal factionalism at Angkor.' *Journal of Southeast Asian Studies* 16(2): 226–244.

31 Also Higham (2001), 70

32 Coe (2003), 108; Higham (2001), 70.

33 Page 113, Hagesteijn, R. R. (1986). "'Trading places': Political leadership in early south east Asian states.' In Van Bakel, M. A., Hagesteijn, R. R., and Van De Velde, P. (eds.). *Private Politics: A Multi-Disciplinary Approach to 'Big-Man' Systems.* Volume 1. Leiden: Brill, pp. 105–116.

34 Coe (2003), 109; Higham (2001), 73–75.

35 Coe (2003), 112.

36 Coe (112), 112.

37 Higham (2001), 93–94.

38 Coe (2003), 115.

39 Higham (2001), 107–109.

40 Coe (2003), 115.

41 Coe (2003), 122.

42 Higham (2001), 114.

43 Coe (2003), 115.

44 Coe (2003), 122.

45 Coe (2003), 122; Higham (2001), 120–121.

46 Coe (2003), 128.

47 Taylor (1999), 170.

48 Taylor (1999), 169.

49 Taylor (1999), 170.

50 Higham (2001), 9.

51 Zephir (1998), 92.

52 Coe (2003), 122–124.
53 Coe (2003), 128.
54 Coe (2003), 130.
55 Page 132, Thompson, A. (2006). 'Buddhism in Cambodia: Rupture and continuity.' In Berkwitz, S. C. (ed.). *Buddhism in World Cultures: Comparative Perspectives.* Santa Barbara: ABC Clio, pp. 129–168.
56 Zephir (1998), 94–95.
57 Page 11, Corfield, J. (2009). *The History of Cambodia.* Santa Barbara: Greenwood Press.
58 Page 195, Jessup, H. I. (2004). *Art and Architecture of Cambodia.* London: Thames and Hudson.
59 Higham (2001), 140; Zephir (1998), 95.
60 Jessup (2004), 195–196
61 Coe (2003), 208.
62 Coe (2003), 210, 213.
63 Hagesteijn (1987), 154.
64 See Coe (2003), 131–194; and Zephir (1998), 104–109.
65 Taylor (1999), 163.
66 Coe (2003), 224.
67 Kiernan, B. (2008). *The Pol Pot Regime: Race, Power, and Genocide in Cambodia under the Khmer Rouge, 1975–1979.* New Haven: Yale University Press.
68 Page 54, Winter, T. (2007). *Post-Conflict Heritage, Postcolonial Tourism: Culture, Politics and Development at Angkor.* London: Routledge.
69 Winter (2007), 58.

13.   The Incredible Survival of Rapa Nui

1   Quoted on page 147, Hunt, T. L. and Lipo, C. P. (2011). *The Statues That Walked: Unravelling the Mystery of Easter Island.* New York: Free Press.
2   Palmer, J. L. (1870). 'A visit to Easter Island, or Rapa Nui, in 1868.' *Journal of the Royal Geographical Society of London* 40: 167–181.
3   Shepardson, B. L. (2005). 'The role of Rapa Nui (Easter Island) statuary as territorial boundary markers.' *Antiquity* 79: 169–178.
4   Page 517, Peiser, B. (2005). 'From genocide to ecocide: The rape of Rapa Nui.' *Energy and Environment* 16(3 & 4): 513–539.
5   Palmer, J. L. (1869–1870). 'A visit to Easter Island, or Rapa Nui.' *Proceedings of the Royal Geographical Society of London* 14(2): 108–120.
6   Palmer (1869–1870), 118.
7   Holton, G. E. (2004). 'Heyerdahl's Kon Tiki theory and the denial of the indigenous past.' *Anthropological Forum* 14(2): 163–181.
8   Page 210, Bahn, P. and Flenley, J. (1992). *Easter Island, Earth Island.* London: Thames and Hudson.
9   Peiser (2005), 513.
10 Diamond, J. (1995). 'Easter Island's end.' *Discover Magazine* 16(8): 63–69.

11 Page 72, Fischer, S. R. (2005). *Island at the End of the World: The Turbulent History of Easter Island*. London: Reaktion Books.

12 Mulloy, W. (1970). 'A speculative reconstruction of techniques of carving, transporting and erecting Easter Island statues.' *Archaeology & Physical Anthropology in Oceania* 5(1): 1–23.

13 Quoted on page 486, Hunt (2007). 'Rethinking Easter Island's ecological catastrophe.' *Journal of Archaeological Science* 34: 485–502.

14 Ponting, C. (2007). *A New Green History of the World: The Environment and the Collapse of the Great Civilizations*. Revised edition. London: Penguin.

15 Ponting (2007), 1–7.

16 Flenley, J. (2002). 'The Easter Island catastrophe.' Environmental catastrophes and recoveries in the Holocene, August 29 – September 2, 2002. Department of Geography & Earth Sciences, Brunel University, Uxbridge, UK. Available at: http://atlas-conferences.com/c/a/i/q/91.htm

17 Bahn and Flenley (1992), 214.

18 Diamond, J. (2005). *Collapse: How Societies Choose to Fail or Succeed*. London: Penguin.

19 Diamond (1995); Page 77, Flenley, J. and Bahn, P. (2002). *The Enigmas of Easter Island*. Oxford: Oxford University Press.

20 Flenley and Bahn (2002), 164.

21 Hunt, T. L. and Lipo, C. P. (2006). 'Late colonization of Easter Island.' *Science* 311: 1603–1606.

22 Flenley and Bahn (2002), 167, 176.

23 Lipo, C. P., Hunt, T. L., and Hundtoft, B. (2010). 'Stylistic variability of stemmed obsidian tools (mata'a), frequency seriation, and the scale of social interaction on Rapa Nui (Easter Island).' *Journal of Archaeological Science* 37: 2551–2561.

24 Pages 566–567, Pollard, J., Paterson, A., and Welham, K. (2010). '*Te Miro o'one*: the archaeology of contact on Rapa Nui (Easter Island).' *World Archaeology* 42(4): 562–580; pages 254–268, Routledge, K. (1919/2005). *The Mystery of Easter Island*. New York: Cosimo Classics.

25 Diamond (1995).

26 Diamond (2005), 90–91.

27 Hunt (2007), 498.

28 Fischer (2005), 87–92; Peiser (2005), 533.

29 Palmer (1869–1870), 119.

30 Metraux, A. (1937). 'The kings of Easter Island.' *The Journal of the Polynesian Society* 46(182): 41–62.

31 Hunter-Anderson, R. L. (1998). 'Human vs climatic impacts at Rapa Nui: Did people really cut down all those trees?' In Stevenson, C. M., Lee, G., and Morin, F. J. (eds.). *Easter Island in Pacific Context: South Seas Symposium*. Santa Barbara: Easter Island Foundation, pp. 85–99.

32 Shepardson (2005); pages 70–71, Tainter, J. A. (2006). 'Archaeology of overshoot and collapse.' *Annual Review of Anthropology* 35: 59–74.

33 Page 418, Mieth, A. and Bork, H.-R. (2010). 'Humans, climate or introduced rats – which is to blame for the woodland destruction on prehistoric Rapa Nui?' *Journal of Archaeological Science* 37: 417–426.

34 Flenley and Bahn (1992), 172–173.

35 Hunt, T. L. (2006). 'Rethinking the fall of Easter Island.' *American Scientist* 94: 412–419; Hunt (2007).

36 Routledge (1919/2005), 233.

37 Mieth and Bork (2010), 423.

38 Hunter-Anderson (1998), 92–93.

39 Page 52, Rull, V. et al. (2010). 'Palaeoecology of Easter Island: Evidence and uncertainties.' *Earth Science Reviews* 99: 50–60.

40 Diamond (1995).

41 Lipo, Hunt, and Hundtoft (2010).

42 Bahn and Flenley (1992), 98–100; Flenley and Bahn (2002), 96.

43 Stevenson, C. M., Ladefoged, T. N., and Haoa, S. (2007). 'An upland agricultural residence on Rapa Nui: Occupation of a *hare oka* (180473G) in the Vaitea region.' *Archaeology in Oceania* 42(2): 72–78.

44 Lightfoot, D. R. and Eddy, F. W. (1994). 'The agricultural utility of lithic-mulch gardens: Past and present.' *GeoJournal* 34(4): 425–437.

45 Pages 398–401, Hanbury-Tenison (2010). *The Oxford Book of Exploration.* Oxford: Oxford University Press.

46 Palmer (1870), 168–169.

47 Whistler, W. A. and Elevitch, C. R. (2006). '*Broussonetia papyrifera* (paper mulberry). Available at: www.agroforestry.net/tti/index.html

48 Best, E. (1925). *The Maori Canoe.* Wellington: W. A. G. Skinner, Government Printer, pp. 302–304; Flenley and Bahn (2002), 159.

49 Hanbury-Tenison (2010), 399.

50 Best (1925), 304–305, 310.

51 Hunter-Anderson (1998), 87–88.

52 Palmer (1870), 111.

53 Fischer (2005), 89.

54 Fischer (2005); Flenley and Bahn (2002), 156–157.

55 Lipo, Hunt, and Hundtoft (2010); Bloch, H. (2012). 'If only they could talk.' Available at: http://ngm.nationalgeographic.com/print/2012/07/easter-island/bloch-text

56 Hamilton, S., Thomas, M. S., and Whitehouse, R. (2011). 'Say it with stone: Constructing with stones on Easter Island.' *World Archaeology* 43(2): 167–190; Richards, C. et al. (2011). 'Road my body goes: Re-creating ancestors from stone at the great *moai* quarry of Rano Raraku, Rapa Nui (Easter Island).' *World Archaeology* 43(2): 191–210.

57 Routledge (1919/2005), 167–174.

58 Hunt and Lipo (2011), 153.

59 Page 382, Anderson, A. (2002). 'Faunal collapse, landscape change and settlement history in Remote Oceania.' *World Archaeology* 33: 375–390.

60 Hunt and Lipo (2011), 148–153.

61 Pollard, Paterson, and Welham (2010).

62 Rainbird, P. (2002). 'A message for our future? The Rapa Nui (Easter Island) ecodisaster and Pacific island environments.' *World Archaeology* 33: 436–451.

63 Rainbird (2002), 448.

64 Peiser (2005).

65 Mulrooney, M. A. et al. (2009). 'The myth of AD 1680: New evidence from Hanga Ho'onu, Rapa Nui (Easter Island).' *Rapa Nui Journal* 23(2): 94–105; Mulrooney, M. A. et al. (2010). 'Empirical assessment of a pre-European societal collapse on Rapa Nui (Easter Island).' In Wallin, P. and Martinsson-Wallin, H. (eds.). *The Gotland Papers: Selected Papers from the VII International Conference on Easter Island and the Pacific: Migration, Identity, and Cultural Heritage.* Visby: Gotland University Press, pp. 141–154.

66 Stevenson, C. M. et al. (2015). 'Variation in Rapa Nui (Easter Island) land use indicates production and population peaks prior to European contact.' *Proceedings of the National Academy of Sciences. Early Edition.* Available at: www.pnas.org/cgi/doi/10.1073/pnas.1420712112

67 Fischer (2005), 135–198.

68 Bloch (2012).

69 Page 87, McLaughlin, S. (2004). '*Rongorongo* and the rock art of Easter Island.' *Rapa Nui Journal* 18(2): 87–94.

14. Conclusions

1 Quoted on page 3, Seitz, J. L. and Hite, K. A. (2012). *Global Issues: An Introduction.* Fourth edition. Chichester: Wiley-Blackwell.

2 The Guardian. (2015). 'ISIS extremists bulldoze ancient Assyrian site near Mosul.' Available at: www.theguardian.com/world/2015/mar/05/islamic-state-isis-extremists-bulldoze-ancient-nimrud-site-mosul-iraq

3 Matthews, M. (2009). 'Apocalypse Now: Breakdown or breakthrough?' *Psychological Perspectives* 52: 482–494.

4 'One in seven (14%) global citizens believe end of the world is coming in their lifetime.' Available at: www.ipsos-na.com/news-polls/pressrelease.aspx?id=5610

5 Miller, E. D. (2012). 'Apocalypse now? The relevance of religion for beliefs about the end of the world.' *Journal of Beliefs and Values: Studies in Religion & Education* 33(1): 111–115.

6 Milbraith, L. W. (1996). 'Envisioning a sustainable society.' In Slaughter, R. A. (ed.). *New Thinking for a New Millennium.* London: Routledge, 185–197.

7 Page 372, Williams, R. P. (2002). Rethinking disaster-induced collapse in the demise of the Andean highland states: Wari and Tiwanaku. *World Archaeology* 33: 361–374.

8 Page 11, Diamond, J. (2005). *Collapse: How Societies Choose to Fail or Succeed.* London: Penguin.

9 Pages 141–142, Dincauze, D. F. (2000). *Environmental Archaeology: Principles and Practice.* Cambridge: Cambridge University Press.

10 Page 173, Stone, R. R. (2012). *Art of the Andes: From Chavin to Inca.* Third edition. London: Thames and Hudson.

11 Tennie, C., Call, J., and Tomasello, M. (2009). 'Ratcheting up the ratchet: On the evolution of cumulative culture.' *Philosophical Transactions of the Royal Society B* 364: 2405–2415.

12 Rogers, A. D. and Laffoley, D. d'A. (2011). International Earth system expert workshop on ocean stresses and impacts. Summary report. IPSO Oxford, 18pp.

13 Hoffman, M. et al. (2010). 'The impact of conservation on the status of the world's vertebrates.' *Science* 330: 1503–1509.

14 Barnosky, A. D. et al. (2011). 'Has the Earth's sixth mass extinction already arrived?' *Nature* 471(7336): 51–57.

15 Milbraith (1996), 186–187.

16 Page 57, Zencey, E. (1988). 'The present case: Apocalypse and ecology.' *North American Review* 273: 54–57.

17 UNEP Global Environment Alert Service (2012). *One Planet, How Many People? A Review of Earth's Carrying Capacity.* Available at: http://na.unep .net/geas/getUNEPPageWithArticleIDScript.php?article_id=88

18 Stamp, G. (2010). *Lost Victorian Britain: How the Twentieth Century Destroyed the Nineteenth Century's Architectural Masterpieces.* London: Aurum Press; Worsley, G. (2011). *England's Lost Houses: From the Archives of Country Life.* London: Aurum Press.

19 Stone, L. (1991). 'The public and the private in the stately homes of England, 1500–1990.' *Social Research* 58(1): 227–251.

20 Zhou, L. et al. (2004). 'Evidence for a significant urbanization effect in climate on China.' *Proceedings of the National Academy of Sciences* 101(26): 9540–9544.

21 For example, Lord Rogers' 2005 report *Towards a Strong Urban Renaissance.* Urban Task Force. Available at: http://www.integreatplus.com/sites/ default/files/towards_a_strong_urban_renaissance.pdf

22 Linebaugh, K. (2011). 'Detroit's population crashes.' *The Wall Street Journal.* Available at: http://online.wsj.com/article/SB100014240527487 04461304576216850733151470.html

23 Whitford, D. (2009). 'Can farming save Detroit?' *CNNMoney.com.* Available at: http://money.cnn.com/2009/12/29/news/economy/farming_ detroit.fortune/. Dolan, M. (2010). 'Less than a full service city.' *The Wall Street Journal.* Available at: http://online.wsj.com/article/SB10001424052 748703727804576011761173192434.html

24 Broadway, M. (2009). 'Growing urban agriculture in North American cities: The example of Milwaukee.' *Focus on Geography* 52(3): 23–30; Platt, E. (2011). 'Nine meals away from anarchy.' *New Statesman* (27th June): 24–27.

25 Page 143, Krautheimer, R. (2000). *Rome: Profile of a City, 312–1308.* Princeton: Princeton University Press.

26 McPhail, R. I., Galinie, H., and Verhaege, F. (2002). 'A future for dark earth?' *Antiquity* 77(296): 349–358.

27 Krautheimer (2000), 66.

28 Page 904, Grafton, A., Most, G. W., and Settis, S. (eds.). (2010). *The Classical Tradition*. Cambridge: Harvard University Press.

29 Quoted on page vii, Rees, M. J. (2008). 'Foreword.' In Bostrom, N. and Cirkovic, M. M. (2008). *Global Catastrophic Risks*. Oxford: Oxford University Press, pp. vii–xi.

30 Bostrom, N. and Cirkovic, M. M. (2008). *Global Catastrophic Risks*. Oxford: Oxford University Press.

31 Castells, M. (2010). *The Rise of the Network Society*. Second edition. Chichester: Wiley-Blackwell.

32 Knight, L. (2013). 'Cyprus crisis: What are capital controls and why does it need them. Available at: www.bbc.co.uk/news/business-21937615

33 Page 17, The World Economic Forum. (2014). *Global Risks 2014, Ninth Edition*. Geneva: World Economic Forum.

34 Fan, K.-W. (2010). 'Climatic change and dynastic cycles in Chinese history: A review.' *Climatic Change* 101: 565–573; Li, F. (2006). *Landscape and Power in Early China: The Crisis and Fall of the Western Zhou*. Cambridge: Cambridge University Press; Zhang, D. D. et al. (2005). 'Climate change, social unrest and dynastic transition in ancient China.' *China Science Bulletin* 50: 137–144; Zhang, D. D. et al. (2006). 'Climatic change, wars and dynastic cycles in China over the last millennium.' *Climatic Change* 76: 459–477.

35 Huffman, T. N. (1972). 'The rise and fall of Zimbabwe.' *Journal of African History* 13(3): 353–366; Huffman, T. N. (2008). 'Mapungubwe and Great Zimbabwe: The origin and spread of social complexity in southern Africa.' *Journal of Anthropological Archaeology* 28: 37–54; Pikirayi, I. (2001). *The Zimbabwe Culture: Origins and Decline of Southern Zambezian States*. Walnut Creek: AltaMira; Pikirayi, I. (2005). 'The demise of Great Zimbabwe, AD 1420–1550: An environmental re-appraisal.' In Green, A. and Leech, R. (eds.). *Cities in the World, 1500–2000*. Post-Medieval Archaeology, Monograph 3. Leeds: Society for Post-Medieval Archaeology; Pikirayi, I. (2013). 'Great Zimbabwe in historical archaeology: Reconceptualizing decline, abandonment, and reoccupation of an ancient polity, AD 1450–1900.' *Historical Archaeology* 47(1): 26–37.

36 Page 206, Demarest, A. (2014). 'The Classic Maya collapse, water, and economic change in Mesoamerica: Critique and alternatives from the 'wet' zone.' In Iannone, G. (ed.). *The Great Maya Droughts in Cultural Context: Case Studies in Resilience and Vulnerability*. Boulder: University Press of Colorado, pp. 177–206.

37 Seitz and Hite (2012).

38 Page 133, Orwell, G. (1940). 'My country left or right.' In *Essays*. London: Penguin, pp. 133–138.

Bibliographical Essay

The interested reader or student of collapse may wish to delve deeper or follow up on specific instances of collapse, but the literature on collapse is extensive and is to be found spread across specialist and popular books and academic journals of many disciplines. This essay describes only a few of those books and journals that are important or easy to get hold of (the reader should also refer to the endnotes for each chapter). More extensive bibliographies can be found in G. D. Middleton (2012) 'Nothing lasts forever: Environmental discourses on the collapse of past societies.' *Journal of Archaeological Research* 20(3): 257–307 and in the works referred to below.

Useful general archaeology books are *The Human Past: World Prehistory & The Development of Human Societies* (second edition, Thames and Hudson, 2009) edited by Chris Scarre, which is an excellent and affordable introduction to many of the societies and traditions examined in this book; it also contains some discussion of collapses and transformations. The *Oxford Handbooks in Archaeology* (and *Handbooks in Classics and Ancient History*) series is good, with volumes devoted to specific areas such as Anatolia, Bronze Age Greece, the Levant, and Mesoamerica. The three-volume *Cambridge World Prehistory* (Cambridge University Press, 2014), edited by Colin Renfrew and Paul Bahn, also contains much relevant discussion.

1. Introducing Collapse

In addition to this one, three other new volumes on collapse have been/are being published in 2017. These are: Scott A. Johnson's *Why Did Civilizations Fail?* (Routledge), which adopts an environmental slant in an examination of several instances of collapse, but Johnson does not seek to explain any of these solely by blaming environmental problems, which makes it a more useful contribution to the literature. The other two are edited volumes, quite different in nature. The first is: Tim Cunningham and Jan Driessen's (eds.) *Crisis to Collapse: The Archaeology of Social Breakdown*, the published results

423

of an workshop of archaeologists, working on different areas and cultures, at Louvain University in 2015; the second addresses collapse as a wider social discourse across multiple genres and will be important for examining how collapse is imaged and imagined – Alison Vogelaar, Brack Hale, and Alexandra Peat (eds.) *The Discourses of Environmental Collapse* (Routledge).

Still key readings are the two books published in 1988: Joseph A. Tainter *The Collapse of Complex Societies* (Cambridge University Press) and Norman Yoffee and George L. Cowgill (eds.) *Collapse of Ancient States and Civilizations* (University of Arizona Press). The first reviews numerous cases of collapse, analyses various explanatory theories, and proposes an economic theory of collapse; however, it is now dated in its case studies and sources. The second offers an important series of useful and stimulating essays by different authors focusing on examples and theories of collapse and decline. David Webster's *The Fall of the Ancient Maya: Solving the Mystery of the Maya Collapse* (Thames and Hudson, 2002), whilst specifically addressing the Classic Maya collapse, offers a good introduction to collapse generally and to many explanatory theories which crop up in other cases.

Jared Diamond's *Collapse: How Societies Choose to Fail or Succeed* (Penguin, 2005) includes several case studies of ancient collapses, generally attributing them to ecological damage or environmental change. Diamond's book must be read alongside the essays in Patricia A. McAnany and N. Yoffee (eds.) *Questioning Collapse: Human Resilience, Ecological Vulnerability, and the Aftermath of Empire* (Cambridge University Press, 2010); written by specialist archaeologists and historians. This volume offers different interpretations of and perspectives on the collapses that Diamond discusses and focusses more on the resilience of human communities. In addition, J. A. Tainter's 2008 essay 'Collapse, sustainability, and the environment: How authors choose to fail or succeed.' *Reviews in Anthropology* 37: 342–371 is a thoughtful review of Diamond's and three other authors' books on collapse, with some general discussion of his own views.

For climate collapse theories, starting points are Harvey Weiss and Raymond S. Bradley's 2001 article 'What drives societal collapse?' *Science* 291: 609–610 and the popular article by Michael Marshall (2012) 'Climate change: The great civilization destroyer.' *New Scientist* 215(2876): 32–36; also see the books of *Brian Fagan: The Little Ice Age: How Climate Made History, 1300–1850* (Basic Books, 2000), *The Long Summer: How Climate Changed Civilization* (Basic Books, 2004), *The Great Warming: Climate Change and the Rise and Fall of Civilizations* (Bloomsbury, 2008), and *Floods, Famines, and Emperors: El Nino and the Fate of Civilizations* (revised edition, Basic Books, 2009) and Ian Whyte's *World Without end? Environmental Disaster and the Collapse of Empires* (I.B. Tauris, 2008). For environmental damage theories, see Clive Ponting's *A New Green History of the World: The Environment and the Collapse of the Great Civilizations* (revised edition, Penguin, 2007) and, for an archaeological account, Charles L. Redman's *Human Impact on Ancient Environments* (University of Arizona Press, 1999).

Three recent articles address collapse from an archaeological perspective: Karl Butzer (2012) 'Collapse, environment, and society.' *Proceedings of the National Academy of Sciences* 109(10): 3632–3639, K. Butzer and Georgina

H. Endfield (2012) 'Critical perspectives on historical collapse.' *Proceedings of the National Academy of Sciences* 109(10): 3628–3631, and Guy D. Middleton (2012). 'Nothing lasts forever: Environmental discourses on the collapse of past societies.' *Journal of Archaeological Research* 20(3): 257–307. These authors are sceptical about purely environmental explanations of collapse. Andrew Lawler offers a brief but interesting discussion of the current views of several archaeologists in 'Collapse? What collapse? Societal change revisited.' *Science* 330: 907–909 (2010).

Two works focus specifically on what happens after collapse. The first is J. A. Tainter 'Post-collapse societies.' In G. Barker (ed.) *Companion Encyclopedia of Archaeology* (Routledge, 1999), pp. 988–1039 and the second is Glenn M. Schwartz and John J. Nichols (eds.) *After Collapse: The Regeneration of Complex Societies* (University of Arizona Press, 2006). Both offer general comments on collapse and post-collapse periods as well as examine specific cases; the latter, a very useful book, is up-to-date and written by subject specialists in archaeology.

2. Egypt: The Old Kingdom Falls

An important discussion of the Old Kingdom collapse and the First Intermediate Period is Stephan Seidlmayer 'The First Intermediate Period (c. 2160–2055 BC).' In I. Shaw (ed.) *The Oxford History of Ancient Egypt* (Oxford University Press, 2000), pp. 108–136. Environmental approaches are found in the still influential paper by Barbara Bell (1971) 'The Dark Ages in ancient history: 1. The first Dark Age in Egypt.' *American Journal of Archaeology* 75: 1–26 and Fekri A. Hassan (2007) 'Droughts, famine, and the collapse of the Old Kingdom: Re-reading Ipuwer.' In Z. Hawass and J. Richards (eds.) *The Art and Archaeology of Ancient Egypt: Essays in Honour of David B. O'Connor. Vol. 1.* (Conseil Supreme des Antiquites de'l Egypte, 2007), pp. 357–377. The last two should be read along with Nadine Moeller (2005) 'The First Intermediate Period: A time of famine and climate change?' *Ägypten und Levante* 15: 153–167 as well as Seidlmayer (2000).

General works that also discuss the collapse and change, the FIP and the sources for it, are Marc Van De Mieroop's *A History of Ancient Egypt* (Blackwell, 2011) and Toby Wilkinson's *The Rise and Fall of Ancient Egypt* (Bloomsbury, 2010).

3. Akkad: The End of the World's First Empire

Benjamin R. Foster's *The Age of Agade: Inventing Empire in Ancient Mesopotamia* (Routledge, 2016) came out too late to be referred to in the text, but contains a historical overview and a section about Akkadian collapse. Mario Liverani's *The Ancient Near East: History, Society and Economy* (Routledge, 2014) covers a swath of Near Eastern history from the Neolithic to Persian times, in which various empires and collapses, including Akkadian and Ur III, are examined.

Specific works on the Akkadian collapse include: H. Weiss and M.-A. Courty *et al.* (1993) 'The genesis and collapse of third millennium north Mesopotamian civilization.' *Science* 261: 995–1004, and later works by Weiss, which should be read along with Richard L. Zettler (2003) 'Reconstructing the world of ancient Mesopotamia: Divided beginnings and holistic history.' *Journal of Economic and Social History of the Orient* 46: 3–45 [republished in N. Yoffee and B. L. Crowell (eds.). (2006). *Excavating Asian History: Interdisciplinary Studies in Archaeology and History.* University of Arizona Press, pp. 113–159.].

An interesting assessment of environmental hazards in Mesopotamia is Tate Paulette 'Domination and resilience in Bronze Age Mesopotamia.' In J. Cooper and P. Sheets (eds.) *Surviving Sudden Environmental Change: Answers from Archaeology* (University of Colorado Press, 2012), pp. 167–195. Arne Wossink's *Challenging Climate Change: Competition and Cooperation among Pastoralists and Agriculturalists in Northern Mesopotamia (c. 3000–1600 BC)* (Sidestone Press, 2009) is a recent review. Also key is Aage Westenholz's 'The Old Akkadian Period: History and culture.' In Sallaberger, W. and Westenholz, A. *Mesopotamien. Akkade-Zeit und Ur III-Zeit.* Orbis biblicus et Orientalis 160/3 (Universitatsverlag Freiburg Schweiz, 1999), pp. 17–117.

Mario Liverani's chapter 'The fall of the Assyrian empire: Ancient and modern interpretations.' In S. E. Alcock, T. N. D'Altroy, K. D. Morrison, and C. M. Sinopoli (eds.) *Empires* (Cambridge University Press, 2001), pp. 374–391 is also a useful and interesting discussion of Mesopotamian collapses and what they meant within Mesopotamian culture.

General works that include discussion of collapses in the Near East include M. Van De Mieroop *A History of the Ancient Near East, ca. 3000–323 BC* (second edition, Blackwell, 2007) and Gwendolyn Leick's very readable *Mesopotamia: The Invention of the City* (Penguin, 2001).

4. The Indus Valley: A Truly Lost Civilisation?

The starting place for views on the Harappan culture is now Robin Coningham and Ruth Young's *The Archaeology of South Asia: From the Indus to Asoka, c. 6500 BCE – 200 CE* (Cambridge University Press, 2015), which has a full discussion of the transformation of Indus society. Rita Wright's *The Ancient Indus: Urbanism, Economy, and Society* (Cambridge University Press, 2010) is another recent discussion. J. M. Kenoyer's *Ancient Cities of the Indus Valley Civilization* (Oxford University Press, 1998) is a very readable and extremely attractive and well-illustrated introduction to the archaeology and culture of the Indus Valley, with a chapter on the transition from the Harappan to the Late Harappan and historic periods. His chapter 'The archaeological heritage of Pakistan: From the Palaeolithic to the Indus civilization.' In Roger D. Long (ed.) *A History of Pakistan* (Oxford University Press, 2015), pp. 1–90 is also a good recent summary.

An article in *Science* brings together a range of ideas on the Indus collapse: A. Lawler (2008) 'Indus collapse: The end or beginning of an Asian culture?' *Science* 320: 1281–1283. Important discussion is also found in Gregory L. Possehl (1997) 'The transformation of the Indus civilization.' *Journal of*

World Prehistory 11: 425–472, which has been republished in Possehl's *The Indus Civilization: A Contemporary Perspective* (AltaMira Press, 2002).

5. The End of Minoan Crete

Treatment of the Minoan collapse can be found in Jan Driessen and Colin F. MacDonald *The Troubled Island. Minoan Crete Before and After the Santorini Eruption* (Aegaeum 17, University of Liege, 1997), which discusses the possible long-term social effects of the Santorini/Thera eruption. A review of (fairly) recent archaeological research on the period can be found in Paul Rehak and John G. Younger's article 'Neopalatial, Final palatial and Postpalatial Crete.' In T. Cullen (ed.) *Aegean Prehistory: A Review* (Archaeological Institute of America, 2001), pp. 383–473.

There are also relevant chapters in two recent handbooks: Erik Hallager (2010) 'Crete.' in E. H. Cline (ed.) *The Oxford Handbook of the Bronze Age Aegean* (Oxford University Press, 2010), pp. 149–159; and Laura Preston 'Late Minoan II to IIIB Crete.' In C. W. Shelmerdine (ed.) *The Cambridge Companion to the Aegean Bronze Age* (Cambridge University Press, 2008), pp. 310–326, as well as the older Ken A. Wardle 'The palace civilizations of Crete and Greece.' In B. Cunliffe (ed.) *The Oxford Illustrated Prehistory of Europe* (Oxford University Press, 1994), pp. 202–243.

For Crete from 1200 BC and after, see Saro Wallace's *Ancient Crete: From Successful Collapse to Democracy's Alternatives, Twelfth to Fifth Centuries BC* (Cambridge University Press, 2010).

6. The Kingdoms of Mycenaean Greece

There are several books on the collapse, the latest, with a good discussion of the archaeological background and the various theories, is Eric Cline's *1177 BC: The Year Civilization Collapsed* (Princeton University Press, 2014), which deals with Greece and the eastern Mediterranean. Also see Oliver Dickinson *The Aegean from Bronze Age to Iron Age: Continuity and Change Between the Twelfth and Eighth Centuries* (Routledge, 2006) for the collapse period and after. Robert Drews' *The End of the Bronze Age: Changes in Warfare and the Catastrophe ca. 1200 BC* (Princeton University Press, 1993) is still good and critically examines a range of theories; he offers a military explanation of the collapse. Guy D. Middleton *The Collapse of Palatial Society in Late Bronze Age Greece and the Postpalatial Period* (Archaeopress, 2010) is a fairly up-to-date examination, which refers also to the Hittite and Classic Maya collapses.

There are several useful chapters in recent archaeological handbooks: Sigrid Deger-Jalkotzy 'Decline, destruction, aftermath.' In C. W. Shelmerdine (ed.).*The Cambridge Companion to the Aegean Bronze Age* (Cambridge University Press, 2008), pp. 387–415 and Oliver Dickinson 'The collapse at the end of the Bronze Age.' In Cline, E. H. (ed.) *The Oxford Handbook of the Bronze Age Aegean* (Oxford University Press, 2010), pp. 483–490.

Older but still useful is Mervyn Popham 'The collapse of Aegean civilization at the end of the Late Bronze Age.' In B. Cunliffe (ed.) *The Oxford Illustrated Prehistory of Europe* (Oxford University Press, 1994), pp. 277–303.

An new paper by A. Bernard Knapp and Sturt W. Manning, 'Crisis in context: The end of the Late Bronze Age in the eastern Mediterranean.' in the *American Journal of Archaeology* 120(1), January 2016, appeared too late to be properly considered properly in this book. However, it is an up-to-date and thorough treatment, which questions the increasingly prominent climatic data and explanations and privileges human agency.

7. The Hittites and the Eastern Mediterranean

For Hittite history, Trevor Bryce's *The Kingdom of the Hittites* (new edition, Oxford University Press, 2005) is the standard work in English with a good discussion of the collapse and the eastern Mediterranean around 1200 BC. Marc Van De Mieroop's *The Eastern Mediterranean in the Age of Ramesses II* (Blackwell, 2010) also deals with collapse in the eastern Mediterranean, emphasising social factors. Bryce's 2005 article 'The last days of Hattusa.' *Archaeology Odyssey* 8(1): 32–41, 51 is an interesting short treatment.

For the post-Hittite period, see T. Bryce *The World of the Neo-Hittite Kingdoms* (Oxford University Press, 2012) and J. D. Hawkins (2009) 'Cilicia, the Amuq, and Aleppo: New light in a dark age.' *Near Eastern Archaeology* 72: 164–172.

On Cyprus see A. Bernard Knapp's *The Archaeology of Cyprus: From Earliest Prehistory through the Bronze Age* (Cambridge University Press, 2013); and Louise Steel's *Cyprus Before History: From the Earliest Settlers to the End of the Bronze Age* (Duckworth, 2004).

For the eastern Mediterranean more generally, and the Sea Peoples, the literature is vast. Good sources include: Ann E. Killebrew and Gunnar Lehmann's edited volume *The Philistines and Other 'Sea Peoples' in Text and Archaeology* (Society of Biblical Literature, 2013); A. B. Knapp and Peter van Dommelen (eds.). *The Cambridge Prehistory of the Bronze and Iron Age Mediterranean* (Cambridge University Press, 2014); and Margreet L. Steiner and Ann E. Killebrew (eds.) *The Oxford Handbook of the Archaeology of the Levant c. 8000-332 BCE* (Oxford University Press, 2014). These contain much up-to-date evidence and opinion and the reader can chase the copious references for other views.

8. The Fall of the Western Roman Empire

There are plenty of books dealing with the collapse of Rome or parts of the empire. A few recent works include: Neil Christie *The Fall of the Western Roman Empire: An Archaeological & Historical Perspective* (Bloomsbury, 2011), which, as the title says, combines archaeological and historical approaches in a refreshing way; Adrian Goldsworthy *How Rome Fell: Death of a Superpower* (Yale University Press, 2009); Guy Halsall *Barbarian Migrations and the*

Roman West, 357–568 (Cambridge University Press, 2007); Peter Heather *The Fall of the Roman Empire: A New History* (Pan Macmillan, 2005); and Bryan Ward-Perkins *The Fall of Rome and the End of Civilization* (Oxford University Press, 2005) are all good too. James J. O'Donnell *The Ruin of the Roman Empire: A New History* (Ecco, 2008) offers some different perspectives.

Donal Kagan's *The End of the Roman Empire* (D. C. Heath, 1992) contains excerpts from older works addressing the fall of Rome. Thomas F. X. Noble (ed.) *From Roman Provinces to Medieval Kingdoms* (Routledge, 2006) gathers together more recent essays on a number of relevant topics.

For Late Antiquity, the classic book is Peter Brown's influential *The World of Late Antiquity* (Thames and Hudson, 1971). Two papers also worth reading for their perspectives are: Greg W. Bowersock (1996) 'The vanishing paradigm of the fall of Rome.' *Bulletin of the American Academy of Arts and Sciences* 49: 29–43; and Walter Goffart (2008). 'Rome's final conquest: The Barbarians.' *History Compass* 6(3): 855–883.

A series of interesting and relevant articles were published in the *Journal of Late Antiquity* 2(1) in 2009.

Dealing with Rome and post-imperial times two chapters in George Holmes (ed.) *The Oxford Illustrated History of Medieval Europe* (Oxford, 1988) are relevant: Thomas Brown's 'The transformation of the Roman Mediterranean, 400–900,' pp. 1–62; and Edward James' 'The northern world in the Dark Ages, 400–900,' pp. 63–114.

John Drinkwater and Hugh Elton's *Fifth-Century Gaul: A Crisis of Identity?* (Cambridge University Press, 1992) is a scholarly work with chapters dealing with aspects of change in post-Roman Gaul. Also of interest are Chris Wickham's *The Inheritance of Rome: A History of Europe from 400 to 1000* (Penguin, 2009); and Peter Wells' *Barbarians to Angels: The Dark Ages Reconsidered* (W. W. Norton, 2008).

Useful general textbooks are: Stephen Mitchell's *A History of the Later Roman Empire, AD 284–641* (Blackwell, 2007); and David Potter's *Rome in the Ancient World: From Romulus to Justinian* (Thames and Hudson, 2009). Sam Moorhead and David Stuttard's *AD 410: The Year that Shook Rome* (British Museum Press, 2010) is a good well-illustrated book on the sack of Rome.

9. Collapse and Revolution in Mesoamerica

On Rio Viejo, see Arthur A. Joyce *et al.* (2014). 'Political transformations and the everyday in Postclassic Oaxaca.' *Ancient Mesoamerica* 25(2): 389–410; A. A. Joyce and E. T. Weller (2007). 'Commoner rituals, resistance, and the Classic-to-Postclassic transition in ancient Mesoamerica.' In N. Gonlin and J. C. Lohse (eds.) *Commoner Ritual and Ideology in Ancient Mesoamerica* (University Press of Colorado), pp. 143–184; and A. A. Joyce, L. Arnaud Bustamente, and M. Levine (2001). 'Commoner power: A case study from the Classic Period collapse on the Oaxaca coast.' *Journal of Archaeological Method and Theory* 8(4): 343–385.

For Teotihuacan, recent work is summarised in Deborah L. Nichols (2015) 'Teotihuacan.' *Journal of Archaeological Research* 24(1): 1–74, which contains extensive references. An important new textbook is George L. Cowgill *Ancient Teotihuacan: Early Urbanism in Central Mexico* (Cambridge University Press, 2015), which devotes a chapter to the collapse. There are also relevant chapters in Takeshi Inomata and Ronald W. Webb (eds.) *The Archaeology of Settlement Abandonment in Middle America* (University of Utah Press, 2003), in particular those by Linda Manzanilla, 'The abandonment of Teotihuacan,' pp. 91–102, and William T. Sanders, 'Collapse and abandonment in Middle America,' pp. 193–202; the book is useful for considering the phenomenon of site abandonment generally. William T. Sanders and S. T. Evans' chapter 'Rulership and palaces in Teotihuacan.' In J. J. Christie and P. J. Sarro (eds.) *Palaces and Power in the Americas: From Peru to the Northwest Coast* (University of Texas Press, 2006), pp. 256–284 discusses the changes through time at Teotihuacan and also its foreign relations.

Rene Millon's chapter 'The last years of Teotihuacan dominance.' In N. Yoffee and G. L. Cowgill (eds.) *The Collapse of Ancient States and Civilizations* (University of Arizona Press, 1988), pp. 102–164 is still important. Two essays by George Cowgill are also still useful: (1997) 'State and society at Teotihuacan, Mexico.' *Annual Review of Anthropology* 26: 129–161 and (1997). 'An update on Teotihuacan.' *Antiquity* 82: 962–975. A paper by Sarah C. Clayton will also be of great relevance but appeared too late to be consulted here: 'After Teotihuacan: A view of collapse and reorganization from the southern Basin of Mexico.' *American Anthropologist* 118(1): 104-120 (2016).

There is now *The Oxford Handbook of the Archaeology of Mesoamerican Archaeology*, edited by Deborah L. Nichols and Christopher A. Pool (Oxford University Press 2012) The general textbook on ancient Mexico by Susan Toby Evans contains good discussion of Teotihuacan, as well as other Mesoamerican sites and collapses: *Ancient Mexico & Central America* (Thames and Hudson, 2004). Also useful is David Webster and S. T. Evans 'Mesoamerican civilization.' In C. Scarre (ed.) *The Human Past: World Prehistory & the Development of Human Societies* (second edition, Thames and Hudson, 2009), pp. 594–639.

10. The Classic Maya Collapse

As with the Roman Empire, there are many contributions to the debate on the Maya collapse. Arthur A. Demarest's 2013 paper 'The collapse of the Classic Maya kingdoms of the southwestern Peten: Implications for the end of the Classic Maya civilization.' In M.-C. Arnauld and A. Breton (eds.) *Millenary Maya Societies: Past Crises and Resilience*. Electronic document, published online at Mesoweb: www.mesoweb.com/publications/MMS/2_Demarest.pdf is an excellent starting point as is James J. Aimers' (2007) paper 'What Maya collapse? Terminal Classic variation in the Maya Lowlands.' *Journal of Archaeological Research* 15: 329–377, which reviews the many theories of collapse and current research up to the date of his paper. David Webster's *The Fall of the Ancient Maya: Solving the Mystery of the Maya*

Collapse (Thames and Hudson, 2002) also offers a very readable discussion of theories of collapse. All three of these are useful readings about collapse generally. Also see Webster's chapter 'The Classic Maya collapse.' In D. L. Nichols and C. A. Pool (eds.) *The Oxford Handbook of Mesoamerican Archaeology* (Oxford University Press, 2012), pp. 324–334. A new book will also be important: Gyles Iannone, Brett A. Houk, and Sonja A. Schwake (eds.) *Ritual, Violence, and the Fall of the Classic Maya Kings* (University of Florida Press, 2016). New works will keep appearing and views modified and refined.

For more in depth and specific research on numerous sites the chapters in A. A. Demarest, Prudence M. Rice, and Don S. Rice (eds.) *Terminal Classic in the Maya Lowlands: Collapse, Transition and Transformation* (University Press of Colorado, 2004) are important contributions.

For the megadrought theory of collapse, see Richardson B. Gill *The Great Maya Droughts: Water, Life, and Death* (University of New Mexico Press, 2000), which must be read with G. Iannone (ed.) *The Great Maya Droughts in Cultural Context: Case Studies in Resilience and Vulnerability* (University Press of Colorado, 2014).

Demarest's collapse chapter in his *Ancient Maya: The Rise and Fall of a Rainforest Civilization* (Cambridge University Press, 2004) focuses on the role of human conflict in the Maya collapse; a forthcoming new edition will present new evidence, ideas, and interpretations.

11. Collapse in the Andes

On the Moche, see Garth Bawden's *The Moche* (Blackwell, 1999) and more recently E. P. Benson's *The Worlds of the Moche on the North Coast of Peru* (University of Texas Press, 2012). Jeffrey Quilter (2002). 'Moche politics, religion, and warfare.' *Journal of World Prehistory* 16(2): 145–195 is a useful article.

Alan L. Kolata *The Tiwanaku: Portrait of an Andean Civilization* (Wiley-Blackwell, 1993) and John Wayne Janusek *Ancient Tiwanaku* (Cambridge University Press, 2008) both contain chapters on the Tiwanaku and Wari collapses, as well as discussions of the culture and interpretations of the Tiwanaku phenomenon. The Tiwanaku collapse is dealt with in depth in Janusek's fascinating 2004 article 'Collapse as cultural revolution: Power and identity in the Tiwanaku to Pacajes transition.' *Archaeological Papers of the American Anthropological Association* 14: 175–209, which gives interesting views on the nature of this particular collapse, some of which can be usefully applied to other examples.

12. Angkor and the Khmer

Good general accounts include Charles Higham's *The Civilization of Angkor* (Phoenix, 2001), Michael Coe's more archaeological and well-illustrated *Angkor and the Khmer Civilization* (Thames and Hudson, 2003), and Thierry Zephir's *Khmer: Lost Empire of Cambodia* (Thames and Hudson, 1998). Bruno Dagens' *Angkor: Heart of an Asian Empire* (Thames and Hudson, 1995) is a good, well-illustrated introduction to the city of Angkor. Also very useful is Miriam T. Stark (2006). 'From Funan to Angkor: Collapse and regeneration in Ancient Cambodia.' In Schwartz, G. M. and Nichols, J. J. (eds.). *After Collapse: The Regeneration of Complex Societies*. Tucson: Arizona University Press, pp. 144–167.

The environmentalist position can be found in: Richard Stone (2009). 'Divining Angkor.' *National Geographic* 216(1): 26–55; Mary Beth Day *et al.* (2012) 'Paleoenvironmental history of the West Baray, Angkor (Cambodia).' *Proceedings of the National Academy of Sciences* 109(4): 1046–1051 and Brendan Buckley *et al.* (2010). 'Climate as a contributing factor in the demise of Angkor, Cambodia.' *Proceedings of the National Academy of Sciences* 107(15): 6748–6752.

A useful introduction to wider southeast Asia, including Angkor and its neighbours, is Keith W. Taylor's chapter 'The early kingdoms.' In N. Tarling (ed.) *The Cambridge History of Southeast Asia. Volume One Part One. From Early Times to c. 1500* (Cambridge University Press, 1999), pp. 137–182.

13. The Incredible Survival of Rapa Nui

Christopher M. Stevenson *et al.* (2015). 'Variation in Rapa Nui (Easter Island) land use indicates production and population peaks prior to European contact.' *Proceedings of the National Academy of Sciences*. Available at: www.pnas .org/cgi/doi/10.1073/pnas.1420712112 provides a new interpretation of population changes on Easter Island and reviews recent and earlier views.

Useful works on Easter Island that discuss collapse are: Terry Hunt and Carl Lipo's *The Statues that Walked: Unravelling the Mystery of Easter Island* (New York: Free Press, 2011) and Steven R. Fischer (2005). *Island at the End of the World: The Turbulent History of Easter Island* (Reaktion Books, 2005); also John Flenley and Paul Bahn *The Enigmas of Easter Island* (Oxford University Press, 2002). T. Hunt and C. Lipo have also published a number of relevant papers on Easter Island the collapse.

A new book, J. J. Boersema's *The Survival of Easter Island: Dwindling Resources and Cultural Resilience* (Cambridge University Press, 2015), came out too late to be referred to properly here, but will contain relevant discussion of collapse and resilience on Easter Island.

14. Conclusions

A few sources of interest are: Daron Acemoglu and James A. Robinson's *Why Nations Fail: The Origins of Power Prosperity and Poverty* (Profile Books Ltd, 2012), which is a great antidote to the persistent determinist theories of development, with ideas applicable to ancient collapses; and Anthony D. Barnosky *et al.* (2011). 'Has the Earth's sixth mass extinction already arrived?' *Nature* 471(7336): 51–57; Nick Bostrom and Milan M. Cirkovic *Global Catastrophic Risks* (Oxford University Press, 2008); Michael Hoffman *et al.* (2010). 'The impact of conservation on the status of the world's vertebrates.' *Science* 330: 1503–1509; Trevor Palmer *Perilous Planet Earth: Catastrophes and*

Catastrophism through the Ages (Cambridge, 2003); A. D. Rogers and D. d'A Laffoley (2011). 'International Earth system expert workshop on ocean stresses and impacts.' Summary report. IPSO Oxford, 18pp; John L. Seitz and Kristen A. Hite *Global Issues: An Introduction* (fourth edition, Wiley-Blackwell, 2012); The World Economic Forum (2014). *Global Risks 2014, Ninth Edition.* Geneva: World Economic Forum; UNEP Global Environment Alert Service (2012). *One Planet, How Many People? A Review of Earth's Carrying Capacity.* Available at: http://na.unep.net/geas/getUNEPPageWithArticleIDScript .php?article_id=88.

Index